AUSTRIAN STUDIES
VOLUME 32
2024

VOL. 32   2024

AUSTRIAN STUDIES

Volume Editors: ANDREA CAPOVILLA,
KATYA KRYLOVA, and MARLEN MAIRHOFER
General Editors: DEBORAH HOLMES,
CAITRÍONA NÍ DHÚILL and DORA OSBORNE
Reviews Editor: KATYA KRYLOVA
Editorial Assistant: MICHAEL POWER

Reading Bachmann Now

Modern Humanities Research Association

Notes for Contributors giving guidance on the form in which to submit papers can be found at: **www.austrian.mhra.org.uk**

The **Modern Humanities Research Association** was founded in Cambridge in 1918 and has become an international organization with members in all parts of the world. It is a registered charity number 1064670, and a company limited by guarantee, registered in England number 3446016. Its main object is to encourage advanced study and research in modern and medieval European languages, literatures, and cultures by its publication of journals, book series, and its Style Guide. Further information about the activities of the Association and individual membership may be obtained from the Membership Secretary, email membership@mhra.org.uk, or from the website at: **www.mhra.org.uk**

ISSN 1350–7532 (print)   ISSN 2222–4262 (online)
ISBN 978-1-83954-266-4

Contents

Contents

Contents

Abbreviations

The following abbreviations have been used throughout this volume for frequently referenced editions of Bachmann's works and letters.

AGB   Ingeborg Bachmann, Anrufung des Großen Bären, ed. by Luigi Reitani (Piper, Suhrkamp, 2022)

BG   Ingeborg Bachmann, *Das Buch Goldmann*, ed. by Marie Luise Wandruszka (Piper, Suhrkamp, 2017)

DJ   Ingeborg Bachmann, *Das dreißigste Jahr*, ed. by Rita Svandrlik with Silvia Bengesser and Hans Höller (Piper, Suhrkamp 2020)

GuI   Ingeborg Bachmann, *Wir müssen wahre Sätze finden. Gespräche und Interviews*, ed. by Christine Koschel and Inge von Weidenbaum (Piper, 1983)

HB2020   *Bachmann-Handbuch. Leben — Werk — Wirkung*, ed. by Monika Albrecht and Dirk Göttsche, 2nd edn (Metzler, 2020)

KS   Ingeborg Bachmann, *Kritische Schriften*, ed. by Monika Albrecht and Dirk Göttsche (Piper, 2005)

LG   Ingeborg Bachmann, *Letzte, unveröffentlichte Gedichte, Entwürfe und Fassungen*, ed. by Hans Höller (Suhrkamp, 1998)

SE   Ingeborg Bachmann, *Sämtliche Erzählungen* (Piper, 2016)

SG   Ingeborg Bachmann, *Sämtliche Gedichte* (Piper, 2003)

TKA   Ingeborg Bachmann, *Todesarten-Projekt: Kritische Ausgabe*, ed. by Monika Albrecht and Dirk Göttsche, 4 vols (Piper, 1995)

W   Ingeborg Bachmann, *Werke*, ed. by Christine Koschel, Inge von Weidenbaum and Clemens Münster, 4 vols (Piper, 1978)

In translation

BFRG   Ingeborg Bachmann, *The Book of Franza and Requiem for Fanny Goldmann*, trans. by Peter Filkins (Northwestern University Press, 2010)

CW   *The Critical Writings of Ingeborg Bachmann*, ed. and trans. by Karen R. Achberger and Karl Ivan Solibakke (Camden House 2021)

DS   Ingeborg Bachmann, *Darkness Spoken: The Collected Poems*, trans. by Peter Filkins (Zephyr Press, 2019)

MB   Ingeborg Bachmann, *Malina*, trans. by Philip Boehm (Penguin Modern Classics, 2019)

TPL   Ingeborg Bachmann, *Three Paths to the Lake*, trans. by Mary Fran Gilbert (Holmes & Meier, 1997)

TY   Ingeborg Bachmann, *The Thirtieth Year*, trans. by Michael Bullock (Holmes & Meier, 1995)

Correspondence

IB/HWH   Ingeborg Bachmann and Hans Werner Henze, *Briefe einer Freundschaft*, ed. by Hans Höller (Piper, 2004)

IB/PC   Ingeborg Bachmann and Paul Celan, *Herzzeit. Briefwechsel*, ed. by Bertrand Badiou, Hans Höller, Andrea Stoll and Barbara Wiedemann (Suhrkamp, 2008)

Introduction:
Reading Bachmann Now

ANDREA CAPOVILLA,
KATYA KRYLOVA AND MARLEN MAIRHOFER

Ingeborg Bachmann Centre; University of Aberdeen; Salzburg

There are many reasons to read Bachmann now: her work and legacy are very much alive. She was a cosmopolitan, transnational and rebellious thinker whose work has considerable intellectual reach and political urgency. Her poetry, prose, radio plays and critical writings — such as the *Frankfurter Poetikvorlesungen* [Frankfurt Lectures on Poetics], which she inaugurated — continue to inspire discussion and analysis.

Ingeborg Bachmann also is, and long has been, a media icon in various guises. Every year in June since 1977 the city of her birth, Klagenfurt, holds the 'Tage der deutschsprachigen Literatur' [Festival of German-Language Literature], the largest German-language literary event, where the coveted 'Bachmannpreis' [Bachmann Prize] is awarded. This competition, which is held in front of an audience and broadcast on live television, provides new generations of writers with an opportunity to present their work to an interested public and often marks the beginning of successful writing careers. While the texts do not necessarily reference Bachmann, the location and framing of the event emphasize her continued significance to the contemporary literary scene. Displays of photographs of her and various works of art relating to her, as well as recent films which expressly engage with the biographical figure of Bachmann (notably, Ruth Beckermann's *Die Geträumten* [The Dreamed Ones], 2016, and Margarethe von Trotta's *Ingeborg Bachmann — Reise in die Wüste* [Journey into the Desert], 2023), confirm her status as a literary figurehead, particularly in the German-speaking context. In addition to the annual 'Tage der deutschsprachigen Literatur', the house she grew up in will open its doors as a museum in 2025. Years after her death, images of Bachmann still appear on the covers of periodicals, such as the double portrait of her and Max Frisch in the style of Andy Warhol gracing the cover of *Die Zeit* in November 2022, captioned with the headline 'Eine Jahrhundertliebe' [a love story for the ages].[1] Despite Bachmann's famed discretion, her life continues to attract sensationalist and hyperbolic media depictions, in the

[1] 'Ingeborg Bachmann und Max Frisch — eine Jahrhundertliebe', *Die Zeit*, 10 November 2022, on the occasion of the publication of the Bachmann/Frisch correspondence.

Austrian Studies 32 (2024), doi:10.1353/aus.00001, pp. 1–12

genre of the 'sensationelle[n] Enthüllungen aus den österreichisch-ungarischen Schlafzimmern' (TKA, III.1, p. 670) ['sensational revelations from Austro-Hungarian bedrooms', MB 266] that Bachmann herself decried in *Malina*.

That the Ingeborg Bachmann Centre for Austrian Literature and Culture in London bears her name is testimony to Bachmann's literary centrality. Her work connects incisively with the Austrian literary tradition cut off by the fascist period; at the same time, it radically challenges the postwar status quo and continues to inspire readers and artists in a variety of genres. As has often been noted, Bachmann frequently references major Austrian modernist writers and thinkers in her texts, especially Robert Musil, Joseph Roth, Hugo von Hofmannsthal and Ludwig Wittgenstein. However, as the present volume demonstrates, the intertextual quality of her writing extends far beyond Austrian literature and beyond the male literary canon.

The year 2023 was the fiftieth anniversary of Bachmann's untimely death in Rome and 2026 will see the centenary of her birth. Exhibitions dedicated to her have recently been hosted at the Literaturmuseum in Vienna and the Literaturhaus in Munich, and conferences held in London, Rome, Salzburg and Munich; the last of these was hosted by and featured early career researchers, including Anna Seethaler and Sebastian Schönbeck, who also contribute to this volume. The past few years have seen a number of new Bachmann publications appear from the writer's literary estate in the Salzburg Bachmann Edition. These have yielded fresh insights into her oeuvre, such as the collection of her writings on medicine and psychiatry in the volume *Male oscuro*.[2] Additionally, English translations of Bachmann's works, including — significantly — her philosophical and critical writings,[3] are bringing her to ever wider audiences. In preparation for this volume, several workshops and a symposium facilitated scholarly debate and exchange. The editors would like to thank the Bachmann scholars, translators and editors who contributed in many ways to *Reading Bachmann Now*, in particular Barbara Agnese, Merve Emre, Uta Degner, Peter Filkins, Tess Lewis, Lyn Marven, Áine McMurtry and Dora Osborne. We would also like to thank Heinz Bachmann, whose memories of his sister have recently been published,[4] for giving us permission to use one of the series of photos he took of Bachmann in Rome in 1962 for our front cover. The coming years will continue to see new departures in Bachmann research, locating her ever more

[2] Ingeborg Bachmann: '*Male oscuro*': *Aufzeichnungen aus der Zeit der Krankheit. Traumnotate, Briefe, Brief- und Redeentwürfe*, ed. by Isolde Schiffermüller and Gabriella Pelloni (Piper, Suhrkamp, 2017). Henceforth, referred to as MO, followed by page number. The general editors of the Salzburg Bachmann Edition are currently Uta Degner and Irene Fußl, with the assistance of Silvia Bengesser.

[3] *The Critical Writings of Ingeborg Bachmann*, ed. and trans. by Karen R. Achberger and Karl Ivan Solibakke (Camden House, 2021). Henceforth, referred to as CW, followed by page number.

[4] Heinz Bachmann, *Ingeborg Bachmann, meine Schwester: Erinnerungen und Bilder* (Piper, 2023).

firmly in the transnational intellectual context that nurtured her works and to which they contributed, for example Marlen Mairhofer's forthcoming study *In Austausch begriffen: Ökonomien der Differenz bei Marlen Haushofer, Ingeborg Bachmann und Hélène Cixous* [In Terms of Exchange: Economies of Difference in Marlen Haushofer, Ingeborg Bachmann und Hélène Cixous]. Further translations are also due to appear (for example, Tess Lewis's translation of Bachmann's early novella *Das Honditschkreuz* [The Honditsch Cross]), as well as further volumes in the Salzburg Bachmann Edition.

Born in 1926 in Klagenfurt (Carinthia), nestled in the 'Dreiländereck' [three-country triangle] between Austria, Slovenia and Italy (W, II, p. 417), Bachmann came of age in the final years of the Second World War. Her impressions of this time would be posthumously published as *Kriegstagebuch* [War Diary].[5] Bachmann's contemporary and long-time close friend Ilse Aichinger was the first Austrian-Jewish writer directly to address the extermination of the country's Jewish inhabitants in her short prose text *Das vierte Tor* [The Fourth Door, 1945] and in her novel *Die größere Hoffnung* [The Greater Hope, 1948]. Shaped by her friendships with Aichinger and Paul Celan, and by her youthful encounter with Jack Hamesh, a Viennese Jew who had escaped on a Kindertransport to England and returned to Austria as a British soldier, Bachmann embarked on a lifelong and incisive literary and theoretical engagement with the legacy of fascism. This work was irredeemably complicated by her close relationship with her father, who served as an officer in both world wars and was also, like many members of the Carinthian middle class, an early member of the Nazi Party. As Merve Emre has pointed out, the 'figure of the Nazi father [...] haunts all her novels'.[6] Bachmann left Carinthia in 1945 and soon settled in Vienna, where she completed a doctorate in philosophy. She also worked for the radio, including the US-controlled broadcaster *Rot-Weiß-Rot* [Red-White-Red] in occupied Vienna, where she wrote scripts for the popular show *Die Radiofamilie* [The Radio Family].[7] Her dissertation was on the critical reception of Martin Heidegger's existential philosophy; although receptive to his philosophy of language, she was largely critical of his work and alert to his fascist past. Instead, she turned to Wittgenstein's philosophy of language, and one of her innumerable intellectual merits is that she championed both Wittgenstein and Robert Musil when they were still underappreciated in postwar Germany and Austria.

Bachmann rose to prominence in the 1950s with her two poetry collections *Die gestundete Zeit* [Borrowed Time, 1953] and *Anrufung des großen Bären*

---

[5] Ingeborg Bachmann, *Kriegstagebuch* (Suhrkamp, 2010); Bachmann, *War Diary*, trans. by Mike Mitchell (Seagull Books, 2014).

[6] Merve Emre, 'The Meticulous One', *The New York Review of Books*, 22 October 2020, <https://www.nybooks.com/articles/2020/10/22/ingeborg-bachmann-meticulous-one/> [accessed 13 August 2024].

[7] Ingeborg Bachmann, *Die Radiofamilie*, ed. by Joseph McVeigh (Suhrkamp, 2011); Bachmann, *The Radio Family*, trans. by Mike Mitchell (Seagull Books, 2014).

[Invocation of the Great Bear, 1956]. Her lyrical musicality and distinctive blending of classical rhythms and metres with avant-garde aesthetics and political acuity were enthusiastically received by critics and readers alike; the press claimed her as an instant modern classic.[8] She then ostensibly turned away from poetry, claiming in an interview that it would be good to pause at a point where she felt a sense of mastery (see GuI, p. 40). Although she did in fact continue to write poetry in more experimental forms, deliberately setting aside her command of rhyme and metre, from the early 1960s onwards she concentrated on her prose work. This was marked by an attentiveness to the recent past haunting postwar Austria and a precise diagnosis of contemporary social mores, combined with the utopian impulse that pervades all her writing, encapsulated by Bachmann herself in the phrase 'ein Tag wird kommen' [a day will come] (GuI, p. 145). When she turned her focus to prose, she was criticized by precisely those critics who had praised her poetry and termed her a 'gefallene Lyrikerin' [fallen poetess].[9] The gist was that she should remain within the box into which the male literary establishment had placed her, a beautiful 'lady poet' writing beautiful poems. This kind of critical attitude engendered restrictive misreadings of her complex and multi-layered prose works as well as of her poems.

Bachmann published little throughout the 1960s but was at work continuously. In her lifetime she completed two extraordinary collections of short stories and the novel *Malina*. The larger part of her writings has, however, been published since her death in 1973 in Rome, where she had lived on and off for many years in what she herself described as a 'Doppelleben' [double life]: 'mit dem einen Teil bin ich immer in Österreich, mit dem anderen hier' [one part of me is always in Austria, the other here] (GuI, pp. 65 and 121). Following the first posthumous publication of a four-volume collection of her writing in 1978, including an edited version of her fragmentary *Todesarten* [Ways of Dying] cycle, a new wave of feminist-oriented readings of Bachmann's work emerged.[10] As has been variously pointed out, this feminist reception had its pitfalls as well, at times reducing her characters and also their author to little more than helpless victims of the aftermath and the continuities of fascism post-1945.

In 1995 Monika Albrecht und Dirk Göttsche completed a critical edition of the 3,000 pages of the *Todesarten* cycle fragments, which is the current basis for scholarly engagement with these texts. The year 2017 saw the publication of the first volume of the Salzburg Bachmann Edition, which plans to produce

---

[8] See for example the much-discussed cover story 'Bachmann: Stenogramm der Zeit', *Der Spiegel*, 18 August 1954, pp. 26–29, including photos of the author in Rome.

[9] The extraordinarily influential Marcel Reich-Ranicki in his review of Bachmann's short story collection *Simultan*; 'Am liebsten beim Friseur', *Die Zeit*, 29 September 1972, supplement p. 8.

[10] *Ingeborg Bachmann: Werke*, ed. by Christine Koschel, Inge von Weidenbaum and Clemens Münster (Piper, 1978). Subsequently referred to as W, followed by volume and page number.

critical editions of all previously published texts and to publish all of her as yet
unpublished papers by 2030. It is the result of cooperation between the Literary
Archive at the Austrian National Library (ÖNB) and the Literature Archive
Salzburg (LAS), as well as between Bachmann's two publishers, Suhrkamp and
Piper. It will eventually encompass around thirty volumes of prose, poetry,
diaries, and around ten volumes of correspondence.

The challenge set by Bachmann's writing practice, as evident in the
approximately 27,000 manuscript sheets she left behind, has already been
described by Monika Albrecht and Dirk Göttsche. They argue that alongside the
printed volumes a complementary digital edition, which did not come to pass,
would have been necessary to capture adequately the text fragments and variants
of her *Todesarten* project.[11] Bachmann frequently retyped passages, thereby
editing her texts time and time again. Moreover, large parts of the *Todesarten*
project remain fragmentary, due to the fact that Bachmann abandoned some of
them, as well as to her sudden premature death. Therefore, the *Todesarten* texts
do not take the form of a linear, continuous work, but rather resemble a gigantic
rhizome that offers countless ways to 'enter' and 'exit' her work, challenging
the reader to respond to this simultaneity. In the introduction to '*Senza casa*',
a volume of Bachmann's autobiographical sketches, notes and diary entries,
and the tenth volume of the ongoing Salzburg Bachmann Edition, Hans Höller
cites Bachmann's fictitious commentary in *Malina* on the editorial process:[12]
'in diesen ganzen staubigen verbleichten Blättern und Papierfetzen, darin wird
sich eines Tages kein Mensch auskennen' (TKA, III.1, p. 632) ['all these yellowed
pages and scraps of paper completely covered with dust, someday no one will be
able to find their way around in them'] (MB, pp. 241–42). The ongoing efforts
to edit Bachmann's oeuvre are proof that generations of scholars keep looking
for their 'way around' in it, accompanied by curious readers who share a keen
interest in reading Bachmann 'now'.

Höller, who is intimately familiar with Bachmann's work and was one
of the first critics to recognize the political implications of her poetry, also
emphasizes that Bachmann refuted victimization: 'Was ihr wichtig blieb:
kein Opfer zu sein' [What continued to matter to her: not to be a victim].[13]
Unfortunately, scholarship did not always live up to that premise and has
persisted in reading both the author and her (female) characters as victims,
often blurring the lines between the two.[14] The interest in Bachmann's life,

[11] Monika Albrecht and Dirk Göttsche, 'Vom Schicksal eines elektronischen
Editionsvorhabens', in '*Über die Zeit schreiben*': *Literatur- und kulturwissenschaftliche
Essays zu Ingeborg Bachmanns 'Todesarten'-Projekt*, ed. by Monika Albrecht and Dirk
Göttsche (Königshausen & Neumann, 1998), pp. 247–50.
[12] Hans Höller, 'Vorwort', in Ingeborg Bachmann, '*Senza casa*': *Autobiographische Skizzen,
Notate, und Tagebucheintragungen*, ed. by Isolde Schiffermüller, Gabriella Pelloni and Silvia
Bengesser (Piper and Suhrkamp, 2024), pp. 7–11 (p. 8).
[13] Ibid., p. 11.
[14] For more on this, see Renate Langer, 'Schmerzensfrau und Immaculata: Bruchlinien im

her relationships and the harrowing circumstances of her death have at times overshadowed and even obscured her writing. This tendency is intensified by the sheer volume of fascinating photographs and video portraits of her, which, however, are often framed by questionable conjectures.[15] In recent years, Bachmann has also been subject to new fictionalized film treatments. Renowned documentary filmmaker Ruth Beckermann's *Die Geträumten* (2016) focuses on the love story of Bachmann and Paul Celan, filtered through the lens of two actors (Anja Plaschg and Laurence Rupp) and their emotions and conversations while recording the dramatic correspondence of the poets at the legendary and now defunct ORF-Funkhaus [Austrian Broadcasting House] in Vienna. Blending documentary and fiction in a screenplay co-written with Ina Hartwig, *Die Geträumten* is the first film in which Beckermann has worked with actors. Its premise centres, in a more delimited sense, on a question that is also key to this volume: what does it mean to read Bachmann (and, in *Die Geträumten*, also Celan) now? As Beckermann put it, she was interested in 'how [...] young people today [would] respond to these letters and the language they use? It was an experiment.'[16] Beckermann's experiment worked insofar as we see the actors engage with the letters long after they have read the selected correspondence aloud in the Funkhaus studio, discussing what they might have done in the same circumstances, or being visibly moved by the intensity of the emotion conveyed in Bachmann's and Celan's missives. The actors' 'offstage' breaks occupy almost as much screen time as the reading aloud from the correspondence. Eschewing any straightforward reconstruction (although Plaschg bears more than a passing resemblance to Bachmann) through the avoidance of period costume or shooting locations other than the radio studio (a medium that is strongly associated with the author), the film puts Bachmann's writing centre stage and allows it to resonate across time. Bachmann's words, spoken by Plaschg, close the film, with the diegesis moving through from an early letter to Celan to the ending of the 'Prinzessin von Kagran' [Princess of Kagran] fragment from *Malina* respectively. The passage of time between the late 1940s, when Bachmann and Celan first began their correspondence, and today is elided, as the two twenty-something actors stand as proxy readers for the audience, through whom we register the impact that Bachmann's writing can continue to have on twenty-first century readers.

While Beckermann's film is content to allude to the biographical figure of

---

Bachmann-Bild', in *Mythos Bachmann: Zwischen Inszenierung und Selbstinszenierung*, ed. by Wilhelm Hemecker and Manfred Mittermayer (Zsolnay, 2011), pp. 54–71 (pp. 58–59).

[15] For more on this, see: J. J. Long, 'Ingeborg Bachmann: Zur fotografischen Konstruktion einer Dichterin', in *Mythos Bachmann*, pp. 203–21; Manfred Mittermayer, 'Gefilmt und verfilmt: Bewegte Bachmann-Bilder im Dokumentar- und im Spielfilm', in *Mythos Bachmann*, pp. 222–40.

[16] Ruth Beckermann, as cited in '"This Love Has the Character of a Dream." Interview with Karin Schiefer', *Austrian Films*, January 2016, https://www.austrianfilms.com/news/en/bodythis_love_has_the_character_of_a_dreambody [accessed 23 August 2024].

Bachmann, veteran New German filmmaker Margarethe von Trotta's *Ingeborg Bachmann — Reise in die Wüste* (2023), the first biopic of the author, takes an altogether different approach. Through meticulous attention to the *mise-en-scène*, encompassing costumes, on-location shooting (including in Rome and Egypt) and casting (especially that of Vicky Krieps as Bachmann), von Trotta's film largely focuses on Bachmann's relationship with Frisch and its aftermath and presents us with a portrait of the Austrian author that we have become familiar with — that of the glamourous but fragile literary star. Yet von Trotta is also keen to underline Bachmann's status as a woman making her way in a decidedly patriarchal postwar literary world, something that Andrea Stoll also emphasizes in her biography.[17] As such, Bachmann becomes part of the weave of von Trotta's on-screen women pioneers across the ages, including Hildegard von Bingen, Rosa Luxemburg, Hannah Arendt and, controversially, Gudrun Ensslin. Von Trotta's films repeatedly focus on the personal as political; in *Reise in die Wüste* too, we see the on-screen Bachmann argue with Frisch (played by Ronald Zehrfeld) about whose turn it is to do the washing-up at the expense of valuable writing time. The struggle for equality, not least through creative self-realization, memorably and enigmatically depicted in Bachmann's *Malina*, is here reduced to a rather banal disagreement about household chores. It is an incomplete, but also not wholly inaccurate, presentation of a writer who stated 'die Ehe ist eine unmögliche Institution. Sie ist unmöglich für eine Frau, die arbeitet und die denkt und selber etwas will' [marriage is an impossible institution, impossible for a woman who works and thinks, and who wants to achieve something herself] (GuI, p. 144), a Bachmann *bon mot* that was widely utilized to promote *Reise in die Wüste*.[18] By definition, one roughly two-hour fictional film cannot fully encompass or reflect a life — instead von Trotta's film presents us with her own reading of Bachmann's biography from a contemporary vantage point, she too is reading Bachmann *now*. Yet it also invites further readings and portraits of the author. The centenary of Franz Kafka's death in 2024 has led to a proliferation of on-screen depictions of the Prague author, including a TV mini-series by Daniel Kehlmann and David Schalko, as well as a biopic directed by the renowned Polish director Agnieszka Holland. It is likely that, as time wears on, Bachmann's life, as well as her work, will continue to fascinate, and the number of medial depictions by new generations of creatives will continue to rise.

Bachmann is a complex and intriguing writer, who also worked on her own image and public persona. This perhaps found its apex during her years in Rome, as the well-connected European intellectual. As more and more of her private letters and diaries become public, her image continues to be reconsidered.

---

[17] Andrea Stoll, *Ingeborg Bachmann: Der dunkle Glanz der Freiheit* (C. Bertelsmann, 2013).

[18] See, for example, Josef Grübl, 'Lieben und schreiben', *Süddeutsche Zeitung*, 17 October 2023, <https://www.sueddeutsche.de/muenchen/kino-muenchen-margarethe-von-trotta-ingeborg-bachmann-city-kino-1.6288950> [accessed 23 August 2024].

Certainties will remain elusive, as any autobiographical text, such as a letter or a diary, will reflect a specific moment in time and any interpretation will remain an approximation. Yet Bachmann continues to inspire rhetorical extremes in her readers, such as when Sigrid Löffler concludes her review of 'Senza casa', paraphrasing Kleist's farewell letter to his half-sister, with the words: 'Die Wahrheit ist, dass ihr auf Erden nicht zu helfen war' [The truth is that she could not be helped on earth].[19] Peter Filkins is at work on the first major biography of Bachmann in English, which will be published by Yale University Press. His aim is to 'demythologize Bachmann's life and career by contextualizing both through historical research'.[20] Rather than trying to fit Bachmann into any one role, Filkins

> aims to show how the many sides of Bachmann make her ultimately unknowable. The result will be a portrait of the many paradoxes threading through Bachmann's life, but one that will delineate how her writing tapped the same in deftly exploring the complex interplay of language, identity, and the self.[21]

Reading Bachmann Now focuses on the author's texts rather than on her persona. Her texts play with (auto)biographical elements, but never in a straightforward manner, and her inter- and intratextual references contribute to the dense weave of her writing and its dialogical character. In a 1971 interview Bachmann stated 'Man muss überhaupt ein Buch auf verschiedene Arten lesen können und es heute anders lesen als morgen' (GuI, p. 100) [You have to be able to read a book in different ways and read it differently today than you will tomorrow]. And also differently from yesterday, one might add. It is the aim of this volume to present a broad variety of ways of reading Bachmann 'now'. These readings, which focus on Bachmann's short stories as well as on her poetry, on private correspondence as well as on her late prose, approach her work from many different angles. Through reading and re-reading Bachmann, we may also re-evaluate our own ways of reading other (female) authors, as well as our ways of academic thinking and speaking.

While some of the contributions in this volume take a broad, often comparative approach, by linking Bachmann to other authors, artists and intellectuals through the centuries and by asking how her texts respond to the pressing issues of her time, others take the form of close readings, uncovering still more layers of meaning in her work. Ecocritical and decolonial readings are presented alongside inquiries into the complex fields of translation, gender, and even neurophysiology. Several of the contributions read Bachmann *with*

---

[19] Sigrid Löffler, 'Liebhaberin ohne festen Wohnsitz', *Süddeutsche Zeitung*, 23 July 2024, <https://www.sueddeutsche.de/kultur/ingeborg-bachmann-senza-casa-hans-werner-henze-klagenfurt-gesamtausgabe-lux.7pHB6vQv1Bris4WEMz8VQh?reduced=true> [accessed 24 July 2024].
[20] Peter Filkins in an email to the editors, 16 July 2024.
[21] Ibid.

other canonical writers and texts, mutually illuminating both. Bachmann's short story 'Unter Mördern und Irren' (1961) [Among Murderers and Madmen] can be read on one level as an account of the continuity of fascism in postwar Austria, as many in positions of power took up their posts again or never left them. Bachmann's story stages an encounter of perpetrators and victims which is in equal measure realistic and surreal. Eluding easy interpretation is the figure of the murderer who resisted murdering under the Nazi regime. By linking 'Unter Mördern und Irren' to Herman Melville's seminal short story 'Bartleby, the Scrivener' (1853), Caitríona Leahy enquires into the terms and conditions of agency in Bachmann's work. Focusing on acts of not-doing and the dialectical relationships they do (not) take place in, her reading shows how literature challenges its own as well as the reader's possibilities of agency.

Following the award of the Büchner prize to Bachmann, an interviewer asked her if she wanted to represent nature in her poetry. She replied that she was not interested in nature as it is commonly understood in the context of poetry. This reaction might be seen as resistance to being labelled a conventional writer of nature poetry — a sentiment also expressed by Ilse Aichinger when she described nature in an interview as a 'Konter-Punkt' [counterpoint].[22] Nonetheless, it is the case that the non-human living world features prominently in Bachmann's poetics; in ways that are just beginning to be grasped, the threat of natural destruction is central to her diagnosis of violence. Conor Brennan suggests an ecocritical reading of the suffering of animals and the symbolism of butchery and meat in the *Todesarten* project, taking his cue from Bachmann's statement that her fragmentary novel cycle is 'eine einzige große Studie aller möglichen Todesarten' (GuI, p. 66) [a single great study of all possible ways of dying]. Lina Užukauskaitė discusses the role of the floral in Bachmann's poetic dialogue with Paul Celan, examining Bachmann's floral figures in the intermedial and transmedial context of their reworking in works of art by Anselm Kiefer and Cy Twombly. Focusing especially on the contrasts and equivalences that can be observed between text and image, Užukauskaitė traces how the artists engage in poetic dialogue with Bachmann through their transmedial exploration of flowers and other 'natural' figures.

A number of contributions in the volume explore Bachmann's engagement with Egypt in her poetry and in the unfinished *Todesarten* project. Teresa Ludden examines scientific coloniality in *Das Buch Franza*, arguing that the web of associations in Bachmann's uncompleted text may be read as allusions to colonial logics of dispossession that generate property and knowledge. Ludden reads scientific praxis, as it is depicted in *Das Buch Franza*, as emerging through the libidinal economy of White Archaeology and in connection with colonial extraction. Thomas Pekar's contribution analyses sexual-political positioning in Bachmann's poem 1957 'Liebe: Dunkler Erdteil' [Love: The Dark Continent].

---

[22] 'Gespräche aus vielen Jahren', in Ilse Aichinger, *Es muss gar nichts bleiben. Interviews 1952–2005* (Edition Korrespondenzen, 2011), pp. 159–62 (p. 162).

The poem is first contextualized with reference to the political climate of the late 1950s, the 1956 Suez Crisis and the decolonization process. From there, Pekar proceeds to explore its depiction of masochistically oriented sexuality from a psychoanalytical perspective. Via a lens of what he calls 'speculative philaelogy', Artur R. Boelderl seeks to establish an underlying possibility for 'Egypt' to function as the common 'ground' between Bachmann, Robert Musil, Paul Celan and Anselm Kiefer. In doing so, Boelderl establishes a poetological siblinghood and intertextual web between these figures that, as he argues, both transcends and enhances the philological correspondences between their works.

Several contributions offer new readings of Bachmann's landmark novel *Malina*. Anna Seethaler reads *Malina* from the perspective of care work and its relation to female authorship. In the novel the narrating 'Ich' [I] is shown to be both a woman who is taking care of herself, thereby creating a sort of 'Kunstfigur' [artificial character] for her lover Ivan, as well as being a writer. Seethaler shows how these roles are in constant tension with each other, thereby shedding light on how Bachmann portrays her protagonist as a female author of the twentieth century. In close scrutiny of a passage in *Malina*, where 'Ich' envisions 'perfecting' ('vollenden') her 'Du' (you) for Ivan, Sebastian Schönbeck explores Bachmann's use of personal pronouns in the novel as well as in her Frankfurt Lectures. By reading Bachmann in conjunction with linguists and sociologists such as Émile Benveniste and Norbert Elias, Schönbeck shows how a literary text like *Malina* may broaden and deepen our understanding of the ways pronouns create and structure relationships.

Several contributions focus on significant constellations and relationships, or on encounters and dialogues. In his article on love and friendship in the correspondence between Ingeborg Bachmann and Hans Werner Henze, Tobias Heinrich shows how the writer and the gay composer move back and forth not only between languages, but also between different forms of relationships. Their plans to live together, even possibly to marry, which are discussed in their letters, cause Bachmann to reflect on her needs as well as her expectations of life as a writer and a woman. Till Greite discusses Berlin as a place of disturbance, focusing on one of the most memorable literary constellations in the postwar city, that between Bachmann and the Polish émigré Witold Gombrowicz. The meeting of the two authors took place in 1963, facilitated by the American Ford Foundation's Artist-in-Residence programme. Greite retraces their unique attunement to this uncanny city, haunted at every turn by its traumatic recent past.

Roberto Interdonato explores the affinities between Bachmann and the Italian writer Anna Maria Ortese. A modern classic in her native country, Ortese has been cited as a major influence by Elena Ferrante, and recently rediscovered for an English-language readership through the translation of her *Neapolitan Chronicles* (1953) by Ann Goldstein and Jenny McPhee.

Interdonato analyses the thematic overlap between Bachmann and Ortese in their descriptions of postwar Naples and in their short stories concerned with sight and vision in their respective post-fascist societies. Mercer Greenwald stages an encounter between Bachmann and the great Brazilian writer Clarice Lispector, taking Hélène Cixous and her *Three Steps on the Ladder of Writing* (1994) as the link between the two. Exploring figurations of the mirror, the echo and the fragmentation of the apostrophic subject, Greenwald builds on the readings of Cixous to uncover further resonances between Bachmann's and Lispector's voices.

Several of the contributions engage with the possibilities and challenges of translation. Claudia J. Fischer and Vera San Payo de Lemos follow the winding paths of translation as movement in Bachmann's short story 'Simultan' through the lens of Transfiction Studies. The authors, who translated the story into Portuguese, pay particular attention to the way Bachmann's protagonist is trying to communicate with her surroundings as well as herself, encountering both uncertainty and revelation. In its themes and composition, the story, so they argue, reflects on the process of translation itself. Ewa Siwak compares Philip Boehm's retranslation of *Malina*, published by Penguin Modern Classics as well as New Directions in 2019, with his previous translation of two decades earlier. Boehm was able to make use of new research findings and go back to the original sources of some of the intertextual references. Moreover, Siwak establishes how the translator's position and practice evolved insofar as his updated version attends closely to *Malina*'s politics and protofeminist voice.

Liselotte van der Gucht and Gunther Martens's article explores embodiment and neurodiversity in *Malina* and in the short stories 'Alles' [Everything] and 'Ihr glücklichen Augen' [Oh Happy Eyes]. Drawing on concepts from Neurodiversity Studies, they demonstrate how Bachmann's writings offer a nuanced and empathetic portrayal of cognitive differences and challenge conventional understandings of disability and neuronormativity. Informed by Bachmann's own engagement with the fields of medicine and psychiatry, the article makes a case for including Bachmann in recent debates, not only in the Medical Humanities, but also in Critical Disability Studies.

In a close reading of the poems 'Die gestundete Zeit' [Borrowed Time], 'Anrufung des großen Bären' [Invocation of the Great Bear], 'Tage in Weiß' [Days in White] and 'An die Sonne' [To the Sun], Sabine I. Gölz sets out the poems' radical break with the established interpretative horizon, which is gendered and which we as gendered readers are schooled to perpetuate. Gölz's readings show the radical and poetico-political impetus of Bachmann's early poetry, which has frequently been obscured. Discussing Bachmann's lectures on poetics together with an essay by Friedrich Kittler, Gölz argues that her writing allows us to deconstruct the traditional model of 'writing as coding' and thereby disrupt the literary and theoretical canon. Her contribution challenges us to subvert our habitual interpretative direction and to re-read the purported master texts of the (male) literary canon through Bachmann's lens, rather than framing her work by them.

Taken together, the contributions in this volume offer new possibilities and ways of thinking about and reading Bachmann's work. They invite us to reappraise and enlarge our existing understanding of the author's oeuvre, as well as that of other authors and thinkers. In connection with her work on one of the last short stories published during her lifetime, 'Drei Wege zum See' [Three Paths to the Lake, 1972], Bachmann asserted that 'Österreich — das ist etwas, das immer weitergeht für mich' [Austria is something that always continues for me, on and on] (GuI, p. 121). In the same manner, her work continues on — not remaining static words on the page, but becoming ever richer through the renewed act of reading Bachmann *now*.

Unterwegs zu Bachmann (via Melville): Re-reading 'Unter Mördern und Irren'

CAITRÍONA LEAHY

Trinity College Dublin

I

There are many ways in which the opening line of Bachmann's 1961 short story 'Unter Mördern und Irren' [Among Murderers and Madmen] resonates with the task of reading Bachmann now. The forthright 'Die Männer sind unterwegs zu sich' (DJ, p. 94) [Men are on their way to themselves] chimes with the tenor of this moment — here, now — reading (with) the Salzburg edition as a more extensive Bachmann emerges, volume by volume.[1] Underway in this reading project, *unterwegs zu Bachmann*, engaged by a story about men who are underway, we are included in its logic: 'Wir sind in Wien, mehr als zehn Jahre nach dem Krieg' (DJ, p. 94) [We are in Vienna, more than ten years after the war] says the narrator. The implication is clear: we, the reader, are in the sights of the text; we, the reader, reading Bachmann now, are underway too, among those who kill and those who go astray,[2] in territory elsewhere described as '[d]ie wirklichen Schauplätze, die inwendigen, von den äußeren mühsam überdeckt' (W, IV, p. 342) [the real crime scenes, the internal ones, carefully covered over by the external ones].

The story of 'Unter Mördern und Irren' is the story of a crime that is both external and internal. The crime is perpetrated by murderers and madmen on the way to themselves, becoming themselves by murdering and erring. The victim of that crime is a self-proclaimed murderer whose error in life is his failure to complete his journey to selfhood. This man, 'unterwegs zu sich' (DJ, p. 94) [underway to himself], chooses not to arrive at himself; he chooses not to murder, not to act out of and towards his own self-defined being, leaving himself suspended on a journey that incites both violence and re-reading.

This article responds to and confirms that incitement by re-reading the matter of the murderer's stalled journey under the heading of agency. It is the murderer's ability to act and not to act that brings the double nature of

---

[1] Translations are by the author.

[2] Entry 'Irre', *Digitales Wörterbuch der deutschen Sprache*, n.d. <https://www.dwds.de/wb/Irre> [accessed 18 October 2023].

Austrian Studies 32 (2024), doi:10.1353/aus.00002, pp. 13–26
© Modern Humanities Research Association 2024

his agency into view: the agent — by definition a person who acts — brings together the two activities of being and doing. He is the person who does; his being is defined by doing. In the story, the question of agency envelops all the characters individually, but it is also presented as the collective doing and being of a quietly murderous society, acting by omission as well as commission. In addition, the story's insistence on including the agency of the reader within its own thinking and doing is a crucial dimension of its concerns. It is not about what had been (done) then, ten years previously, what was being done now, still, ten years later; it is extended into the reading underway now — 'wir', individually and collectively, *unterwegs* to being readers by 'doing reading'. This is what really matters about 'Unter Mördern und Irren': in its precision focus on the point where agency becomes visible as a decision in one individual life, it succeeds in unlocking a contagious logic. At stake in the decision of one person on how to 'do being' are the terms and conditions of everyone else's existence. These terms and conditions illuminate the relationships between the individual and the collective, between reading and reasoning, and between copying and murdering. To help us read the story in this way, we will proceed via Herman Melville's 1853 short story 'Bartleby, the Scrivener' — another story about a man who fails to act in fulfilment of his name. Bartleby, the scrivener who chooses not to scriven, has much to contribute to our re-reading, now, of a murderer who chooses not to murder.

II

The reading proposed here is not the first to foreground the metaphor of being *unterwegs*. This is unsurprising given the prominence of the semantic field of journeys in all the stories of *Das dreißigste Jahr* and the defining, existential frame of reference established in the title story. When the everyman protagonist 'in sein dreißigstes Jahr geht' (DJ, p. 26) [goes into his thirtieth year] and loses his sense of infinite possibility, his life is condensed to its core questions — where to go, what to do, who to be — and to facing the terms and conditions of his pathway choice. Stepping this way or that, to be a doer or a thinker, a revolutionary or an idler, all choices converge on the possibility or impossibility of a self-determined life: to what extent is a different way, ever — in its own moment, now — possible? To what extent are directions and choices already prescribed by what has already been, by paths already taken and characters (both human and linguistic) already set down? With that, 'Das dreißigste Jahr' defines its temporal step as a decisive one not just in determining the direction of life's journey, but also in uncovering how agency is defined by and entangled with language.

The Salzburg edition approaches the metaphor of being *unterwegs* from a different perspective. It draws our attention to the far-reaching potency of the semantic field of pathways, by situating the short story volume in Bachmann's writing career. Under the heading 'Der lange Weg zur Prosa' (DJ, p. 211) [The long path to prose], the editorial commentary frames the collection as an important milestone in a number of respects. It notes Bachmann's own description of it already in 1957: 'Er wird keine Erzählungen im engeren Sinne enthalten' [It will not contain stories, in the strict sense of the term], she says, 'eher Versuche, einen eigenen Weg für mich zu finden' [but rather attempts on my part to find my own path] (DJ, p. 214). This 'eigene[r] Weg' [own path], Bachmann's own particular way, can itself be read in a number of ways. It signifies in the first instance the move from poetry to prose — not, as we now know, a clean or sudden move, but a move nonetheless. It is, she will later say, an 'Umzug im Kopf' [a house-move in my head], an 'Übersiedlung' [migration] (DJ, pp. 215–16). These various forms of relocation are not just metaphors; the move to prose is happening while Bachmann herself is moving between America, Germany, Italy, Austria and France, establishing clear resonance between her own life and what Arturo Larcati terms the nomadic subjectivity seeking itself out at the heart of her prose.[3] The search for a way to go, a way to be, has a number of different dimensions. Being *unterwegs* in the world, and *unterwegs* in the language worlds of literature and philosophy, are manifestations of the one existential journey; to be is to be — hither and thither — underway.[4]

The whither question — to where are we *unterwegs*? — is posed, often and literally, in the opening lines of the stories in *Das dreißigste Jahr*. Where are we going when we walk down Radetzkystraße ('Jugend in einer österreichischen Stadt') [Youth in an Austrian Town], when we approach the apartment door ('Alles') [Everything], when the last guests leave ('Ein Schritt nach Gomorrha') [A Step towards Gomorrah], when we come through a clearing ('Undine geht') [Undine goes]? But Bachmann's most famous iteration of the question is its plaintive, existential formulation in the opening line of the poem 'Reklame' [Advertising], composed in the same period as work is beginning on the 'attempts' of *Das dreißigste Jahr* (W, I, p. 114). Here, the 'Wohin aber gehen wir' [But where are we going] question is revealed to be a question of agency — 'was sollen wir tun' (W, I, p. 114) [what should we do]. It is a question that refers not just to the doings of the poem's 'wir' [we], it also implicates the reader and binds them into its direct reference to what the poem itself does. What the poem does

---

[3] Arturo Larcati's study *Ingeborg Bachmanns Poetik* (Wissenschaftliche Buchgesellschaft, 2006) brings together the many different aspects of Bachmann's references to journeys and pathways. Of particular significance for present purposes is Larcati's interpretation of Bachmann's utopia as a mode of being and doing that brings a deterritorialized language practice to bear on the stubbornly immovable, repetitive frames of collective identity and politics in postwar Austria. See especially pp. 186–240.

[4] See Bachmann's description of being in literature as a 'verzweiflungsvolle[s] Unterwegsseins' (KS, p. 345) [being underway in a state of desperation] in the fifth Frankfurt Lecture, 'Literatur als Utopie'. The phrase referred to above is not translated literally and loses some of the impact of the metaphor in the extended formulation 'desperately and incessantly striving towards the utopia of language' (CW, p. 330).

is to constitute itself by doing, specifically, by going-doing language, from line to line, carrying on speaking until 'Totenstille | eintritt' (W, I, p. 114) [deathly silence | steps in]. In short, underway in Bachmann are characters, their readers and language itself, and in each case the journey is defined by the exercise of agency.

Where that agency is thought of in terms of the stepping or not stepping of protagonists and readers, in a direction to be decided and to an end that is at once outward-looking and self-reflexive, one is already, with Bachmann, in the company of Kafka, thinking with both of the agency of literature. Kafka's presence here is also noted by the editors of the Salzburg edition, who compare their own task as re-readers of Bachmann to that of Bachmann as a re-reader of Kafka in 1953. Marking the reissue of *Amerika* as part of Max Brod's Kafka edition that year, Bachmann authored a radio-essay focusing on the haplessness of Karl Roßmann as a protagonist and the wider significance of haplessness as a mode of being.[5] For Bachmann, Roßmann's defining feature is his childlike nature, which propels his tumbles from one misfortune to the next; it is also, however, what makes it possible for him to rise and move on, again and again. In yielding to the failure of 'Tatkraft' (KS, p. 91) [the capacity to accomplish]. Roßmann moves through the world, ultimately — according to Bachmann — more successfully than his wilful adult counterparts in *Der Prozeß* [*The Trial*] and *Das Schloß* [*The Castle*].

For the Salzburg editors, Roßmann's mode of being *unterwegs* in the world as one who repeatedly falls and gets up again, is echoed in *Das dreißigste Jahr*. More significant than this narrow similarity, however, is the editors' appeal via Bachmann's *Amerika* essay to a shared investment in reading as a utopian act. It is this shift away from looking at the 'Gangart' (KS, p. 263) [gait] of protagonists to focus instead on the rhythms that underpin the production and consumption of literature per se that brings us to the heart of the matter of literature's agency in any given moment of its reading. The *Amerika* essay concludes with this wide-angle perspective on why, now, in 1953, the time is ripe for reading Kafka again: 'Dichtern wird man in der Stille gerecht, denn wenn alle Deutungen veraltet und alle Erklärungen verbraucht sind, erklärt sich ihr Werk aus der unverbrauchbaren Wahrheit, der es sich verdankt' ['Poets are accorded their due in periods of calm, for when all interpretations have become outdated and all exegeses are worn out, their work reveals itself by way of the inexhaustible truth to which it is beholden'] (KS, p. 95; CW, p. 122; translation amended).

The Kafka reference and the expansive framework in which it is placed bring echoes of their own, however: Bachmann writes elsewhere too of the inexhaustibility of literature, about its capacity to fall and get up again, about the literary characters who enact that and about the utopian nature of that mode of being. At the furthest reach of this phenomenon Bachmann places

---

[5] For the background to its publication, see the commentary on Bachmann's radio-essay in KS, pp. 549–51.

the heroism of Samuel Beckett's Mahood, the unnamable (migrating between names) speaker of the novel *The Unnamable*, a being beyond identity, history, experience or any content of which to speak. Unable to move, Mahood's only investment in being *unterwegs* on the journey of life is his determination to go on speaking 'ich werde also weitermachen, man muß Worte sagen, solange es welche gibt' ['I'll go on, you must say words, as long as there are any'] (KS, pp. 304–06; CW, p. 304). This version of doing being as doing language resonates with Bachmann's conception of utopia as outlined throughout the Frankfurt Lectures and which culminates in the stand-alone, apodictic line 'Es gilt, weiterzuschreiben' ['We must continue to write'] (KS, p. 348; CW, p. 332). This is literature's task and the purpose of its agency — its 'Unterwegssein' (KS, p. 345) [being underway] to utopian language, its marching on and mumbling on.

For all the emphasis on literature's inexhaustible 'weitermachen' [going on], however, Bachmann's focus (and ours too) is on the underside of motion, that is to say, on the still grounds of its definition. She describes the journey of literature and the manner in which it is *unterwegs* by attending to those moments where it is marked by an apparent failure to be in motion: moments of withdrawal, pause, resistance and silence. All writers, she argues, conscious of the inadequacy of their language, contain within themselves the seeds of the so-called 'end of literature'. This 'end of literature' cannot offer narrative support to any particular story of the journey of literature because it is not in the first instance historically anchored; it is to be found across historical periods and in always individual, never collective forms of expression. Thus Tolstoy's self-loathing, Gogol's and Kleist's burning of their works, Grillparzer's and Mörike's falling silent — these all endings in themselves — are to be considered, in Bachmann's view, important precursors of the more famous twentieth-century versions of literature's stalling. Here, the story of Hofmannsthal's fictional seventeenth-century writer, Lord Chandos, whose language crisis breaks the ties that bind the self to the world, is considered the original of what follows — the falls out of language and reality and selfhood that feature in Rilke, Musil and Benn. These various falls, endings, stallings, 'Stürze ins Schweigen' ['plunges into silence'] come from the individual experience of an assault on language, where a 'moralischer, erkenntnishafter Ruck' ['moral, epistemological jolt'] has occurred (KS, p. 263; CW, p. 269). Jolts alter the 'Gangart' [gait] and trajectory of a writer — '[d]ieses Richtungnehmen, dieses Geschleudertwerden in eine Bahn' ['this setting of a course, this being catapulted into a trajectory'] (KS, p. 264; CW, p. 270; translation amended). This phenomenon which is the motor of newness in literature and language assumes in Bachmann's telling a fateful form. It is 'Richtung' [direction] made absolute that makes a writer ineluctable, but ineluctable too is his own fated task: 'Weil er Richtung hat, weil seine Bahn zieht wie den einzigen aller möglichen Wege [...] Weil er von sich weiß, ich bin unausweichlich, und weil er nicht ausweichen kann selber, enthüllt sich ihm seine Aufgabe' ['Because he has direction and maintains that direction as the only possible one among many [...] Because he asserts of himself that "I am undeflectable", and because he cannot sidestep, his mission is revealed to him'] (KS, p. 264; CW, p. 270; translation amended).

In summary then, we are noting here two key aspects of Bachmann's telling of literature's journey to itself, which is at the same time its exercise of agency in acknowledgement of its task. The journey's most crucial junctures are where and when a jolt inscribes itself in the gait and direction of language as it moves forward. The impact may occasion a lurch forward, but it may also occasion the opposite — namely a fall inwards, a falling down, falling silent, a moment of stalling in the journey of literature. Secondly, when literature picks itself up and 'goes on' after the fall, it becomes defined by a kind of inevitability vis-à-vis itself; it cannot but fulfil its mission to journey ever onwards, *unterwegs* — unavoidably — to itself. This is how literature does its own being. Paradoxically then, the point at which literature is most assuredly marking its own way comes about when it stalls; and its agency is strongest when it surrenders to its own mission. All of this happens, in Bachmann's telling, in two dimensions at once: one concerned with literature itself as a story (the Chandos dimension), one concerned with the stories told within literature (the Roßmann dimension). The former looks to the grand scale — the story of the 'whither' of literature, and the what and how of language; the latter looks to the individual, to those whose journeys are defined by versions of not stepping, and whose agency is thus expressed negatively. They are the stumblers, fallers and refusers who reveal the nature of agency and the story of literature as they go, and don't go.[6]

There is one more piece of Bachmann's framework to be put in place before we come back to 'Unter Mördern und Irren'. We have seen above how the hapless Karl Roßmann is read as a key figure, not just in *Das dreißigste Jahr*, but in Bachmann's work as a whole. I wish to extend this line of argument by suggesting that as a character defined by his 'fehlende Tatkraft' [lack of capacity to do], Roßmann has an important counterpart in Bachmann's literary-historical writings (KS, p. 91). That counterpart (which is also the term for one of two copies of a legal document) is Bachmann's Iago, of whom she writes: 'Jago ist das extremste Beispiel für das, was ein Mensch vermag' ['Iago is the most extreme example of what a human being is capable of'] (KS, p. 407; CW, p. 241). There are no limits to Iago's capacity to do, to cause others to do, to cause others to die. This capacity is both the driving force of Shakespeare's play and Verdi's opera and the monstrous zenith of human agency. It is 'von einer Art, die wir noch nicht einmal verstehen gelernt haben, obwohl soviel Hundertjahre über dieses Stück hinweggegangen sind' ['in a way that we have not yet learned to comprehend, despite the centuries that have elapsed since the play was written']

---

[6] Rachel MagShamhráin explores the 'static' underside of journeying and movement in Bachmann's work and its significance for literature in the post-pandemic world in 'Don't Go! Some Agoraphobic Postulates for a Post-Travel World Derived from Ingeborg Bachmann's "Probleme Probleme"', *Austrian Studies*, 31 (2023), pp. 16–35.

(KS, p. 407; CW, p. 240). Placing side by side Bachmann's readings of these two characters — one whose agency is expressed in its suspension and one whose agency is expressed in being unlimited — the overarching, underpinning question concerning humans then becomes: on the spectrum between Karl Roßmann and Iago, between the absence and excess of 'Tatkraft' [capacity to do], how to be — or rather, how to do being — without being a murderer. This question, articulated in the ungainly expression of what is in terms of what is done or not done and set against the backdrop of the self-reflection of literature, is the shared preoccupation of Bachmann and Melville.

III

When the men in 'Unter Mördern und Irren' step into the Kronenkeller, they adopt the action-words that build worlds and worldviews out of language: 'die Männer redeten und meinten und erzählten wie die Irrfahrer und Dulder, wie die Titanen und Halbgötter von der Geschichte und den Geschichten' (DJ, p. 94) [the men discussed and opined and told stories, like the wanderers and sufferers, the Titans and demigods of history and stories]. This is a world of manly agency, imagined in stories, realized in history, and remembered and regenerated in the circles of the Kronenkeller. Placed so ostentatiously in the inherited linguistic field of myths which interpolates the men before they say or do at all, they have their being only as bit players in a web whose weave already looms. Their agency must find its feet and its language in an imposed relation to paths already laid down and stories ripe for retelling and reliving. From this perspective, the conceptual field of the story seems closely aligned to that of the title story of the collection, 'Das dreißigste Jahr'; there too, the protagonist seeks a pathway and a language of agency, a mode of being and doing between inheritance and freedom. In 'Unter Mördern und Irren' that narrative is more difficult to discern, because it is played out in a collective, the members of which are not characters as such, but rather placeholder biographies representing strands of the general population 'nach dem Krieg' (DJ, p. 94) [after the war]. This men's circle, in other words, does not exist in and of itself, and is not self-constituting. Rather it is an illustration and a microcosm of the greater social imaginary, something with a history, a language, a path and a destiny, and something whose dispersed, collective agency is difficult to locate. Where, when and in whose name it acts may be difficult to pinpoint, but that it acts is clear. It acts to reproduce itself — by keeping on going, by doing in the present what was done in the past, by copying and replicating.

This, of course, is one of Bachmann's most enduring themes: the reproduction of fascism in the lives and the stories of a time called 'nach dem Krieg' (DJ, p. 94) [after the war]. And in this story as elsewhere, as everywhere, it is a gendered reproduction. While the men conceive of themselves as heroes and adventurers, the women, confined to pre-ordained passivity, can only dream of murder. The men are constitutively *unterwegs*; they are 'ihre ausgefahrenen, ausgerittenen, nie nach Hause kommenden Männer' (DJ, p. 95) [their journeyed out, ridden out, never homecoming men]. The women — their collective counterparts — are at home, 'angekommen bei ihren wahrhaftigsten Tränen' (DJ, p. 95) [having arrived at their most authentic tears], willing the myriad deaths of their men.

Much of the narrative of 'Unter Mördern und Irren' is concerned with identifying the tangled individual threads of the men's collective being and doing. Much of that is done by establishing a matrix of resistance and compliance with which to classify the characters. In this regard, their characterization schematizes that central exercise of individual agency — resisting or complying in the Nazi years, resisting or complying now, 'nach dem Krieg' (DJ, p. 94) [after the war], with the enduring transhistorical demands of social organization and social self-replication, and with the mythologies 'von der Geschichte und den Geschichten' (DJ, p. 94) [of history and stories] that underpin all of that. The active and passive Nazis, the active and passive victims, now sit together in their circle, and try to take their next collective step. What matters about that step is whether it will retrace practised actions, or whether it will forge what Bachmann finds modelled in literary history — some Büchneresque 'Inkonsequenz' (W, IV, pp. 278–93) [inconsistency], that is to say, a resistance to being consistent with what has always been the case.[7] Will what follows copy the past, write the same history-stories again, or with an altered gait and 'lebhaft mit dem Kommenden befasst' [actively focused on what is yet to come] will it, like the protagonist of 'Das dreißigste Jahr', heed its own closing instruction to 'steh auf und geh' [stand up and go] on a path not yet laid down (DJ, p. 71)?

The verbal acts of the men — their 'reden', 'meinen' and 'erzählen' (DJ, p. 94) [talking, opining, storytelling] — are measured against their established characters and their past deeds, as outlined by the narrator. They reveal themselves in their own speaking either in accordance with or in contradiction of what lies within and behind them. To make visible — literally — the truth or untruth of the way in which they present themselves, the story features a vagrant sketch artist who captures their images as they sit in the circle. The men are thus explicitly confronted with the gap between self-presentation and truth; they are made to see and read themselves. A second outsider figure is introduced into the circle as 'der Unbekannte' [literally: the unknown man], a man who presents himself by telling his own backstory.[8] This is the story

---

[7] Bachmann uses this term from Georg Büchner's novella *Lenz* as a central motif in her acceptance speech for the Büchner Prize, *Ein Ort für Zufälle* [A Place for Coincidences]. The word 'Inkonsequenz' describes a break with the logic of continuity and replication and reason.

[8] In *Malina* the protagonist signs letters using the designation 'Eine Unbekannte' [an unknown woman] as a proper name. Its purpose is to counter the assumption that that which has a name and a place in language is known and captured in and by that name. It acts therefore as a placeholder within language for that which is withheld. See W, III, pp. 9–337; as well as the Fourth Frankfurt Lecture: 'Namen' ['Names'] (KS, pp. 312–28; CW, pp. 306–20).

of his failed journey to himself. In his own telling, 'der Unbekannte' is a murderer — that is who he is, that is his destiny and he is eager to fulfil it. But this given 'Bestimmung' [destiny] is never realized.[9] The 'murderer' never acts in accordance with his character because the conditions imposed on his actions destroy its proper truth — that is to say its purity. For this 'murderer' to murder, the act must stand as the pure expression of his given character, his 'Bestimmung'. His doing must proceed purely and solely from his being, and it must anchor that true doing of being in a true word-name: 'Mörder' [murderer]. In contrast to this (perversely) prelapsarian ideal, the conditions appending to murder during the war are corrupted. In war one murders not because one must act out the truth of one's being, but because identities, concepts, mythologies, ideas stand to be eliminated, not with guns even, but with metaphors. One set of words — 'Polacken, Amis, Schwarze' [Polacks, Yanks, Blacks] — is to be erased by another — ' "Ausradieren", "aufreiben", "ausräuchern" ' [wipe out, grind down, burn out] (DJ, pp. 119–20). From the uncompromising perspective of the 'murderer', such words occlude the possibility of doing in accordance with being in a way that would be 'deutlich, nicht blumig' (DJ, p. 119) [clear, not flowery]. Moreover, in concealing and misnaming the acts they describe, they reveal language itself to be a potential, displaced domain of murder most foul. And so the story of the unknown man becomes the story of language. In this story, the particular, the individual, is murdered by the general, the collective. That collective acts in the name of a past, still underway, still ordaining (another 'Bestimmung') what can and cannot come into being, what can and cannot be done. The person who falls outside of this determination names (in the name 'der Unbekannte') the point at which names and words become only placeholders for what cannot be accommodated. The failure of the unknown man to be an agent for his own identity, to do murder as a murderer, is a failure to step into a language in which *bestimmte* terms and conditions apply. This is, as everyone in the story agrees, the act — or failure to act — of a madman.

[9] The 'murderer' (who never murdered) repeatedly uses the term 'bestimmt' [destined/ordained/set down in language/certain] in describing the force of certain knowledge that his being a murderer was not a decision, act or development in which he played any part. It was his given destiny, the intended destination of his life's journey, 'unterwegs zu sich'. This emphasis on 'Bestimmung' is underscored by the narrator, who notes that the 'murderer' addresses his remarks to no 'bestimmten Zuhörer' [particular/predetermined listener]. It suggests that the 'Bestimmung' of the murderer to realize his destiny by murdering has a counterpart in the 'Bestimmung' of all potential listeners to listen (and all potential readers to read) (DJ, p. 117).

IV

I want to suggest here that the act of 'der Unbekannte' in not acting bears fruitful comparison with Herman Melville's character, Bartleby the Scrivener. Bartleby is a man also defined by a failure to act, but even more than that by the contagious phrase that expresses that failure: 'I would prefer not to'.[10] His existence is played out in language. He is a copyist, employed to replicate originals, to reproduce precisely what already is. In other words, he is a man whose very profession is based on the prohibition of difference in language (and by extension, in law). And the test of his copying skills is the simultaneous, synchronized reading of original and copies by multiple readers. In this way, any difference introduced by the scribe is brought to light and erased. It is, to be sure, a very particular mode of reading that patrols and controls both the text and its scrivener and safeguards the production of reproduction.

Bartleby's withdrawal from this activity on the grounds that he would 'prefer not to' makes him the scrivener who does not scriven, a man at odds with his own name-designation. This alone sets him apart from the other characters in the story, whose names are transparently, descriptively 'true'. But there is more to Bartleby's self-description than the phrase that famously defines him as one who resists by resisting definition. He also insists repeatedly and conspicuously, and as if to qualify his preference for preferring not to: 'I am not particular' (B, p. 36). To be particular means to have one's singularity borne out by the fact of having preferences. When Bartleby says 'I am not particular', he is saying 'I have no preferences'; the man who prefers not to has no preferences. He is also denying the very individuality that his act of denial expresses. Characterized by his speaking, Bartleby is therefore a man indifferent to the demand for consistency — a fatal flaw in a copyist. Moreover, he speaks as one indifferent to the existence of difference, on which the meaning making of language depends. If the word 'not' establishes no difference from that to which it refers, then the poles of yes and no, of assent and dissent, resistance and compliance, lose the clarity on which the expression of response and preference, and with that the expression of the self and its place in life and language, depend. Bartleby's particularity points forward to that place where, as Bachmann describes it, language seems to will its own end by making visible its 'Unzulänglichkeit' [inadequacy]; it is 'irreführend [...] verwerflich [...] beliebig, befangen [...] der Wahrheit immer etwas schuldig' ['misleading [...] reprehensible [...] arbitrary, biased [...] always [...] fall[ing] short of the truth'] (KS, p. 258; CW, pp. 265–56). The shortfall of language in respect of truth and the consequences of that for writing and writers when 'kein Auftrag mehr da ist von oben und überhaupt kein Auftrag mehr kommt, keiner mehr täuscht' ['there is no longer

---

[10] Herman Melville, *Bartleby, the Scrivener: A Story of Wall-Street*, in Herman Melville, *Billy Budd, Sailor and Selected Tales*, ed. by Robert Milder (Oxford University Press, 1998), pp. 3–41 (p. 11 and throughout). References to this volume will henceforth be given in the text as B followed by the page number(s).

a commission from a higher authority, no longer any commission, none to deceive us any longer'] (KS, pp. 257–58: CW, p. 265) — this, I would argue, is the context in which Bartleby's preferences and particularity in the face of his commission ('Bestimmung') is to be considered. He belongs in Bachmann's literary history of those who stumble and mumble and fall silent; of all that fall (so to speak) and 'alles, was der Fall ist' [all that is the case].[11] In other words, read with Bachmann, Bartleby finds his particular tribe.

When Gilles Deleuze reads Bartleby, he too is concerned with particularity. Deleuze is one of those prominent philosophers — the list also includes Jacques Derrida, Maurice Blanchot, Giorgio Agamben, Michael Hardt and Antonio Negri — whose attention to the story is indicative of the prominent contagion of its attraction, outside the story as well as within it. As the narrator within the text notes, Bartleby has 'turned the tongues' of all others in the office, who now pepper their sentences with 'preferring' (B, p. 25). But that is only the beginning of its contagion — a generation on from famous philosophers 'reading Melville now', today Bartleby inspires accounts of his significance that prefer not to agree with what has already been said, but find themselves nonetheless within its sphere.[12]

Deleuze's reading of Bartleby's particularity is not as the counterpart of preference as I have read it above, but rather as the counterpart of universality. The claim not to be particular is, says Deleuze, a claim to be universal; it 'subsists once and for all and in all cases'.[13] This way of understanding Bartleby's particularity is also supported by the open-endedness of the 'preferring not to' phrase, which can be completed in any given way. In the 'agrammaticality' of its formula, which, as Deleuze describes it, 'annihilates "copying", the only reference in relation to which something might or might not be preferred', Bartleby's stated preference undermines the capacity of language per se to refer: 'it hollows out a zone of indetermination that renders words indistinguishable, that creates a vacuum within language'.[14] In other words, regardless of whether we approach Bartleby's defining sentence as a signifier of individual or universal

---

[11] Samuel Beckett, *All That Fall and Other Plays for Radio and Screen*, preface and notes by Everett Frost (Faber, 2009). The second reference here is to the famous opening line of Ludwig Wittgenstein's *Tractatus logico-philosophicus: Logisch-philosophische Abhandlung*, 28th edn (Suhrkamp, 2003), 'Die Welt ist alles, was der Fall ist' [The world is everything that is the case]. Bachmann writes in the original version of her essay 'Ludwig Wittgenstein — Zu einem Kapitel der jüngsten Philosophiegeschichte' [Ludwig Wittgenstein — On a Chapter of Most Recent History of Philosophy] that Wittgenstein's understanding of the sentence ('der Satz') fixes reality as 'yes' or 'no' (KS, p. 61). The German word 'Satz', as well as meaning sentence, also designates what is set down, what belongs together and — contrarily — a leap or jolt.
[12] See Emile Bojesen and Ansgar Allen, 'Bartleby is Dead: Inverting Common Readings of Melville's *Bartleby, the Scrivener*', *Angelaki*, 24.5 (2019), pp. 61–72.
[13] Gilles Deleuze, 'Bartleby; or The Formula', in Gilles Deleuze, *Essays Critical and Clinical*, trans. by Daniel W. Smith and Michael A. Greco (Verso, 1998), pp. 68–90 (p. 69).
[14] Ibid., p. 73.

agency and identity ('I am particularly unparticular' or 'I am universal'), his mode of being (that is to say, preferring not to) brings the reader to the same point: standing on the threshold between the inside and outside of language where the terms and conditions of speech acts become visible.

Giorgio Agamben follows this lead (or contagion) in looking to the manner in which language seems to expose and simultaneously hold fast to its own suspension of meaning. He describes Bartleby's 'preferring not to' as an act of 'stepping forward and stepping backward at the same time'.[15] It is, he says, a phrase that makes the absence of a referent spin back on itself: '*I would prefer not to prefer not to prefer not to ...*'[16] It is, for our purposes here, a perfect performance of copying, a production of the ineluctable logic of reproduction. Even as Bartleby establishes the redemptive possibility of resistance as negation — no more copying — in his expression of preference for 'not', he exposes the destructive terms of the language which that gesture must inhabit: language entraps that which enters it. Bachmann's *Malina* narrator, who signs herself 'eine Unbekannte' [an unknown woman], describes this bind: 'die Sprache ist die Strafe. In sie müssen alle Dinge eingehen und in ihr müssen sie wieder vergehen nach ihrer Schuld und dem Ausmaß ihrer Schuld' (W, III, p. 97) ['language is punishment. All things must enter it and perish there according to their sin and the scale of their sin'].[17]

In its hovering between affirmation and negation, consent and refusal, Agamben goes on to argue that Bartleby's 'preferring not to' presents a fundamental insult to Leibniz's principle of sufficient reason; it thwarts the demand of the philosopher-reader to trace what is back to its sources and forward to its consequences. The narrator's initial response to Bartleby reads as follows:

> With any other man I should have flown outright into a dreadful passion, scorned all further words, and thrust him ignominiously from my presence. But there was something about Bartleby that not only strangely disarmed me, but in a wonderful manner touched and disconcerted me. I began to reason with him. (B, p. 13)

What takes place, Agamben goes on, say the thinkers of reason, must have a reason, otherwise there is only the will of men inhabiting and shaping a fairy tale world.[18] Bartleby's preference-no preference gives no reason and admits of no narrator's reasoning; it is, in other words, the very definition

[15] Giorgio Agamben, 'Bartleby, or On Contingency', in Giorgio Agamben, *Potentialities: Collected Essays in Philosophy*, ed. and trans. by Daniel Heller-Roazen (Stanford University Press, 1999), pp. 243–71 (p. 255).

[16] Ibid., p. 255. Italics in original.

[17] Agamben quotes these lines in his reading of Kafka's Penal Colony as a text about the punishment machine of language. Giorgio Agamben, *Idea of Prose*, trans. by Michael Sullivan and Sam Whitsitt (SUNY Press, 1995), p. 115.

[18] Agamben, 'Bartleby', p. 258. Here Agamben is referring to Christian Wolff commenting on the work of his teacher, Leibniz.

of 'Inkonsequenz', as described by Bachmann reading Büchner in Berlin, a city of 'Zufälle' (W, IV, p. 278) [coincidences] where things and people befall one another without reason. But 'Inkonsequenz' — the kind of madness that upends everyone else's reason — is itself most consequential, especially when it pitches its tent right in the centre of language production and prefers not to budge. Bartleby is, after all, above all, a 'motionless young man', of 'long-continued motionlessness' (B, pp. 10, 21). (It is no great surprise that Bartleby became a point of reference for the Occupy (Wall Street) Movement.)[19] And so, even when the firm moves elsewhere, Bartleby remains, 'like the last column of some ruined temple, [...] standing mute and solitary' (B, p. 27). When he occupies the stairwell, Bartleby resembles Kafka's Odradek, inhabiting a space without having a place or executing a task, preferring not to do, but persisting in being.[20] Both figures are tolerated on the basis that they are not 'ordinarily human' (B, p. 12); both inspire a will to reason and acute anxiety in the narrators whose task it is to tell their stories. Both narrators worry that their subjects will outlive them. Melville's narrator worries that Bartleby will be murdered, worries about his own capacity for murder and eventually presents this ominous assessment of things to Bartleby: 'one of two things must take place. Either you must do something, or something must be done to you' (B, p. 35). Where reason is thwarted, murder is incited. Not stepping into a language in which the terms and conditions of reason apply prompts the speaking and doing of others. These are the terms and conditions made visible by Odradek — a being without linguistic or genetic source, and without 'Bestimmung' — and lived to their logical conclusion by the scrivener who prefers not to scriven and the murderer who prefers not to murder.

In place of Bartleby's speaking, the narrator speaks; and in accumulated layers thereafter, readers read, again, now. In Jacques Derrida's reading of *Bartleby*, it is this structure of reading itself that is to the fore. The narrator is both a man of law and an analyst who is provoked into reading — that is to say, analysing and writing the story of Bartleby — by Bartleby's failure to 'render reason'.[21] To analyse is — traced to its Greek origins — to untie, to untangle, to acquit.[22] Analysis, it follows, is called for, but also resisted, when things are in a knot, when someone prefers (k)not to. Here, where unyielding characters loom, where the weave of the story is tangled, its threads entwining and unravelling — Odradek-like — in disorderly fashion, here reading is called for.[23]

---

[19] See Bojesen and Allen, 'Bartleby is Dead'; and on the relationship between work, occupation and Bartleby's immobility, see Michael Hardt and Antonio Negri, *Empire* (Harvard University Press, 2000), pp. 203–04.

[20] Franz Kafka, 'Die Sorge des Hausvaters' [literally, The Worry of the House-Father] in Franz Kafka, *Sämtliche Erzählungen*, ed. by Paul Raabe (Fischer, 1970), pp. 139–40.

[21] Jacques Derrida, 'Resistances', in *Resistances of Psychoanalysis*, trans. by Peggy Kamuf, Pascale-Anne Brault and Michael Naas (Stanford University Press, 1998), pp. 1–38 (p. 5).

[22] Ibid., pp. 3, 27.

[23] Odradek is made of, among other things, bits of unravelling thread.

What is disorderly and disordered must act or be acted upon in accordance with that determination ('Bestimmung') and remove itself or be removed. Bartleby ends, like 'der Unbekannte' — among murderers and madmen. What Bartleby and 'der Unbekannte' have in common is that they reach beyond a shared 'failure' to act, to step reasonably into their designated place in language and in being — the copier by copying, the murderer by murdering — and point to the possibility within language, within 'Geschichte und Geschichten' (DJ, p. 94) [history and stories], of facing the full import of the (k)not/'preferring not to' of being and doing 'Unterwegssein' (KS, p. 345) [being underway]. To prefer not to, is not just to reproduce, not just to retrace the paths and words of old patterns of being and doing what has already been determined, by the names and habits and inhabitants of collectives. Reading the failed scrivener and the failed murderer in light of one another and in light of what they share with Kafka makes visible their common conviction: failure to comply with the reasonable terms and conditions of language carries a death sentence. But it also animates literature.

The potential for this animation to occur depends on the reader — the addressee of the declared not/knot. Bartleby, it is rumoured, once worked in the Dead Letter Office, the destiny-destination ('Bestimmung') of letters whose intended readers cannot be found. He knows therefore the fragility of what the scribe trusts when he trusts in language. It is knowledge he shares with the narrator of Bachmann's *Malina*, endlessly writing letters which 'nicht den Weg der Verschickung gehen, sondern den Weg des Abfalls' [do not go the way of dispatch, but rather the way of refuse (literally, what falls off)], and endlessly signing herself 'Eine Unbekannte'.[24] The addressee of such writing can only be a reader who knows that the source that commits itself to doing language, by being in language is, as a matter of truth, *unbekannt*. It is both the peril and the potentiality of language and literature that this is so. Those — like Bachmann — who step into language to make visible its murderous or redemptive terms and conditions are both sacrificed to and make possible the agency of literature — that is to say, its potential to be a literature that does.

---

[24] For an extensive contextualization of this phenomenon in Bachmann's work as a whole, see Sigrid Weigel, *Ingeborg Bachmann: Hinterlassenschaften unter Wahrung des Briefgeheimnisses* (Zsolnay, 1999), pp. 543–58 (p. 553).

From *Todesarten* to *Artensterben*: Re-reading Bachmann through an Ecocritical Lens

CONOR BRENNAN

St John's College, University of Oxford

I

In a TV broadcast from 1964, an interviewer points out to Ingeborg Bachmann that the words used most frequently in her poetry — night, light, eyes, wind, land, sun, sky, and sea — are, in many ways, 'Standardworte der konventionellen Naturlyrik' [the standard words of conventional nature poetry]. Bachmann, who has been fiddling idly with the lever of her typewriter, places her hands down and looks at him. Her expression is impassive; it contains, perhaps, just a hint of exasperation. The interviewer, unperturbed, asks: 'Wollen Sie Natur in Ihrer Lyrik wiedergeben?' [Do you wish to represent nature in your poetry?]. After a beat, Bachmann replies: 'Nein, gewiss will ich das nicht. Die Natur, oder was man im Zusammenhang mit Lyrik unter Natur versteht, interessiert mich überhaupt nicht' [No, I certainly don't. Nature, or what is usually meant by nature in the context of poetry, doesn't interest me at all].[1]

To contemporary ecocritical eyes, it is a fascinating exchange. The verb the interviewer uses — 'wiedergeben' — does not mean strictly 'to represent', but to reflect or reproduce; literally, to 'give back'. It is a clumsy choice for Bachmann's poetry, which is highly stylized, anything but mimetic. More intriguing, however, is Bachmann's response. It tells us emphatically, if we did not know already, what kind of ecological writer Bachmann is not: she is not a Lake Poet or a literary eco-activist espousing the sublime and the beautiful in Nature with a capital N. Nonetheless, although she clearly rejects this characterization of her writing, she does not say simply that 'nature' does not interest her — meaning, presumably, the aspects of the physical world and biosphere that her go-to nouns commonly designate. Instead, she specifies that the real object of her indifference is *what is usually meant by nature in the context of poetry*. 'Ich

[1] 'Ingeborg Bachmann erhält den Georg-Büchner-Preis 1964', ARD Mediathek, 6:02 <https://www.ardmediathek.de/video/kultur-im-norden/ingeborg-bachmann-erhaelt-den-georg-buechner-preis/ndr/Y3JpZDovL25kci5kZS9jOWRjMmQ4MyozMzNjLTQzMzktODA1MCoxODZhYmVhNmVmMTA> [accessed 16 July 2024], my translation.

Austrian Studies 32 (2024), doi:10.1353/aus.00003, pp. 27–40

glaube nicht,' she concludes, 'dass ich zu den Gräserbewisperern gehöre' [I do not believe that I am one of those who whisper to the grasses].[2]

What Bachmann's response leaves open is the possibility of a different understanding of ecological writing. Bachmann's rejection of what is usually understood by nature in poetic contexts recalls the ideas of the well-known ecocritic Timothy Morton, for instance, who argues in *Ecology without Nature* that the very attempt to cordon off 'Nature' or 'the environment' from ourselves is part of the problem. 'Putting something called Nature on a pedestal and admiring it from afar', Morton writes, 'does for the environment what patriarchy does for the figure of Woman'.[3] Their work attempts to counteract this view with a more expansive understanding of what it means to 'be ecological', an understanding that includes the synthetic and the aesthetic. Morton's big claim that 'all art is ecological' rests partly on perceived analogies between how we relate to art and how we relate to animals and other non-human lifeforms, as kinds of attention to something beyond the self.[4] In a similar way, Bachmann's reply indicates that she thinks of the nouns the interviewer lists both as symbolic or associative references to something else, and as allusions to other texts and poets in a textual, aesthetic realm: the word 'Gräserbewisperer', as she points out in the interview, was coined by Gottfried Benn.[5] At the same time, the very ambition and expansiveness of a literary project like *Todesarten* — which Bachmann envisaged as 'eine einzige große Studie aller möglichen Todesarten' (GuI, p. 66) [a single great study of all possible ways of dying'; or 'all possible types of death'] — invites us to think beyond the specific forms of violence Bachmann was concerned with, and to extend her insights to the systems underpinning environmental destruction and ecocide. Reading Bachmann now, in a time of ecological crisis, some of the 'Todesarten' that such a project brings to mind most readily are the industrial slaughter of animals and the destruction of the biosphere, including in its extreme consequence of *Artensterben* [extinction of species].

This article, then, will present the case for reading Bachmann as an ecological writer — not in the terms of 'konventionelle Naturlyrik' [conventional nature poetry] offered by the hapless interviewer, but with reference to her particular

---

[2] Ibid., 6:09.

[3] Timothy Morton, *Ecology without Nature: Rethinking Environmental Aesthetics* (Harvard University Press, 2009), p. 5.

[4] 'Your indifference to ecological things', Bachmann might be pleased to hear, 'is exactly the sort of place where you will find the right kind of ecological feeling' (Timothy Morton, *Being Ecological* (MIT Press, 2018), p. 125). For Morton, this is why 'being able to *appreciate* ambiguity is at the basis of being ecological [...] *You don't know why you should care*: isn't that what we are all feeling when we experience something beautiful? How come this chord sequence is making tears run down my face? Reasons for being nice to other lifeforms abound, but around them there is a ghostly penumbra of feelings of appreciating them for no reason at all' (ibid.).

[5] 'Ingeborg Bachmann erhält den Georg-Büchner Preis 1964', 6:15.

aesthetic and the philosophical concerns of her prose. The central examples I will draw on here are the many images of suffering animals in Bachmann's fiction, which are viewed by the protagonists of *Todesarten*, in particular, as ciphers or mirrors of their own plight. The propulsive, associative style of much of Bachmann's prose, which serves to connect the victims of various types of violence — not always in an equal relation — will form the crux of the argument. The article considers two distinct ways of thinking about this associative aesthetic, each with its own implications for reading Bachmann ecocritically. Bachmann's aesthetic will be analysed first in terms of 'multidirectional' narration, and, secondly, in the older language of archetypes. In each instance, comparisons will be drawn with prominent contemporary writers whose work chimes with Bachmann's in various ways, including the Polish Nobel laureate Olga Tokarczuk, the Korean writer and recent Nobel winner Han Kang, and the Irish playwright Marina Carr. The strong resonances between Bachmann's writing and these recent texts — all of which are more overtly 'ecological' in content than the *Todesarten* cycle — demonstrate both the potential and the need for new, ecologically inflected readings of Bachmann's singular body of work.

II

Before turning to the case of *Todesarten* specifically, it is worth examining one key image from Bachmann's earlier prose that chimes with and helps to clarify some of the ideas presented by Morton. The image is that of 'das blaue Wild' ['the blue deer'] (W, II, p. 159; TY, p. 78) from the story 'Unter Mördern und Irren' (1961) [Among Murderers and Madmen]. It provides a useful touchstone for the more expansive idea of ecological fiction, because we can think of this 'blue deer' or 'blue game' as an animal, but also as art and — as I will argue later — as an archetype.[6] The story centres on a circle of men during a night on the town in postwar Vienna, and on the various ways in which they avoid facing up to the consequences of the wartime past. Anticipating the *Todesarten* texts, however, these are not only modern men in postwar Vienna, but also hunters and storytellers in a kind of primordial desert space: they 'kommen geradewegs aus den Redaktionen und den Bürohäusern, aus der Praxis und den Ateliers und treffen uns, heften uns auf die Fährte, jagen [...]' ['come straight from publishing houses and office blocks, from surgeries and studios, and meet, take up the trail, hunt (...)'] (W, III, p. 159; TY, p. 77, lightly edited). Within the realist scaffolding of Vienna after the war, the men settle down 'am Feuer

---

[6] While the German word 'Wild' is used to refer to any animals targeted by hunters — and indeed, the transformation of anything 'wild' into 'quarry' or a 'game' is exactly what is at issue in reading Bachmann's patriarchal figures ecologically — the proximity to the common word 'Rotwild' [red deer] suggests the more specific translation, also chosen by Michael Bullock in his published version (TY, p. 78).

[...] in der Nacht und der Wüste, in der sie waren' ['by the fire (...) in the night and the desert in which they were'] (W, II, pp. 159; TY, p. 78). What they are hunting, meanwhile, is 'das blaue Wild' ['the blue deer'], which appears first as 'das Beste, was wir verloren haben' ['the best that we have lost'] (W, II, pp. 159; TY, p. 77).

In keeping with Morton's alignment of the ecological and the aesthetic, 'das blaue Wild' can certainly be understood as art — the phrase is an allusion to the poetry of Georg Trakl, where it crops up quite frequently, often appearing as something like the soul.[7] In its non-mimetic appearance, it recalls the paintings of 'Der blaue Reiter' produced by several of Trakl's Expressionist contemporaries. The 1913 painting *Tierschicksale* [*Animal Fates*] by Franz Marc, for instance — who, like Trakl, was to become a casualty of the Great War one year later — features a blue deer in the centre, in an uncharacteristically dark version of the many colourful animals in Marc's paintings, most famously three tranquil blue horses. This is significant partly because 'das blaue Wild' is linked in Bachmann's story to the voices and identities that are silenced or othered in order for the 'Herrenrunde' ['men's circle' (TY, p. 78) or 'circle of masters'] to stay on track, such as the women confined at home or, more centrally in the story, the Jewish victims of the Holocaust. The idea of blue animal paintings as 'entartete Kunst' [degenerate art] links 'das blaue Wild' to the victims of fascism through the process of cordoning off and rejection from the self: in the us-and-them logic of fascism, paintings of blue animals are as alien as Jews. The men in the story seem to feel the loss of the blue deer profoundly: they 'jagten das blaue Wild [...], und solange es nicht zurückkehrte, blieb die Welt ein Wahn' ['hunted the blue deer (...) and so long as it did not come back the world remained a madness'] (W, II, p. 172; TY, p. 90). At the same time, they relate to it only by hunting it, and though they claim to be searching for the blue deer, they do their best not to listen to what it has to say. It is only in the silences that its voice is heard: 'wenn keinem ein Witz einfällt oder eine Geschichte, die unbedingt erzählt werden muß, wenn keiner gegen das Schweigen aufkommt und jeder in sich versinkt, hört hin und wieder einer das blaue Wild klagen — noch einmal, noch immer' ['when nobody thinks of a joke or a story that must definitely be told, when nobody assails the silence and everyone sinks into himself, someone now and then hears the blue deer lament — once more, still'] (W, II, p. 159; TY, pp. 77–78).

In Morton's view of ecology as coexistence, the men's longing for the blue deer — which they themselves have driven away and seek to destroy — can be understood as a longing for otherness itself. 'When you experience beauty', Morton writes, 'you experience evidence in your inner space that at least one

---

[7] Versions of the phrase ('Blaues Wild' and 'ein blaues Wild') occur in the poems 'An die Schwester', 'Elis', 'Passion', 'Sommersneige', 'Nachtseele', 'An Luzifer', and 'Am Abend'. Georg Trakl, *Dichtungen und Briefe*, ed. by Walther Killy and Hans Szklemar (Otto Müller Verlag, 1971), pp. 32–33; 48–49; 68–69; 75; 107–08; 186–87; 189–90.

thing that isn't you exists'.[8] 'Das blaue Wild' seems to exemplify this point perfectly: it is a beautiful phrase, a beautiful image. Morton characterizes the experience of beauty as 'an evanescent footprint in your inner space — you don't need to prove that things are real by hitting them or eating them'.[9] While Bachmann might agree with the reading of beauty as the evidence of something other than oneself, she takes a markedly less optimistic view of how humans — and particularly men — respond to such an experience. Instead of 'a nonviolent coexisting without coercion',[10] her work imagines would-be masters whose primary impulse towards otherness is to coerce, possess and dominate it, and who destroy the object of their desire in the process. These figures are then left once again 'in [ihrem] Wahn' ['in (their) madness'] (W, II, p. 186; TY, p. 104), trapped in their heads, longing for a way out that they have themselves foreclosed. In a twenty-first century reading context, this appears not least as an apt allegorical depiction of the relationship between humans and other species. The narrator of 'Unter Mördern und Irren' — a conscientious objector who nonetheless, by the end of the story, is horrified to find blood on his hands — was, for Bachmann, a figure mired in the complexities of Austrian postwar guilt. In a contemporary ecocritical reading, however, his condition might be seen to anticipate what Timothy Clark terms 'Anthropocene horror': the guilt that arises 'from living in a context of latent environmental violence and feeling personally trapped in its wrongs'.[11]

The image of the blue deer also provides a useful entry point into discussions of the associative logic at work in much of Bachmann's prose, including the *Todesarten* texts. Its otherness, as I have already suggested, is aligned in the text with the ideologically constructed otherness of Jewish Holocaust victims. As the story's 'Herrenrunde' gathers, missing one or two of its regulars, their friend Mahler comments darkly to the narrator and Friedl: 'Wir sind heute nur drei Juden' ['There are only three of us Jews here this evening'] (W, II, p. 161; TY, p. 79). This is a strange comment, as immediately signalled in Friedl's reaction: 'Friedl starrte ihn verständnislos [...] an [...], wohl weil er dachte, daß er doch gar kein Jude sei, und Mahler war es auch nicht, sein Vater vielleicht, sein Großvater — Friedl wußte es nicht genau' ['Friedl stared at him uncomprehendingly (...), no doubt because he thought he wasn't a Jew at all, and nor was Mahler, his father perhaps, his grandfather — Friedl didn't know exactly'] (W, II, p. 161; TY, p. 79). The characters in question, that is, are not Jewish in any straightforward sense. Instead, Mahler is pointing to an associative truth. In the exclusionary logic of fascism, and of the group's ringleaders, the narrator's faction — made

---

[8] Timothy Morton, *Dark Ecology: For a Logic of Future Coexistence* (Columbia University Press, 2016), p. 149.

[9] Ibid.

[10] Ibid.

[11] Timothy Clark, 'Ecological Grief and Anthropocene Horror', *American Imago*, 77.1 (2020), pp. 61–80 (p. 62).

up of wartime conscientious objectors — does not fully belong among the 'Herren' [men/masters]. Mahler's comment, then, hits on a truth of sorts, in that it exposes the arbitrariness of the concept 'Jew' as constructed in Nazi ideology.

Viewed in this light, 'Unter Mördern und Irren' is an early example of how Bachmann's fiction links various types of violence: most famously patriarchy and fascism, but also the violence of colonialism, as highlighted in other contributions to this volume. This approach of linking the victims and the perpetrators of quite different types of violence is not without its difficulties and its detractors, most visibly in the case of *Das Buch Franza* [*The Book of Franza*]. Franza's pronouncements that 'Ich bin von niedriger Rasse. Oder müsste es nicht Klasse heißen' ['I am from a lower race. Or perhaps it's a class'] (W, III, p. 413; BFRG, p. 79) and 'Ich bin eine Papua' ['I am a Papuan'] (W, III, p. 414; BFRG, p. 80) conflate radically different types of oppression in a way that sits uneasily with many readers.[12]

One theoretical paradigm for analysing and defending this type of writing is Michael Rothberg's concept of 'multidirectional memory', which has been applied to Bachmann's work by scholars like Tessa Wegener.[13] The term was coined by Rothberg to describe texts that 'connect instances of institutional violence and social injustice that are apparently separate in place and time', and is offered as a counter-model to 'competitive memory', which creates a priority-queue understanding of history in which vaster injustices like the Holocaust leave no space for the commemoration of other atrocities.[14] This has proved to be a controversial argument particularly in Germany, where a translation of Rothberg's book in 2021 ignited a public debate about the uniqueness of the Holocaust dubbed 'Historikerstreit 2.0'.[15] What Rothberg

---

[12] This is reflected in critical attempts to read the text as a deliberate portrayal of self-blindness on Franza's part, setting her statements at an ironic distance from the narrative voice. Sara Lennox points to multiple textual hints that 'readers should regard Franza's own judgments with some scepticism', from a late draft that 'clearly pokes fun' at Franza's white saviour complex to the 'ubiquitous bottles of Coca-Cola she drinks along her journey' (Sara Lennox, *Cemetery of the Murdered Daughters: Feminism, History, and Ingeborg Bachmann* (University of Massachusetts Press, 2006), pp. 275–76). Lennox's argument is picked up and elaborated on by Heidi Schlipphacke, who maintains that 'the "symbolic" [...] and, I would add, formalist nature of Bachmann's use of tropes of oppression in the Franza fragment point to a conflicted textual irony' (Heidi Schlipphacke, 'Postmodernism and the Place of Nostalgia in Ingeborg Bachmann's *Franza* Fragment', *The German Quarterly*, 79.1 (2006), pp. 71–89 (p. 73)).

[13] Tessa Wegener, 'Blurred Spaces and Belated Shock: The Poetics of Multidirectional Memory in Ingeborg Bachmann's *The Book of Franza*', *Women in German Yearbook*, 30 (2014), pp. 1–22.

[14] Robert Dixon, 'Circles of Violence: Historical Constellations in *Death of a River Guide* and *The Sound of One Hand Clapping*', in *Richard Flanagan: Critical Essays*, ed. by Robert Dixon (Sydney University Press, 2018), pp. 21–41 (pp. 32–33); see Michael Rothberg, *Multidirectional Memory: Remembering the Holocaust in the Age of Decolonization* (Stanford University Press, 2009).

[15] See Jürgen Habermas, 'Der neue Historikerstreit', *Philosophie Magazin*, 6 (2021), pp.

has in mind are first and foremost the connections between the Holocaust and European colonialism, aligning his study in obvious ways with the concerns of *Das Buch Franza*. Another type of victim evoked very often in *Todesarten*, however — as well as in the work of several authors Rothberg mentions directly, among them W. G. Sebald[16] — are suffering animals, which we can start to think about through the example of 'the blue deer'. We have already seen that Bachmann, in her own time, was not much concerned with literal animals; instead, 'das blaue Wild' is a kind of condensed poetic image for all that is excluded from and hunted by the 'Herrenrunde' [men's circle/circle of masters]. But the idea of multidirectionality raises the intriguing prospect that metaphors and comparisons can work in both directions: that the emphasis can begin to flow back towards the source of the metaphor. Even if suffering animals are invoked by Bachmann only to provide an image for the plight of women within patriarchy, or for Jewish Holocaust victims, this very comparison might allow for empathy to reflect back on the literal animal being used in the service of metaphor.

This is the move that Carol J. Adams refers to as 'restoring the absent referent'.[17] In her foundational work *The Sexual Politics of Meat* (1990), Adams argues that there is an intimate connection between the way women and meat are represented in Western culture, which she locates in the 'cycle of objectification, fragmentation and consumption [that] links butchering with both the representation and reality of sexual violence'.[18] Adams draws on a long tradition of feminist writing that includes Woolf's *Three Guineas*, which she quotes to the effect that 'scarcely a human being in the course of history has fallen to a woman's rifle; the vast majority of birds and beasts have been killed by you, not us'.[19] Her key concern is with restoring what she calls the 'absent referent': the real, experiencing animal made absent in the act of butchering it into parts; in the use of different language for meat than for living animals; and in the use of both meat and animals for the purposes of metaphor.[20] In *Todesarten*, as I have already suggested, these animals crop up frequently, offering the female protagonists a view of their own fate. In *Das Buch Franza*, Franza recognizes herself in a camel slaughtered for a wedding

---

10–11; Michael Rothberg, 'Lived Multidirectionality: "Historikerstreit 2.0" and the Politics of Holocaust Memory', *Memory Studies*, 15.6 (2022), pp. 1316–29.

[16] Rothberg, *Multidirectional Memory*, pp. 27–28.

[17] Carol J. Adams, *The Sexual Politics of Meat: A Feminist-Vegetarian Critical Theory*, (Continuum, 1990; facsimile repr. 2010), p. 66.

[18] Ibid., p. 73. Adams regularly updates her website with recent illustrations of her argument from popular and online culture: Carol J. Adams, 'Examples of the Sexual Politics of Meat' <https://www.caroljadams.com/examples-of-spom> [accessed 3 February 2023].

[19] Adams, *The Sexual Politics of Meat*, p. 66.

[20] Ibid, pp. 66–67. Adams's second example of how animals are rendered into 'absent referents' in the production of meat — through language — does not always apply in German.

feast, thinking: 'Das Kamel, sie hatten das Kamel getötet. Ich weiß, wie ich aussehe. Ich sehe aus wie das Kamel, das mich ansieht' ['The camel, they had killed the camel. I know what I look like. I look like the camel that is looking at me'] (W, III, p. 440; BFRG, p. 113, lightly altered). *Malina*'s Ich explains to Ivan that she is trying 'mich in das Leben einer Fliege hineinzudenken oder in das Leben eines Kaninchens, das im Labor für einen Versuch mißbraucht wird, in eine Ratte, die man abspritzt, aber die doch noch einmal haßvoll zum Sprung ansetzt' ['to imagine myself as a fly or a rabbit being abused in some laboratory experiment, or a rat, which has been injected but, full of hate, makes one final jump'] (TKA, III.1, p. 621; MB, p. 232): an undertaking Ivan no more understands or approves of than he does the manuscript titled *Todesarten*. Bachmann's earliest sketches for the novel fragment first published as *Requiem für Fanny Goldmann* [*Requiem for Fanny Goldmann*], now re-edited as *Das Buch Goldmann* [*The Book of Goldmann*], centre on Fanny's identification with slaughtered and butchered animals after she has been exploited by the writer Anton Marek, who has gutted her lived experience and selfhood in turning her into a novel. Reading Marek's book, Fanny is overcome with the sensation that she has been ' "ausgeschlachtet" [...], ja es heißt ausgeschlachtet, so heißt es [...] er hatte sie ausgeweidet, hatte aus ihr Blutwurst und Braten und alles gemacht, er hatte sie geschlachtet sie war geschlachtet' (BG, pp. 16–17) ["butchered" (...), yes they call it butchered, that's what it's called (...) he had gutted her, had made blood sausage and roast and everything out of her, he had slaughtered her she was slaughtered; my translation]. She cannot bear 'diese Schande, daß sie hier geschlachtet, gekocht und geräuchert worden war, wie ein Schwein' ['this disgrace, namely the disgrace of her having been sliced up, boiled, and smoked like a pig'] (BG, p. 17; BFRG, p. 190).

The most common way of reading these images — one that aligns with Bachmann's non-*Gräserbewisperer* status — is as a kind of visceral metaphor for the violence patriarchy inflicts on women. 'The first metaphor', as John Berger puts it, 'was animal'.[21] But the very idea of *Todesarten* as a project opens up the possibility of attending to animal victims and their deaths in their own right. One major contemporary writer whose work chimes with Bachmann's in this regard is the Polish writer Olga Tokarczuk. Tokarczuk shares Bachmann's philosophical, historical and formal ambition, but places ecological concerns and the suffering of animals front and centre, reversing the direction of many of Bachmann's comparisons. A character in Tokarczuk's novel *Flights* (*Bieguni*, 2007; trans. by Jennifer Croft, 2017), for instance, recalls the *Todesarten* project in unexpected ways. Where *Todesarten* appears in part as an elaboration of the thought that fascism begins in the relationships between people, that it is 'das erste in der Beziehung zwischen einem Mann und einer Frau' (GuI, p. 144) [the first thing in the relationship between a man and a woman], this character — an animal rights activist the narrator meets in an airport — argues that 'in

---

[21] John Berger, *About Looking* (Pantheon, 1980), p. 5.

reality, everywhere is the same. In terms of animals. In terms of how we interact with animals.'[22] Where Bachmann sets out to compile a compendium 'aller möglichen Todesarten' [of all possible ways of dying], this airport acquaintance is gathering as many stories as possible of how animals are abused, exploited and killed, wishing to write 'an exhaustive volume that leaves out no crime, from the dawn of the world to our time. It will be humanity's confessions.'[23]

In keeping with the notion of 'confession', one of the ways in which Tokarczuk's writing reverses the emphasis of Bachmann's associative narration is in literalizing religious metaphors, many of them arising from the Catholic cultural context shared by both writers. The word that occurs to Fanny for the book Marek produces, which she perceives as her own life and flesh, is 'Bibel' [Bible]. She is, she thinks, the 'Lamm Gottes' (BG, p. 17) [Lamb of God], who has been slaughtered 'auf 386 Seiten Bibel' (BG, p. 19) [over 386 pages of Bible], while Marek has achieved success as 'der Bibelschreiber, der Passionsschilderer [...] mit der Schlachtung, dem Ölberg und dem Essigschwamm' ['this biblical scribe, this depictor of the Passion [...] with the slaughter, the Mount of Olives and the vinegar sponge'] (BG, p. 18; BFRG, p. 191, lightly edited). Here we see a religious variation of animals as the 'absent referent' or 'the first metaphor', the sense in which 'Lamm Gottes' [Lamb of God] is meant. For Caitríona Leahy, this version of the relationship between metaphor and its 'real', absent referent is crystallized in the Eucharist as interpreted literally (in Catholicism) or figuratively (in the Protestant tradition).[24] The issue raised by this doctrinal difference, Leahy points out, is 'very often a feature of interpretations and depictions of metamorphosis': its 'proximity to the discourse of the aesthetic (symbolism, metaphor, etc.), and the way in which the aesthetic "steps in" to provide explanation (reason, *Grund*) when the means by which we verify the real [...] is inadequate'.[25] The 'metamorphosis' at issue here, in other words, is

---

[22] Olga Tokarczuk, *Flights*, trans. by Jennifer Croft (Fitzcarraldo, 2017), p. 72. See also Conor Brennan, 'Fallmeister Franza: Journeys of Mastery in Ransmayr and Bachmann', *Austrian Studies*, 31 (2023), pp. 194–210 (p. 206).

[23] The vast scope and religious overtones of this imagined project are in keeping with Bachmann's ambitions for the *Todesarten* cycle as a whole, as her reported preference for the biblical titles *Das Buch Malina*, *Das Buch Franza* and *Das Buch Goldmann* attests. Marie Luise Wandruszka quotes a letter from Bachmann to her publisher Siegfried Unseld, in which Bachmann elaborates on her preference for the title *Das Buch Malina*: 'Das Buch/ MALINA [...] Es kann nicht anders heissen. [...] Ueber den "biblischen" Ton dieses Titels, die mögliche Anmassung, die darin liegt, habe ich natürlich auch nachgedacht [...] selbst wenn man diesen Ton im Ohr haben sollte dabei — er stört mich nicht, es hat auch damit für mich eine Richtigkeit' (BG, 285) [The Book of/MALINA [...] It cannot be called anything else [...] Of course I have also thought about the 'biblical' tone of this title, the possible presumptuousness that it contains [...] even if one should have this tone in one's ear — it doesn't bother me, even that has a kind of rightness for me].

[24] Caitríona Leahy, *'Der wahre Historiker': Ingeborg Bachmann and the Problem of Witnessing History* (Königshausen & Neumann, 2007), p. 112.

[25] Ibid.

a question of direction: of whether we read animals 'away' from themselves, in aesthetic association with something else, or use their metaphorical connection with human victims to direct empathy back towards them. In a simple reversal, the airport activist in Tokarczuk's *Flights* offers a literal reading of the 'Lamm Gottes', holding up the triptych *Adoration of the Mystic Lamb* as supposed proof that 'the true God is an animal'.[26] Another prominent novel by Tokarczuk, meanwhile — *Drive Your Plow over the Bones of the Dead* (*Prowadź swój pług przez kości umarłych*, 2009; trans. by Antonia Lloyd-Jones, 2019) — sees the vegetarian narrator Janina Duszejko buffeted back and forth between the Lamb and flesh of God as symbol and as material while she sits in a Catholic Mass:

> 'O Lamb of God...' the words thundered overhead, and I heard a strange noise, a faint thudding sound from all directions — it was people beating their own chests as they prayed to the Lamb. [...]
>
> I couldn't stop wondering what they had in their bellies. What they had eaten today and yesterday, whether they had already digested the ham, whether the Chickens, Rabbits and Calves had already gone through their stomachs yet. [...]
>
> Father Rustle was now coming along the railing, accompanied by an altar boy, feeding them their next bit of meat, this time in symbolic form, but nevertheless meat, the body of a living Being.
>
> It occurred to me that if there really was a Good God, he should appear now in his true shape, as a Sheep, Cow or Stag, and thunder in a mighty tone.[27]

These examples highlight an interesting connection between Bachmann's associative prose and ideas of empathy, identification and consumption. Identification — particularly identification with animals — is closely linked across all the texts at hand to ideas of consumption, either by 'consuming' the reality of the other or being consumed by it in turn. For Fanny and Franza, identification with animals and other victims appears to coincide with the loss of a stable self; if Fanny's consciousness seems to roam around in search of images in which to moor itself, it is because Marek's book has destroyed her own understanding of who she is. Like Franza, trapped in the cage of Jordan's notes (W, III, p. 407), she identifies with other prisoners and other victims in the midst of her own annihilation. While the killing and consumption of animals can provide a salient image for — and literal parallel to — other forms of violence, in narrative terms, this often seems to require that the protagonist themselves be in some way consumed by the comparison. As Leahy writes of the first-person narrator of *Malina* — who tries and fails to rescue herself from disappearance by 'grounding' herself in texts such as the Christian story of the passion — 'to predicate the possibility of selfhood on a model of intersubjectivity

---

[26] Tokarczuk, *Flights*, pp. 73–74.

[27] Olga Tokarczuk, *Drive Your Plow over the Bones of the Dead*, trans. by Antonia Lloyd-Jones (Fitzcarraldo, 2019), p. 234.

makes for a potentially fatal vulnerability: one might be drowned rather than saved in the texts of others'.[28]

This aspect of Bachmann's associative aesthetic can be traced across a good deal of contemporary ecological writing, particularly where it intersects with feminist thought. Along with the works of Tokarczuk, a further notable example can be found in Han Kang's novel *The Vegetarian* (채식주의자, 2007; trans. by Deborah Smith, 2015), which links the oppression of women in South Korean society to industrial slaughter and meat eating. The novel's plot unfolds from the decision of the previously conforming protagonist, Yeong-hye, to stop eating meat after the connection between her own suffering and that of slaughtered animals begins to haunt her in her dreams. In a manner markedly reminiscent of the *Todesarten* texts, this empathic pain is treated by those around her as a pathology and as unwelcome resistance, and eventually leads to Yeong-hye's destruction at the hands of the society in which she lives. Like Fanny and Franza before her, Yeong-hye becomes lost in identification with others in ways that dissolve the boundaries of her selfhood, carrying symptoms on her own body of ills arising elsewhere. Her deterioration is, in many ways, a Bachmann-esque development: the reactions of those around her to her decision to stop eating meat determine the course it takes, reflecting the insight that individual acts of privation are not only self-inflicted.[29] By the end of the novel, Yeong-hye is committed to hospital and believes that she needs only sunlight to survive, as she is becoming a plant; the novel leaves both the literal, magical realist interpretation and the pathological reading open. The female protagonists of *Todesarten*, particularly Franza and Fanny, are characterized both by an apparent excess of empathy and by their seemingly inexorable fate, which involves playing out the logic of the patriarchal structures in which they are trapped. This logic demands that they must die and must disappear from the narrative, except in the incomplete memories of Martin Ranner, or the 'butchered' account offered by Marek. The same is true, to an extent, of Yeong-hye in *The Vegetarian*: she, too, is viewed only through the eyes of her small-minded husband; her brother-in-law, who develops a sexual fascination with her; and finally her sister, who witnesses her apparent decline towards a death of starvation. Ultimately, *The Vegetarian* demonstrates a difficulty that could not be more relevant to ecological readings of *Todesarten*; namely, that 'the link between veganism and insanity for women is impossible to navigate', with the renunciation of meat-eating often appearing as 'the first step towards mental illness and possibly death for women who feel they have no other option but to starve to avoid inscription within the patriarchy'.[30]

---

[28] Leahy, *Der wahre Historiker*, pp. 193–94.

[29] I am grateful to Caitríona Leahy for this observation about Bachmann's work.

[30] Laura Wright, 'Veganism and Disordered Eating', in *The Edinburgh Companion to Vegan Literary Studies*, ed. by Laura Wright and Emelia Quinn (Edinburgh University Press, 2022), pp. 167–82 (pp. 168–69). In literal terms, it should be noted that *Malina* refers

III

Reading Bachmann's associative narration in terms of 'multidirectionality', and alongside key instances of contemporary ecological fiction, it becomes increasingly conceivable that we should count animal deaths among the real deaths of *Todesarten*. At the same time, this approach remains perhaps too literal — too one-sided — to provide a full and satisfying account of how Bachmann's overall aesthetic can be read ecocritically. I would like to end, then, by considering a different way of reading Bachmann's associative prose: not as multidirectional writing, but as fiction that deals in archetypes. These archetypes might be seen to include the nightmarish father figures of *Malina* and *Das Buch Franza*, but also the vision of the men as hunters in the mythical desert space of 'Unter Mördern und Irren', as well as 'das blaue Wild' itself.

Rothberg's concept of 'multidirectional memory' remains caught on a level between the abstract and the specific: it hinges on the question of whether commemoration of one given atrocity can help to draw attention to another, a hypothesis that has been challenged on practical as well as ethical grounds. What his thinking does not aim at is the level of symbolic abstraction, the underlying level of patterns and paradigms that fascinates both Bachmann and many of her twenty-first century heirs. What interests these writers is not only the correspondence between one or more specific contexts, but also the ways in which patterns that run deeper still — the patterns of dreams and myths — can be used to connect different manifestations of violence, and to plant these connections deep within the mind of the reader. The sense of these structures as underlying and pre-existing the context in which they manifest themselves is captured, for instance, in Bachmann's image of 'das Virus Verbrechen' ['the virus of crime'] (W, III, p. 341; BFRG, p. 3), and in her designation of fascism as 'das erste in der Beziehung zwischen einem Mann und einer Frau' (GuI, p. 144) [the first thing in the relationship between a man and a woman] — implying an element that precedes the relationship, that is always already inherent in it. Bachmann's writing, which is always restlessly in search of the causes for already-existing effects, finds these on the one hand in recognizable and realistic social settings; and on the other hand, on an underlying level of myth and archetype. This latter word refers both to something original, ancestral

---

to vegetarianism derisively as an example of misguided asceticism and male social control over women. In discussing how it is often the most pathetic men who drive women to the extremes of suicide and self-destruction, Ich relates to Malina the case of Erna Zanetti, who overdoses on sleeping pills after a relationship with a theatre scholar: 'er hat ihr auch noch das Rauchen abgewöhnt, weil er keinen Rauch verträgt. Ob sie vegetarisch essen mußte, weiß ich nicht, aber es werden schon noch ein paar schlimme Dinge gewesen sein' (TKA, III.1, p. 612) ['he also got her to stop smoking, because he couldn't stand the smoke. I don't know whether she had to become a vegetarian or not, but I'm sure some other horrible things happened as well'] (MB, p. 227). In keeping with Bachmann's barbed reference to 'grass-whisperers', the tone of these comments within the text is darkly humorous, and Malina laughs despite himself.

and prior to reason, as in the Jungian understanding of archetypes as images hard-wired into the collective unconscious; and also to an aesthetic device that functions as a trope or shorthand. This archetypal mode is where I perceive the echoes of *Todesarten* in the final contemporary intertext to which I will refer: the one-woman play *iGirl* by Irish playwright Marina Carr.

'Unter Mördern und Irren', we recall, gives us an emptied-out desert space in which the men appear as hunters: a mythic originary level underlying postwar Vienna. *iGirl* operates by putting a similarly emptied-out world onstage, where it represents the last days of *homo sapiens*. The only character onstage is Girl, who speaks both in her own voice and in the voices of historical and mythical figures such as Oedipus and Joan of Arc, offering glimpses of how this desolate future came about. In keeping with Carr's feminist concerns, gender is an important component of the play: Girl is 'I Girl | Girl of the cursed | Breasts | Daughter of homo | Sapiens'.[31] As in *Todesarten* and the other contemporary intertexts discussed here, gender is associated with both sacrifice and consumption: speaking in the voice of Joan of Arc, Girl proclaims 'I have become | The Sunday roast | That the world eats, | And excretes'.[32] The play, however, does not content itself with this connection between gender, identification and consumption; instead, it suggests more extreme and ambiguous resonances that chime even more strongly with the associative aesthetic of Bachmann's prose. In a text that knows it is 'So Anthropocene',[33] the central version of *Todesarten* that *iGirl* is concerned with is that of extinction, of *Artensterben*. The representation of guilt and human destructiveness in the play powerfully recalls Bachmann's hunters and their blue deer: the archetypal other they have destroyed or driven away, and which they now long for and hear lamenting. 'The wrong species | Survived', Girl tells us, 'If you look at the deer | The doe | [...] Weeping behind the leaves |You know | The wrong species | Came to the fore'.[34] What *iGirl* seems to suggest, then, is that the same destructive paradigm that drives the various types of violence in *Todesarten* is also at the heart of ecocide and the destruction of the biosphere. The extreme, archetypal origin story the play offers for humankind is that we killed and ate our closest relative, the Neanderthals, who are portrayed as 'gentle' and 'mute', and are linked to animal victims in a series of Bachmann-esque associations: 'They were deer', Girl tells us, 'Before doe | Was invented'.[35] This non-realist understanding of what it means to be 'deer' — to be other, to be prey, to be eaten — brings us full circle to the valences of 'das blaue Wild', and to Morton's understanding of the ecological as a relationship to something outside the self.

---

[31] Marina Carr, *iGirl* (Faber, 2021), p. 13.
[32] Ibid., p. 17.
[33] Ibid., p. 82.
[34] Ibid., p. 4.
[35] Ibid., p. 14.

IV

Whether we consider Bachmann's unique prose style in the framework of multidirectionality or the language of archetypes, it seems clear that her aesthetic approach and thematic concerns resonate well beyond their immediate context. To read her work now is to follow its associative logic past the structures of patriarchy and fascism, allowing it to encompass the victims of ecocide and industrial slaughter. If we take seriously Bachmann's ambition to compile a vast compendium of all possible 'Todesarten', then this project surely extends to the forms of violence and disappearance that shape our twenty-first century context, foremost among them the horror of *Artensterben*. This intuition is confirmed by the striking parallels between Bachmann's prose and the works of prominent contemporary writers grappling with ecological themes. At the same time, these contemporary intertexts prove a point that might come as a relief to Bachmann: then, as now, those producing the most interesting ecological writing do not belong 'zu den Gräserbewisperern' ['among the grass-whisperers'].[36]

---

[36] 'Ingeborg Bachmann erhält den Georg-Büchner-Preis 1964', 6:15.

Scientific Coloniality, Nubia and the Dynamics of Dispossession in *Das Buch Franza*

TERESA LUDDEN

Newcastle University

I

In the prefaces to *Das Buch Franza* [*The Book of Franza*], written in 1966, Bachmann draws attention, albeit in codified form, to the importance of a geopolitical moment in the history of the world as central to her book (TKA, I, p. 73).[1] By quoting part of a line from Rimbaud's *Une saison en enfer* (1873) [*A Season in Hell*] she refers to the Columbian encounter with the inhabited geographies of the New World: 'Les blancs débarquent. Le canon! Il faut se soumettre au baptême, s'habiller, travailler' [The whites land. The cannon! We have to submit to baptism, clothing, work].[2] Rimbaud imagines cannon fire, the whites disembarking from ships, subjugation through slavery and Christianity. He conjures the moment that, to quote Áime Césaire, 'Christian pedantry laid down the dishonest equations *Christianity = civilization, paganism = savagery*, from which there could not but ensue abominable colonialist and racist consequences.'[3] As Césaire writes, the colonial invasions were not the benevolent bequest of 'progress' and 'civilization' as propagated by European myths but rather wholesale plunder, evil social arrangements, expropriation, 'forced labor, intimidation, pressure, the police, taxation, theft, rape, compulsory crops, contempt'.[4]

When Bachmann mobilizes Rimbaud's phrase rendered in German as 'die Weißen kommen' [the whites are coming] or simply 'die Weißen' [the whites], which is a leitmotif throughout *Das Buch Franza*, it becomes a shorthand way to allude to colonial expropriation and dispossession across subjective and territorial registers. Moreover, the phrase resounds in the continuous present, which has the effect of questioning the linear movement of history, implying that what happened in the past is not over but ongoing in the here and now.[5] While

---

[1] The prefaces were written to precede public readings in Zurich of the work-in-progress. The prefaces are accorded a central status in the scholarship as illuminating the poetics of the entire *'Todesarten'*-project (HB2020).

[2] See Albrecht and Göttsche's note, TKA, II, pp. 485–86.

[3] Áime Césaire, *Discourse on Colonialism* (Monthly Review Press, 2000), p. 33.

[4] Ibid., p. 42.

[5] On this notion see Ariella Aïsha Azoulay, *Potential History: Unlearning Imperialism* (Verso, 2019).

Austrian Studies 32 (2024), doi:10.1353/aus.00004, pp. 41–63

in the preface she alludes to the concept of the human as a construct the whites
cast in their own image and positioned at the apex of a hierarchized taxonomy
of creation, by virtue of their self-authored descriptions of their so-called
superiority (TKA, II, p. 73), in the text itself such theoretical reflections find
material resonances in allusions to land dispossession, biopolitics, the praxis of
scientific disciplines and social reality in contemporary Nubia.

My reading of Bachmann's images and metonyms draws on critical race
and decolonial perspectives to place front and centre the notions of inhuman,
scientific disciplinarity as an allegory of colonial logics, and the mechanisms
that produce and justify dispossession.[6] Taking inspiration from Sylvia
Wynter's important philosophy, there will be a focus on epistemological
production and enclosure in specific historical and socio-economic contexts.
Wynter articulates how colonialism was central to the formulation of Western
conceptualizations of the human and how the inhuman was/is produced as
the co-constitutive other of the human.[7] As Walter Mignolo explains, it is
imperative to see that 'the Human is a product of a particular epistemology and
implicit in this epistemological framework are the worldviews of those who
have been cast as non-Human or less than human'.[8] I argue that Bachmann's
text allegorizes modes of epistemological enclosure through images that draw
attention to the material effects of the conceptual apparatus. In the existing
scholarship, Bachmann's writing has been understood as critiquing patriarchal
and fascist structures;[9] here, the multidimensional webs of associations are read
as alluding to colonial logics. I draw connections between the textual analogies
to bring together notions of knowledge production, scientific coloniality and
systematic theft as a mode of generating property.[10] I link images of proprietary

[6] The concept of racial capitalism, originally formulated by Cedric J. Robinson, informs
my re-reading of Bachmann's texts. For an excellent mobilization of the concept in relation
to colonial property laws, see Brenna Bhandar, *The Colonial Lives of Property: Land, Law
and Racial Regimes of Ownership* (Duke University Press, 2018).

[7] Sylvia Wynter, 'Unsettling the Coloniality of Being/Power/Truth/Freedom: Towards the
Human, After Man, Its Overrepresentation — An Argument', *The New Centennial Review*,
3.3 (2003), pp. 257–337.

[8] Walter Mignolo, 'Sylvia Wynter: What does it mean to be Human?', in *Sylvia Wynter.
On Being Human as Praxis*, ed. by Katherine McKittrick (Duke University Press, 2015), pp.
106–24 (p. 108).

[9] See, among others: HB2020; Sigrid Weigel, *Ingeborg Bachmann: Hinterlassenschaften
unter Wahrung des Briefgeheimnisses* (dtv, 2003); Caitríona Leahy, *Der wahre Historiker:
Ingeborg Bachmann and the Problem of Witnessing History* (Königshausen & Neumann,
2007); Merve Emre, 'The Meticulous One', *The New York Review of Books*, 22 October 2020
<https://www.nybooks.com/articles/2020/10/22/ingeborg-bachmann-meticulous-one/>
[accessed 27 August 2024]. The character Dr Körner, whom Franza visits, experimented on
female prisoners in concentration camps in National Socialist Germany. Herbert Uerlings
argues that he is based on Dr Hans Eisele, a former SS captain and convicted war criminal
living in Cairo. See Herbert Uerlings, *'Ich bin von niedriger Rasse': (Post-)Kolonialismus und
Geschlechterdifferenz in der deutschen Literatur* (Böhlau, 2006).

[10] See Robert Nichols, *Theft is Property! Dispossession and Critical Theory* (Duke University

relations and scientific disciplinarity as a material praxis to the key phrase (and reference to Nietzsche) 'den privaten Wissensdurst eines Wissenschaftlers' (TKA, II, p. 216) [private thirst for knowledge of a scientist] to articulate the text's allusions to the material economies emerging from the libidinal forces of Western epistemologies. I argue that the associations, especially in conjunction with the repetition of Rimbaud's phrase 'the whites are coming', allude to what Alexander G. Weheliye calls 'racializing assemblages' as 'a set of sociopolitical processes that discipline humanity into full humans, not-quite-humans, and nonhumans'.[11]

My interpretation centres on the third chapter of *Das Buch Franza*, 'die ägyptische Finsternis', which reworks material from the *Wüstenbuch* (1964) [Desert Book], an unpublished text Bachmann wrote after returning from a trip to Egypt and Sudan. The protagonist is a mentally ill white woman called Franza who is a fugitive from a mental asylum in which she has been forcibly incarcerated by her psychiatrist husband, Jordan. Her brother, Martin, a geologist-cum-historian, takes her with him on a research trip to Egypt. In the second chapter Franza voices several anti-colonial statements.[12] In these sections Franza also recounts her experiences of being subjected to what we would now call coercive control by Jordan.[13] In the third and final chapter set in Egypt and Sudan in 1964 she suffers many episodes of breakdown. At the end of the text, she is raped by a white man at the base of the pyramids and afterwards smashes her head against the ancient stone structure and dies while cursing the whites.

Postcolonial readings of *Das Buch Franza* have concentrated on the white tourist gaze and critical exoticism,[14] addressing the ways in which the text criticizes, and is complicit with, systems that exclude and render others inferior.

Press, 2020).

[11] Alexander G. Weheliye, *Habeas Viscus: Racializing Assemblages, Biopolitics, and Black Feminist Theories of the Human* (Duke University Press, 2014), p. 4.

[12] Lilian Friedberg's reading of these sections is exemplary. She articulates how the text identifies colonialism with genocide, '"Verbrechen, die ich meine..."': *Manners of Death* as Thickly Descriptive Translation of *Todesarten*', *Monatshefte*, 94.2 (2002), pp. 189–208.

[13] Bachmann would not have known the term, but she describes the phenomenon, including controlling behaviour, physical and emotional abuse, marital rape and a forced abortion. Coercive control became a criminal offence under English and Welsh law in 2015. There is no direct equivalent in Austria where such acts would be tried under the EU domestic abuse laws. Gendered violence will not be the focus of this article for reasons of space. The topic is too important to treat tangentially.

[14] See Monika Albrecht, '"Sire, this village is yours". Ingeborg Bachmanns Romanfragment *Das Buch Franza* aus postkolonialer Sicht', in *Über die Zeit schreiben: literatur- und kulturwissenschaftliche Essays zu Ingeborg Bachmanns 'Todesarten'-Projekt*, ed. by Monika Albrecht and Dirk Göttsche, 3 vols (Königshausen & Neumann, 2004), III, pp. 159–72. See also Moustapha M. Diallo, '"Die Erfahrung der Variabilität": Kritischer Exotismus in Ingeborg Bachmanns *Todesarten*-Projekt im Kontext des interkulturellen Dialogs zwischen Afrika und Europa', in *Über die Zeit schreiben*, ed. by Monika Albrecht and Dirk Göttsche, 3 vols (Würzburg: Königshausen & Neumann, 1998), I, pp. 33–58.

However, they tend to focus on the inner contradictions of Western civilization and do not emphasize enough that modernity was planetary and not European.[15] While existing interpretations have argued that Bachmann reuses dominant Western codes to criticize them,[16] I uncover more subterranean lines of critique by foregrounding how the text alludes to the forces that produce these codes. This means attending to the grammars of dispossession, the material economies and processes of extraction and accumulation that continue to shape our contemporary global inequalities. *Das Buch Franza* attempts to foreground the 'inhumanity that delivered the human' by finding ways to highlight what Kathryn Yusoff calls the 'warp of dispossession'.[17] Yusoff is referring to the historical institution of slavery and the theft of indigenous land, colonial crimes that are forgotten when narratives of a common humanity are uncritically mobilized.[18] To smooth away the warp is to forget the world-historical event of slavery that created a category of non-being which 'taints' humanism;[19] to forget that the category of the inhuman was created to justify expropriation and colonial accumulation of capital.[20]

The second section below analyses the references to the colonial roots of archaeology and Egyptology in *Das Buch Franza*; the third focuses on the importance of Wadi Halfa and the flooding of Nubia in 1964 when the Aswan High Dam was opened. I read this as Bachmann's intuition of the dynamics of land dispossession, and of the 'fleshy surplus'[21] created by the neocolonial accumulation of capital. Linking the two sections is what I call White Archaeology. Bachmann uses the words 'die Weißen' with their connotations of colonial terror to describe the archaeologists' plundering of the ancient Egyptian tombs. She introduces this phrase when Franza contradicts Martin's racist lectures in which he berates the Bedouins for thieving while not seeing the devastation wrought by Western archaeology. Franza thereby uncovers the colonial roots of Western narratives of salvage and custodianship which are

---

[15] See Dirk Göttsche, 'Die Schwarzkunst der Worte: Zur Barbey und Rimbaud Rezeption in Ingeborg Bachmanns "Todesarten"-Zyklus', *Jahrbuch der Grillparzer Gesellschaft*, 3.17 (1991), pp. 127–67. See also Enrique Dussel, *Ethics of Liberation: In the Age of Globalization and Exclusion* (Duke University Press, 2013).

[16] See Sara Lennox, *Cemetery of the Murdered Daughters: Feminism, History, and Ingeborg Bachmann* (University of Massachusetts Press, 2006).

[17] Kathryn Yusoff, *A Billion Black Anthropocenes or None* (University of Minnesota Press, 2019), p. 5. Yusoff's antiracist materialist mode of reading brings together the economic, the political, the epistemological and the ontological to illuminate recursive racial logics.

[18] Ibid.

[19] Paul Gilroy argues that humanism has been tainted through systematic inhumanism and calls for an anti-race humanism. See Paul Gilroy, *Between Camps: Race, Identity and Nationalism at the End of the Colour Line* (Penguin, 2000), p. 18.

[20] I am drawing with a very broad brush on the black intellectual tradition — W. E. B. DuBois, C. L. R. James, Frantz Fanon — through Wynter's use of these writers. For an explanation of the differences between the black anti-racist tradition and liberal anti-racism see Arun Kundnani, *What Is Anti-Racism and Why It Means Anti-Capitalism* (Verso, 2023).

[21] Weheliye, *Habeas Viscus*, p. 8.

still relied upon today by the bastions of world culture in the Global North.[22] White Archaeology is an allegory both of colonial systematic theft and of knowledge production within fields of meaning (knowledge not as 'discovery' but as production of that which it presupposes). As Bachmann's images of the violent unwrapping of mummified bodies conveys, 'biopolitical subjectivation' appears as a mechanism to legitimize regimes of ownership (of knowledge and property).[23] Furthermore, White Archaeology symbolizes a specific modality of dispossession articulated by Robert Nichols in reference to land theft from Indigenous peoples. Colonization involves a

> unique species of theft for which we do not always have adequate language. Dispossession of this sort combines two processes typically thought distinct: it transforms nonproprietary relations into proprietary ones while, at the same time, systematically transferring control and title of this (newly formed) property. It is thus not (only) about the *transfer of* property but the *transformation into* property. In this way, dispossession creates an object in the very act of appropriating it.[24]

As I will argue below, the epistemological violence of White Archaeology becomes visible as acts of making and taking — exemplified in Bachman's images of mummified bodies exposed in the institution of the museum, which I link to racial capitalism — and as erasure, as legitimizing the silencing of alternative epistemologies and different modes of being.

In the second section, I use critical ethnic studies to argue that White Archaeology symbolizes the actual UNESCO campaign to save the ancient monuments of Nubia from the Aswan High Dam's floodwater. The High Dam at Aswan brought millions of acres under irrigation for the production of cotton for the export market and both symbolizes liberation from colonialism on the part of a successful postcolonial nation — Bachmann's text subtly celebrates the demise of British colonialism when Franza visits Suez[25] — and represents what many saw as the ensuing era of neocolonialism.[26] The building of the dam created a lake (known as Lake Nasser in Egypt and Lake Nubia in Sudan), which submerged Nubian settlements and necessitated the forced displacement

---

[22] See, among others: Dan Hicks, *The Brutish Museums: The Benin Bronzes, Colonial Violence and Cultural Restitution* (Pluto, 2020); Alice Proctor, *The Whole Picture: The Colonial Story of the Art in our Museums and why we need to talk about it* (Cassell, 2020); Azoulay, *Potential History*. The literature and activism on restitution is vast. See, for a prominent example, Felwine Sarr and Benedicte Savoy, *Restitution of African Cultural Heritage: Towards a New Relational Ethics* (Ministère de la Culture, 2018).

[23] Judith Butler and Athena Athanasiou, *Dispossession: The Performative in the Political* (Polity, 2013), p. 2.

[24] Nichols, *Theft is Property!*, pp. 30–31.

[25] Dane Kennedy terms Suez the 'tragi-comic death knell of the British Empire'. The British prime minister resigned in disgrace. See Dane Kennedy, *Decolonization: A Very Short Introduction* (Oxford University Press, 2016), p. 60.

[26] Kwame Nkrumah, *Neo-colonialism: The Last Stage of Imperialism* (Nelson, 1965, facsimile repr. Panaf, 1974).

of 90,000 Nubian people.[27] From 1960 to 1980 UNESCO ran a campaign to salvage the ancient monuments of Nubia, which was dominated by the Global North and laced with coloniality. White Archaeology valued the ancient structures over the contemporary Nubian culture which they did little to save; it was complicit in praxes that displaced Nubia from the history of civilization and produced the contemporary Nubian population as less-than-human by excluding them from the institutional history of the human. Although Bachmann does not mention the particular campaign, I link the criticisms of White Archaeology to the concrete experiences of land dispossession and displacement in Wadi Halfa, an important centre of Nubian culture, which I interpret as the missing heart of Bachmann's unfinished text. The planned sections set in Aswan and Wadi Halfa remain lacunae in the final version of the posthumously published text. I read around the edges of the final version and draw on the *Wüstenbuch* in order to foreground the narrator's experiences in Wadi Halfa.

Bachmann hints that Nubia is the final destination of her critique but she never quite arrives at this point because she did not complete the sections set in Aswan and Wadi Halfa, the town she visited in 1964 shortly before the area was flooded. Bachmann does not invent characters who give voice to the lived experience of race. There is much that she does not say. We could read Idris Ali's novel *Dongola. A Novel of Nubia* alongside *Das Buch Franza* to underscore this point. Ali's characters express being abandoned by the world which saved the ancient monuments and left modern Nubia to its fate.[28] Nevertheless, to interpret Wadi Halfa as Franza's self-destructive identification with victims is to fail to understand the significance of the place and people,[29] both in terms of the role that the desert plays in the text as a whole and as concrete manifestations of resistance that point to the non-inevitability of Western-authored scripts. I read Bachmann's obscure images as allusions to the existence of alternative modalities of relations and being that fall through the parameters of Western epistemologies.

II

By placing an exponent of Western science in Egypt and Sudan in 1964 Bachmann signals a concern with Western knowledge production and dissemination in global geographies. Martin might be a benign brother in Austria, but when the

---

[27] William Carruthers, *Flooded Pasts: UNESCO, Nubia, and the Recolonization of Archaeology* (Cornell University Press, 2022).

[28] Idris Ali, *Dunqula: Riwaya Nubiyya* (al-Hai'a al-Misriyya al-'Ama li-l-Kuttab, 1993); Idris Ali, *Dongola: A Novel of Nubia*, trans. by Peter Theroux (University of Arkansas Press, 1998). This is the first Nubian novel to be translated into English.

[29] This assumption undergirds most of the scholarship. See, among others, Lennox, *Cemetery of the Murdered Daughters*; Georgina Paul, *Perspectives on Gender in Post-1945 German Literature* (Camden House, 2009); Peter Filkins's introduction to his translation of *Das Buch Franza* (BFRG, p. xiii).

siblings arrive in Egypt he represents colonial Western science (and not a tourist as the scholarship has interpreted him). His field trip to Egypt is financed with European research funding. His disciplines are geology and history (TKA, II, p. 71), a strange combination that can be understood as symbolizing the bridging of the natural sciences and the humanities in the German ideal of *Wissenschaft*, knowledge production broadly conceived. Further connotations accrue. Martin stands for scientific humanism through his association with the American Egyptologist James Henry Breasted, whose book he is reading.[30] Breasted was the founder of the Oriental Institute at the University of Chicago, a research institution that positioned itself between palaeontology, anthropology, ethnology, history and sociology as a laboratory for the systematic analysis of the origins of civilization.[31] More concretely still, Martin seems to combine the types of scientists building the Aswan High Dam and working for the UNESCO campaign in 1964 as a geologist and an historian/Egyptologist involved in the huge documentation project. By association, he is a symbol of scientific coloniality and aligned with White Archaeology; this is underlined in the passage where he meets his archaeologist friend in the exclusive Cairo Tower restaurant which revolves to give panoramic views of the river Nile and surrounding land. Franza says that 'Martins Leute deuteten auf die Stadt hinunter, stolz, als hätten sie nicht nur den Verabredungsplatz so gut gewählt, sondern Kairo und den Nil dazu erschaffen' ['Martin's people gestured proudly toward the city below as if they not only had chosen such a good meeting place but had created Cairo and the Nile for it as well'] (TKA, II, p. 292; BFRG, p. 122) The revolving glass windows and the height of the tower recall the colonial apparatus of surveys and mapping and suggest abstraction through property relations from the land that the Westerners think has been arranged at their feet for their enjoyment.[32] In an image at the end of the text that suggests the Aryanization of Egyptology,[33] Martin insists on trampling over the pyramids, displaying that he owns the means of production of knowledge and controls the narratives about civilization. The image evokes the construction of the idea of a racially pure Europe through the omission of African history in Western origin stories.[34]

---

[30] Peter Filkins identifies the book as Breasted's *History of Egypt* and tells us that Bachmann owned a German translation (BFRG, p. 222). Breasted was educated in Germany.

[31] See Vanessa Davies, 'Egyptological Conversations on Race and Science', *Rockefeller Archive Center*, n.d. <https://rockarch.issuelab.org/resources/29650/29650.pdf> [accessed 2 May 2024].

[32] See Iyko Day, 'Eco-Criticism and Primitive Accumulation in Indigenous Studies', in *After Marx. Literature, Theory, and Value in the Twenty-First Century*, ed. by Colleen Lye and Christopher Nealon (Cambridge University Press 2022), pp. 40–54.

[33] See Mark Bernal, *Black Athena: The Afroasiatic Roots of Classical Civilisation* (Rutgers University Press, 1987).

[34] See Cedric J. Robinson, *Black Marxism* (Penguin, 2021).

The coloniality that is clearly expressed in the images of Martin climbing to the top of the pyramid is also in evidence in his research trip to the Valley of the Kings. In Luxor, upon looking into the empty tombs and not wanting to see the gaping spaces, Franza feels debilitating 'Schande' [shame]; the searing intensity and bodily affect is politicized (de-individualized) to evoke a sense of intolerable desecration. Bachmann creates a sense of occlusion and deracination that resonates indeterminately. She repeats the word 'Schändung/ schänden' [defilement, violation and desecration] three times: 'Sie haben die Gräber geschändet. Martin dachte zuerst, sie denke an die Grabräuber von seinen Vorlesungen. [...] Nein, die Weißen. Die Archäologen. Sie haben die Toten weggeschleppt' (TKA, II, p. 274) [They have violated the graves. At first Martin thought she was thinking of the grave robbers he mentioned in his lectures. [...] No, the whites. The archaeologists. They dragged off the dead].[35] White Archaeology is an allegory of colonial extraction, here named by Franza as the agent behind the plunder, which suggests theft of land and belongings, displacement, and the destruction of indigenous social worlds. The use of 'die Weißen' here creates echoes with the passages in the previous chapter where Franza condemns the whites for stealing 'Bodenschätze' [treasures of the ground] from non-European peoples. But the register of desecration in relation to dispossession suggests that this is not merely the theft of objects; it expresses the loss of something of immeasurable moral worth.[36] In the particular context, it is the lifeworld of an ancient culture which appears to be stolen and appropriated by being transformed into White Archaeology's property.

The digging up and displacement of the bodies is only the first of many layers of desecration. The Luxor passage is linked to the images at the Egyptian Museum (Egyptian Museum of Antiquities) in Cairo which Martin and Franza visit. The stolen mummified bodies are on display in a building that is especially symbolic of colonial power. Built on the orders of British colonialists in 1902 and adorned with Latin inscriptions to its founding fathers, the Egyptian Museum represents the colonial consumption of 'Ancient Egypt' driven by a combination of imperial capitalism and European idealism. Bachmann alludes to the recursive nature of dispossession. If the first violation is tearing the bodies from the land, the second is their unwrapping (which Bachmann evokes with visceral horror as we will see below) and the third their exposure in the museum. The fourth layer of violence is the photographing of the mummies on display, which evokes a range of associations, from the archaeological archive, to the role of art history in ethnographic objectification, to the uses to which photography was put as an imperial technology.

Franza vomits at the entrance to the hall of mummies (TKA, II, pp. 273–74) and in earlier versions she spits vomit at the photographers. The passages stress the sense of horror and desecration by evoking the exposed skulls:

[35] My translation. See also Peter Filkins (BFRG, p. 109).
[36] Nichols, *Theft is Property!*, p. 29.

Das Grauen für 45 Piaster Eintritt, für 5 Piaster wäre das ganze Museum zu sehen, aber hier drängen sie sich, nicht die Grabschänder, Soldatenhorden und Beduinen auf Schatzsuche, sondern das Publikum, die Leicas im Anschlag, die von Gier entstellten Gesichter bis dicht über die Grabsärge gesenkt, Breughelfiguren aus Holland, aus Deutschland, aus Dänemark [...] Farbfilm oder nicht, das ist die Frage. (TKA, II, pp. 289–90)

[For forty-five piastres one gains entrance to such horror; for five piastres one can see the entire museum. But it's here (the mummy room) that they flock, not the 'violators of graves', the hordes of soldiers and Bedouins in search of treasure, but rather the crowds of spectators, the public, armed with cameras, their faces distorted by rapacious greed, gathering thick as flies around the coffins, Brueghel-like figures from Holland, from Germany, from Denmark, [...] Whether to use color film or not, that is the question.] (BFRG, p. 120)[37]

Franza repeats here that it is not the Bedouins who are the force of devastation. Although the Dutch, Danish and German photographers appear to be tourists (or perhaps journalists), the word 'Publikum' encompasses audience, spectators and customers, and this expresses the commercial and scientific apparatus of White Archaeology. The photographers are proxies for White Archaeology, pointing to its inherently colonial roots and its vast photographic archive.[38] They symbolize an attitude of avaricious capture and enclosure associated with the act of photographic reproduction, itself a key component in the inhumanizing assemblage that transforms a body into a thing and into the property of White Archaeology. The abomination is White Archaeology, not the exposed skulls themselves. Photography in the colonial museum metonymically points to the epistemological production of the category of the inhuman within the grammars of archaeology and Egyptology.[39] Moreover, the very expensive Leica cameras evoke the wealth of the whites in conjunction with this scene of abjection, thus underscoring accumulation by dispossession.[40] I will come back to the price of the entrance ticket below.

[37] Translation modified. Filkins mistranslates 'Gier' as curiosity (Neugier). 'Gier' encompasses uncontrollable desire (to get something/own something), the demand for pleasure and drive for gratification, greediness, rapaciousness, hunger, thirst, lust, etc. The word is important as Nietzsche uses it in relation to 'Wissenslust' and 'Finderglück' (see below).

[38] As Christina Riggs writes, archaeology and Egyptology are unthinkable without the photographic archive which shaped ideas of what was ancient. These disciplines are also historically synonymous with ethnographic objection, but their roots are rarely scrutinized. See Riggs, 'Sitting Uncomfortably', christinariggs.com, 13 June 2021, <https://www.christinariggs.com/2021/06/13/sitting-uncomfortably/> [accessed 14 May 2024].

[39] See also Bachmann's note: 'Sudan: es sei verboten, bei hoher Strafe "human beings" zu photographieren. Den Nil und alles andere habe ich vergessen, dieses Verbot nicht' (TKA, IV, pp. 386) [The sign in Sudan said: 'it is forbidden to photograph human beings. Large fines issued for breaking this prohibition.' I have forgotten the Nile and everything else, but not this prohibition].

[40] David Harvey, The New Imperialism (Oxford University Press, 2003).

The word 'Gier' links the Leicas as extractive technology to the libidinal drive of White Archaeology, that is, to the insatiable forces of desire fuelling knowledge production. The passage in the museum needs to be read in relation to an earlier section in which Bachmann uses the phrase 'den privaten Wissensdurst eines Wissenschaftlers'. Before continuing with the analysis of White Archaeology, we need to make a detour through this strand in the web of allusions. It comes in the context of Franza describing to Martin how Jordan turned her into a psychiatric case study:

> Die Strategie, die Berechnung. Versprich mir, daß du nie rechnen wirst. Man hat mich benutzt, ich bin in einen Versuch gegangen, ein Objekt für den privaten Wissensdurst eines Wissenschaftlers. Körperbau wurde mit festgestellt, Typenlehre, und Charakter, mich wunderts nur, daß er nicht meine Handschrift zur Untersuchung gegeben hat. Ich muß lachen. Das sollen sie jetzt in Firmen, das ist Usus, Träume, ja, auch, habe ich pflichtschuldigst erzählt. (TKA, II, pp. 216–17)

> [The strategy, the calculation. Promise me that you'll never be calculating. I've been used, I've been part of an experiment, an object for the private thirst for knowledge of a scientist. The physique was assessed, gauged for its type, and character, myself only surprised that he didn't submit my handwriting to analysis. I have to laugh. They do that in companies these days. Including dreams as well, I related everything in a dutiful manner.] (BFRG, p. 71, translation modified)

On the contextual level Franza is explaining about Jordan keeping notes on her. Bachmann stresses that psychiatry's core business is probing and penetrating the object of study for the purpose of differentiation and the extraction of labour. Her allusion to human resources departments hints that the disciplinary practices of defining, recognizing, quantifying and identifying are intimately linked to calculating and evaluating the exchange value of a person who will be reduced to, or abstracted into, monetary value. This is sinister, but Bachmann also mocks psychiatry as ludicrously paranoid in its drive to lay bare the object completely, demanding to know all, watching for her to expose herself, even invading her dreams and penetrating the idiosyncrasies of her handwriting.

The phrase 'Wissensdurst eines Wissenschaftlers' [thirst for knowledge of a scientist] is an important reference to Nietzsche's criticism of the insatiable Socratic 'thirst for knowledge' in *Die Geburt der Tragödie*. Nietzsche uses the words 'Wissenslust' and 'Wissensgier' [desire or craving for knowledge][41] to express the drive fuelling theoretical modes of knowing as represented by Socrates, the 'Mystagogen der Wissenschaft' [mystagogue of science],[42] the forerunner of the theoretical man of philosophy and science in the nineteenth century. Socrates is 'das Urbild des theoretischen Optimisten' ['the prototype

---

[41] Friedrich Nietzsche, *The Birth of Tragedy*, trans. by Walter Kaufmann (Vintage, 1967), p. 138.
[42] Nietzsche, *Die Geburt der Tragödie*, p. 82; *The Birth of Tragedy*, p. 96.

of the theoretical optimist'], who believes in the 'Ergründlichkeit der Natur der Dinge' ['the fathomableness of the nature of things'] and values above all the 'Mechanismus der Begriffe, Urtheile und Schlüsse' ['mechanism of concepts, judgements and conclusions'] as the most noble human capabilities.[43] Theoretical man's thirst for knowledge might be culturally privileged as the foremost attribute of the highest form of being, but Nietzsche uncovers the more murky forces. He takes Socrates's gaze to be a function of 'eine grosse Cyklopenauge' ['one great Cyclopean eye'].[44] What Nietzsche implies by the Cyclops analogy is, to quote Glen Baier:

> that there is a singularity to Socrates' vision. He only 'looks' with one thing, and that is his eye as directed by his desire. In addition, the exaggerated nature of his eye makes it invasive in that it constantly probes the world.[45]

His desire to see things as closely as possible, to relentlessly expose all, according to Baier, points towards his 'deep-seated dread of ontological diversity'.[46] When the theoretical man looks at the world, he does not accept it as it is in all its heterogeneity and variety; instead 'it is with a superior attitude of making the world conform to the ideals of the theoretical man'.[47] Thus, far from being a noble characteristic, theoretical man's insatiable 'Finderglück' [finder's happiness], to use Nietzsche's word, becomes synonymous with self-centred reduction of everything to himself. His 'far-reaching devotion to homogeneity' means that he reproduces himself and his worldview when he looks at the world.[48] 'Wissensdurst' implies the thrill of 'discovery' that has very little to do with actually finding or meeting the world's heterogeneity but rather can be more accurately seen as the drive to produce fictitious projections that reflect theoretical man's desire. 'Wissensdurst' at the most fundamental level is the invention of value.

Bachmann uses Nietzsche to criticize scientific disciplinarity. Her word 'Berechnung' [calculating] stresses an obsession with quantity and measurement, and knowing appears synonymous with 'feststellen' [establishing]. She evokes the circular nature of this form of knowledge, which produces that which it presupposes. Further, the passage alludes to how the cyclops eye manifests itself as a denigrating attitude towards difference, which resonates on at

---

[43] Nietzsche, *Die Geburt der Tragödie*, p. 83; *The Birth of Tragedy*, p. 97.

[44] *Die Geburt der Tragödie*, p. 73; *The Birth of Tragedy*, p. 89.

[45] Glen Baier, 'Nietzsche's Diagnosis of Socrates in *The Birth of Tragedy*: Voyeurism and the Denigration of Difference', in *Nietzsche and the Politics of Difference*, ed. by Andrea Rehberg and Ashley Woodward (De Gruyter, 2022), pp. 54–74 (p. 56).

[46] Ibid., p. 55.

[47] Ibid. Baier quotes and explains the following: 'wohin er seine prüfenden Blicke richtet, sieht er den Mangel der Einsicht und die Macht des Wahns und schliesst aus diesem Mangel auf die innerliche Verkehrtheit und Verwerflichkeit des Vorhandenen. Von diesem einen Punkte aus glaubte Sokrates das Dasein corrigiren zu müssen', Nietzsche *Die Geburt der Tragödie*, p.71.

[48] Ibid., p. 56.

least two levels; first, within Europe the cyclops eye of psychiatry delineates between the irrational and rational, and second, outside Europe, the cyclops eye resolves difference into taxonomy and race. Especially multidimensional are the sentences that evoke the probing cyclops eye directed at the exposed body. It becomes more than a singularity of vision; it is, to speak with Kathryn Yusoff, a 'technology of matter', disciplining the body, desiring and imagining the properties of matter.[49] Franza describes how Jordan classified her body type and character, and defined her personality type (deeming it to be excessively carnal) as linked to her body shape. The term 'Typenlehre' [typology] refers to systematic classification according to general type and is especially connected to the scientific practices of biology, psychology and archaeology. Bachmann places this term in conjunction with the words 'Körperbau' [physique] and 'Persönlichkeit' [personality] to allude to classification based on a combination of physical and moral attributes. Her sentences evoke scientific racism, taxonomic comparison and the material effects of disaggregation within systems of knowledge. They resound in relation to the cyclops eye to allude to scientific method and its attitudes towards, and treatment of, matter. As Yusoff shows, there is traffic between the inhuman and matter and the inhuman and race.[50] Bachmann hints at these co-implications which can also be linked to Wynter's analysis of the processes whereby non-being is created within governing Western descriptive statements of the human.[51]

The word 'private' in the phrase 'private thirst for knowledge' in Franza's description of her husband and his treatment of her is highly allegorical. It serves to shift the focus from the content of knowledge to the economies that drive production within autopoietic fields of meaning. The words 'private thirst' render knowledge production akin to a bodily urge at the level of the organism. They allude to how fields of meaning are driven by rapacious and not entirely rational or controllable forces, and crucially to how they are ineluctably self-centred and self-serving, geared to the preservation and reproduction of themselves. This goes against the conventional view of scientific projects as unbiased and value-free, which can come to function as an ideal.[52] Further connotations associated with the word 'private' link disciplinarity with private ownership. This hints at the conjunction of inquisitive and acquisitive qualities in the cyclops eye. That is, desiring/defining/evaluating the properties of an object is intrinsic to the mechanisms that generate property. Thus science's central feature of striving towards the total categorization of matter is linked to the creation, not of 'a new material object but of a juridical and conceptual object — an abstraction — that serves to anchor relations, rights, and ultimately,

---

[49] Yusoff, *A Billion Black Anthropocenes or None*, p.14.
[50] Ibid.
[51] Wynter, 'Unsettling the Coloniality of Being/Power/Truth/Freedom', p. 274.
[52] See Thomas Nagel's criticism of scientism in *The View from Nowhere* (Oxford University Press, 1989).

power'.[53] Franza's mockery of Jordan reveals the ostensibly noble pursuit of knowledge to be the self-legitimizing mechanisms that securitize accumulation by producing the stability of the object as property.

While colonialization is only implicit in the 'Wissensdurst' passage, the associations created via Rimbaud's phrase 'die Weißen kommen', which above we associated with historical and present-day ongoing colonial and racist dispossession, allow us to glean that thirst for knowledge is associated with the colonists' thirst for land and gold. Bachmann's associative-poetic genealogical critique hints at the forces fuelling the particular species of colonial theft found in colonial extraction and regimes of property. Although the text does not explicitly say so, the cyclops eye can come to be associated with the brutal calculative logic that 'encodes the enslaved and land as inhuman property' as a 'tactic of empire and European world building'.[54] The register of materiality and corporeality in the text — the sand, mud, sweat, blood — attempts to find ways to allegorize what Nietzsche does not comment on: what it is to be on the receiving end of the cyclops eye. One way Bachmann does this is through the treatment of mummified bodies.

We can now return to the criticisms of White Archaeology in the Egyptian Museum in Cairo. The 'cyclops eye' appears in the guise of the whites' camera lenses thrust up close to the mummified bodies as an image of making in the very act of taking. White Archaeology reproduces itself as owner of knowledge through the production and appropriation of the object as inert matter. Bachmann's analogy stresses the multiple levels of violence required to underwrite and securitize possession. In the *Wüstenbuch* the narrator goes further than Franza (whose vomiting — the contents of the pool of sick described in detail — mutely expresses the intolerable scenario at the museum) and imagines revenge on the archaeologists:

> Aber ich habe für Amenophis geweint, wegen der Barbarei der Archäologen. Das sind keine Menschen. Sie haben seinen Körper angerührt. Das war zu viel. Sie haben ihm die Leintücher von den Knochen gerissen, ihn ausgestellt für 45 Piaster, einen Leichnam, einen Totenschädel, der es ihnen heimzahlen wird. [...] Es wird alles heimgezahlt werden, jede Schändung. (TKA, I, p. 269)

> [But I cried for Amenophis on account of the barbarity of the archaeologists. They are not human. They have touched his body. That was too much. They have torn the linen bandages from his bones, put him on display for 45 piastres, a corpse, a skull that will get his own back. ...] Everything will exact its revenge, every desecration.][55]

This passage resounds in many valences. Most obviously, it is an image of White Archaeology violently extracting monetary value from a lifeless African body

---

[53] Nichols, *Theft is Property!*, p. 31.
[54] Yusoff, *A Billion Black Anthropocenes or None*, p. 68.
[55] All translations of the *Wüstenbuch* are my own.

and while it does not refer directly to enslavement,[56] it alludes to colonialism
as a necropolitical force. Achille Mbembe, developing Fanon's understanding
of colonialism as genocidal, shows how in historical and contemporary
configurations of racism, groups and populations are systematically produced as
lifeless or less-than-human.[57] White Archaeology appears here as an inherently
necropolitical power based on the subjugation of the inhumanized body. In
a political-economic register, the mummified body in Bachmann's passage is
clearly commoditized in the institution of the colonial museum which extracts
surplus value from it. She tells us how expensive the entrance ticket to the
exhibition is; the ancient bodies on display are generating wealth for Europeans
and elites. This refers us to the fetishization and commercialization of Egyptian
artefacts and to the capitalist colonial context within which the scientific
disciplines of Egyptology and archaeology operate. From 1902 until 1979 there
was a sale room in the Egyptian Museum of Antiquities where officials plied
their lucrative international trade in Egyptian art. The passage makes visible
the logics of racial capitalism by emphasizing that accumulation is fuelled
by exploitation, expropriation and dispossession. Visceral images foreground
the effects of racial capitalist logics on the bodies of the dispossessed. The
emphasis is on the praxis of tearing off the mummies' bandages rather than
the individual pharaoh in question, stressing the obscene levels of violence
required to produce property, value and 'knowledge'. The mention of bones
in this context is particularly striking: are we to imagine the force used as so
extreme that skin and flesh come away too? Or have skin and linen melded,
so that when the wrappings are torn off, it is akin to layers of skin and flesh
themselves being ripped away? Either way, Bachmann's image speaks of paring
back to the bone, of flaying. It draws attention to the fleshy body that delivers
the abstraction of the value-form and recalls Karl Marx's imagery in *Capital*
where value is repeatedly described as the *Gallerte* (gelatine) of the human
body.[58] In Bachmann's scenario, however, the flayed body is not hidden behind
the commodity form but itself constitutes the main attraction at the museum.
The abstraction of value and the matter of the racialized body become one and
the same. The bones make the dynamics of dispossession fully visible in the

---

[56] The text has a more explicit reference to enslavement in the image of the couple that
the narrator sees on a platform at the train station in Cairo. The man has tied his wife
with ropes and is violently pulling her hair. The narrator of *Wüstenbuch* and Franza in the
final version at first interpret the vignette as the woman being attacked and enslaved by a
mad man but a passer-by explains to her in English that it is the woman who is mentally
ill and requires restraint. It is a disturbing image that suggests, at the same time, slavery,
patriarchal violence and the abuse of the mentally ill (TKA, I, p. 274 and TKA, II, pp. 306–09
and BFRG, p. 131).
[57] Achille Mbembe, *Critique of Black Reason*, trans. by Laurent Dubois (Duke University
Press, 2017).
[58] Karl Marx, *Capital vol 1*, trans. by Ben Fowkes (Penguin, 1976), for example pp. 128, 135,
141. *Das Kapital: Kritik der politischen Ökonomie Buch 1* (Otto Meissner, 1867), p. 767.

here and now. If the empty tombs in Luxor, whence these bodies were taken, are, as we argued above, lacunae alluding to the destruction of social worlds and indigenous knowledge caused by the trauma of colonial violence, these gaps are rendered visible in the imagery of the flayed bones.

We can read the unwrapping as defining the boundaries of ownership, through the material dynamics of being produced, as inhuman, as an effect of power. In this passage the Nietzschean cyclops eye moves into the realm of biopolitics. There are dimensions of perversity here when Bachmann describes the body as violated by the archaeologists' touch, stressing again the valence of desecration. The ancient Egyptian practice of wrapping dead bodies was associated with notions of the secret and the sacred; the body was hallowed through wrapping. The unwrapping and merciless exposure symbolize immeasurable sacrilege while the context — that of the abuse of corpses — reinforces the sense of the alien nature of proprietary and commodified models of personhood. Dispossession resounds here in a scene that problematizes the notion of (self-)ownership while foregrounding acts of appropriation as intrinsic to the libidinal economy of White Archaeology. The abuse of the mummified bodies highlights the dynamics that legitimize the accumulation of knowledge in the museum and functions metonymically as an allusion to colonial power. Unwrapping or unrolling suggests that something is being revealed (the discovery of knowledge) but Bachmann's focus on the violence makes us see that something is being produced, knowledge and property generated. Again, dispossession is creating an object in the very act of appropriating it. This is analogous too with the birth of fields of meaning. As Christina Riggs explains, unrolling mummies helped define archaeology as a discipline,[59] a discipline inextricably linked to the production of race as Debbie Challis shows.[60]

Unwrapping the mummy becomes an allegory of the material economy that emerges through the libidinal economy of White Archaeology. It is by drawing attention to the slide between persons and the inhuman in the image of the materiality of bones that the text offers resistance by recalling the warp of dispossession. The exposed bones can be read as a form of what Dan Hicks calls 'necrology'. Hicks argues that foregrounding death and loss in the 'world culture' museum can have a decolonial force by drawing attention to colonial histories that are usually disavowed.[61] Bachmann's text also stresses the continuity of colonial logics in current local and global economic arrangements. In all the drafts she wrote of this passage, she mentions the exact price of the entrance ticket to the mummy room and thus reminds the reader of multiple forms of exclusivity: the wealth of the white photographers/White Archaeology, and

---

[59] Christina Riggs, *Photographing Tutankhamun* (Routledge, 2018), p. 10.
[60] See Debbie Challis, *The Archaeology of Race: The Eugenic Ideas of Francis Galton and Flinders Petrie* (Bloomsbury, 2014).
[61] See Hicks, *The Brutish Museums*.

the colonial origins of the Egyptian Museum, which was not originally built for Egyptians at all but for Europeans. Since the museum purports to curate the origins of human civilization, unequal access underscores the enclosure of the human that is going on within the institution. Moreover, and crucially, it points to ongoing occlusions. Forty-five piastres would be considerably more than a day's pay for the Nubian adults and children lifting and moving the stones for the white archaeologists.[62] We can read the mummified body finally as pointing to the real living bodies in Nubia under the regime of racial capital. It is to the multiple forms of dispossession in Nubia that my next section on Wadi Halfa turns.

III

It is difficult to know how to interpret the sections of *Das Buch Franza* that Bachmann did not complete. While I argue that Wadi Halfa is the emotional and political heart of the text, it is, crucially, the *missing* centre of the (unfinished) text. Bachmann clearly found it difficult to integrate Wadi Halfa into a narrative and this non-integration is significant because it means that Wadi Halfa is not straightforwardly represented. It is untenable for a critical interpretation, then, to turn Wadi Halfa into a symbol of anything. Nonetheless the connection between Wadi Halfa and White Archaeology needs to be made. Bachmann herself does not join up the dots by mentioning the UNESCO international salvage campaign in Nubia.[63] This historical context can help explain the presence of the white archaeologists in the text, however, and also offers a concrete manifestation of the dynamics of dispossession in which land dispossession is mirrored by occlusion from narratives of civilization and development. Importantly, the historical context allows images of Nubian resistance to come to the fore.

The key image from *Wüstenbuch* is the narrator clinging to Wadi Halfa as it is submerged:

> Ich fahre nach Wadi Halfa. Daran kann ich mich klammern. Denn es wird untergehen. / Ein Abend im Sudan, auf der Höhe von einer Stadt, die es in kurzer Zeit nicht mehr geben wird. Alle Dörfer sind schon leer, die letzten Frauen sind verschifft, die Männer sind längst ausgezogen, in die neuen Unterkünfte. Aber da ist noch diese Stadt, ein Anflug von Leben, und das Flirren von grünen Mücken in jedem Augenblick [...]. (TKA, I, p. 278)[64]

> [I am going to Wadi Halfa. I can cling on to it. For it will go under. An evening in Sudan, high up in the town which will soon no longer exist. All

---

[62] William Carruthers includes an image of the University of Chicago Oriental Institute's Nubian payroll for January and February 1963 where adult men earned 30 piastres a day, and boys 25 piastres. This document brings to light the exploitation of Nubian child labour. See Carruthers, *Flooded Pasts*, p. 204.

[63] To my knowledge Bachmann scholarship has not mentioned the UNESCO campaign. Herbert Uerlings writes on the historical context of the Cold War and decolonization. See Uerlings, 'Ich bin von niedriger Rasse', pp. 146–51.

[64] The solidus denotes a large gap between the sections of text in Bachmann's notebook.

the villages are empty, the last women sent away on ships, the men have moved out long ago into the new houses. But the town is still here, a hint of life and the buzzing of green flies fills every moment.]

This quotation refers to the real events. The opening of the Aswan High Dam flooded Nubian land and necessitated the forced displacement of 90,000 Nubian people who were re-settled in two new settlements hundreds of miles apart — al-Nuba al-Jadida (New Nubia) in Egypt and Khashm El Girba in Sudan.[65] As Nichols writes, to 'relocate an entire human community to some other place is to fundamentally and irrevocably transform it (moreover, most people view their homelands as nonfungible, to the point that adequate compensation cannot, even in principle, be given for their irredeemable loss or destruction)'.[66] Several thousand Halfawis refused to be moved and lived in temporary dwellings close to the edge of the new lake until the authorities finally started to rebuild a new Wadi Halfa in 1970. It is presumably these Halfawi people whom Bachmann visited in 1964 and described in the *Wüstenbuch*. They are alluded to obliquely in the closing pages of the final version of *Das Buch Franza*, as the rebels who topple the Sudanese government (TKA, II, p. 332).[67]

To cling to Wadi Halfa as it is submerged is to foreground the dynamics of land dispossession. Rather than generating property for colonists, dispossession here is associated with the relation between centre and periphery and the state's power to render the land waste and control populations in the service of development. Moreover, there are again multiple layers of dispossession. Adding to the loss of land and ways of life caused by the flooding and forced expulsion, the UNESCO Nubian monument salvage campaign itself compounded dispossession through actions which assumed ownership of Nubian heritage while ignoring contemporary Nubian voices. This was dominated by the Global North and involved dismantling and moving ancient structures to higher ground and to museums worldwide.[68] As Nancy Reynolds notes, it rested on the

claim of the international right to the area's ancient heritage. While this claim accorded ancient Egypt a foundational role in Western civilization, it nevertheless replicated a Eurocentric and teleological narrative that dismissed modern Egypt as culturally insignificant and challenged its national sovereignty.[69]

---

[65] According to Carruthers this fashioned Nubians into modern Egyptian and Sudanese citizens with coherent identities and separated them off as a distinct and second-class category: Carruthers, *Flooded Pasts*, p. 9.

[66] Nichols, *Theft is Property!*, p. 76.

[67] See Uerlings, 'Ich bin von niedriger Rasse', pp. 146–51. Part of the protests concerned the inadequate compensation they received for the flooding of their land.

[68] Carruthers, *Flooded Pasts*, pp. 25–64. Carruthers makes clear that the UNESCO salvage campaign was a colonial operation.

[69] Nancy Reynolds, 'Building the Past: Rockscapes and the Aswan High Dam in Egypt', in *Water on Sand: Environmental Histories of the Middle East and North Africa*, ed. by Alan Mikhail (Oxford University Press, 2012), pp. 181–206 (p. 192).

Countries that funded the massive documentation and restoration project were entitled to half of the artefacts found on their sites. Entangled with this dominance of the Global North was also a certain Egypto-centric bias which disadvantaged Nubia and Sudan. Many decisions on what to save were governed by Western commercial values, and research institutions and museums played a role in the differential treatment of Egyptian Nubian and Sudanese Nubian structures.[70] The contemporary Nubian population who lived next to the ancient temples were disregarded by the Western archaeologists who ignored their calls to move their villages, saints' shrines and gravesites to resettlement sites.[71] There was a double occlusion of the Nubian local population both by the international campaign and by the Egyptian state. As William Carruthers argues, Egyptian officialdom 'conflated the predominately black populations of Nubia and Sudan as natural objects of their rule'.[72]

While Bachmann alludes to the decolonial importance of the Aswan High Dam by having Franza read newspaper reports, it is also associated with the power of the state and Franza is not depicted visiting it, although she glimpses the Soviet leader's boat passing by on the occasion of the sluice gates opening on 15 May 1964. This distance kept from the dam is contrasted with the narrator's physical presence in Wadi Halfa just before it is flooded. There is lengthy narration of the days spent in Wadi Halfa in the *Wüstenbuch*.[73] The enduring impression is that of generous hospitality shown towards the white foreign narrator. The town seems to have ceased functioning normally, and no shops or markets are open. After a long passage describing her search for food and water during the day, in the evening the narrator sees Halfawi people in the streets and asks where she can buy provisions. They take her to a small house on the edge of town where she is invited in by a Halfawi family who share their food with her. She stays until late at night, leaving in the pitch darkness. These experiences feed into images that are used in the final version of *Das Buch Franza*. The shared meal in particular appears in the phrase: 'vier schwarze Hände und eine weiße Hand sind abwechselnd im Teller' (TKA, II, p. 332) [four black hands and a white one take turns eating from the bowl]. In the sentimental closing sections of the final version when Franza is dying, she describes this meal as the best she ever ate (TKA, II, p. 332). This apparent intimation of racial harmony can appear politically naïve, but also, as Uerlings argues, as a depiction of racial inequality.[74] However, the meanings associated with this image are much wider. As I explain below, the experience of being together in this Halfawi home is important for a political re-reading of the Nubian desert as fundamental to the text's notion of holding the governing codes in abeyance. In the *Wüstenbuch* the

---

[70] Ibid., p. 193.

[71] Ibid., pp. 182 and 194.

[72] Carruthers, *Flooded Pasts*, p. 30.

[73] See TKA, I, pp. 237–85. Although it is based on Bachmann's experiences, the *Wüstenbuch* is not simply a travel journal.

[74] See Uerlings, 'Ich bin von niedriger Rasse', p. 150.

image appears as part of a longer narrative that describes being together with Nubian hosts in their home. The writing evokes the lifeworld of the narrator's hosts and is shot through with the awareness of the power her whiteness affords her. She is embarrassed about eating their bread; she thinks it is the last piece in Wadi Halfa as she has been unable to find any bread anywhere during the day. The experience consists of being together as bodies, without language: 'Die Welt ist Geste, Gang, Licht, Dunkel, Warten, redelos' (TKA, I, p. 282) [The world is gesture, gait, light, darkness, waiting, speechless]. Inside this Halfawi home the narrator sees herself through the eyes of the child who briefly wakes up and is shocked to see a white face: 'ein nacktes dunkles Kind, das kurz aufweint, in ein weißes Gesicht starrt, aufbegehrt, sich beruhigt' (TKA, I, p. 282) [a naked, black child cries briefly, stares into a white face, protests and quietens down]. This could be read as an attempt to make the white narrator the object of the child's gaze, but the momentary flashing up of the face also recalls photography and ethnographic objectification and can appear like a snapshot of a moment with the white woman holding the camera that captures the child's cry. These unfinished drafts suggest Bachmann's uncertainty as to whether writing the Nubian cry might contribute to the mechanisms that dispossess, and the question remains whether the unheard textual cry can draw attention to the dynamics of dispossession by alluding to what we cannot hear.

We can re-read several of the images in the final version as allegories that frame this question. The striking image of Franza being buried alive in the alluvial mud of the Nile evokes the process of being silenced while attempting to speak the silencing; the image of gagging on unheard words makes silence concrete and material: 'Bei dem ersten unhörbaren Wort bröckelte ihr der Sand in den Mund [...] in den Mund rann Sand, in die Augen [...] wenn sie schrie, dann würde der Sand zustoßen und ihr die Luftröhre füllen' (TKA, II, p. 270) [at the first inaudible word the sand crumbled into her mouth, sand ran into her mouth, into her eyes [...] if she screamed the sand would close over completely and fill her windpipe]. The corporeal imagery alludes to lived experience and to the dynamics of dispossession from the side of the dispossessed. That this is an oblique reference to Nubian history and experience can be inferred from the fact that this burial occurs on the very same day that the dam's sluice gates are opened:

> Dann werden sie die Schleusen öffnen, das Wasser wird kommen. Die Geschichte wird den Wassertag verzeichnen. Und ich war lebendig begraben. Meine Geschichte und die Geschichten aller, die doch die große Geschichte ausmachen, wo kommen die mit der großen zusammen. Immer an einem Straßenrand? Wie kommt das zusammen? (TKA, II, p. 270)

> [Then they will open the sluices, the water will come out. History will dub it the Day of Water. And I was buried alive. My story and the story of all those who make up the larger history, how do these find a place within the whole of history [come together with the larger history, TL]. Are they always left by the side of the road? How do they find a place?] (BFRG, p. 107)

This is the closest the final version of *Das Buch Franza* comes to bringing the High Dam and the flooding of Nubia together. Franza asks about the relation between unheard histories and History with a capital H. Although Bachmann frames the question through the metaphor of historiography, the affect associated with being buried alive and the corporeal and material registers emphasize a concrete sense of dispossession, alluding to embodied histories and geographies that remain unheard within hegemonic structures of knowledge and power. The imagery of annihilation is brought into conjunction with the question of the institutional formations of History (of which the museum is a part). It raises the issue of erasure as a deliberate effect of these formations of History.[75] In the context of land dispossession in Nubia and the UNESCO project to salvage/write the History of civilization, the image alludes to those intentionally omitted. As Brenna Bhandar writes,

> peruse any legislation relating to the enclosure or appropriation of land, and you will be hard-pressed to find references to those whose land was being enclosed or stolen. Whether this was about common lands being enclosed or indigenous lands being appropriated by colonial authorities, those being dispossessed never appear in the text, as if they did not exist at all.[76]

Bachmann's striking image of matter speaking itself as the sand fills the windpipe expresses the silencing in material gulps and thus draws attention to Nubian culture, which appears to assert itself as alluvial agency even while in the throes of drowning in mud and grit raised by the building of the dam and the salvage campaign.[77]

The imagery of the desert also needs to be understood in relation to real lifeworlds in Nubia — and specifically that shared meal with the Halfawi hosts. In the *Wüstenbuch* it is made clear that the meanings attached to the desert can be traced back to the narrator's experiences in Wadi Halfa. The Nubian desert is said to possess revelatory powers, but the real revelation comes from being in that Halfawi home:

> Ich bin also zu einer Predigt gekommen, die niemand gesprochen und unter keinem Tempeldach gehalten hat, zur Predigung der Wüste und unformulierter Gesetze, zu Schlucken, Bissen, Gängen, Schlafarten, die [...] auf ihre Stunde gewartet haben, [...] auf das Halleluja des Überlebens im Nichts [...]. (TKA, I, p. 283)
>
> [Hence I came to a sermon that was spoken by no one and was not delivered in a temple; to the desert preaching the lesson of the unformulated laws, to

---

[75] Azoulay, *Potential History*.

[76] See Brenna Bhandar, 'Organised State Abandonment: The Meaning of Grenfell', *CLT*, 21 September 2018 <https://www.criticallegalthinking.com/2018/09/21/organised-state-abandonment-the-meaning-of-grenfell/> [accessed 27 August 2024].

[77] Both the dam and the salvage campaign involved the massive movement of stone. Images of workers moving stones for the dam and for the salvage campaign blurred into each other. Gamal Abdel Nasser depicted the High Dam as a modern pyramid. See Reynolds, 'Building the Past', p. 201.

gulping, chewing, ways of walking and sleeping that have waited for their hour, for the hallelujah of survival in the Nothing.]

I understand this complex passage, not as saying that the desert equates to the inchoate, but that in the desert the narrator encountered ontological diversity, and here it is clear that this diversity is the specificity of the movements of particular bodies, the gait and ways of living and being of her Halfawi hosts. The notion of the Nothing here is recalled in the closing sentence of the final version that describes the 'Finsternis' (TKA, II, p. 333) [darkness] as absolute. Bachmann's use of the Nothing alludes to Heidegger's interpretation of Kant's transcendental object. This is a concept of which we have no knowledge but need to presume as the ground or conditions of possibility for knowledge. The desert is aligned with the Nothing in a transcendental sense. As Heidegger writes:

> Das X ist ein 'Etwas', wovon wir überhaupt gar nichts wissen können. Es ist aber nicht deshalb nicht wißbar, weil dieses X als ein Seiendes 'hinter' einer Schicht von Erscheinungen versteckt liegt, sondern weil es schlechthin kein möglicher Gegenstand eines Wissens, d. h. des Besitzes einer Erkenntnis von Seiendem, werden kann. Es kann dergleichen nie werden, weil es ein Nichts ist.
>
> Nichts bedeutet: nicht ein Seiendes, aber gleichwohl 'Etwas'. Es 'dient nur als Correlatum', d. h. es ist seinem Wesen nach reiner Horizont. Kant nennt dieses X den 'transzendentalen Gegenstand' [...].
>
> [...] Dieser Horizont ist freilich nicht Gegenstand, sondern ein Nichts, wenn Gegenstand so viel bedeutet wie thematisch erfaßtes Seiendes.[78]

> [The X is a 'Something' of which in general we can know nothing at all. But it is not therefore not knowable, because as a being this X lies hidden 'behind' a layer of appearances. Rather, it is not knowable because it simply cannot become a possible object of knowing, i.e., the possession of a knowledge of beings. It can never become such because it is a Nothing.
>
> Nothing means: not a being, but nevertheless 'Something'. It 'serves only as *correlatum*', i.e., according to its essence it is pure horizon. Kant calls this X the 'transcendental object' [...].
>
> [...] This horizon is indeed not object but rather a Nothing, if by object we mean a being which is apprehended thematically.][79]

The notion of the pure horizon is aligned with the desert and transformed by Bachmann into the thought of Nothing as suspension as a force of resistance. The idea of the Something = X that cannot be known is politicized in the context of a critique of dispossession because the Nothing cannot be the possession of anyone; it does not even 'belong' to everyone equally.[80] The Nothing neutralizes

---

[78] Martin Heidegger, *Gesamtausgabe*, ed. by Friedrich-Wilhelm von Herrmann, 5th edn, 102 vols (Vittorio Klostermann, 1991), III (*Kant und das Problem der Metaphysik*), pp. 122–23. Heidegger is quoting Kant, *Critique of Pure Reason*, A250–51. See Immanuel Kant, *Critique of Pure Reason*, trans. by Norman Kemp Smith (Macmillan, 1929), pp. 267–68.

[79] Martin Heidegger, *Kant and the Problem of Metaphysics*, trans. by Richard Taft, 5th edn (Indiana University Press, 1997), pp. 86–87.

[80] I diverge here from the existing interpretations which read the desert as a moral absolute

the overlay of significations and governing codes — not by overcoming them, but in the sense of constituting a transcendental dimension and allowing us to conceive of a transcendental dimension (in this phenomenal, not another, world) in which the categories cannot yet be employed. It foregrounds the notion of the Something/Nothing that precedes any conceptual organization or realization of property relations, a pre-given lifeworld to which the governing conceptual apparatus does not have a necessary connection.

This holding in abeyance opens a space for material diversity. When articulated in this valence, the desert is not an exotic otherness but alludes to the dispersed material multiplicities of human lives. It is this heterogeneity that appears under threat from the coming flood. The ensuing complex image in the quotation above oscillates between destruction and the expectation of resurrection in the Nothing. Bachmann reworked this passage in the closing paragraphs of the final version of *Das Buch Franza* to express a variation on this idea. Here the passage evokes the Halfawi lanterns suspended ('Aufheben'), not swept away, in the floodwater (TKA, II, p. 333). This is an image of Nubian resistance and again refers to the narrator's experience in Wadi Halfa as the lanterns are held by her hosts to guide her back to her lodgings. The lanterns symbolize a fugitive alluvial ontology and recall the Halfawis who refused to be displaced to the designated resettlement sites but remained on the edge of Lake Nubia, dismantling and rebuilding their dwellings each time the floodwaters rose.[81] If, on one level, the floodwaters represent the homogenizing and racializing effects of neocolonial capitalism, the transcendental Nothing that is associated with the flooded Nubian desert holds open a space for the unformulated, that is, for the un-writing and rewriting of laws.[82]

The notion of material heterogeneity as a force for the reformulation of the conceptual apparatus is also a call for being human otherwise. My final and concluding example privileges a surreal image, that of the black sea cucumber on the beach at Safaga. In this scene Franza collapses while experiencing hallucinations after placing the stranded sea cucumber back into the sea. The scene is in both the *Wüstenbuch* and the final version of *Das Buch Franza*, and ends with the phrase: 'Die arabische Wüste ist von zerbrochenen Gottesvorstellungen umsäumt' (TKA, II, p. 288) [the Arabian desert is surrounded by shattered conceptions of God].[83] In both versions the crumbling

---

and as an entity with which Franza identifies. For example, see Stephanie Bird, *Women Writers and National Identity* (Cambridge University Press, 2003), p. 31. In my reading, the desert is a transcendental condition of experience; morals and identity are neither here nor there.

[81] Carruthers, *Flooded Pasts*, p. 190: 'Nubian mobility could never entirely be controlled, and the new Wadi Halfa stands today as material evidence of the failure of officialdom to implement such regulation in the face of still-resonant affective ties to place.'

[82] The pronoun 'I' in literature for Bachmann is similarly a transcendental horizon, a placeholder for the diversity of the human voice, as she describes in 'The Third Frankfurt Lecture: Concerning the I' (CW, 305).

[83] In the Wüstenbuch the phrase is 'Ich bin in einer Wüste, die von zerbrochenen Gotteserwartungen umsäumt ist' (TKA, I, p. 273). This is Bachmann's reworking of a

of the concepts of God on the edge of the desert opens onto an alternative: the inhuman black body of the sea creature. In the *Wüstenbuch*, the sea cucumber is an apparition that emerges from the fragmentation at the limits:

> ein zerbrochenes Bild [...] ganz schwarz, vor lauter Licht und Wüste, es war so und es <war> zerbrochen. [...] als ich näher kam lag am Strand eine Seetolle, ein schwarzer Kloß aus Fleisch, kaum dreißig Zentimeter lang, ein schwerbewegliches Stück Meeresfleisch. Das war die Erscheinung. Ich sah aber Gott. (TKA, I, pp. 276–77)

> [a shattered image [...] everything completely black blinded by light and desert, it was broken as I came nearer, on the beach lay a sea creature, a black clump of flesh, barely thirty centimetres long, a fleshy sea animal. That was the appearance. But I saw God.]

Here the sea cucumber is broken into pieces; in the final version the marine animal is shrivelled up but not destroyed:

> Gott kommt auf mich, und ich komme auf Gott zu. Sie lief wieder und weinte, weinte [...] und da lag Er vor ihr, ein schwarzer Strunk, aus dem Wasser geschwemmt, eine Seewalze, ein zusammengeschrumpftes Ungeheuer, keine dreißig Zentimeter lang, in dem ein leises Leben war. (TKA, II, pp. 286–87)

> [God comes towards me and I come towards God. She ran again and cried, cried [...]. [...] and there He lay before her, a black stump, washed up by the tide, a sea cucumber, a shrivelled-up monster, barely thirty centimetres in length, which was just about still alive.]

In this version it is the protagonist who appears broken, but her breakdown is not the real focus; instead, the passages ask us to imagine that God is a black sea cucumber. At the risk of translating what is surrealist anti-narrative into a political message, this evokes replacing the extrahuman, eternal authority with the body of the sea cucumber. Strictly speaking, not all concepts have been shattered; rather the image militates for a different kind of concept. The text is not longing for a non-conceptual oblivion or Utopia. The image speaks of uncovering material differences that are very much in this world precisely by centralizing the inhuman body without making it into a new norm. The sea cucumber survives by sifting through material fragments at the bottom of the deepest oceans. As such it is linked by association to listening to the materialities of submerged histories and paying attention to material economies. It is described as black flesh, but it is not a symbol of a 'racialized other'; to interpret it as such would only reuse the colonial codes. Rather the symbol speaks of getting lost from the human,[84] becoming unmoored from colonial systems of knowledge, orientating towards other versions of the human that are unheard within the dominant epistemologies of the West.

quotation from T. E. Lawrence's *The Seven Pillars of Wisdom*, of which she owned a German translation. See TKA, II, p. 487.
[84] On this idea, see Bayo Akomolafe, *These Wilds beyond our Fences: Letters to my Daughter on Humanity's Search for Home* (North Atlantic Books, 2017).

Sexual-Political Positioning in Ingeborg Bachmann's Poem 'Liebe: Dunkler Erdteil' [Love: The Dark Continent]

THOMAS PEKAR

Gakushuin University, Tokyo

In this article, I will argue in three steps that Bachmann's poem 'Liebe: Dunkler Erdteil' [Love: The Dark Continent], first published in 1957, develops a sexual-political positioning that later became of great importance to her, especially in her novel *Das Buch Franza* (TKA, II) [*The Book of Franza*]. To accomplish this, the political content and context of the poem will be examined first, followed by an analysis of its sexual imaginings, with the aim of integrating these two components to clarify its sexual-political positioning. The nine-stanza poem follows a relatively conventional structure with verse metre (pentameter iambic hendecasyllables) and rhymes (interrupted cross-rhyme). A speaker addressed as 'dich/du' [you] and not specified in detail,[1] which one could intuitively interpret as 'female' (however, at no point in the poem is the gender of this 'you' explicitly named), is drawn to a distant land, a blend of tropical and desert (arid) landscapes evoking Africa or, as subsequent analysis will reveal, Egypt. The poem's figurative language, which includes references to 'Tropenregen' [tropical rain], 'Gold und Elfenbein' [gold and ivory], 'Büffelherde' [buffalo herd], 'Karawanen' [caravans], 'Wüstenland' [desert land], 'Lianen' [liana ropes], 'Gazellen' [gazelles], 'Korallen' [corals], and more, creates an atmosphere of an ambiguous, exotic reality, a characteristic that has been subject to critical observation on numerous occasions. Gerhard Härle, for example, attributed to the poem an accumulation of exotic stereotypes, aesthetically anachronistic and irritating even for the 1950s.[2]

---

[1] On this term see Jochen Petzold, *Sprechsituationen lyrischer Dichtung: Ein Beitrag zur Gattungstypologie* (Königshausen & Neumann, 2012), pp. 137–38.

[2] See Gerhard Härle, 'Topographien der Leidenschaft: Der Liebesdiskurs Ingeborg Bachmanns zwischen Exotismus und Transkulturalität', in *Poetik des Widerstands: Eine Festschrift für Werner Wintersteiner*, ed. by Artur R. Boelderl and others (StudienVerlag, 2020), pp. 147–69 (p. 149); see also Áine McMurtry: '[T]he 1957 poem presents an array of images relating to animals and nature which correspond to traditional Western renderings of the exotic' in McMurtry, *Crisis and Form in the Later Writing of Ingeborg Bachmann: An Aesthetic Examination of the Poetic Drafts of the 1960s* (Modern Humanities Research Association, 2012), p. 65.

Austrian Studies 32 (2024), doi:10.1353/aus.00005, pp. 64–76
© Modern Humanities Research Association 2024

There, in this faraway fictional place, the speaking instance masochistically submits to an all-powerful 'schwarzen König' [black king]. This submission is consistently celebrated in the poem in various images and can certainly be read in a sexual sense. For example, the fifth stanza reads:

> Er, fellig, farbig, ist an deiner Seite,
> er greift dich auf, wirft über dich sein Garn.
> Um deine Hüften knüpfen sich Lianen,
> um deinen Hals kraust sich der fette Farn. (SG, p. 168)

> [He, hairy, brightly colored,[3] is by your side;
> He snatches you up, throws over you his snare.
> Soon long liana ropes will bind your hips,
> Your throat is ruffled with a lush fern collar.] (DS, p. 323)

The black king falls upon the 'you' bound by lianas and ferns (in the seventh stanza a chromium-plated snake — as 'Schmuck und Handschelle' [ornament and handcuff] — still hang from the arm of the speaking instance),[4] which could be read as an — at least implied — masochistic sex act. Only in the penultimate, eighth stanza, can a deviation from this absolutely asymmetrical positioning be seen — an active black king contrasts with a 'you' who passively tolerates.[5] Here, a change might be possible, because the black king appears to give up the emblems of power:

> Er gibt Insignien aus seinen Händen.
> Trag die Korallen, geh im hellen Wahn!
> Du kannst das Reich um seinen König bringen,
> du, selbst geheim, blick sein Geheimnis an. (SG, p. 169)

> [He gives to you insignia from his hands.
> Wear the corals, walk in deluded raiment!
> You can deprive the kingdom of its king,
> For it's you who, secretly, has seen his secret.] (DS, p. 325)

This transfer of power through the change of the emblems of rule towards the 'you' is not realized in the end, however, but the omnipotence of the black king, metaphorized as a panther — which could be an allusion to Rilke's famous poem 'Der Panther' (1903) [The Panther][6] — is restored in the ninth and last stanza more gloriously than ever:

---

[3] Bachmann, on the other hand, seems to address the specific skin colour — in the sense of 'farbig' (= 'coloured').

[4] Härle, 'Topographien der Leidenschaft', p. 155.

[5] It corresponds to this binary opposition that almost all verbs of the poem, such as 'zeigen' [show], 'jagen' [chase], 'befehlen' [command], 'ziehen' [draw], 'verwerfen' [reject], 'wählen' [choose], 'peitschen' [lash], 'sehen' [see], 'greifen' [snatch], etc., are assigned to the black king; further, natural objects (such as 'Monde' [moons] or 'Sand' [sand]), plants and animals, are depicted as representatives for him.

[6] Rainer Maria Rilke, *Gedichte: Erster Teil* (Suhrkamp, 1987), p. 505.

Um den Äquator sinken alle Schranken.
Der Panther steht allein im Liebesraum.
Er setzt herüber aus dem Tal des Todes,
und seine Pranke schleift den Himmelssaum. (SG, p. 169)

[On the equator all barriers are lowered.
The panther lives alone by love's own laws.
He crosses over from the valley of death,
Trailing the heavens' fabric in his claws.] (DS, p. 325)

Examining the political significance of this poem, it is evident that its composition and publication coincide with the Suez Crisis of 1956. This crisis, a pivotal moment in European colonial history, as well as in the histories of Africa and Egypt, is subsequently extensively referenced by Bachmann in *Das Buch Franza* [*The Book of Franza*].[7] Prior to writing this book, Bachmann had visited the region in the spring of 1964 during her trip to Egypt and Sudan.[8] In a way, the poem 'Liebe: Dunkler Erdteil' can be seen as a preview of that journey and that novel.

In July 1956, the charismatic Egyptian president Nasser nationalized the Suez Canal, which had until then been majority-owned by the British–French Suez Canal Company, in order to be able to pay the costs for the construction work on the Aswan Dam from the canal usage fees. In response to this, France, Great Britain and Israel attacked Egypt at the end of October 1956. The aim was also to overthrow Nasser, who had been demonized to a certain extent in the West. The Soviet Union, as well as the United States, condemned this attack and exerted great diplomatic pressure, which is why Great Britain, France and Israel had to cease hostilities and withdraw. For the two European colonial powers, Great Britain and France, the fiasco of the Suez Crisis practically meant the end of their colonial ambitions. The dissolution of the British Empire, which still existed in large parts of the world at that time,[9] and of the French colonial empire was accelerated by this withdrawal.[10] Nasser was celebrated as defender of the Arab cause and hero of decolonization; a nimbus arose around him, also in connection with his ideas of unifying the Arab world.

Of course, it would be too simplistic to say that the powerful 'black king' in 'Liebe: Dunkler Erdteil', who shows 'die Raubtiernägel' [the predatory nails] in

---

[7] See TKA, III, pp. 91–92 and 250.
[8] I will not go into the biographical details of this journey here. Following the trip, Bachmann first initially distilled her impressions and experiences in her *Wüstenbuch* [Desert Book], which later became incorporated into her fragment *Das Buch Franza* [*The Book of Franza*], as part of her novel project *Todesarten* [*Ways of Dying*]. However, she broke off work on *Franza* in 1966.
[9] India and Pakistan had become independent in 1947. The extensive decolonization of Africa then took place in the 1960s.
[10] After giving independence to Tunisia and Morocco in 1956, France tried to keep Algeria as part of its territory, which led to the bloody Algerian War from 1954 to 1962.

the first line of the first stanza,[11] can be equated with Nasser and his political power, but it can be considered likely that Western media coverage of this popular politician, in which he was often placed in ancient Egyptian contexts, could have influenced Bachmann's conception of the poem.[12]

It can be said that the Suez Crisis was a concrete event that could be recognized as signifying the end of European colonialism — or, at the very least, that Bachmann, like many others, could have interpreted this crisis in this manner.[13] The beginning of this colonialism, as is well known, can be dated back to the so-called 'discovery' of America by Christopher Columbus in 1492. The Enlightenment philosopher Georg Christoph Lichtenberg formulated a revealing aphorism: 'Der Amerikaner,[14] der den Columbus zuerst entdeckte, machte eine böse Entdeckung' [The American, who first discovered Columbus, made an evil discovery].[15] Lichtenberg's aphorism makes a fictitious change of perspective insofar as he claims to speak from the perspective of a non-European. There is a long tradition for this change of perspective, which, with reference to colonial history, goes back to the sixteenth-century Dominican Bartolomé de Las Casas, who was one of the harshest critics of the *Conquista*, the 'conquest' of Central and South America by Spanish and Portuguese soldiers that followed Columbus. Las Casas tried to adopt the perspective of the natives and victims of this conquest of the Americas by writing — as he himself said — 'si Indus esset', as if he were a Native American.[16]

Another voice of this change of perspective, and one that was important for Bachmann, was the French lyricist Arthur Rimbaud, who in his book *Une saison en enfer* (1873) [*A Season in Hell*] puts the primal scene of the appearance

---

[11] The English translation says: 'the panther's claws' (DS, p. 323). In the original text, the panther is not mentioned until the final stanza.

[12] For example, Nasser, who was also called 'the red pharaoh' in Western media, was featured on the covers of *Time* magazine on 26 September 1955 and 27 August 1956, in such a way that his portrait is shown against ancient Egyptian background images, such as hieroglyphs, pharaohs armed with modern rifles on the 1956 cover, or pyramids. See <https://content.time.com/time/covers/0,16641,19550926,00.html> and <https://content.time.com/time/covers/0,16641,19560827,00.html>; see also the later 29 March 1963 cover, where Nasser's profile is superimposed onto that of the Sphinx; <https://content.time.com/time/covers/0,16641,19630329,00.html> [accessed 25 July 2023].

[13] The end of European colonialism also signified the realization that Europe or European culture 'is no longer the unquestioned and dominant centre of the world': Robert J. C. Young, *White Mythologies: Writing History and the West*, 2nd edn (Routledge, 2004), p. 51. This is a view that Bachmann certainly shared. See also Sara Lennox, *Cemetery of the Murdered Daughters: Feminism, History, and Ingeborg Bachmann* (University of Massachusetts Press, 2006), pp. 4–5.

[14] By which is meant here the Native American.

[15] Georg Christoph Lichtenberg, *Schriften und Briefe. Zweiter Band. Sudelbücher II. Materialhefte, Tagebücher*, ed. by Wolfgang Promies, 2nd edn (Hanser, 1975), p. 166.

[16] Las Casas cited in Mariano Delgado, '"Columbus noster est": Der Wandel des Kolumbusbildes und der Entdeckung Amerikas', *Schweizerische Zeitschrift für Religions- und Kulturgeschichte*, 100 (2006), pp. 59–78 (p. 63).

of the European 'explorers' in a land unknown to them into the 'Schreckensruf'
(TKA, II, p. 73) [cry of terror], thus articulated under certain circumstances by
'natives': 'Les blancs débarquent' [The white men are landing].[17] Furthermore,
he undertakes an inversion of the Western racialized binary by describing
himself as 'de race inférieure' [of inferior race].[18] Bachmann brings both
sentences together for her novel *Das Buch Franza* and repeats them constantly.[19]

Such a change of perspective can also be found in Bachmann's poem 'Liebe:
Dunkler Erdteil', namely in the final line of the first stanza, which begins with
the appearance of the 'black king':

> Der schwarze König zeigt die Raubtiernägel,
> zehn blasse Monde jagt er in die Bahn,
> und er befiehlt den großen Tropenregen.
> Die Welt sieht dich vom andren Ende an! (SG, p. 168)

> [The black king holds aloft the panther's claws
> And chases ten pale moons around like prey,
> Invoking great tropical rain that begins to fall.
> The world is looking at you in a different way!] (DS, p. 323)

In particular, the final line of this stanza can be linked to the end of colonialism,
connected with the Suez Crisis. The formerly colonized world now looks as
an emancipated, independent subject upon Europe.[20] An inversion of this
kind — which decentres the colonizer's point of view and centres that of the
colonized — goes some, but only some, way towards indicating the immense
complexities of coloniality and its destructive aftermaths, as theorized by anti-,
post- and decolonial thinkers since Frantz Fanon. Following on from the
far-reaching analysis of complex interlocking issues — from the formation of
economic world systems since early modernity, the development of global trade
under capitalism, imperial and colonial regimes of resource extraction, the
epistemic violence of Eurocentric and white-supremacist racial ideology and its
internalization and contestation by minoritized and subaltern populations and

---

[17] Arthur Rimbaud, *Une Saison en Enfer: Eine Zeit in der Hölle. Französisch / Deutsch*,
trans. by Werner Dürrson (Reclam, 1970), p. 20; Arthur Rimbaud, *Complete Works*, trans.
by Paul Schmidt (Harper Perennial, 2008), p. 223.

[18] Rimbaud, *Une Saison en Enfer*, p. 14; Rimbaud, *Complete Works*, p. 221.

[19] These can also already be found in *Ein Ort für Zufälle* [*A Place for Coincidences*] and then
later in the *Wüstenbuch* [Desert Book]: 'Die Weißen kommen, ich bin von niedriger Rasse'
(TKA, I, p. 180; see also p. 257, p. 283 and the commentary on p. 596, and TKA, II, pp. 34, 278
and the commentary pp. 485–86) [The whites are coming, I am of a low race]. This racial
inversion culminates in the sentence '[I]ch bin eine Papua' (TKA, II, p. 232) [I am a Papuan].
On the problematization of this attitude, see, among others, Gisela Brinker-Gabler, 'Andere
Begegnung: Begegnung mit dem Anderen zwischen Aneignung und Enteignung', *Seminar*,
29 (1993), pp. 95–105; and on Bachmann's reception of Rimbaud: Dirk Göttsche, '"Die
Schwarzkunst der Worte" — Zur Barbey- und Rimbaud-Rezeption in Ingeborg Bachmanns
Todesarten-Zyklus', *Jahrbuch der Grillparzer-Gesellschaft*, 3.17 (1991), pp. 127–62.

[20] The turn is less clearly expressed in the English translation. In the original, it says: 'Die
Welt sieht dich vom andren Ende an!' (SG, p. 168) — [from the *other* end!].

people of colour — recent theories of intersectionality as defined by Kimberlé Crenshaw have begun to elucidate the fateful cross-cutting of gender and race that is at the heart of this poem. It falls beyond the scope of this article to provide a fuller theoretical contextualization of the issues raised in the poem, but the political-historical complexes addressed by anti- and postcolonial theory, decolonial thinking and intersectional analysis are immensely relevant to a reading of it now.[21]

With this political-theoretical context in mind, then, one might observe more keenly a Copernican turn in the poem, in which the European is no longer in the colonial position of an active and penetrating bearer of the gaze, but is shifted into the other position of passive, gazed at and penetrated. The significance of the 'black king' is not only political, then, but leads to the centre of what one might call Ingeborg Bachmann's private mythology. In this king one can recognize the figure of the ancient Egyptian god of death, rebirth and the Nile, Osiris, who was often depicted in black,[22] whereby blackness is a symbol of fertility, referring to the colour of the dark alluvial land of the Nile; thus, Egypt was also called *kemet*, the black land, by its inhabitants.[23] With this Egyptian god, one is in an extensive intertextual field of reference for this poem, which was of the highest importance for Bachmann.[24] Above all, Osiris refers to Robert Musil's poem 'Isis und Osiris' (1923),[25] which Bachmann quotes in her radio essay, written around 1952, about Musil's fragmentary epochal novel *Der Mann ohne Eigenschaften* [*The Man without Qualities*]. In her comments on it,

[21] The following studies give some theoretical background to these reflections: Frantz Fanon, *Black Skin, White Masks*, trans. by Charles Lam Markmann (Grove Press, 1967); Edward W. Said, *Orientalism* (Pantheon, 1978); Ngugi wa Thiong'o, *Decolonising the Mind: The Politics of Language in African Literature* (Currey, 1986); Gayatri Chakravorty Spivak, 'Can the Subaltern Speak', in *The Post-colonial Studies Reader*, ed. by Bill Ashcroft (Routledge 1995), pp. 28–37; Kimberlé Crenshaw, *On Intersectionality: Essential Writings* (The New Press, 2019).

[22] Plutarch writes that the Egyptians gave Osiris a black skin colour. See Plutarch, *Drei religionsphilosophische Schriften. Über den Aberglauben. Über die späte Strafe der Gottheit. Über Isis und Osiris. Griechisch-deutsch*, ed. and trans. by Herwig Görgemanns, 2nd edn (Artemis & Winkler, 2009), p. 173.

[23] Egon Friedell, *Kulturgeschichte Ägyptens und des Alten Orients: Leben und Legende der vorchristlichen Seele* (Beck, 1936, facsimile repr. 1998), p. 108. As Lennox notes, one can understand Egypt also as 'a site outside the boundaries of the west and [...] [as] a stage of psychic development before "the Greeks" (i.e., the Oedipus complex, patriarchy) assume control'. See Lennox, *Cemetery of the Murdered Daughters*, p. 38.

[24] Bachmann was familiar with ancient Egyptian myths and had Friedell's *Kulturgeschichte Ägyptens* in her possession. See Susanne Bothner, *Ingeborg Bachmann: Der janusköpfige Tod. Versuch einer literaturpsychologischen Deutung eines Grenzgebietes der Lyrik unter Einbeziehung des Nachlasses* (Peter Lang, 1986), p. 311. References to Celan's poem 'In Ägypten' [In Egypt], published in 1948 and later dedicated to Bachmann, certainly also feature in 'Liebe: Dunkler Erdteil', but cannot be addressed here.

[25] Robert Musil, *Gesamtausgabe: In Zeitungen und Zeitschriften 1922–1924 II*, ed. by Walter Fanta (Jung und Jung, 2020), p. 282.

Bachmann emphasizes that, in this poem, Musil 'variiere' [varies] the central love theme that unfolds in the novel — in connection with the famous 'andere Zustand' [other state] — and that a 'traumhafte Lösung' (KS, p. 119) [dreamlike solution] is found here with regard to the theme of sibling love. Bachmann seems to be following Musil's statement that his poem 'in nucleo den Roman enthalte' [contains the novel in nucleo].[26]

To what extent this is correct is open for discussion — Musil never actually finds a 'solution' in his fragmentary novel, but gives a multitude of variations of this love. In any case, Bachmann associates a heightened, different state with Isis and Osiris, which, on the one hand, comprises a utopian component, and on the other hand is understood as a state of love. Thus, in the radio essay, Bachmann speaks of Musil's 'Utopie dieses "anderen Zustands"' [Utopia of that 'other state'] (KS, p. 120; CW, p. 143) and of the fact that his 'Weg des Denkens [...] mit dem der Liebe zusammen[fällt]' [path of thought coincides with that of love] (KS, p. 118; CW, p. 141).

This is of crucial importance for Bachmann's own conception of love, which contains precisely these two elements of the 'utopian' and the 'other', whereby the utopian element is linked to a fictitious faraway place (non-Europe) and the moment of the 'other' is connected to an unconventional form of love, which in Bachmann's work — as will be shown — bears strongly masochistic traits. Musil could have been one of the models for this masochistic turn of the other love state, less in his novel *The Man Without Qualities* than in his short story collection *Vereinigungen* [Unions], known to Bachmann.[27] In the first of the two stories comprising the collection, 'Die Vollendung der Liebe' [The Perfecting of Love], the protagonist Claudine gives herself over to a random man, in order to be able to experience a kind of heightened union with her absent lover through this masochistically experienced sexual act.[28]

In a draft letter by Bachmann from 1957 about a planned journey, addressed to her friend Hans Werner Henze, these two moments are brought together with regard to her poem 'Liebe: Dunkler Erdteil'. Bachmann first writes about her 'ungewöhnliche Entscheidung' [unusual decision] that will take her 'ich weiss nicht wie viele Kilometer von hier' [I don't know how many kilometres away from here], to 'das andre Ende der Welt' [the other end of the world]. She undertakes this journey, she continues, in order to understand the 'Leere' [emptiness] she has 'erlitten' [suffered] (IB/HWH, p. 153).[29] Then, in an address

---

[26] Robert Musil, *Tagebücher*, ed. by Adolf Frisé (Rowohlt, 1983), p. 846.

[27] She owned the prose edition of Musil edited by Adolf Frisé (see KS, p. 668), in which these novellas are found.

[28] Robert Musil, 'Die Vollendung der Liebe', in *Gesamtausgabe: Bücher I*, ed. by Walter Fanta (Jung und Jung, 2019), pp. 365–426.

[29] In fact, no major journey by Bachmann took place at this time, but Alfred Andersch had suggested a 'North Africa trip' to Morocco to her, with the goal of a well-paid radio reportage. See Monika Albrecht and Dirk Göttsche, 'Leben und Werk im Überblick — eine Chronik', in HB2020, pp. 3–23 (p. 10). However, Bachmann was not able to realize this idea

to Henze, she proceeds:

> Ich liebe Dich noch, aber ich werde das immer tun [...] — und da gibt
> es etwas anderes, das zerstört und zerstörerisch ist, alles oder nichts in sich
> dazu angetan, mich einmal wissen zu lassen, was ich wert bin und was ich
> nicht wert bin, und ich bin es, Hans, ich allein, die die Dinge so auf die
> Spitze treibt, denn die Männer sind Feiglinge, [sic]
> Es ist merkwürdig, dass ich vor kurzem etwas über diesen dunkeln
> Erdteil geschrieben habe, und nun gehe ich wirklich dorthin, und ich fühle
> diese [sic] alten starken Mut[.] (IB/HWH, p. 154)

> [I still love you, but I always will [...] — and there is something else that
> is destroying and destructive, all or nothing in itself, capable of letting me
> know for once what I am worth and what I am not worth, and it is I, Hans,
> I alone, who pushes things too far, because men are cowards, [sic]
> It is strange that I recently wrote something about this dark continent,
> and now I am really going there, and I feel this old strong courage.]

The men Bachmann refers to here as 'cowards' are European men with
their conventionally bourgeois-individualized understanding of love, which,
however, as the historical experience of fascism shows, is inscribed with great
destructive potential. The counter-place to Europe would then be Africa,
the African love that Bachmann names in an unpublished poem entitled
'Auflösung' [Dissolution]:

> Ich rufe Dich von der Straße,
> komm, hab schwarzes Haar, sei jung,
> sei hart, tu weh, hier wo alle blond sind,
> terra nova, Africa, ultima speranza.[30]

> [I call out to you from the street,
> Come, have black hair, be young,
> Be hard, hurt me, here where everyone is blond,
> Terra nova, Africa, *ultima speranza*.] (DS, p. 595)

What we find here, as in 'Liebe: Dunkler Erdteil',[31] is an idealization of the
Other, here: the African love. Bachmann thus follows the racist cliché of the
greater sexual powers of Blacks, to which, for example, the Cameroonian
postcolonialist historian Achille Mbembe, following the colonialism critic
Franz Fanon, has drawn attention. Fanon showed that 'der Ursprung des
archaischen Rassismus und seiner Negrophobie, sein schwankendes Objekt,
in der Angst vor der "halluzinierenden sexuellen Potenz" [liege], die dem
Neger unterstellt wird. Für die Mehrheit der Weißen, schreibt Fanon, stehe der
Schwarze für ungehemmten Geschlechtstrieb' [the origin of archaic racism and

of a trip to Africa until 1964, as mentioned above.

[30] Ingeborg Bachmann, *Ich weiß keine bessere Welt: Unveröffentlichte Gedichte*, ed. by
Isolde Moser, Heinz Bachmann, and Christian Moser (Piper, 2000), p. 168.

[31] It can be argued that in this poem Bachmann combines the mythological blackness of
Osiris with the 'authentic' blackness of Africans, so to speak.

its Negrophobia, its fluctuating object, [lies] in the fear of the 'hallucinating sexual potency' imputed to the Negro. For the majority of whites, Fanon writes, the Black stands for unrestrained sexual drive'.[32] In Bachmann's case, however, this racist stereotype is positively subverted.[33]

This other — here, black — love is masochistically structured, or rather its masochistic experience constitutes precisely its otherness. However, it is exactly for this reason that it is 'love' in the proper and emphatic sense, which now illuminates the title of Bachmann's poem, which could perhaps be paraphrased thus: if one wants to experience what love really is, one must go to Africa, the 'Dark Continent', that, since Freud, is not only a geographical designation, but also denotes hidden (female) desires. This term 'Dark Continent', as well as the two terms 'Fetisch' [fetish] and 'Tabu' [taboo],[34] that appear in the poem (in the sixth and seventh stanzas) refer to its psychoanalytical layers of meaning.[35] With the title of the poem, Bachmann alludes to one of Freud's most famous quotations. He wrote in 1926: 'Vom Geschlechtsleben des kleinen Mädchens wissen wir weniger als von dem des Knaben. Wir brauchen uns dieser Differenz nicht zu schämen; ist doch auch das Geschlechtsleben des erwachsenen Weibes ein *dark continent* für die Psychologie' [We know less about the sexual life of little girls than of boys. But we need not feel ashamed of this distinction; after all, the sexual life of adult women is a 'dark continent'[36] for psychology].[37]

In 'Liebe: Dunkler Erdteil', Bachmann seems to agree with Freud's allegorization of female sexuality as an unexplored continent. She recognizes in this sexuality — or in the masochistic form thereof described here — potential possibilities for a utopian understanding of love that is no longer bourgeois

---

[32] Achille Mbembe, *Kritik der schwarzen Vernunft*, trans. by Michael Bischoff (Suhrkamp, 2017), p. 212.

[33] On racist stereotypes in Bachmann's work, consider also this line from her poem 'Harlem': 'Die schwarze Stadt rollt ihre weißen Augen' (SG, p. 125). The English translation attempts to avoid this stereotypical black–white contrast: 'The ghetto rolls along with wide white eyes' (DS, p. 169).

[34] Both terms can also be found in Friedell in connection with Egyptian cults. See Friedell, *Kulturgeschichte Ägyptens und des Alten Orients*, p. 138.

[35] In a draft for a preface to *The Book of Franza*, Bachmann refers to Freud and the 'unentdeckten Sacher-Masoch' (TKA, II, p. 16) [undiscovered Sacher-Masoch]. Bachmann's library included two books by Sacher-Masoch: see TKA, II, p. 468 and Christine Kanz, 'Psychologie, Psychoanalyse und Psychiatrie in Bachmanns Werk', in HB2020, pp. 223–36 (p. 224).

[36] In English in the original.

[37] Sigmund Freud, 'Die Frage der Laienanalyse: Unterredungen mit einem Unparteiischen' (1926), in *Sigmund Freud: Schriften zur Behandlungstechnik. Studienausgabe. Ergänzungsband*, 6th edn (Fischer, 1975), pp. 271–349 (p. 303); Sigmund Freud, 'The Question of Lay Analysis' (1926), in *Sigmund Freud: The Standard Edition of the Complete Psychological Works*, trans. and ed. by James Strachey and Anna Freud, 24 vols (The Hogarth Press, 1959, facsimile repr. 1991), XX, pp. 179–258 (p. 212). Immediately following this passage, Freud formulates his controversial thesis of female penis envy. This thesis, as well as Freud's allegorization of female sexuality as a dark continent, has of course been met with much criticism, but it points to the confluence of colonialism, gender and racism.

or Western 'white'.[38] In any case, the other two psychoanalytic terms of the poem, fetish and taboo,[39] from the sixth and seventh stanzas, also point in this direction. These stanzas read:

> Aus allen Dschungelnischen: Seufzer, Schreie.
> Er hebt den Fetisch. Dir entfällt das Wort.
> Die süßen Hölzer rühren dunkle Trommeln.
> Du blickst gebannt auf deinen Todesort.
>
> Sieh, die Gazellen schweben in den Lüften,
> auf halbem Wege hält der Dattelschwarm!
> Tabu ist alles: Erden, Früchte, Ströme ...
> Die Schlange hängt verchromt an deinem Arm.
>
> (SG, pp. 168–69)
>
> [From every jungle recess: sighs and screams.
> He lifts the fetish. You have no reply.
> Sweet wooden sticks begin to beat dark drums.
> You stare transfixed, seeing where you will die.
>
> Look, gazelles are floating on the breeze,
> Only halfway down bends the date's ripe swarm!
> Everything is taboo: earth, fruit, streams ...
> The snake hangs shimmering upon your arm.]
>
> (DS, pp. 323 and 325)

With the fetish, a masculine-phallic dimension is called up, to which the 'you' in the poem reacts with silence and inaction: banished, it can only stare at the place where it will die.[40] However, one could also see in the poem a certain subversion of this quite clichéd situation, because — if one considers the fetish as one of the 'Insignien' [insignia] mentioned in the eighth stanza — it is, in a sense, movable, which means that it is *not* to be understood as genuinely masculine at all. Accordingly, Freud understood the fetish as the imaginary 'Phallus des Weibes (der Mutter)' [absent female phallus],[41] which Judith Butler follows up with the fictional 'lesbian phallus'.[42] The equation fetish =

---

[38] On this fundamental understanding of the poem, see also Lennox, who writes that the poem 'represents Africa as a lush and exotic realm of sexuality beyond the repressive boundaries established by Europeans'. Lennox, *Cemetery of the Murdered Daughters*, p. 270.

[39] Moreover, both terms originate from non-European areas: taboo is originally a Polynesian word, while fetish comes from the Portuguese (*feitiço*) and denoted sorcery and witchcraft among the African and West Indian natives.

[40] The poem speaks of 'Todesort' (SG, p. 168) [place of death], which already anticipates Bachmann's later novel project *Todesarten* [*Ways of Dying*].

[41] Sigmund Freud, 'Fetischismus' (1927), in *Sigmund Freud: Psychologie des Unbewußten. Studienausgabe*, 10 vols (Fischer, 1982), III, pp. 379–88 (pp. 383–84); Sigmund Freud, 'Fetishism' (1927), in *Sigmund Freud: The Standard Edition of the Complete Psychological Works*, trans. and ed. by James Strachey and Anna Freud, 24 vols (The Hogarth Press, 1961, facsimile repr. 1986), XXI, pp. 149–57 (p. 155).

[42] See Judith Butler, *Bodies That Matter: On the Discursive Limits of 'Sex'* (Routledge, 1993), pp. 28–30.

phallus = male power thus only works at first glance, since it is quite possible for the woman to have the phallus in the sense of a 'fictitious possession' — as Butler says: ' "the" lesbian phallus is a fiction'[43] — or rather, she also originally possessed it, as a fictitious maternal one. The Osiris myth, Musil in his poem about it, and Bachmann too, all draw attention to the artificiality and transferability of the phallus, which is perfectly in line with Butler's thesis that 'the phallus is a transferable phantasm'.[44]

The second psychoanalytic term, taboo, known primarily from Freud's essay *Totem and Taboo* (1912–13), signifies in the poem the excessive and completely arbitrary power of the black king, who declares natural conditions, such as fruits and streams, to be forbidden, taboo objects or realms. This is also shown in these lines from the second stanza: 'Dort aber liegst du immer auf den Knien, | und er verwirft und wählt dich ohne Grund' [But there you always fall upon your knees, | and he chooses and rejects you without grounds] (SG, p. 168; DS, p. 323). For Weigel, this line of the poem is an example of the motif of the 'Negation einer Erklär- oder Begründbarkeit der Liebe' [negation of an explicability or justifiability of love] that is frequent in Bachmann's work.[45]

If, in the psychoanalytical context, the fetish declares the masculine-phallic power to be decisive for the conventional organization of sexuality, which in Bachmann's poem is acknowledged and, as elaborated above, only somewhat subverted, the concept of taboo is also connected with a principle that is fundamental for the organization of 'normal' sexuality: namely that of the prohibition of incest.[46] This prohibition does not matter in the poem, but it becomes an important plot element in Bachmann's *Franza* novel, following Musil's *Mann ohne Eigenschaften*. The theme of incest, which plays a central role in the latter book, is taken up in Bachmann's novel with regard to the shaping of the warm and caring relationship between the siblings Martin and Franza.

---

[43] Ibid., p. 52.

[44] Ibid., p. 53, see also pp. 32–33.

[45] Sigrid Weigel, *Ingeborg Bachmann: Hinterlassenschaften unter Wahrung des Briefgeheimnisses* (Zsolnay, 1999), p. 154.

[46] Freud explains 'the two fundamental prohibitions of totemism' with the fact that the 'band of brothers' kill the violent original father, and now, out of their consciousness of guilt, they forbid 'the killing of the totem, the substitute for their father' as taboo, just as they also, in order to avoid quarrels among themselves, establish the prohibition of incest as a second fundamental taboo: 'Thus the brothers had no alternative, if they were to live together, but [...] to institute the law against incest by which they all alike renounced the women whom they desired and who had been their chief motive for despatching their father.' See Sigmund Freud, 'Totem and Taboo: Some Points of Agreement between the Mental Lives of Savages and Neurotics' (1912–13), in *Sigmund Freud: The Standard Edition of the Complete Psychological Works*, trans. and ed. by James Strachey and Anna Freud, 24 vols (The Hogarth Press, 1955, facsimile repr. 1962), XIII, pp. 1–162 (pp. 143–44).

In conclusion, one can argue that Bachmann's poem 'Liebe: Dunkler Erdteil' primarily articulates itself through contradictions evident on both the political and the erotic-sexual level.[47] It celebrates decolonization,[48] particularly in light of its relevance to the Suez Crisis, by aligning with the redistribution or reversal of colonial power structures. Bachmann achieves this by positioning the speaking instance of the poem in an absolutely powerless position — this can be seen as the decisive structural formula for this poem.[49]

The possibility of a fundamentally non-European perspective is also pointed out, which places Bachmann in a long (European) tradition dating back to Las Casas. However, the poem juxtaposes this notion with its use of exotic imagery and perpetuation of (philo-)racist stereotypes about Black sexuality. Regarding the contradiction on the erotic-sexual level, the poem articulates a sexuality or eroticism that goes beyond bourgeois European norms, which are named as 'white'.[50] A literary model for this heightened understanding of love is Musil's 'other state'. This state would correspond in Lacanian terminology to the concept of *jouissance*, linked to femininity and poetry by Julia Kristeva and others.[51] This heightened state of love could also be interpreted as a social utopia, as hinted at in the poem by the term 'Liebesraum' [space of love].[52] In *The Book of Franza*, an embodiment of this space of love as a social utopia, implying a peaceful community without racial differentiations, can be seen in Franza's shared meal with Arabs 'aus einem Teller' [from one plate].[53]

[47] From a feminist point of view, one could say that these contradictions can be read as 'a representation of the degree to which racialized and imperial fantasies are constituent elements of the European female psyche'. See Lennox, *Cemetery of the Murdered Daughters*, p. 270.
[48] On the not always unproblematic connection between Bachmann and (post-)colonialism, see the research overview in Monika Albrecht, 'Bachmann in postkolonialer Sicht', in HB2020, pp. 378–82.
[49] This also occurs through Franza's desert journey, which is described in *Franza* with the term 'die ägyptische Finsternis' [the Egyptian darkness] (TKA, II, pp. 61, 90 and 248; BFRG, p. 146). This expression is known to have been taken by Bachmann from Friedell, where it appears as a marginal section heading, next to which one can read: '*Islam* ist ein Infinitiv und bedeutet "sich ergeben" (in den Willen Allahs)' [*Islam* is an infinitive and means 'to surrender' (to the will of Allah)]: Friedell, *Kulturgeschichte Ägyptens und des Alten Orients*, p. 123. However, this religious aspect, which plays a central role, for example, in Michel Houellebecq's scandalous novel *Soumission* (2015) [*Submission*], is not present in Bachmann's work.
[50] The destructive, fascist characteristics of this sexuality are elaborated by Bachmann in *The Book of Franza* and condensed in the scene when Franza is raped by a 'white man' at the Cheops pyramid (TKA, II, pp. 125–26 and 319–23; BFRG, pp. 138–40).
[51] See Julia Kristeva, *Revolution in Poetic Language*, trans. by Margaret Waller (Columbia University Press, 1984), p. 17 and passim.
[52] In the English translation, the term 'Liebesraum' is somewhat unfortunately paraphrased as 'love's own laws' (DS, p. 325).
[53] In the submerged Wadi Halfa — flooded by Lake Nasser, created by the Aswan Dam — Franza shares, shortly before the flooding, a simple meal with other Arabs, prepared by a young Arab woman, which for her is an experience of true communion. Lennox refers to

In 'Liebe: Dunkler Erdteil', it is contradictory that the sexuality occurring within or constituting this space of love is clearly marked by violent and masochistic connotations.[54] In Bachmann's poems and novels, two protagonists appear quite often: a black (or Arabic) sadistic man (or men) and a white masochistic woman.[55] As shown, however, Bachmann subverts this asymmetrical power and love dynamic in the poem by drawing attention to the transferability of the fetish/phallus, essentially anticipating current insights such as those expressed by Judith Butler.[56]

The contradictions discussed in this article cannot be resolved, but only identified. The question remains, of course, why Bachmann chooses this masochistic perspective in the poem, later continued in *Franza* and indeed in other parts of her oeuvre.[57] Attempts at an answer are given, for example, by Weigel, who criticizes Bachmann's tendency to identify with victims, especially Jewish victims of the Holocaust.[58] Höller draws attention to a poetological dimension of masochism or destructiveness when he says that Bachmann exposed herself to it 'um diese geradezu physisch erfahrene Gewalt sprachlich bearbeiten zu können' [to address this violence, almost physically felt, through language].[59] Positively speaking, one could view this masochism as a poetically courageous attempt to delve into unknown realms of the soul, into the human 'Abgründigkeit und Hintergründigkeit' (TKA, ii, p. 16) [unfathomableness and profundity], in order to expand the field of what can be articulated.

this scene as 'the only utopian moment of the novel' and that Franza finds here a 'connection to a community in a setting that is almost religious, a kind of last supper' (Lennox, *Cemetery of the Murdered Daughters*, pp. 22 and 180). In its English translation, the novel also ends with a recollected evocation of this meal (see BFGR, 146).

[54] However, *jouissance* and masochism need not be contradictory; on their compatibility, see, for example, Lennox, *Cemetery of the Murdered Daughters*, p. 261.

[55] Two examples: the protagonist in Bachmann's *Wüstenbuch* [Desert Book] gives herself in an orgy to two Arabs (see TKA, i, p. 180), while Countess Kottwitz's sexuality (in drafts of the Kottwitz story as part of *Requiem für Fanny Goldmann*) — to say it in the words of Sara Lennox — 'is "awakened" only when she is "raped" by an African student with proverbially prodigious sexual capabilities' (Lennox, *Cemetery of the Murdered Daughters*, p. 26). Like 'Liebe: Dunkler Erdteil', other poems by Bachmann deal with these racialized sexual fantasies: 'Terra Nova' [Terra Nova], 'Immer wieder Schwarz und Weiss' [Always Black and White], 'Auflösung' [Dissolution], 'Ich habe euch, meine Spießer' [I did it with pleasure, you prudes] (see DS, pp. 588–89, 592–93, 594–95, 596–97).

[56] The fact that Bachmann shares or partially anticipated the insights of feminist scholars is a recurring theme in Bachmann scholarship. See, for example, Lennox, *Cemetery of the Murdered Daughters*, pp. 19–20.

[57] From the perspective of the genesis of her oeuvre, the relationships between Bachmann's poetry and prose works would be quite close at this crucial point.

[58] Weigel, *Ingeborg Bachmann*, p. 475.

[59] Hans Höller, 'Die Infragestellung des Scheincharakters der Kunst: "Keine Delikatessen"', in LG, pp. 81–93 (p. 88).

Ingeborg Bachmann *In Egypt* with Robert Musil, Paul Celan and Anselm Kiefer: An Exercise in Speculative Philaelogy (or *Art Will Survive its Ruins*, Artists Will Not)

ARTUR R. BOELDERL

University of Klagenfurt

> The books are always books of *life* (their archetype would be the *Book of Life* kept by the God of the Jews) or of *survival* (their archetype would be the *Books of the Dead* kept by the Egyptians). — JACQUES DERRIDA[1]

I

Reading Bachmann Now, 'Bachmann jetzt lesen': to me, here and now, this is to say reading Bachmann *with*, reading now *with* Bachmann, reading *along with* Bachmann's Now, reading the *Now* with Bachmann. On the one hand, this represents a fairly general, even easily generalizable, hypothesis concerning the genuine meaning of intertextuality, according to which all texts are sibbed with one another, no text exists on its own, every text is inscribed in a genealogy, its genealogy — which at the same time is not exclusively its alone — whereby it only becomes legible against its background. On the other hand, with respect to Bachmann, the said state of affairs represents quite a precise, indeed a Bachmann-specific, hypothesis suggesting that the *intertextuality* of the texts of this particular author announces itself both literally and metaphorically as *siblinghood*, that is, as a certain kind of kinship which owes less to free choice than to what Jacques Lacan called a forced choice.[2]

In other words — and I am hereby composing myself to transfer to Bach-

---

[1] Jacques Derrida, 'Edmond Jabès und die Frage nach dem Buch', in *Die Schrift und die Differenz*, trans. by Rodolphe Gasché (Suhrkamp, 1976), pp. 102–20 (p. 120), my English trans. See Jacques Derrida, 'Edmond Jabès and the Question of the Book', in Derrida, *Writing and Difference*, trans. by Alan Bass (University of Chicago Press, 1978), pp. 64–78 (p. 78): 'Books are always books of *life* (the archetype would be the Book of Life kept by the God of the Jews) or of *afterlife* (the archetype would be the Books of the Dead kept by the Egyptians).' Derrida's original text was first published as *L'écriture et la différence* (Seuil, 1967).

[2] See Jacques Lacan, *The Four Fundamental Concepts of Psychoanalysis: The Seminar of Jacques Lacan. Book XI (1963–1964)*, ed. by Jacques-Alain Miller, trans. by Alan Sheridan (W. W. Norton, 1977), p. 212.

Austrian Studies 32 (2024), doi:10.1353/aus.00006, pp. 77–90
© Modern Humanities Research Association 2024

mann, in an admittedly unseemly reduction, an approach developed and tested in the context of my work on MUSIL ONLINE, with this older Austrian fellow writer of hers: One cannot read Bachmann *now*, not *anymore* perhaps, without *With*, that is to say: one cannot read her alone, on her own, without also reading her contexts, which may be *pretexts* as in the case of Musil or *co-texts* as with Celan, as well as *post-texts* like Anselm Kiefer's paintings, which in turn refer to both Bachmann and Celan and even to Musil. The latter are, of course, not texts in the literal sense of the term, or not *just* (or not *yet*?) texts, indeed, if considered rightly, they are *more* than texts in all the cases mentioned, namely *books*, whole books or half books, unfinished (like Musil's *Man without Qualities*), open, and opened ones (like the Torah that actively calls for ever new commentaries), such as are uninscribed (blank) and unwritten (conceived only, for instance), burnt in part and partly burnt (as in various acts of so-called auto-da-fés past and present), both in the literal and in the figurative sense (e.g. when Kiefer exposes leaden books to fire), historically as well as metaphorically and, in Bachmann's case, even metonymically, palimpsests (if unintentionally, different from Artaud's practice of burning holes in his manuscripts and drawings with cigarettes).[3] They are, therefore, at the same time also less than books, not books, not any more, or at least not a *book*, less than any *one book*, less than *the book* at any rate, even less perhaps than a text that is still in a book; damaged books, if you will, in the sense that Adorno had in mind when he chose to characterize his *Minima Moralia* in its subtitle as *Reflections from Damaged Life*,[4] thus emphasizing that such books are less *and* more than just books because they are writing (*écriture*) whose place nevertheless remains *the book*, yet certainly no longer this or that one, nor the ideal, unwritten book in the sense of Mallarmé's *livre irréalisé*,[5] but rather the book *in* the book, the book without beginning and without end that is both preceded and followed by countless books — no totality of all books promising to round or close itself teleologically or even eschatologically, no wholeness or integrity of the book as such and no sum of all real and possible books, rather the book in the plural, an *oversum* qua *gestalt* that cannot be reduced to the sum of its parts nor

---

[3] See Paule Thévenin and Jacques Derrida, *Antonin Artaud: Zeichnungen und Portraits*, trans. by Simon Werle (Schirmer/Mosel, 1986). For the texts by Thévenin and Derrida in English, see Paule Thévenin and Jacques Derrida, *The Secret Art of Antonin Artaud*, trans. by Mary Ann Caws (MIT Press, 1998).

[4] See Theodor W. Adorno, *Minima Moralia: Reflections from Damaged Life*, trans. by Edmund F. N. Jephcott (New Left Review Editions, 1974).

[5] See Jacques Derrida, *Writing and Difference*, trans. by Alan Bass (Routledge & Kegan Paul, 1978), p. 25; see also Artur R. Boelderl, 'Vom *Livre irréalisé* zum *Texte hyperréalisé*? Ein Abriss der Fragestellungen, Problemfelder und Lösungsansätze im Zusammenhang mit der Entwicklung von Kommentarstrukturen und Modellkommentaren für eine interaktive Kommentierung der Schriften Robert Musils im Internetportal MUSIL ONLINE', *Zeitschrift für digitale Geisteswissenschaften*, special volume 2 (2018): *Digitale Metamorphose: Digital Humanities und Editionswissenschaft*, ed. by Roland S. Kamzelak and Timo Steyer, doi: 10.17175/sb002_010

deduced or projected from the same: an image of the book whose individual pages (and individual books), like splinters of a broken mirror in the context of Jewish mysticism,[6] point from afar to a pre-lost whole or wholeness that, more desired than assumed or presupposed, disappears or remains invisible in the transparency of its material — glass, fired from hot sand — and can at best be guessed from the shadows of its outlines against an overbright source of light.

In short, according to my double proposition, the form of Bachmann's intertextuality — which allows us to fathom her books in the act of reading both the finished and the unfinished ones alongside each other, including first and foremost but not exclusively those belonging to the *Todesarten* [*Ways of Dying*] project, such as, in particular, *The Book of Franza* and the 'Desert Book' — is *siblinghood* (1) and its content or thematic point of reference is *Egypt*. More precisely, 'Egypt' forms an *intercontext* for Bachmann (2), from which the intertextuality that exists between her texts and those of Musil and Celan on the one hand, and Anselm Kiefer's paintings on the other, transcending genres and being transtextual, even transmedial, can be grasped and made productive for attempts at interpretation in literary studies: 'Egypt' is therefore an intercontext common to them all. The approach I am advocating here thus clearly draws on previous research and pertinent insights by others.[7] At the same time, the present article seeks to establish what I suggest is an underlying condition of

---

[6] See, for example, Gershom Scholem, *Von der mystischen Gestalt der Gottheit: Studien zu Grundbegriffen der Kabbala* (Rhein-Verlag, 1962), and, with respect to Celan, Rüdiger Sünner, 'Gottes zerstreute Funken: Jüdische Mystik bei Paul Celan', in *Okkulte Kunst*, ed. by Alexander Graeff (transcript, 2019), pp. 127–46.

[7] Such as, for instance: Barbara Agnese, 'Isis und Osiris: Mythos und Doppelgeschlechtlichkeit der Seele bei Robert Musil und Ingeborg Bachmann', in *Mythos und Geschlecht — Mythes et différences des sexes: Deutsch-französisches Kolloquium*, ed. by Françoise Rétif and Ortrun Niethammer (Winter, 2005), pp. 73–84; Franziska Frei Gerlach, 'Auf Sand gebaut. Anselm Kiefers Antrag zur Geschwisterschaft an Ingeborg Bachmann', *Jahrbuch der deutschen Schillergesellschaft: Internationales Organ für neuere deutsche Literatur*, 44 (2000), pp. 235–64; Frei Gerlach, 'Geschwisterschaft in Wort und Bild: Ingeborg Bachmann und Anselm Kiefer', *Freiburger FrauenStudien*, 1 (2000), pp. 169–91; Frei Gerlach, 'Sandkunst.:Korrespondenzen zwischen Anselm Kiefer, Paul Celan und Ingeborg Bachmann', in *Poetiken der Materie: Stoffe und ihre Qualitäten in Literatur, Kunst und Philosophie*, ed. by Thomas Strässle and Caroline Torra-Mattenklott (Rombach, 2005), pp. 225–42; Annette Gilbert, ' "Es ist erstaunlich, wie man oft eben das findet, was man sucht." Anselm Kiefer im Gespräch mit Ingeborg Bachmann über Geschichte, Zeit und Utopie', in *'Mitten ins Herz': KünstlerInnen lesen Ingeborg Bachmann*, ed. by Brigitte E. Jirku and Marion Schulz (Peter Lang, 2009), pp. 73–97; Bettina von Jagow, 'Liebe und Tabu: Zum Kulturtransfer des Isis-Osiris-Mythos in die Moderne: Ingeborg Bachmanns *Der Fall Franza* und Robert Musils *Isis und Osiris*', *Orbis Litterarum*, 58 (2003), pp. 116–34; Karina von Tippelskirch, 'Angrenzen: Anselm Kiefer und Ingeborg Bachmann', in *'Die Waffen nieder! Lay down your weapons!' Ingeborg Bachmanns Schreiben gegen den Krieg*, ed. by Karl Ivan Solibakke and Karina von Tippelskirch (Königshausen & Neumann, 2012), pp. 173–84; and with regard to the impact of 'Egypt' in the Western history of ideas in general and for literary theory in particular, see Artur R. Boelderl, *Literarische Hermetik: Die Ethik zwischen Hermeneutik, Psychoanalyse und Dekonstruktion* (Parerga, 1997).

the possibility for 'Egypt' to function as the 'common ground' between Musil, Celan, Bachmann and Kiefer, a philological as well as philosophical ground at that, which has been merely touched upon hitherto rather than expressly taken into account as seriously as it deserves to be. My exploration of 'Egypt' as intercontext thus deliberately runs the risk of drawing somewhat bolder conclusions than the aforementioned studies.

In the words of Celan and Musil: 'Everything is more than it is, everything is less.'[8] I have dealt with the striking intertextuality between these two authors elsewhere by discussing this very verse from Celan's 'Cello-Einsatz' [Cello Entry],[9] or rather its inversion cited here — 'everything is less than it is, everything is more' (the correct sequence);[10] and the way in which everything is simultaneously less and more than it is, is Egyptian (from which one can, at the same time, tell the indissoluble entanglement of form and content, since it is in each case a variant of what one could call an *Egyptian siblinghood*): in Musil as in Celan and in Bachmann — via the latter two authors' shared posthumous mediation of the former — as Anselm Kiefer sensitively registers and points (or paints) out. This is certainly not to say that this attribute means exactly the same thing in all three authors, no more than the narration of a concrete myth according to Lévi-Strauss may be regarded as congruent or identical with this very myth, while the latter still unmistakably shines through all its more or less divergent versions and can be identified as such. Thus, in Celan, 'Egyptian' can clearly reference, in an isotopic manner, via the sand or the grain of sand, the snow and the snowflake. It finds its common ground, across the blatant climatic and geographic as well as temperature and colour difference, in the crystalline quality of both; and thus, in Bachmann, 'Egypt' can just as easily border on Bohemia without any poetological rupture, as Bohemia itself can lie by the sea — after all, Shakespeare's reference text, which is the inspiration for the latter 'impossibility', already speaks of the 'deserts of Bohemia', at whose shores the travellers' ship unexpectedly arrives.[11] After all, there are ice deserts just as there

---

[8] Robert Musil, *Der Mann ohne Eigenschaften. Roman*, ed. by Adolf Frisé (Rowohlt, 1952), p. 1381 (written after 16 February 1936, see Musil, *Klagenfurter Ausgabe: Kommentierte Edition sämtlicher Werke, Briefe und nachgelassener Schriften. Mit Transkriptionen und Faksimiles aller Handschriften*, ed. by Walter Fanta with the collaboration of Rosmarie Zeller (DVD-ROM, Klagenfurt 2009, Update 2015), 'III: *Der Mann ohne Eigenschaften*: Lesetexte: *Stumm und die Propheten*'; see also Musil, *Gesamtausgabe*, v: *Der Mann ohne Eigenschaften. Roman*, ed. by Walter Fanta (Jung und Jung, 2016), pp. 423–24.

[9] See Artur R. Boelderl, '"Alles ist mehr, als es ist" — Prothesen zu einer Begegnung von Musil "und" Celan *In Aegypten*', in *Paul Celan — 'sah daß ein Blatt fiel und wußte, daß es eine Botschaft war': Neue Einsichten und Lektüren*, ed. by Martin A. Hainz (Frank & Timme, 2022), pp. 153–81.

[10] Paul Celan, 'Cello-Einsatz', written on 24 December 1964, from *Atemwende* (1967); in *Die Gedichte: Neue kommentierte Gesamtausgabe in einem Band*, ed. with commentaries by Barbara Wiedemann (Suhrkamp, 2018), pp. 203–04 (p. 204).

[11] See *A Winter's Tale* III, 3, line 1439, First Folio Edition 1623: [Antigonus] 'Thou art perfect then, our ship hath toucht vpon | The Desarts of Bohemia.'; the German edition by Schlegel and Tieck indicates the very location as 'Bohmen. Eine wüste [!] Gegend am Meer'.

are sand deserts, both of which metaphorically border on the very sentiments also associated with the ocean, indicating places or regions where one easily gets lost and feels alone and abandoned while at the same time somehow strangely attracted and even contained, if only temporarily and/or counter-intuitively (as is the case, for instance, in the *Book of Franza* when the protagonist has herself virtually interred in wet sand and barely escapes suffocation from the rapidly drying and thus solidifying loam). Against this background, 'Böhmen liegt am Meer' [Bohemia Lies by the Sea], Bachmann's 'last poem', her own favourite, written in the immediate temporal context of her journey to Egypt in 1964 after a visit to Prague with Adolf Opel, which paved the way for their ensuing trip to the Orient, also echoes the aforementioned turn of phrase found in Musil and Celan as to the Being-more-and-less of everything, when the narrator says in the third-to-last verse: 'ich grenz, wie wenig auch, an alles immer mehr' (LG, p. 117) [I border, however little, on everything more and more].

II

In further pursuit of the traces opened up by these initial suggestions, the testing of my proposition takes the shape of an *exercise in speculative philology*, by which expression I proactively adopt a formulation that may well be read in a critical manner and affirmatively turn it to the positive or constructive side; I even radicalize the speculative dimension of my approach — which I admittedly would prefer to be understood in a non-pejorative, namely philosophical, sense — by overlaying the philological part with what I call, with a deliberately mannered neologism, 'philaelogy'. For it is to Philae that we must go, at least in spirit, in order to gauge what 'Egyptian siblinghood' between Bachmann, Musil, Celan and Kiefer may perhaps mean; and in so doing, I also assume, by the way, that the philological facts that form the basis for this venture have long been on the table, even more: that they are known to all of us who have read and seen the works of these artists, so that there is no longer any need for *philological* research in the original or disciplinary sense in order to seriously pursue the epistemological interest described. What is needed, rather, is a *philosophical* reflection on these essentials with which previous research has hitherto provided us, a form of philology heightened — or exaggerated, if you like — to the affective dimension, a *philophilology* along the lines of the late Werner Hamacher (who unfortunately, as far as I know, wrote or left nothing about Bachmann or Musil, but correspondingly more about Celan),[12] which betakes itself with open and reading eyes to the shoals of the arts, shoals in the lake, in the sea, in the mountains, in the forest, in the desert or in a combination of these that has been raised to the umpteenth power of peril — as is the case, for instance, in Philae.

[12] See Artur R. Boelderl, 'HEIMlich : HAMacher : am HEIMischsten — Dieser ebenso diskrete wie obskure Affekt der Philonatologie', *Triëdere: Zeitschrift für Theorie, Literatur und Kunst*, 23 (2022), pp. 111–26.

So I take to heart the advice, supposedly given by Mark Twain, according to which writing is easy, you just have to cross out the wrong words, 'wrong' meaning 'unnecessary' in our case, and I apply it to my contribution insofar as I vow to say nothing that I think I may take for granted, on my side as much as on the readers',[13] and rather concentrate on what, to my knowledge, has not yet been said, by asking what I believe to be the crucial question (at least for my own reading, that is), namely: What does 'Egyptian' mean here? — and at the same time proposing a provisional answer. 'Egyptian' stands for an unthinkable-ancestral, unavailable-withdrawn, misunderstood-incomprehensible, yet also unmistakably conspicuous, a- or pre-rational rather than irrational ('non-ratioïd' in Musil's terms) *relatedness*, more darkly felt than cognitively experienced, an affinity that one has not chosen, that has no (biological or genealogical, historical or cultural) reason or cause one could state beyond doubt, but rather represents that abyss which is the sky as one sees it below when, according to Celan, one walks on one's head. This is a relationship that is not accessible to any hermeneutic approach aimed at understanding, one that has found its powerful expression in the mythical figure of the Egyptian Hermes Trismegistus as the incarnation of the god Thoth, companion of Osiris, the god of the dead, and inventor of language and writing as well as patron of books and libraries, to whom the so-called hermetic tradition, or Hermeticism, harks back.[14] In short, to claim that Musil, Celan, Bachmann and Kiefer are acquainted with each other in Egyptian siblinghood is tantamount to saying that they are relatives in the *hermetic* spirit. It is a crystal-clear Hermeticism, of course, along the lines of the 'daylight mysticism' in Musil to which Bachmann already referred in her radio essays dedicated to him and his *Man without Qualities* (as well as to his poem *Isis und Osiris*),[15] not an esoteric, darkly brooding Hermeticism of the kind that Musil severely criticized in Klages and Spengler, and Bachmann in Heidegger, and with which (notwithstanding a certain admitted affinity) Celan resolutely forbade himself to be unreflectedly associated by his own critics.[16] As far as Celan the Jew in particular is concerned, this Egypt which, according to a letter to Max Frisch,[17]

---

[13] Much of which is listed in footnote 8.

[14] See Boelderl, *Literarische Hermetik*.

[15] See Robert Musil, 'Isis und Osiris', *Prager Presse*, III, 116, 29 April 1923 (literary supplement 'Dichtung und Welt', no. 15, p. 1); *Die Neue Rundschau*, XXXIV, 5, 1923, p. 464; reprint in *Patmos. Zwölf Lyriker*, ed. by Ernst Schönwiese (Johannes-Presse, 1935), pp. 49–50; see also Musil, *Gesamtausgabe*, X: *In Zeitungen und Zeitschriften II (1922–1924)*, ed. by Walter Fanta (Jung und Jung, 2020), p. 282.

[16] See, for instance, Joanna Klink, 'You: An Introduction to Paul Celan', *The Iowa Review*, 30.1 (2000), pp. 1–18 (p. 2). Klink links this attribution to two aspects of Celan's work: his dialogue with the Kabbalah scholar Scholem and his engagement with the tradition of *poésie pure* in poets such as Éluard or Char, referring back to Mallarmé, and she also mentions his interest in alchemy.

[17] 'nun werde ich, obgleich ich mich keineswegs erinnere, jemals aus Ägypten ausgezogen zu sein, dieses Fest [sc. die jüdischen Ostern, Pessach] feiern, in England [...]' (IB/PC, p. 165)

he knew he had never left, also woefully integrates the Kabbalistic trait of his own poetic language. Taking this fact into account, one could rephrase Celan's rejection of the expression 'hermetic' with respect to his poetry somewhat more diligently and precisely thus: While the attribution, particularly if made by literary critics with a more or less reproachful undertone, was certainly terminologically incorrect or at least misleading, it was undoubtedly well founded. Celan's poems are indeed *hermetic*, in exactly the same sense as Egyptian hieroglyphs are undoubtedly hermetic in terms of their simultaneous legibility and illegibility (both before and after Champollion — decipherability is only marginally involved in this question). At the same time, like the hieroglyphs, they are by no means *esoteric*, insofar as they never set out to cryptologize themselves, count on their illegibility or even play with it (bet on it, as it were). Such obscuration nevertheless occurs regardless of the intention of the message, inevitably and necessarily (unlike in the case of esotericism, which, with the promise of the complete decipherability of its message, functions according to a kind of 'brachial hermeneutics', so to speak, whose forced 'success' depends on the restriction of the number of addressees to the initiated, i.e. those in the inner circle of the respective tradition). Against this background, the often invoked illegibility of Musil's *Man without Qualities* and the inaccessibility of Celan's poems are on the same level, in that they are the result and manifestation of a kindred poetological attitude to do with 'Egypt'.[18]

III

In the case of Ingeborg Bachmann, Celan's 'wie alles Verlorene nahe Schwester-gestalt' [sister figure, close like all that is lost],[19] if such a shortcut were permitted, the pre-lost Egypt begins and ends, as indicated, in Philae. In this landscape, the Egyptian desert, the only one 'for which eyes are made', the condition of seeing is complete darkness. In other words, its demise, impending since time immemorial and in perpetuity, in the waters of the rising and falling

[now, although I have no recollection of ever having left Egypt, I shall celebrate this feast [sc. Pessach/Passover, the Jewish Easter] in England [...]]. See also Giorgio Agamben, 'Ostern in Ägypten', in Giorgio Agamben *Die Erzählung und das Feuer* trans. by Andreas Hiepko (Fischer, 2017), pp. 73–77.

[18] It is worth mentioning that this is in keeping with the famous bon mot of the Kabbalah scholar Gershom Scholem with whom Celan was well familiar, having read his works and also met him personally, as Harold Bloom reports: 'When, in my puzzlement, I attempted to remind him [sc. Scholem] that Gnosticism itself seemed as much a misreading of Plato as of the Hebrew Bible, so that in some strange sense Gnosticism and Neoplatonism both derived from Plato, Scholem replied triumphantly: "Exactly so. And where did Plato get everything from? Egypt, who had it from us!"' See Harold Bloom, 'Scholem: Unhistorical or Jewish Gnosticism', in *Gershom Scholem*, ed. by Harold Bloom (Chelsea House, 1987), pp. 207–20 (p. 216). See also Harold Bloom, *Kafka — Freud — Scholem: 3 Essays*, trans. by Angelika Schweikhart (Stroemfeld/Roter Stern, 1990), p. 72.

[19] Celan, 'Chymisch', from *Die Niemandsrose* (1963) [*No One's Rose*, trans. by David Young, Marick Press, 2014], in *Die Gedichte*, p. 138.

Nile, a decline which even where it seems perfect and irrevocable, as in Philae
— whose place is only gradually taken by Wadi Halfa in the course of the
author's poetic work of integration and alienation of the 'Desert Book' and the
individual text stages of the *Book of Franza* — is not final, either because the
rise of the Nile meter naturally finds its limit, a turning point, and changes to a
fall (which guarantees the fertility of the land under the most adverse climatic
conditions and prompted Herodotus famously to state that Egypt is a gift of
the Nile), or because the rise of the Nile is brought about by human hands, in a
technical way. The flooding of the ancient cultural sites is effected on the one
hand completely and permanently, while on the other hand it is at the same
time and by the same technical means strangely being undone as in Philae and
previously in Abu Simbel.

Like these Egyptian loci in the geographical reality, through the literary
work on the *Book of Franza* as a book within a book, a planned book within the
books of the *Todesarten* project that are designed to be plural, art, too — art 'as
such', if you will — is not lost, but, in accordance with Anselm Kiefer's famous
dictum, it will 'survive its ruins',[20] quite literally: 'Zu der Zeit ging Wadi Halfa
unter' (TKA, II, p. 128) [At that time Wadi Halfa went under] was originally to
be the last sentence of the book.[21] Just like the scraps of quotations scrawled in
Kiefer's deliberately infantile handwriting on pyramidal manifestations of and
from desert sand in his treatments of Bachmann and Celan, notwithstanding
their demise, that is to say their factual decay through erosion and weathering
under the influence of nature as well as society, art remains readable through
the topoi it gives us to see, legible yet always also illegible, as a literary-aesthetic
cast of the Egyptian hieroglyph, as it were, which retains its hermetic secrecy
even after its successful hermeneutic decipherment with the help of the famous
Rosetta Stone in the 1820s by the French linguist Jean-François Champollion,
in a quite Hegelian, threefold sense.

The illegibility is, following Hegel's conception of *Aufhebung*,[22] sublated,
suspended because it has been deciphered; it is at the same time sublated, that is
preserved, because it has not disappeared materially through the decipherment
and remains enigmatic; and it is sublated, elevated, brought to a higher level,
like the Temple of Isis at Philae, which was saved from the rising waters of the
Nile by the construction of a dam and no longer stands where it originally
stood. That is, it has not sunk and yet has perished, while being accessible as
ever — in principle to anyone who knows how to read the signs, at the moment
they read them, namely, to enter the temple or open the book.

---

[20] See Anselm Kiefer, *Die Kunst geht knapp nicht unter: Anselm Kiefer im Gespräch mit Klaus Dermutz* (Suhrkamp, 2010), pp. 228–55, and Kiefer, *L'art survivra à ses ruines/Art Will Survive its Ruins: Anselm Kiefer au Collège de France* (Éditions du Regard, 2011).

[21] See the text-critical commentary in TKA, II, pp. 423–24.

[22] This is a key concept of Hegelian philosophy, present from the early *Phenomenology of Spirit* (1806) onward throughout the development of Hegel's thought; see, for instance, G. W. Hegel, *Phänomenologie des Geistes*, ed. by Hans-Friedrich Wessels and Heinrich Clairmont (Meiner, 2006), p. 80.

IV

Is it an exaggeration to assume that it was not least this experience of the 'Egyptian darkness' as a hermetic twilight that contributed to the restoration of confidence, even euphoria, which Bachmann reported to her travel companion in reality (as opposed to Franza's mood, and fate, in the literary world) in letters after their return from Egypt, and that moreover facilitated the transfer of this experience — which remained essentially the same until the end, regardless of the incompletion of the other novel drafts belonging to the *Todesarten* project with the exception of *Malina* — into a productive writing process? Such an observation does not diminish or detract from the drastic nature of the issues that are tackled in a literary way in this Egyptian-hermetic framework: the tragedy between the individual and collective past, historical and present existence as a woman and victim in a world of male perpetrators. If we were to devote ourselves here to Celan to the same extent as to Bachmann against the same Egyptian background, it would be possible to show in what other, yet readily comparable, way his themes are inscribed in it, or can, to say the very least, be situated on its grounds (as those of a Jew who, unlike Bachmann, has not returned from Egypt but on the contrary, as mentioned, never thought he had left Egypt in the first place). It would become obvious how those themes border on each other and gain their profile in terms of a genuine Hermeticism of poetic expression in each case, for example when they meet in the sand — which for *him*, Celan, trickles 'out of the urns',[23] for *her*, Bachmann, 'out of the hair' ('Das Spiel ist aus', W I, 82–83), in both cases completely unmetaphorically — and at the same time depart from one another on their idiomatic as well as isotopic paths to the *red*, blood-soaked *sand* transformed into mud here and into the *white* crystal of *snow*flakes there, reminiscent of the trickling down of previously ascended ashes (or to the 'Grab in den Lüften' [grave in the air] where one does not lie narrowly in Celan's 'Todesfuge', and to the near-death by suffocation during a playful imitation of being buried alive in moist mud, when this mud hardens more quickly than expected and threatens to make breathing impossible along with movement in Bachmann's *Book of Franza* — here, in Bachmann, that is, where everything *white* and a fortiori *the* whites are being extinguished in contrast to there). 'Unter hundert Brüdern dieser eine. Und er aß ihr Herz, und sie das seine' (W, III, p. 397) [Among a hundred brothers this one. And he ate her heart, and she ate his] — this 'cult phrase' of the Ranner siblings in the *Book of Franza*, taken from Musil's poem *Isis und Osiris* and transformed into the past tense, thus announces an *Egyptian siblinghood* that connects and sustains Bachmann with Musil on one side and, via the latter, with Celan on the other, in terms of their respective poetologies, far beyond this one unfinished book. To mention just one other example, there is also the

[23] This is the title of Celan's first published collection of poems, *Sand aus den Urnen* (Sexl, 1948), which notoriously contained so many misprints and errors that the author chose to withdraw it from circulation.

Kakanian side of Bachmann's affinity with Musil and Celan, the former her immediate fellow countryman, born in Klagenfurt and Carinthia like herself, the latter originally from the formerly Habsburgian Bukovina, both mediated via the semi-fictional topos 'Galicia', not to mention the Galician oil fields with which Ulrich's adversary and alter ego Arnheim is concerned in the *Man without Qualities*, far ahead of his other professed interests in the salon of the Collateral Campaign. And no matter how one might be inclined to assess Anselm Kiefer's preoccupation with the works of Bachmann and Celan in terms of art history or otherwise, his identification and impressive depiction of their subliminal *intertextuality*, or *intercontext* rather, called 'Egypt', constitutes one of his lasting achievements.

The notion that we form of the literary texts in view of Kiefer's paintings gains an additional focus which is not only compatible with our reading of the same, but indeed conducive and enriching, rather than — as Hartmut Böhme believes — directing it in a manner that is at least inappropriate, if not downright inadmissible, or overforming them, as it were, with powerful images, or even covering them up, eclipsing them with a 'metaphysics of painting'.[24] As far as Bachmann in particular is concerned, they rather *reveal* a dimension of her texts that I hope to have brought to the fore here, at least in outline, by introducing and highlighting the keywords 'Egyptian' or 'hermetic' (in a non-pejorative sense), and which also finds its underpinning, beyond any *philologically* sound 'proof', in further evidence — *philaelogical* evidence at that.

> [W]elche Vorstellung von Ägypten hat sich jeder von uns vor Antritt dieser Reise gemacht? [...] Sie nennt natürlich 'Isis und Osiris', Robert Musils einziges Gedicht, ihr liebstes Gedicht, aus dem sie immer wieder gerne zitiert — aber das gilt nicht, denn es sollen ja graphische und nicht Wortbilder sein. [...] die Ägyptologische Abteilung dort [sc. im Kunsthistorischen Museum in Wien] habe sie nicht besonders beeindruckt; dafür aber ein ganz unspektakuläres Fresko im Naturhistorischen Museum, hoch oben an der Wand, das 'Idealbild Pylae', eine romantische Darstellung der alljährlich mit der Flut im Wasser verschwindenden Nilinsel [...].[25]

> [What idea of Egypt did each of us have before embarking on this journey? Of course she mentions 'Isis and Osiris', Robert Musil's only poem, her favourite poem, from which she likes to quote again and again — but that does not apply, for the images are supposed to be graphic, not words. The Egyptology Department there [sc. in the Museum of Fine Arts in Vienna] did not particularly impress her; but a quite unspectacular fresco in the Museum of Natural History did, high up on the wall, the 'Ideal Image of Pylae', a romantic depiction of the island in the Nile that disappears in the water every year with the high tide.]

[24] Hartmut Böhme, '"Mit einem Steingefühl, alterslos": Anselm Kiefers Zyklus für Ingeborg Bachmann', *Neue Zürcher Zeitung*, 6 June 1998, p. 8 <https://www.hartmutboehme.de/media/steingefuehl.pdf> [accessed 15 May 2023].

[25] Adolf Opel, *'Wo mir das Lachen zurückgekommen ist ...' Auf Reisen mit Ingeborg Bachmann* (Langen Müller/Herbig, 2001), pp. 139–41.

[...] die Inbetriebnahme des Nil-Staudammes steht bevor und der Ort Wadi Halfa wird für immer in den Fluten des Nils versinken. Das Schiff soll auch in Abu Simbel anhalten — es ist die letzte Gelegenheit, den berühmten Tempel an der Stelle zu sehen, wo er gebaut worden ist: auch die wird überflutet, und es stehen auch schon Maschinen bereit, die Abu Simbel in Stücke sägen werden, um es dann an einem anderen Standort wieder zusammenzusetzen. *[Sc. wie Isis ihren von ihrer beider Bruder Seth getöteten Mann Osiris; der Mord erfolgt auf hinterhältige Weise dadurch, dass Seth bei einem Fest für Osiris demjenigen eine wertvolle Lade als Geschenk verspricht, der in sie hineinpasst; als Osiris sich in die passgenau für ihn angefertigte Lade legt, klappen Seths 72 Schergen die Lade zu, verschließen den Spalt zwischen Deckel und Wanne mit heißem Blei, Osiris erstickt und wird mit der Lade in den Nil geworfen.]* [...] Obwohl wir eben erst an diesem Ort angekommen sind [sc. in Assuan], der Pforte zum eigentlichen Afrika, will sie gleich zum nächsten, nilaufwärts, weiter in den Süden, als locke dort eine Steigerung der euphorischen Hochstimmung von Assuan. Sie will auch kaum etwas besichtigen in Assuan [...] Der Tempel auf der Insel Philae fällt ohnehin aus, er fällt buchstäblich ins Wasser, denn der Wasserspiegel ist zwischen Jänner und Juli so hoch, dass von der Nil-Insel nichts zu sehen ist; das Fresko im Wiener Museum wird ein 'Idealbild' bleiben, [...] vermutlich für alle Zeiten [...].[26]

[The commissioning of the Nile dam is imminent and the site of Wadi Halfa will sink forever in the floods of the Nile. The ship is also to stop off at Abu Simbel — it is the last chance to see the famous temple at the site where it was built: that, too, will be flooded, and machines are already in place that will saw Abu Simbel to pieces, to be reassembled at another site. *[Sc. much like Isis did with her husband Osiris, after he was killed by their common brother Seth; the murder is carried out in a devious way by Seth promising a valuable ark as a gift to whoever fits into it on the occasion of a feast for Osiris; when Osiris lies down in the ark made to fit him exactly, Seth's seventy-two henchmen snap the ark shut, close the gap between the lid and the tub with hot lead, Osiris suffocates and is thrown into the Nile with the ark].* Although we have only just arrived at this place [sc. in Aswan], the gateway to Africa proper, she wants to go straight on to the next, up the Nile, further south, as if an intensification of the euphoric high spirits of Aswan were enticing there. She also hardly wants to visit anything in Aswan. The temple on the island of Philae is out of the question anyway; it falls through, literally into the water, for the water level between January and July is so high that nothing can be seen of the Nile island; the fresco in the Viennese museum remains an 'ideal image', presumably for all time.]

In the version of the text that, according to the *Kritische Ausgabe*, was read by Bachmann on 9 January 1966 in Zurich, there is still explicit mention of Philae, while in the edited main version it will intermittently have textually sunk in favour of that comparatively unspectacular other place of demise, Wadi Halfa, which has taken over its literary-aesthetic function; its name comes up in the immediate aftermath of the 'Orgia', the orgy of four, which is more implied

---

[26] Ibid., pp. 184–85.

than described:

> Nie mehr die Griechen, nie mehr der neutrale Plural, nichts mehr mit den Griechen, sie ausgestrichen, in Ägypten verfinstert in einer Nacht am Nil, weitergegangen, ausgelöscht, was weiß war, ausgetreten aus dem Plunder Zärtlichkeit, Beteuerung, dem ideologischen Produkt Liebe, der weißen Hysterie aus Inferiorität. [...] Franza kleinlaut: und du, und du? Unter hundert Brüdern. [...] Es ist licht im Zimmer. Der Nil stieg an, sie [sc. mit Achmed und Sallah] gingen und gingen, Franza in ihrer Mitte, ein Wesen, das aufs äußerste zu respektieren war [...]. [...] Achmed und Sallah, unberührt von Kitcheners Tod, Grab, Elephantine und Philae, hofierten Franza schweigend bis zum Nilometer, sie erklärten ihr in schlechtem Englisch, was es mit dem Urmeter auf sich habe. [...] Franza sagte, wir fahren zurück, und stieg zum Boot hinunter. Tote, die erst so kurz begraben sind, interessieren mich nicht. Und Inseln, die unter Wasser sind, sie deutete dahin, [...] wo Philae noch für ein paar Monate lang überschwemmt liegen würde, eh es wieder auftauchen konnte mit dem Isistempel. Und Inseln unter Wasser, das mag hingehen [...] (TKA, II, pp. 32–33)

> [No more the Greeks, no more the neutral plural, nothing more with the Greeks, these wiped out, eclipsed in Egypt in a night on the Nile, moved on, erased what was white, exited from the deadwood of tenderness, assurance, the ideological product love, the white hysteria out of inferiority. Franza meekly: and you, and you? Among a hundred brothers. It is light in the room. The Nile rose, they [sc. with Ahmed and Sallah] walked and walked, Franza in their midst, a being to be respected to the utmost. Ahmed and Sallah, untouched by Kitchener's death, grave, Elephantine and Philae, courted Franza in silence until they reached the Nilometer; they explained to her in bad English what the prototype metre was all about. Franza said, we are going back, and descended to the boat. Dead people only buried very recently do not interest me. And islands under water, she pointed where Philae would lie flooded for a few more months before it could resurface with the temple of Isis. And islands under water, that might do.]

V

Even if and when culture sinks — and its exponents with it, the rulers as well as the ruled, the pharaohs as well as their scribes — art remains afloat or, more precisely, the book does, in Musil, Celan and Bachmann, as well as, in its own way, in Anselm Kiefer. And does the indeterminate-changing final sound -ae of Phil*ae* not contain the aesthetic siblinghood of this literary *orgia* of four authors *In Egypt* across all borders, including not least those between the sexes, whose real or possible rhythm, from the back and forth of sexual encounter via the mirroring or doubling to the exchange not only of perspectives but of bodies, forms a continuous motif in all of them, and contains it in a downright *literal* manner? It is as if the entire name of the site where the temple of Isis once stood, then sank and now stands again, or stands still, literally expresses a certain inclination, *philia*, a striving, *philein*, towards the respective Other, whose mythical allegory is represented by the hermaphrodite or, in the hermetic context, the androgyne. This is the Egyptian siblinghood which resonates in the names Anders (as Ulrich was initially called in Musil's novel) and A*gathe* — Antschel/Celan — Ranner — Anselm.[27]

In the words of the French Egyptian Jewish poet Edmond Jabès:

> We have left our opposite shores and landed in your book.
> — You have not left the book.
> You could not have done it.

> But sometimes the spaces between the lines are so wide that it seems to you that you are treading on new ground, so wide are the margins.

> The book binds us.[28]

> Have you seen how a word is born and dies?
> Have you seen how two names are born and die?
> The word is a kingdom.

> Each letter has its own status, life, and rank. The first [sc. doubled as in B*achmann* — *Franza*] entertains the greatest power; the power of enchantment and obsession.

> United kingdoms, innocent universes that the alphabet conquered and then destroyed at the hands of man.
> You have lost your kingdom.
> I have lost my kingdom, as my scattered brothers have lost almost everywhere in a world that has fed on their scattering.
> Have you seen how a kingdom comes into being and passes away?
> Have you seen how a book is created and passes away?[29]

---

[27] It is also worth noting in this context that Musil chose *Anselm* as the name for the male protagonist of his play *Die Schwärmer* (*The Enthusiasts*, 1921). In the series of photos *Occupations* — in which Kiefer documented how he executed the so-called 'Hitler salute' at historically significant places in Germany, sometimes in women's clothing — the artist was responding, among other things, to precisely this important element of androgyny that can be observed from ancient Egyptian mythology to the realm of modern literature. For more on the issue of sexual relation in general and sex change in particular, as well as on the problematic question of dealing with works of art that polemically reference Hitler(ism), especially from an editorial perspective in the context of MUSIL ONLINE and the inter-discursive commentary developed as an integral feature thereof, see Artur R. Boelderl, *Musil, diskursweise: Wirklich mögliche Kontexte zum 'Mann ohne Eigenschaften'* (Brill/Fink, 2024), chapters 8 and 13 respectively.

[28] Edmond Jabès, *Das Buch der Fragen*, trans. by Henriette Beese (Suhrkamp, 1989), p. 70: '[...] wir haben unsere entgegengesetzten Ufer verlassen und sind in deinem Buch gelandet. | — Ihr habt das Buch nicht verlassen. | Ihr hättet es nicht gekonnt. | Aber manchmal sind die Zwischenräume zwischen den Zeilen so breit, daß euch scheint, ihr tretet auf neuen Boden, so breit sind die Ränder. | Uns bindet das Buch.'

[29] Ibid., p. 177: 'Hast du gesehen, wie ein Wort geboren wird und stirbt? | Hast du gesehen, wie zwei Namen geboren werden und sterben? | [...] / Das Wort ist ein Königreich. | Jedem

Read with respect to the hermetic filiation of Egyptian origin that binds the works of Musil, Celan, Bachmann and Kiefer in and to 'the' book, as I have tried to develop it here, 'going back to Egypt (and returning to Kakania)', as in Musil's case, 'remaining in Egypt, unable to leave', as in Celan's case, and 'going to Egypt for good', as in Bachmann's *Franza*, mean only slightly, yet decisively different, if nonetheless intimately related things whose recognition allows the reader to perceive a 'deeper' level of their poetological siblinghood that both transcends and enhances their philological correspondences.

Buchstaben eignet sein Stand, sein Leben und sein Rang. Der erste [sc. gedoppelt wie in Bachmann — *Franza*] genießt die größte Macht; die Macht der Bezauberung und der Besessenheit. [...] | Vereinte Königreiche, unschuldige Universen, die das Alphabet eroberte und dann durch die Hände der Menschen zerstörte. | Ihr habt euer Königreich verloren. | Ich habe mein Königreich verloren, wie meine zerstreuten Brüder fast überall in einer Welt, die sich an ihrer Zerstreuung genährt hat, verloren haben. | Hast du gesehen, wie ein Königreich entsteht und vergeht? | Hast du gesehen, wie ein Buch entsteht und vergeht?'

Intermedial Relations and Plant Poetics in Ingeborg Bachmann, Cy Twombly and Anselm Kiefer

LINA UŽUKAUSKAITĖ

Paris Lodron Universität Salzburg

In two paintings from the six-part cycle *Untitled (Roses)*,[1] which the American artist Cy Twombly (1928–2011) created in Gaeta in 2008 specifically for the Brandhorst Museum in Munich, the following quotations from Ingeborg Bachmann's poems 'Im Gewitter der Rosen' (1953) [In the Storm of Roses] and 'Schatten Rosen Schatten' (1956) [Shadows Roses Shadows] are woven into the visual work of art:

> Wohin wir uns wenden im Gewitter der Rosen,
> ist die Nacht von Dornen erhellt, und der Donner
> des Laubs, das so leise war in den Büschen,
> folgt uns jetzt auf dem Fuß. (W, I, p. 56)

> [Wherever we turn in the storm of roses,
> the night is lit up by thorns, and the thunder
> of leaves, once so quiet within the bushes,
> rumbling at our heels][2]

> Unter einem fremden Himmel
> Schatten Rosen
> Schatten
> auf einer fremden Erde
> zwischen Rosen und Schatten
> in einem fremden Wasser
> mein Schatten (AGB, p. 76)

> [Under an alien sky
> shadows roses
> shadow
> on an alien earth
> between roses and shadows
> in alien waters
> my shadow][3]

---

[1] See *Cy Twombly: Inscriptions I–VI*, 6 vols, ed. by Thierry Greub, (Fink, 2022), VI, pp. 380–95, 384–85, 392–93. The other four paintings of the cycle quote works by Rainer Maria Rilke, Patricia Waters, Emily Dickinson and T. S. Eliot, see ibid., pp. 386–91, 394–95.

[2] Ingeborg Bachmann, *Darkness Spoken: The Collected Poems*, trans. by Peter Filkins (Zephyr, 2006), p. 57. See Greub, *Cy Twombly: Inscriptions*, VI, pp. 385, 393.

[3] Bachmann, *Darkness Spoken*, p. 29.

Austrian Studies 32 (2024), doi:10.1353/aus.00007, pp. 91–106
© Modern Humanities Research Association 2024

The German-Austrian artist Anselm Kiefer (born 1945) also uses Bachmann's 'Im Gewitter der Rosen' as a literary source in a cycle of canvases, collages, watercolours and sculptures created in 2014; four paintings in this cycle feature explicit references to the poem.[4] Kiefer's eponymous exhibition *Im Gewitter der Rosen* ran at the Thaddaeus Ropac Gallery in Salzburg from March to May 2015.

In what follows, I present a detailed analysis based on the close reading and close viewing of the paintings mentioned above, the literary quotations they incorporate, and the forms of intermediality and transmediality which they instantiate, while also briefly reflecting on their cultural and historical context (*wide reading*). I will show how careful attention to the intermedial image–text relations and the paintings' compositional techniques facilitates understanding of their aesthetic complexity and their creative response to Bachmann's poetry.[5] Finally, I will discuss this complex of image-texts from the perspective of plant philosophy and cultural plant studies, showing how current theoretical and philosophical concerns with the non-human and with vegetal life can offer new frames for reading these works.

The first part of the article explores different modes of referentiality between text and image as these play out in intermedial interactions. Twombly's and Kiefer's paintings are read as instances of productive reception in a specific historical and art-historical context. Moreover, their use of quotations or pre-texts in their artistic work can be understood as cultural acts of memory, within the framework of Renate Lachmann's post-structuralist theory of intertextuality.[6] Close analysis of the works of art renders visible the transgression of medial boundaries as well as the intermedial expansion of artistic language and disciplines. In a second step, my intermedial analysis proceeds to consider transmedial dimensions in dialogue with plant poetics. In this context, transmediality is understood as organic creativity and cross-fertilization of (interdisciplinary) 'texts':[7] the 'source medium' in this case is

---

[4] Anselm Kiefer and Orhan Pamuk, *Im Gewitter der Rosen*, ed. by Arne Ehmann, trans. by Gerhard Meier and Ekin Oklap (Galerie Thaddaeus Ropac, 2015), pp. 10–11, 16–17, 38–41, 46–47. In this cycle, Kiefer also refers to the literary texts of Walther von der Vogelweide and Arthur Rimbaud.

[5] See Thierry Greub, '"... to revalorize Poetry now ...": Zu Twomblys literarischen Einschreibungen', in *Cy Twombly, Bild, Text, Paratext*, ed. by Thierry Greub (Morphomata, 2014), pp. 359–80; Thierry Greub, 'Cy Twomblys "Inverted Archeology"', in *Cy Twombly: Die Werkübersicht*, ed. by Nicola Del Roscio (Schirmer/Mosel, 2014), pp. 227–36, also Greub, *Cy Twombly: Inscriptions*, I, pp. 19, 51, 68, 70–71, 76, 79, 136–37 and figures on pp. 52 and 72, on the relations between text and image and references to Bachmann and Twombly's cycle *Untitled (Roses)*.

[6] Renate Lachmann, *Gedächtnis und Literatur: Intertextualität in der russischen Moderne* (Suhrkamp, 1990); see also Astrid Erll and Ansgar Nünning, 'Literaturwissenschaftliche Konzepte von Gedächtnis: Ein einführender Überblick', in *Gedächtniskonzepte der Literaturwissenschaft: Theoretische Grundlegung und Anwendungsperspektiven*, ed. by Astrid Erll and Ansgar Nünning (De Gruyter, 2005), pp. 1–9 (p. 2).

[7] See Irina O. Rajewsky, *Intermedialität* (Francke, 2002), p. 19; see also footnote 55.

an organic phenomenon of plant life, the rose, whose contexts of meaning are expanded as it is taken up through the disciplines of visual and verbal art and their interactions. The cultural imaginary of plant life, and a heightened awareness of the ecological contexts encoded and reflected in this imaginary, offer new perspectives on Twombly's and Kiefer's creative engagement with the poems of Ingeborg Bachmann.

I

Irina Rajewsky's distinction between 'intermediale Referenz' [intermedial reference] and 'Medienkombination' [medial combination] sheds light on the image–text relations in the works of Twombly and Kiefer under discussion.[8] Intermedial reference involves thematizing, simulating or reproducing within the media-specific means of one's own artistic discipline elements and/or structures of another medium that is conventionally perceived as distinct.[9] In order to determine the specifics of the intermedial reference in the following analyses, I focus first on how the artists quote or reproduce the poetic text, and whether they make changes to the quotation. I attend to the thematic references the artist adopts from the text, asking whether these references are implicit or explicit, whether the artist imitates structural elements of the text in the image, and how the language or (painted) writing within the painting differs from its printed, text-only form. An artist can for example render strange the quotation or the writing through painted handwriting, which can be difficult to read.[10]

Nevertheless, in Twombly's and Kiefer's paintings, two media that are conventionally considered as distinct from one another — text and image — come together to form a medial combination or *Medienkombination*.[11] While continuing to reflect on the specificity of each medium, my investigation allows for the possibility that something 'third' or hybrid might emerge from the text–image combination. I will therefore analyse, not only the differences but also the equivalences between text and image, the possible transgression of their usual boundary, their points of overlap and their mutual transformation.

Contemporary theories of intermediality are indebted, of course, to earlier discourses. Gabrielle Rippl argues for the continued relevance of the Horatian adage *ut pictura poesis*, as well as of Gotthold Ephraim Lessing's terms 'Sukzessivität/Nacheinander' [successiveness] and 'Simultaneität/Nebeneinander' [simultaneity]. The Horatian *ut pictura poesis* suggests a structural text–

[8] Ibid.

[9] Ibid., p. 17.

[10] For further discussion of the represented and the representing medium in the sense of intermediality, see Jens Schröter, 'Intermedialität: Facetten und Probleme eines aktuellen medienwissenschaftlichen Begriffs', *montage/av: Zeitschrift für Theorie und Geschichte audiovisueller Kommunikation*, 7.2 (1998), pp. 129–54 (p. 144).

[11] '[Z]wei konventionell als distinkt wahrgenommene Medien', Rajewsky, *Intermedialität*, p. 13.

image analogy,[12] while Lessing emphasizes differences and rivalry between the respective media in his 1766 treatise *Laokoon: oder Über die Grenzen der Malerei und Poesie [Laocoon: or On the Limits of Painting and Poetry]*. Successiveness means that a work of art articulates itself in time (like poetry or narrative), while simultaneity means that the painting can be grasped at a glance, all at once.[13] For this discussion of Twombly's and Kiefer's Bachmann works, the term 'literariness' will be extended to encompass a quality of the image-text,[14] foregrounding the hybridity of these works and their creative encroachment onto the terrain of literature.[15] The intermedial dialogues between Twombly and Bachmann, and Kiefer and Bachmann, invoke and transform established literary, artistic and aesthetic traditions, including traditions of thinking about the relationships between text and image. Read together, the Twombly–Bachmann and Kiefer–Bachmann image-texts can be said to exemplify the search for a new critical poetics and to demonstrate heightened awareness of the sociocultural and sociopolitical problematics of language and aesthetics in the postwar period.

II

Twombly takes the Bachmann poem 'Shadows Roses Shadows' in the English translation by Peter Filkins (2006) and reproduces it in his painting in a modified form.[16] In terms of Rajewsky's 'intermedial reference', the artist proceeds by modification, omitting the last two lines 'in alien waters | my shadow'.[17] This omission changes the poem's meaning by removing the direct reference to the text subject. The new context of meaning is also formally implemented in the painting, which features several roses, one of which appears to be cut off at the top.[18]

---

[12] See Gabriele Rippl, 'Intermedialität: Text/Bild-Verhältnisse', in *Handbuch Literatur & Visuelle Kultur*, ed. by Claudia Benthien and Brigitte Weingart (De Gruyter, 2014), pp. 139–58 (p. 140).

[13] Ibid., p. 141.

[14] See Jonathan Culler, 'The Literary in Theory', in *What's Left of Theory: New Works on the Politics of Literary Theory*, ed. by Judith Butler, John Guillory and Kendall Thomas (Routledge, 2000), pp. 273–93.

[15] Rainer Leschke uses the terms 'primary' and 'secondary' intermediality, whereby the first term refers to the differences between the media, and the second highlights the indifferences and interferences, namely a place between the media. Rainer Leschke, *Einführung in die Medientheorie* (Fink 2003), pp. 35, 309.

[16] Bachmann, *Darkness Spoken*. Twombly possessed a copy of Bachmann's poems; it remains in his library in Gaeta, which I visited in June 2019. See also Greub, *Cy Twombly: Inscriptions*, I, p. 263.

[17] Greub, *Cy Twombly: Inscriptions*, I, p. 52.

[18] For a more detailed discussion of further aspects of Twombly's creative responses to Bachmann, see Lina Užukauskaité, 'Ingeborg Bachmann und die Kunst: Intermediale Aktionsformen in den Italien-Kunstwerken von Cy Twombly, Elisa Montessori und Marina

Twombly's painterly poetics clearly draw on thematic as well as formal aspects of Bachmann's text: the painting refers to the elements 'roses' and 'shadows', and takes up the principle of repetition and rhythmic structure, along with the resulting structural ambivalence. Ambivalence can be observed in relation to what happens to the text when it is incorporated into the image, and how it is changed by its new medial context, generating uncertainty in the viewer. When one first looks at the large format rose painting from a distance, one is unlikely to realize immediately that there is a text at the top, and less likely still to recognize this as a poem by Ingeborg Bachmann. Rather, the text initially appears to be a blurred line. Visitors to the Brandhorst Museum can find explanatory sheets in the exhibition room providing detailed information on the poems quoted. Only with this help do most viewers become aware of the quotation and are motivated to delve deeper into the text in the picture. As an intermedial reference, the quotation determines the reception process in terms of distance and proximity, setting its viewers in motion and 'inviting' them to come closer to the text-painting. They then realize that the quotation is integral to Twombly's picture, that is, it constitutes a medial combination in Rajewsky's sense. However, the text retains its medial limitations. Within the image, the text does not act according to the laws of simultaneity (*Nebeneinander*); it wants and needs to be read in the mode of Lessing's *Nacheinander*.

The inclusion of the poem in the painting shows the engagement with writing that is a crucial aspect of Twombly's oeuvre as a whole. Twombly applies the poem in red paint to the canvas with a brush, in several layers: after writing, the artist wipes off one layer and applies another. This palimpsestic writing-painting makes the writing or the written image difficult to read, slowing down the reception process. It means that the intermedial reference is rendered strange by the artist. Roland Barthes describes this approach in 1976 as a 'delicate salissure' [a delicate smear],[19] as a result of which many layers are present simultaneously, 'donnent à la toile la profondeur d'un ciel' [giving the canvas the depth of a sky].[20] The quotation written-painted by Twombly is '[u]nnachahmlich' [inimitable],[21] authentic, because it bears his handwriting and his authentic painting gesture.[22] Like a manuscript, Twombly's work 'reconciles poetry and painting in a rare dialogue',[23] allowing viewers to follow the artist's

---

Bindella', *Römische Historische Mitteilungen*, 65 (2023), pp. 605–36 (pp. 616–23).

[19] Roland Barthes, 'Non multa sed multum', in *Catalogue raisonné des oeuvres sur papier de Cy Twombly VI (1973–1976)*, ed. by Yvon Lambert (Multhipla Edizioni, 1979), pp. 5–13 (p. 9).

[20] Roland Barthes, 'Sagesse de l'art', in *Cy Twombly: Paintings and Drawings: 1954–1977* (Whitney Museum of American Art, 1979), pp. 9–22 (p. 10).

[21] Heiner Bastian, 'Semina Motuum', in *Cy Twombly: Letter of Resignation*, ed. by Heiner Bastian (Schirmer/Mosel, 1991), first page, unnumbered pages.

[22] See Christoph Zeller, *Ästhetik des Authentischen: Literatur und Kunst um 1970* (De Gruyter, 2010). Zeller writes for example about 'Authentizität als Tat' [authenticity as action].

[23] Bastian, 'Semina Motuum', p. i.

production process and thus to witness the materiality of his writing-painting technique.[24]

This text–image combination in Twombly's painting extends the possibilities of media by combining them. Through language and image, a poetics of transitions and border crossings is developed, in which a modified poem quotation is combined with modified or abstracted rose images. In his work, Twombly sought multi-perspectival connections between past and present,[25] between inside and outside, between text and image as well as '[a] connection between the physical action and the use of language'.[26] In the abstract rose petals which Twombly creates from spiral lines, as well as in the painted text, one can follow the artist's physical gestures during the production process.

The transformation of the rose petals can be followed from left to right based on a reading direction determined by the colour change. Reading in this direction, the darkening colour can be interpreted as the withering of the flowers. The formal expression of roses also becomes more concrete along this reading trajectory. The criterion of time therefore plays an important role in the narrativity or *Nacheinander* of the painting: the painting takes on the quality of a text, while at the same time continuing to work simultaneously as spatial art (*Nebeneinander*). Twombly's implementation of the Horatian *ut pictura poesis* suggests an analogy between text and image through their combination. This is particularly evident in the predominant horizontality of the verses and the painted roses.

The rose motif itself offers several possible interpretations: riddle, symbol of love and growth, wound, or symbol of ephemerality. At the same time, it opens a contradiction between beauty and pain, as the rivulets of colour evoke dripping blood. According to Luigi Reitani, Bachmann's poem is in intertextual conversation with the poetry of Paul Celan, 'die ähnliche Chiffren enthält' [which contains similar ciphers],[27] for example in 'Schlaf und Speise' [Sleep and Food] and in the verses quoted below from the poem 'Stille!' [Silence!]:

> Stille! Ich treibe den Dorn in Dein Herz,
> denn die Rose, die Rose
> steht mit den Schatten im Spiegel, sie blutet![28]

> [Silence! I drive the thorn into your heart,

---

[24] See *Schreiben als Kulturtechnik: Grundlagentexte*, ed. by Sandro Zanetti (Suhrkamp, 2012), p. 11.

[25] Eleonora Di Erasmo, personal communication, 28 November 2023, Cy Twombly Foundation.

[26] Nicolas Serota, 'History Behind the Thought: An Interview with Cy Twombly', *Cy Twombly: Cycles and Seasons*, ed. by Nicholas Serota (D.A.P., 2008), pp. 43–53 (p. 48).

[27] Luigi Reitani, 'Zur Edition: Aspekte der Überlieferung, Entstehung, Textgenese und Arbeitsweise', in Ingeborg Bachmann, *Anrufung des Großen Bären*, Salzburger Bachmann Edition, ed. by Luigi Reitani, preface by Hans Höller (Suhrkamp, 2022), pp. 255–56.

[28] Paul Celan, *Die Gedichte: Kommentierte Gesamtausgabe in einem Band*, ed. by Barbara Wiedemann (Suhrkamp, 2003), p. 52.

> because the rose, the rose
> stands with the shadows in the mirror, it bleeds!]

The rose as a bleeding wound refers to the violence of recent European history: as is well known, the Second World War, the Nazi regime and the Shoah are confronted at a fundamental level in the work of both Ingeborg Bachmann and Paul Celan. I would argue that Cy Twombly also takes up themes of war and historical violence with the 'bleeding' roses.[29] A fuller exploration of the rose motif and its spectrum of meaning requires engagement with plant poetics and transmedial analysis, to which I will return below.

The lyrical text in the work of art draws our attention to Twombly's principle of poetic painting. Mary Jacobus describes Twombly's 'Mal-Poesie' [paint-poetry][30] — for him the only form of truth[31] — as 'poetry in paint',[32] an interface at which Twombly's reflection on both media is enabled through their merging into one another, their working together and simultaneously. Language, writing and writing processes are all inextricably part of Twombly's aesthetic, which is why Barthes characterizes his paintings and drawings as works of literature or 'writing'.[33] Twombly's — and Kiefer's — paintings are perceivable, according to Andreas Hapkemeyer, 'aus der Perspektive eines erweiterten Literaturbegriffs [from the perspective of an expanded concept of literature].[34] As Hapkemeyer notes, as the works of these artists expand into the realm of language, they gain an affinity with the lyrical, which concerns not only their use of language, but also and above all their way of working.

Because Twombly's paintings are created as hybrid, 'in-between' phenomena, they have been interpreted both as art and as literature, insofar as they participate in both systems at the same time.[35] The location of Twombly's work at this medial intersection prompts a re-examination of the systems of art and literature. This partial participation also marks an effective departure from both of these fields, insofar as Twombly's works belong neither to art nor to literature, but are characterized by a hybrid or palimpsestic quality. Twombly's medial combinations effect genre changes and give rise to new iterations

---

[29] Simon Schama writes about the 'tödliche Spiele' [deadly games] of war and refers to Twombly's works with warships. See Simon Schama, 'Cy Twombly', in *Cy Twombly: Die Werkübersicht*, ed. by Nicola Del Roscio (Schirmer/Mosel, 2014), pp. 11–14 (p. 14).

[30] See Andreas Hapkemeyer, *... und das soll Dichtung sein: Untersuchungen zur 'neuen Sprache' in Lyrik und Kunst seit den 1950er Jahren* (Königshausen & Neumann 2012), p. 114.

[31] Heiner Bastian, 'Einführung: Die Macht der Bilder und der Poesie', in *Cy Twombly: Catalogue Raisonné of the Paintings*, v (1996–2007), ed. by Heiner Bastian (Schirmer/Mosel 2009), pp. 11–21 (p. 12).

[32] Mary Jacobus, *Reading Cy Twombly: Poetry in Paint* (Princeton University Press, 2016), p. 283. According to Jacobus, this is a modified quotation from Marion Junkin — 'I feel that he will develop into a poet in paint' — written 10 May 1950 in an initial recommendation letter to the Virginia Museum of Fine Arts (VMFA).

[33] Roland Barthes, *Cy Twombly* (Merve, 1983), p. 8.

[34] Hapkemeyer, *... und das soll Dichtung sein*, book jacket text.

[35] Ibid., pp. 16–17.

of their pre-texts, dispensing with the need for a clear distinction between original and copy,[36] and demonstrating the cross-fertilization potential of the disciplines of literature and painting. Intermedial expansion of the artistic language entails expansion of the concept of the text. Through multi-layering and entanglement of citations, different modes of referentiality between text and image, and a cross-over between intermediality and memory,[37] Twombly's and Kiefer's works challenge conventional or commonplace understandings of visual art and literary texts.

Almost all of the aspects discussed above also apply to Twombly's expressive blue and (dark) purple rose painting 'Im Gewitter der Rosen' [In the Storm of Roses]. Here, too, the artist omits a line of verse (of leaves, once so quiet within the bushes), thereby changing the intermedial reference and expanding the context of its meaning. The inner connections between the poem and the painting become visible, the painterly constellations of meaning that the text produces, for example, with regard to the 'erhellt[e] Nacht' [brightened night], the trembling 'Gewitter' [storm], the dynamics of the '[W]end[ung]' [turn] and the persecution by 'Donner' [thunder].

In rendering the verbal medium in the visual, Twombly's artistic process requires a particular painterly technique or set of techniques. The poem, applied with a narrower brush, is written in blue on two central panels above the two blue roses. The writing in this work is easily legible and has only one layer of colour. The two middle roses — as the lyrical subjects ('wir' [we]) — 'wenden' [turn] towards each other and correspond via the colour in their centre, so that we can speak of a dialogic narrative principle in Twombly's painting-poetry.

The purple rose on the left side of the painting is clearly different from the three blue roses, while the blue rose on the right side stands out from the two blue roses in the middle of the painting, due to the colour in its heart and the lighter blue surrounding it. The heart of the purple rose is also highlighted with coloured crayon and curling lines. The curling lines, which can also be seen on the other roses, evoke the dynamism and trembling of the storm and thunder. This gives the painting a synaesthetic, visual-acoustic effect, which opens the dimension of *Nebeneinander* or simultaneity in Lessing's sense. One can say that the blue, which is usually a passive colour,[38] is thereby activated.

---

[36] See Uwe Wirth, 'Original und Kopie im Spannungsfeld von Iteration und Aufpfropfung', *Originalkopie: Praktiken des Sekundären*, ed. by Gisela Fehrmann, Erika Linz, Eckhard Schumacher and Brigitte Weingart (DuMont, 2004), p. 22.

[37] As Kirsten Dickhaut notes, the relationships between memory and intermediality have remained under-theorized in scholarship on the latter. See Kirsten Dickhaut, 'Intermedialität und Gedächtnis', in *Gedächtniskonzepte der Literaturwissenschaft*, ed. by Erll and Nünning, pp. 203–26 (p. 207).

[38] Johannes Pawlik, *Theorie der Farbe: Eine Einführung in begriffliche Gebiete der ästhetischen Farbenlehre*, 6th edn (DuMont 1979), pp. 71–72.

III

Four paintings by Kiefer have titles that quote from Bachmann's 'Im Gewitter der Rosen'. In all four paintings, the German-language verses are painted in white against the dark background, as an intermedial reference. The artist's handwriting is easy to read, associatively reminiscent of chalk writing on a school blackboard.

In the first painting *wohin wir uns wenden im Gewitter der Rosen: für Ingeborg Bachmann* [where we turn in the storm of roses: for Ingeborg Bachmann],[39] the order of the verses, the punctuation and the last two verses are modified: '[da]s so leise' [[that] is so quiet] and 'folgt uns jetzt auf dem Fuß' [is now following on our heels] are omitted. The commas from the original poem are missing. Kiefer turns the four-line pre-text into a three-line post-text. After the word 'da' [here] in the painting there is a break, a blank space — 'das' [that] becomes 'da' [here] — so one could say that Kiefer's text is divided into two larger and two smaller parts.

Kiefer's medial combination frames the text as an integral part of the image, inviting the viewer to read. He uses photography and canvas as a background, painting them with acrylic and oil paints, emulsion and chalk. He also applies sediment from electrolysis in layers without a brush. This creates a relief-like texture as well as an abstract spatial depth that is reminiscent of a dark, destroyed (war) landscape ('Nacht', 'Gewitter', 'Donner'). The bright splashes of colour suggest plants ('Laub', 'Büschen'), gesturing towards a present, but broken, vitality ('mit Dornen erhellt', 'Gewitter der Rosen'). The simultaneous effect of the image, in which there is no clear reading direction, stands in clear contrast to the sequentiality of the text: 'Die formale Ungleichmäßigkeit hinterlässt ein Gefühl der Bewegung, die ungerichtet ist' [The formal unevenness leaves a feeling of movement that is undirected].[40] Despite this medial limit, there are both content-related and structural correspondences between text and image: the image, one might say, acquires a literary quality. The break and empty space in the text stand in painful tension to the vision of brokenness and destruction in the image-space; they seem dialectically related to each other. The broken plants (flowers and stalks) in the picture, as in the whole cycle,[41] evoke a destroyed natural landscape, a war landscape, a painful or broken love, revealing 'die thematische Dialektik von Krieg und Frieden, Liebe und Schmerz, Schönheit und Zerstörung' [the thematic dialectics of war and peace, love and pain, beauty and destruction].[42] Kiefer uses plants from his

---

[39] Kiefer and Pamuk, *Im Gewitter der Rosen*, pp. 10–11.

[40] 'Anselm Kiefer. Gewitter der Rosen. 27 März–9 Mai 2015 bei Galerie Thaddaeus Ropac in Salzburg, Österreich', *MEER*, 7 April 2015 <https://www.meer.com/de/14578-anselm-kiefer-gewitter-der-rosen> [accessed 14 Febuary 2024].

[41] Kiefer already uses this iconography in his earlier works, for example in the Paul Celan series.

[42] 'Anselm Kiefer. Gewitter der Rosen. 27 März–9 Mai 2015 bei Galerie Thaddaeus Ropac in Salzburg, Österreich'.

immediate living and working environment in his works.[43] Insofar as these flowers have a connection to his life, they have an autobiographical quality, echoing a connection between reality and fiction, between the imaginary and the biographical, that has often been attested in Ingeborg Bachmann's work.[44]

In the second painting, *im Gewitter der Rosen ist die Nacht*, Kiefer quotes Bachmann's poem 'Aria I', the first verse of which is similar to the poem 'Im Gewitter der Rosen'.[45] From the second verse of 'Aria I', the following two verses are inscribed in the painting with changed punctuation and a lower case 'w' on the first word:

> Wo immer gelöscht wird, was die Rosen entzünden,
> schwemmt Regen uns in den Fluß. O fernere Nacht!
>
> [Wherever what the roses ignite is extinguished,
> rain washes us into the river. Oh, distant night!][46]

The 'entzündeten' [ignited] meadow flowers and two 'Rosen' stand out against the darkness, night sky and extinguishment which dominate in this work of art — as already suggested by its title. In the painted quotation from 'Aria I' the artist also highlights the word 'Rosen' to underline that these roses are to be associated with the power of ignition.

The third painting *wohin wir uns wenden im Gewitter der Rosen* quotes the entire poem 'Aria I':

> Wohin wir uns wenden im Gewitter der Rosen,
> ist die Nacht von Dornen erhellt, und der Donner
> des Laubs, das so leise war in den Büschen,
> folgt uns jetzt auf dem Fuß.
>
> Wo immer gelöscht wird, was die Rosen entzünden,
> schwemmt Regen uns in den Fluß. O fernere Nacht!
> Doch ein Blatt, das uns traf, treibt auf den Wellen
> bis zur Mündung uns nach. (W, I, p. 160)
>
> [Wherever we turn in the storm of roses,
> the night is lit up by thorns, and the thunder
> of leaves, once so quiet within the bushes,
> rumbling at our heels
>
> Wherever what the roses ignite is extinguished,
> rain washes us into the river. Oh, distant night!
> But a leaf that hit us drifts on the waves
> to the estuary after us.][47]

---

[43] For this information I thank Dr Arne Ehmann, Executive Director of the Thaddeus Ropac Gallery Salzburg.
[44] See for example Irene Fußl and Arturo Larcati, *Das Rom der Ingeborg Bachmann* (Edition A. B. Fischer, 2015), p. 14; Sigrid Weigel, *Ingeborg Bachmann: Hinterlassenschaften unter Wahrung des Briefgeheimnisses* (dtv, 2003), pp. i–ix.
[45] Kiefer and Pamuk, *Im Gewitter der Rosen*, pp. 16–17.
[46] Bachmann, *Darkness Spoken*, p. 57.
[47] Ibid., p. 47.

In the bottom of the right-hand corner one can see the dedication 'für I. B.' [for I. B.]. The plants seem broken, the grey-green clouds suggest steam or the aftermath of rain. Compared to the second painting, this one appears darker.

In this fourth painting *wohin wir uns wenden im Gewitter der Rosen*, the poem has likewise been modified.[48] Some words are replaced with new ones, and the punctuation and verse division are changed as shown below:

> Wohin wir uns wenden im Gewitter der Rosen,
> ist die Nacht von Dornen erhellt [[]], und der Donner
> ~~des Laubs, das~~ [der] so leise war in den Büschen,
> ~~folgt~~ uns ~~jetzt~~ [ach] auf dem Fuß.

Kiefer also adds 'o fernere Nacht' [oh distant night] from 'Aria I'. The colours of this painting are more intense compared to those discussed so far: green, red/ orange, yellow, and white sheen against a grey-black background suggest vital forces of nature. The huge plant depicted in the middle of the picture is the poisonous giant hogweed (*Heracleum mantegazzianum*), which causes burns in people and animals when touched. The text is shown in small font, while the colourful plants and the giant hogweed dominate the image, meaning that the dimension of simultaneity (*Nebeneinander*) predominates over that of successiveness (*Nacheinander*).

The ambivalence that constitutes a key structural principle in both Kiefer's and Bachmann's aesthetics — for example in the coincidence of vitality with poison, or of a wound and a flower — is particularly evident in the plants that appear in their works. The red dots in the second and especially in the fourth of Kiefer's *Gewitter der Rosen* images suggest roses and poppies, but also bleeding gunshot wounds. We can claim with Anette Gilbert that 'Nicht der menschliche Körper ist hier also Symptomträger einer verdrängten und zerstörerischen Geschichte, sondern das Material der Kunst' [It's not the human body that is the bearer of a repressed and destructive history here, but rather the material of art].[49] As Karina von Tippelskirch writes, an associative connection can be made to Paul Celan's *Mohn und Gedächtnis* [Poppy and Memory] as well as to Remembrance or Memorial Day, on which fallen soldiers are remembered.[50]

In an interview with Heinz Peter Schwerfel in 2001, Kiefer declared that he felt a 'Geschwisterschaft' [sibling bond] with Ingeborg Bachmann,[51] claiming

---

[48] Ibid., pp. 46–47.

[49] Anette Gilbert, '"Es ist erstaunlich, wie man oft eben das findet, was man sucht." Anselm Kiefer im Gespräch mit Ingeborg Bachmann über Geschichte, Zeit und Utopie', in *'Mitten ins Herz': KünstlerInnen lesen Ingeborg Bachmann*, ed. by Marion Schulz and Brigitte Jirku (Peter Lang, 2009), pp. 73–97 (p. 90).

[50] Karina von Tippelskirch, 'Angrenzen: Anselm Kiefer und Ingeborg Bachmann', in *Die Waffen nieder! / Lay down your weapons! Ingeborg Bachmanns Schreiben gegen den Krieg*, ed. by Karl Ivan Solibakke and Karina von Tippelskirch (Königshausen und Neumann, 2012), pp. 173–84 (p. 183).

[51] Heinz Peter Schwerfel, '"Ich wollte noch einmal neu anfangen": Ein Interview mit Anselm Kiefer', *art — Das Kunstmagazin*, 7 (2001), pp. 14–29 (p. 28).

'Es gibt niemanden, mit dem ich einen so engen Kontakt hätte' [There is no one else with whom I would have such close contact].[52] The artist repeatedly emphasizes the significance of Bachmann and her poems for his work, with regard to creative ethos, artistic commitment, and an awareness of time and history.[53] This temporal and historical dimension is, as we have seen, clearly expressed in the painting cycle *Im Gewitter der Rosen*, through the poison of the giant hogweed and the red colour dots, which associate abstract roses and poppies with bleeding gunshot wounds.

IV

Transmedial analysis helps us to deepen and diversify our insights into these paintings by Cy Twombly and Anselm Kiefer and their response to Ingeborg Bachmann's poetry,[54] enriching our understanding of their entangled themes and motifs, their narrativity and citation modes, as well as their philosophical, literary and ecological resonances. The intermedial approach I have taken up to this point focuses on contact between text and image and the forms of interaction between them. Transmedial analysis goes a step further, illuminating the works of art in a cross-fertilization of 'texts' while tending to emphasize medial non-specificity and the lack of an origin medium in transmedial processes.[55] In the final section of this article, I will bring impulses from transmedial analysis into dialogue with perspectives from interdisciplinary plant studies, re-reading the image–text relations in and between Bachmann, Twombly and Kiefer with a new focus on the vegetal.

The prominence of roses, other plants, natural phenomena and landscapes in the works under discussion allows us to determine a 'plant poetics' at work in the creative dialogue between Bachmann, Twombly and Kiefer.[56] Transmediality allows the cross-media plant-oriented aspects of their works to come to the fore, the similarities in terms of plant themes and structural principles which can be determined independently of any specific media.

---

[52] Ibid.

[53] Gilbert, 'Es ist erstaunlich', p. 75.

[54] See Lina Užukauskaitė, 'Pflanzen und Pflanzenpoetik in Kunst und Literatur: Cy Twomblys Rosengemälde und ihre literarischen Vorlagen (Ingeborg Bachmann, Rainer Maria Rilke)', in *Culture — Environment — Society: Humanities and Beyond*, ed. by Paweł Piszczatowski and Joanna Godlewicz-Adamiec (Vandenhoeck & Ruprecht, 2024).

[55] Rajewsky defines transmediality as follows: 'Medienunspezifische Phänomene, die in verschiedenen Medien mit den dem jeweiligen Medium eigenen Mitteln ausgetragen werden können, ohne daß hierbei die Annahme eines kontaktgebenden Ursprungsmediums wichtig oder möglich ist' [Media-non-specific phenomena that can be executed in various media using the means specific to the respective medium, without the assumption of a contact-providing source medium being important or possible]. Rajewsky, *Intermedialität*, p. 19.

[56] The connection between botanical knowledge, literary textual processes and artistic image processes is relevant here, see Joela Jacobs und Isabel Kranz, 'Einleitung: Das literarische Leben der Pflanzen: Poetiken des Botanischen', *Literatur für Leser*, 40.2 (2017), pp. 85–89.

Transmediality in this case can be understood as organic creativity in the sense of Jacques Derrida's grafting metaphor ('Aufpropfung'),[57] which resonates with the citation methods of Twombly and Kiefer as well as with the cross-fertilization of different concepts and texts from philosophy and Cultural Plant Studies.

First, I would like to address Bachmann's poem 'Schatten Rosen Schatten' and attempt a re-reading with a refreshed focus on the plants. In the poem, the lyrical self speaks of 'Rosen', although this extrinsic speaking does not describe the flowers in detail. Nature is laconically evoked by the additional keywords 'Himmel' [sky], 'Erde' [earth] and 'Wasser' [water]. The missing verbs and punctuation, together with the blank spaces in the poem, allow different connotations and ambiguity. Its predominant principles are openness, ambivalence or paradox, and repetition. The lyrical self, only appearing through the possessive in the final line, is positioned between shadows and roses, between sky, earth and water. There is no further specification of the interaction between plants and humans in the poem. In contrast to the rooted plants, the poem's text subject is unrooted, a stranger who observes their own shadow on the alien water. Bachmann scholars connect this sense of alienation with the historical context of the loss of home and the experience of (moral) exile after the Shoah.[58] Whether the lyrical subject in Bachmann's poem is opposed to nature as a passive object or is connected to it remains an open question.[59] The word 'zwischen' [between] used here might suggest an interweaving of the human and non-human spheres. Bachmann's aesthetic process of evocation creates empty spaces and many different possibilities for reading the poem; we are to continue thinking about it and to reflect anew on the possible relations to, and meanings of, the roses.[60] The blank spaces in the poem may indicate the silent existence of plants that nevertheless communicates itself through scent, touch and sight. Bachmann's aesthetic principles intertwine with the plant world, its openness and vastness, its non-human temporality, its constant growth and decay. These overlaps between the plants and the text allow one to speak of a 'vegetal' aspect of the text and of a 'Poetik des Pflanzlichen' or plant-based poetics.[61]

---

[57] Jaques Derrida, 'Signatur, Ereignis, Kontext', in Derrida, *Limited Inc.*, ed. by Peter Engelmann; trans. by Werner Rappl and Dagmar Travner (Passagen, 2001), p. 27.

[58] See Hans Höller, 'Böhmen liegt am Meer', in LG, pp. 125–26.

[59] See Anke Kramer, 'Plant Studies im Literaturunterricht: Verwebungen von Pflanzen und Menschen bei Karin Peschka', in *Ästhetisierungen der Natur und ökologischer Wandel: Literaturdidaktische Perspektiven auf Narrative der Natur in der deutschsprachigen Gegenwartsliteratur*, ed. by Jan Standke und Dieter Wrobel (WVT, 2021), pp. 203–15 (pp. 204 and 210).

[60] Bachmann herself posited this openness to continual (re-)interpretation as an essential characteristic of literature, for example, in an interview with Toni Kielechner on 9 April 1971, GuI, pp. 95–100 (p. 100).

[61] Urte Stobbe, 'Plant Studies: Pflanzen kulturwissenschaftlich erforschen — Grundlagen, Tendenzen, Perspektiven', *Kulturwissenschaftliche Zeitschrift*, 4.1 (2019), p. 98. See also

What knowledge of roses is conveyed to the reader in this poem by Bachmann? If we take the plant perspective and centre the plants more firmly, an expanded reading of the poem opens up. Drawing on Emmanuele Coccia's philosophy of plants,[62] we can begin to perceive the plants in Bachmann's poem as 'Aktanten'[63] [actants] oder 'Wirkende' [agents],[64] which send an existential message to the lyrical self and the reader. In this respect, plant speech can be characterized as intrinsic speech.[65] It must be emphasized that plant 'agency' cannot be thought of as similar or comparable to human action: it is neither intentional nor individual and cannot be separated from the plants' situation or environment.[66] Nevertheless, plants are actively able to change these surroundings, demonstrating what Stobbe has referred to as 'performative Verhaltensweisen' [performative behaviours].[67] If, according to Emmanuele Coccia, there is no world without plants, that is to say, if plants demonstrate radical 'being-in-the-world' through their 'adhesion [...] to their environment' and their dwelling in a cosmic home between the sun and the earth, then clear differences emerge between the existence of the plants and the existence of the lyrical subject,[68] who is presented in the poem in terms of her mobility, uprootedness and homelessness in the world. Reading with Coccia, the existential message sent by plants can be interpreted as follows in relation to Bachmann's poem. In a learning and attentive engagement with plants, the human lyrical subject can not only assume a new and expanding consciousness, but also acquire the plants' comprehensive form of being which allows for a 'cosmological' rootedness in Coccia's sense,[69] thereby counteracting the feeling of being foreign and homeless.

Thanks to their roots, which mark the beginning of growth while also ensuring further survival, plants are located in both the past and the future.[70] Their very structure, then, suggests non-simultaneity, temporal unboundedness and permanent emergence, all of which work to counteract too elegiac a reading of the poem as the cry of an unrooted subject in an alien or alienated world. A reading that opens the poem to the insights of plant studies and the philosophy

Literaturen und Kulturen des Vegetabilen: Plant Studies — Kulturwissenschaftliche Pflanzenforschung, ed. by Urte Stobbe, Anke Kramer and Berbeli Wanning (Peter Lang, 2022).

[62] Emanuele Coccia, *Die Wurzeln der Welt: Eine Philosophie der Pflanzen*, trans. by Elsbeth Ranke (Carl Hanser, 2018).

[63] Stobbe, 'Plant Studies', p. 101.

[64] Kramer, 'Plant Studies', p. 204.

[65] See Jacobs and Kranz, 'Einleitung', p. 86.

[66] See Yvonne Al-Taie and Evelyn Dueck, 'Einleitung: Blütenlesen — Poetiken des Vegetabilen in der Gegenwartslyrik', in *Blütenlesen: Poetiken des Vegetabilen in der Gegenwartslyrik*, ed. by Yvonne Al-Taie and Evelyn Dueck (Springer, 2023), pp. 1–21 (p. 4).

[67] Stobbe, 'Plant Studies', p. 102.

[68] Coccia, *Die Wurzeln*, pp. 17–18.

[69] Ibid., p. 58.

[70] See Carla Swiderski, 'Restaurationsarbeiten im imaginierten Garten in Hilde Domins *Das zweite Paradies*', *Literatur für Leser*, 40.2 (2017), pp. 153–66 (p. 165).

of plants reminds us that plants are agents, manifesting their presence in such a way as to stimulate people to act, causing processes of transition and transformation.[71] This allows us to see the roses of the poem as more than just a motif, decoration or symbol whose meaning must always be translated back into human terms.[72] A plant-philosophical reading offers an alternative path towards a plant poetics. This is not to claim for Bachmann the kind of concrete political or social engagement with ecological themes that can be found in other German poetry of the 1970s and 1980s;[73] she decidedly refused the epithet 'Gräserbewisperer' [grass whisperer].[74] Yet the focus on plants and non-human or more-than-human nature in the works of art discussed here could be said to anticipate, or participate in, increasing awareness of the unstable and precarious relationships between humans and their environment. Twombly's omission of the two last lines of Bachmann's poem in his painting, which results in the elimination of the only direct reference to the lyric subject, arguably suggests a gentle critique of, or turning away from, anthropocentrism.[75]

Plant poetics also resonate with the mode of citation used by Twombly and Kiefer, according to Jacques Derrida. Derrida describes quoting as a movement of taking something out of one context and inserting it into another, and for this act of citation he uses the metaphor of grafting,[76] the 'greffe citationelle'.[77] In horticultural grafting, two plants are injured and brought together so that they can grow together: a part of the other plant is grafted onto the host plant, and as they grow together the host plant is refined.[78] Derrida uses the term 'grafting' also for the act of writing ('greffe'): the artist — Twombly or Kiefer — writes Bachmann's poem onto his painting; he is a *greffier* in Derrida's sense.[79] By grafting the quotations onto their works, Twombly and Kiefer create transitions, enabling circular communication between Bachmann's text and the later images.[80] Uwe Wirth speaks of grafting as a central figure of the poetics of knowledge and its reinscription; here, the painterly vision arising from the encounter with Bachmann's text is grafted onto the text itself, which in its turn was grafted onto the poetic tradition of rose symbolism.

---

[71] Kramer, 'Plant Studies', pp. 205–06.
[72] As roses and other flowers have long been read in literary studies, see ibid.
[73] See Al-Taie and Dueck, 'Einleitung', p. 2.
[74] 'Ingeborg Bachmann erhält den Georg-Büchner-Preis 1964', ARD Mediathek, 5:44. <https://www.ardmediathek.de/video/kultur-im-norden/ingeborg-bachmann-erhaelt-den-georg-buechner-preis/ndr/Y3JpZDovL25kci5kZS9jOWRjMmQ4MyozMzNjLTQzMzktODA1MCoxODZhYmVhNmVmMTA> [accessed 15 July 2024].
[75] See Al-Taie and Dueck, 'Einleitung', pp. 3–5.
[76] See Uwe Wirth, 'Zitieren Propfen Exzerpieren', in *Kreativität des Findens: Figurationen des Zitats*, ed. by Martin Roussel (Brill, 2012), pp. 79–98 (p. 79).
[77] Jacques Derrida, 'Signature événement contexte', in Derrida, *Marges de la philosophie* (Les Éditions de Minuit, 1972), pp. 365–93 (p. 381).
[78] See Wirth, 'Zitieren Propfen Exzerpieren', p. 79.
[79] See Wirth, 'Original und Kopie', p. 21.
[80] See Wirth, 'Zitieren Propfen Exzerpieren', p. 86.

In the paintings of Kiefer and Twombly, the agency of the plants is also visible. In Kiefer's Bachmann paintings, as we have seen, the assertion of the vital, ever-renewing forces of nature, characterized by recurrence and repetition, can be observed against a dark, ruined war-scape, creating a distinctive ambivalence. Here, the rhythms of nature carry an openness that seems to defy historical destruction. Many plants in these paintings of Kiefer's are broken, but the flowers still continue to grow and bloom. Viewers of Twombly's painting are exposed to the gaze of the plant, to its 'eyes', as Kramer puts it in another context.[81] According to Coccia, flowers are an attractor insofar as they draw the world towards them.[82] Twombly's roses, nuanced in colour and shape, also have an attractive effect on the recipient. The roses depicted can be interpreted on multiple levels: on the one hand, as enigmatic, mysterious and ephemeral; on the other hand, as associated with love, growth, metamorphosis and transformation, thereby opening the contradiction between beauty and pain. The aesthetic principles of the painting — openness, ambivalence, repetition — correspond to the characteristics of plant life. These correspondences allow one to speak of a 'vegetal' quality in Twombly's — and Kiefer's — responses to Bachmann, and of a plant poetics. Approaching Bachmann's poetry, and Twombly's and Kiefer's paintings, through cultural plant studies, we may gain a stronger sense of how these works attempt to rethink humanity's position vis-à-vis non-human life, the earth and the cosmos.[83]

This article is part of the research project *Forms of Interaction Between Art and Literature: Cy Twombly and World Literature from the 18th to the 21st Century* funded by the Austrian Science Fund (FWF, V01024-G).

---

[81] Kramer, 'Plant Studies', p. 208.
[82] Coccia, *Die Wurzeln*, p. 126.
[83] See Al-Taie and Dueck, 'Einleitung', p. 2.

Inhabiting the Mind of a Multilingual Interpreter: Translation, Displacement and Revelation in Bachmann's 'Simultan'

CLAUDIA J. FISCHER and VERA SAN PAYO DE LEMOS

Lisbon University (CEComp / CET)

> Ich mit der deutschen Sprache
> dieser Wolke um mich
> die ich halte als Haus
> treibe durch alle Sprachen
> (W, IV, p. 153)

> [I with the German language
> this cloud around me
> that I hold as a house
> drift through all languages]

In *Über den Humanismus* ['Letter on Humanism'], Martin Heidegger defines language as a space of inhabitation guarded by philosophers and poets: 'Die Sprache ist das Haus des Seins [...] In ihrer Behausung wohnt der Mensch. Die Denkenden und Dichtenden sind die Wächter dieser Behausung' ['Language is the house of being. In its home human beings dwell. Those who think and those who create with words are the guardians of this home'].[1] This evocative definition of language permeates various moments of Bachmann's work, and in particular her short story 'Simultan', published in 1970, twenty years after she wrote and defended a doctoral thesis on Heidegger's philosophy, titled *Die kritische Aufnahme der Existentialphilosophie Martin Heideggers* [The Critical Reception of Martin Heidegger's Existential Philosophy].

As a multilingual interpreter from Vienna living between several languages, Nadja, the main character, deals with feelings of displacement and homelessness. Featuring a journey along the southern coast of Italy, the plot, as well as the narration itself, conveys an idea of instability and perpetual movement in both space and time. More than feeling far away from her roots, Nadja misses the shelter of a stable house of language. The title 'Simultan' refers in the first instance to Nadja's work as a simultaneous interpreter, but other simultaneities

---

[1] Martin Heidegger, *Über den Humanismus* (Vittorio Klostermann, 1949), p. 5; Martin Heidegger, 'Letter on Humanism', trans. by Frank A. Capuzzi, in *Pathmarks*, ed. by William McNeal (Cambridge University Press, 1998), p. 239.

Austrian Studies 32 (2024), doi:10.1353/aus.00008, pp. 107–19

are also hinted at: different thoughts emerge in Nadja's mind concurrently, different languages occur in the same sentence, and the narrator's point of view continually oscillates between first- and third-person perspectives. The instability of the reading process deliberately induced by these narrative strategies leads to a feeling of displacement that ultimately affects the reader as well.

Bachmann describes the story as 'ein simultanes Geschehen und Denken und Fühlen, und Sprachen, die sich nie ganz begegnen, jeder muss den anderen ein wenig übersetzen' (TKA, IV, p. 17) [a simultaneity of events, thoughts and emotions, and languages that never quite meet, everyone has to translate the other a little]. Her concept of translation in this statement seems to bear a broader sense than the usual understanding of translation as a mediation between speakers of different languages: it also must occur between people who share the same language. In a brief note, never published in Bachmann's lifetime but intended to be included in the first publication of the story, translation is acknowledged as a need, a fundamental duty, a human right even: 'Übersetzen ist die erste Pflicht, auch wenn sie nicht in [die] Charta der Menschenrechte aufgenommen ist' (TKA, IV, p. 17) [Translating is the first duty, even if it's not included in the Charter of Human Rights]. It is no coincidence that, in 'Simultan', interpretation carried out by Nadja occurs at international conferences and is primarily linked to global human issues such as disarmament and food security.

In this article we not only argue that translation is, in this broader sense, a significant topic in 'Simultan', but also that Bachmann's text constitutes an example of 'transfiction', an area currently receiving increased attention in Translation Studies. Our own translation of 'Simultan', which directly inspired this investigation, was published in 2023 in an anthology of transfiction.[2] Coined and defined by Klaus Kaindl in 2014 as 'the introduction and (increased) use of translation-related phenomena in fiction',[3] transfiction encompasses all kinds of fiction (literary texts, movies, theatre, dance performance and so on) that have translators and/or simultaneous interpreters as central characters, thus dealing with different aspects of their work and social image. The emergence of transfiction is linked to a turn that took place in Translation Studies at the end of the twentieth century. An ideal of invisibility of the translator, who formerly was considered a silent and faithful servant of the original — the master — was replaced by a new conception that grants translators a space of their own, a right

---

[2] Ingeborg Bachmann, 'Simultâneo', trans. by Claudia J. Fischer and Vera San Payo de Lemos, in *O Irresistível Charme da Tradução... Uma Antologia de Histórias de Tradutores*, ed. by Marisa Mourinha and Marta Pacheco Pinto (Documenta, 2023), pp. 67–99. Together we had already translated *Herzzeit*, the correspondence between Ingeborg Bachmann and Paul Celan, published in Portugal under the title *Tempo do Coração* (Antígona, 2020).

[3] Klaus Kaindl, 'Going Fictional! Translators and Interpreters in Literature and Film: An Introduction', in *Transfiction: Research into the Realities of Translation Fiction*, ed. by Klaus Kaindl and Karlheinz Spitzl (John Benjamins, 2014), pp. 1–26 (p. 4).

to visibility, a right to their own presence (and sometimes even subjectivity) in the creation of the target text.[4] The previous ideal of translation had resulted in the marginalization (displacement) of the translator, whose name sometimes would not even be explicitly mentioned in translated books. Certainly since Lawrence Venuti's claim in *The Translator's Invisibility* (1995), a translator is assumed to be an author who creates original work.

Transfiction Studies can be considered both an offspring and a booster of this turn. Translators increasingly appear on the stage of fiction as characters whose stories are brought to the fore, making tangible to the reader the implications of being a translator or an interpreter. As Rosemary Arrojo points out in *Fictional Translators: Rethinking Translation Through Literature*, it was this increasing visibility of the translator characters in fiction that led to scholarly interest in reading fiction as a form of theory. Evoking the etymology of the word 'theory' and considering it in broader terms as a way of seeing, Arrojo argues that the inner struggles of the characters depicted in fiction, their views on language and interpretation, offer 'unique opportunities for reflection that can be potentially more insightful than those associated with what specialists tend to classify as "real" theory'.[5] In the same year, 2018, Lynne Sharon Schwartz edited the volume *Crossing Borders*,[6] which assembles 'sixteen stories and essays by prominent fiction writers and translators about the way in which translation operates in our lives', as it is described on the publisher's website.[7]

Very recently, in 2023, Marco Miletich published *Transfiction: Characters in Search of Translation Studies*,[8] a collection of essays that explores topics such as the role of the translator in culture and society, gender and translation, and issues regarding power struggles within the translatorial task. Also in 2023, Marisa Mourinha and Marta Pacheco Pinto published *O Irresistível Charme da Tradução...* [The Irresistible Charm of Translation...], a Portuguese anthology of short stories and poems from different literary traditions featuring translators. Mostly dating from the twenty-first and the second half of the twentieth century,[9] these texts gravitate around concepts that have always been associated with the act of translating: mediation, trust, misunderstanding, loneliness,

---

[4] These ways of conceptualizing the relationship between translator and original have been problematized by numerous critics. For a feminist critique of the gendered assumptions underlying the idea of 'faithfulness' see, for example, Rosemary Arrojo, 'Fidelity and The Gendered Translation', *Traduction, Terminologie, Redaction*, 7.2 (1994), pp. 147–63.

[5] Rosemary Arrojo, *Fictional Translators: Rethinking Translation through Literature* (Routledge, 2018), p. 2.

[6] *Crossing Borders: Stories and Essays about Translation*, ed. by Lynne Sharon Schwartz (Seven Stories, 2018).

[7] 'Crossing Borders Stories and Essays about Translation', Seven Stories Press, n.d. <https://www.sevenstories.com/books/4042-crossing-borders> [accessed 8 May 2024].

[8] Marco Miletich, *Transfiction: Characters in Search of Translation Studies* (Vernon Press, 2023).

[9] Among the twenty-one texts in this volume, only Conan Doyle's 'The Greek Interpreter' (1894) and Isaac Babel's 'Guy de Maupassant' (1920–22) antedate Bachmann's story.

poverty, multilingualism.[10] Bachmann's 'Simultan' was published here for the first time in its Portuguese translation.[11]

Probably written in the winter of 1967/68, 'Simultan' was first streamed on 7 October 1968 by the radio station NDR, and, in 1970, published in the journal *Die Neue Rundschau*. In 1972, Bachmann republished it in a book, along with four other short stories: 'Probleme Probleme' ['Problems Problems'], 'Ihr glücklichen Augen' ['Eyes to Wonder'], 'Das Gebell' ['The Barking'], and 'Drei Wege zum See' ['Three Paths to the Lake'].[12] The title chosen for this collection — *Simultan* — repeats, thus foregrounding, the title of the volume's first story.[13] The creation process of the five stories, all of them featuring Viennese women, is recalled by Bachmann in a little-known, posthumously published note with the title 'Hommage an die Wienerin' [Tribute to the Viennese Woman], in these terms:

> Vor etwa vier Jahren schrieb ich die Titelgeschichte Simultan [sic], weil mich etwas daran hinderte, an dem weiterzuschreiben, was die Hauptsache für mich war, die ganze Geschichte ist in einem Tag entworfen worden, und einige Monate später war sie fertig.
>
> Das Vergnügen und Entspannung haben dann bewirkt, dass ich in kurzer Reihenfolge einige andere Geschichten anfing, wieder liegenließ, und sie hatten immer mit Personen zu tun, die am Rande von meinem Hauptbuch lebten, aber dort keinen Platz fanden, Wien aber mitbevölkerten in meinen Gedanken, und nach einiger Zeit merkte ich, dass Simultan, das einfach ein sachlicher Titel war, des Inhalts wegen ganz gut für alle ginge, die ich manchmal für mich, im Scherz 'Wienerinnen' nannte.[14]

> [About four years ago I wrote the title story 'Simultan' because something was preventing me from continuing to write the main thing I was working on. The whole story was drafted in one day and a few months later it was finished.
>
> Pleasure and relaxation then caused me to start a few other stories in quick succession, then drop them again, and they always had to do with people who lived on the fringes of my main book, but who had no place there, but who also co-inhabited Vienna in my thoughts, and after a while I realized that 'Simultan', which was simply a matter-of-fact title, would work quite well content-wise for all those whom I sometimes to myself jokingly called 'Viennese women'.]

By 'my main book' Bachmann means the novel *Malina*, which was published only ten months prior to *Simultan*, the last book published in her lifetime. Temporal and spatial conceptualization are at stake in this intriguing testimony:

---

[10] Ibid., p. 13.
[11] Ibid., pp. 67–99. See also footnote 2.
[12] Titles in English according to TPL.
[13] The title for this English translation of the short story 'Simultan' is 'Word for Word'.
[14] Ingeborg Bachmann, 'Hommage an die Wienerin: Eine unveröffentlichte Skizze', in *Ingeborg Bachmann: Das Lächeln der Sphinx*, special issue of *Du: Die Zeitschrift der Kultur*, 9 (1994), pp. 70–71 (p. 70).

both books were written at the same time, and the characters, who 'co-inhabited Vienna' in her thoughts but 'had no place' in the main book, engendered this short fiction. In these stories the female characters, correspondingly, also feel utterly displaced in their worlds.

When defining translators and interpreters as 'individuals who are constantly in motion or create motion due to their constant movement between languages and cultures',[15] Kaindl argues that their action represents 'the deterritorialisation of humankind perfectly'. Instead of being pictured sitting at a desk in the backstage of events, translators and interpreters become symbols of a new human condition, moving between places and languages, embodying the instability of the modern world. In 2020, picturing contemporary life, Dirk Delabastita claims that 'translation has become a master metaphor epitomizing our present human condition in a globalized and centreless world, evoking the human search for a sense of self and belonging in a puzzling world full of change and difference'.[16]

Although written some decades before what already was called 'a fictional turn in translation studies',[17] Bachmann's story 'Simultan' already fits into the characterization of human life in a modern globalized world, where 'ein simultanes Geschehen und Denken und Fühlen, und Sprachen' (TKA, IV, p. 17) [simultaneity of events and thoughts and emotions, and languages] is an everyday reality. Not yet linked to digital or remote devices, Nadja's mind and body are constantly in motion, travelling around the world from conference to conference, from hotel room to hotel room. This displacement is encapsulated in the evocation of '[ein] Daheim, das nirgends mehr für sie war' (SE, p. 285) ['she was no longer at home anywhere'] (TPL, p. 2).

Nadja's feeling of displacement is mainly language related. She hopes to find a feeling of home through an affair with Ludwig Frankel,[18] a man who, also born in Vienna, supposedly speaks her language. The communication she seeks to have with him seems primarily based on a wish to recover her native tongue, lost amidst the multiplicity of her work languages:

---

[15] Kaindl, *Transfiction*, p. 3.

[16] Dirk Delabastita, 'Fictional Representations', in *Routledge Encyclopedia of Translation Studies*, ed. by M. Baker and G. Saldanha (Routledge, 2020), pp. 189–94 (p. 192).

[17] See Marta Pacheco Pinto, João Ferreira Duarte and Helder Lopes, 'Editor's Introduction: Collectors of Worlds: Translators, History and Fiction', *Dedalus*, 26 (2022), pp. 13–25 (p. 15).

[18] Bachmann's choice of the characters' names in this story, as always, is clearly deliberate and well thought out. Names such as Nadja, Ludwig Frankel, Jean Pierre and Mr Keen, all raise associations with meanings or persons. Nadja, which means hope in Russian and Slovenian, suggests the title of André Breton's second novel; Ludwig Frankel, prompting in the reader's mind Wittgenstein's first name, clearly suggests Jewish origins, whereas Jean Pierre, the name of her former lover, is profoundly Christian. Mr Keen, who bears no first name in the story, is Frankel's colleague at the FAO, who keeps him from progressing in his career. See also Ingeborg Bachmann, 'Der Umgang mit Namen', in *Frankfurter Vorlesungen: Probleme zeitgenössischer Dichtung* (Piper, 1982), pp. 79–96.

> sie beide [hatten] [...] eine ähnliche Art zu sprechen und beiseite zu sprechen [...], vielleicht hatte sie auch nur, nach einem dritten Whisky auf der Dachterrasse im Hilton, geglaubt, er bringe ihr etwas zurück, einen vermissten Geschmack, einen fehlenden Tonfall, ein geisterhaftes Gefühl von einem Daheim, das nirgends mehr für sie war. (SE, p. 285)

> [they had [...] a similar way of talking, the same intonation, perhaps she'd just wanted to believe after that third whiskey on the roof garden at the Hilton that he would give her back something she'd lost, a missing taste,[19] an intonation gone flat, that ghostly feeling of home, though she was no longer at home anywhere.] (TPL, p. 2)

Nadja's professional activity at conferences leads her to a state of utter exhaustion,[20] as textually reinforced by the introjection of other languages (English and Italian) in the German text:

> sie waren immer zu zweit in einer Kabine, nicht wie Pilot und Co-Pilot, nein, natürlich nur, um sofort wechseln zu können nach zwanzig Minuten, das war die vernünftigste Zeit, länger konnte man nicht übersetzen, [...] der reine Wahnsinn, [...] es war dieses fanatisch genaue Zuhören, dieses totale sich Versenken in eine andere Stimme, und ein Schaltbrett war ja einfach zu bedienen, aber ihr Kopf, just imagine, t'immagini! (SE, p. 290)

> [they always worked two in a booth, not like pilot and co-pilot, no, it was only set up like that so you could switch after twenty minutes, that was a reasonable interval, you just couldn't translate longer than that, [...] utter insanity. [...] you had to listen so carefully, fanatically, totally immersed in another voice. A switchboard was comparatively easy to operate, but her head, just imagine, t'immagini!] (TPL, p. 8)[21]

Evoking comparison to the cockpit of an aircraft, this short description summarizes two strenuous aspects of the profession: the extreme concentration required to replace a discourse uttered in another language, combined with the great speed at which this must happen. Unlike pilot and co-pilot, the interpreting colleague does not operate as an assistant, but rather as a substitute who assures a quick rendering. Alienation and the voiding of the self are a result of this physical and mental stress, turning Nadja into a replicating machine:[22]

---

[19] Instead of 'missing taste', we suggest 'missed taste'.

[20] Bachmann herself had experience as a literary translator (she published translations of poems by Ungaretti), but not as a simultaneous interpreter. In an unsent letter to Marcel Reich-Ranicki we learn that she did research on this 'new profession' that, in her words, 'diese armen Menschen zerstört und kaputtmacht' (KS, p. 804) [destroys and damages these poor people].

[21] In the English edition, words that are in English in the source text, as for example 'just imagine', are emphasized by the use of italics, but in this case the translator/editor seems to have forgotten to mark these words.

[22] Áine McMurtry has interpreted Nadja as a 'machinic' figure, an articulation of modern technological enslavement who has informed later writers' critique of neoliberal capitalism. See 'Literary Interventions and Texts in Transit in the Work of Kathrin Röggla', *Austrian Studies*, 26 (2018), pp. 72–90 (pp. 87–90). At the same time, Nadja's fate also resonates with

'Was für ein seltsamer Mechanismus war sie doch, ohne einen einzigen Gedanken im Kopf zu haben, lebte sie, eingetaucht in die Sätze anderer, und musste nachtwandlerisch mit gleichen, aber anderslautenden Sätzen sofort nachkommen' (SE, p. 295) ['What a strange mechanism she was, she lived without a single thought of her own, immersed in the sentences of others, like a sleepwalker, furnishing the same but different-sounding sentences an instant later'] (TPL, p. 13).

Voided of her own thoughts but overfilled by the words of others, she risks getting 'von den Wortmassen verschüttet' (SE, p. 295) ['snowed under by an avalanche of words'] (TPL, p. 14). This strong image — a variation of the former description of Nadja's work as a 'totale sich Versenken in eine andere Stimme' (SE, p. 290) ['totally immersed in another voice'] (TPL, p. 2) — resonates with the line 'Drüben versinkt dir die Geliebte im Sand' (SG, p. 47) ['Over there your love sinks in the sand'] of Bachmann's famous poem 'Die gestundete Zeit' ['Mortgaged Time'],[23] published in her first poetry volume from 1953. An impending threat shadows both texts: the menace of total annihilation of the self when dealing with 'mortgaged time'.

Nadja has met Mr Frankel,[24] who works for the Food and Agriculture Organization (FAO), at one of those exhausting conferences at its headquarters in Rome. During their short romantic getaway, she realizes that they have little in common, apart from their Viennese origins and an international job that involves constant motion around the world, and hence the capacity to communicate in several different languages. Their multilingualism spreads throughout the narrative itself, where foreign words and sentences in Russian, Italian, French, Slovenian, English and Spanish pop up, sometimes defying the comprehension of the reader. Apparently, unlike Nadja in her professional role, the text itself does not always interpret/translate for the reader, who — to return to Heidegger's opening metaphor — is left outside the house of her/his language. Beyond merely understanding the events of the story and the inner workings of the character's mind, the reader experiences these peculiarities at first hand through their own linguistic displacement.

that of Echo: 'Echo could only repeat the words she heard at the end of a sentence and never reply herself', which in the case of the myth led to the disappearance of the nymph's body: 'Wretched and sleepless with anguish, she started to waste away [...] nothing remaining but voice and bone' (Ovid, *Metamorphoses*, trans. by David Raeburn (Penguin Books, 2004), vv. 369 and 394–98).

[23] Ingeborg Bachmann, 'Mortgaged Time', in Bachmann, *In the Storm of Roses: Selected Poems*, trans. and ed. by Mark Anderson (Princeton University Press, 1986), p. 43. This poem has several published English translations by different translators, each one bearing a different title: 'The Respite' (Michael Hamburger, 1967); 'Borrowed Time' (Peter Filkins, 2006); 'Time on Loan' (Mike Lyons and Patrick Drysdale, 2011); 'Deferred Time' (Catherine Rogan, 2019).

[24] The narrator keeps referring to Ludwig Frankel as Mr Frankel, possibly to emphasize the fact that Nadja and he are actually strangers. The song 'Strangers in the Night' mentioned in the story also hints at this fact.

A sense of estrangement permeates the opening of the story, the first paragraph of which confronts the reader with sheer disorientation, in several layers of the narrative. Driving in the dark, the couple looks for a hotel she remembers but whose name she cannot recall. While Nadja does not recognize the place she knew from former trips, the reader is immediately confronted by words in a foreign language (*Bože moj!*, 'My God' in Russian) and by an unstable narrative voice, constantly flipping between inner monologue and free indirect discourse, as well as hesitating between first- and third person-narration:

> Bože moj! hatte sie kalte Füße, aber das musste endlich Paestum sein, es gibt da dieses alte Hotel, ich versteh nicht, wie mir der Name, er wird mir gleich einfallen, ich habe ihn auf der Zunge, nur fiel er ihr nicht ein, sie kurbelte das Fenster herunter und starrte angestrengt seitwärts und nach vorne, sie suchte den Weg, der nach rechts, credimi, te lo giuro, dico a destra, abbiegen mußte. Dann war es also das NETTUNO. (SE, p. 284)

> [Bože moj! were her feet cold, but this finally seemed to be Paestum, there's an old hotel here, I can't understand how the name could have slipped my, it'll occur to me in a second, it's on the tip of my tongue, but she couldn't remember it, rolled down the window and strained to see out to the side and ahead, she was looking for the road that should branch off to the right, credimi, te lo giuro, dico a destra. Ah there it was, yes, the Nettuno.] (TPL, p. 1)

However, when the headlights are turned on, directional signs appear on the road, offering orientation — not only for Nadja, but also for the reader, since the narrator's point of view and the syntax tend to stabilize:

> Als er an der Kreuzung verlangsamte und den Scheinwerfer aufblendete, entdeckte sie sofort das Schild, angeleuchtet im Dunkel, unter einem Dutzend Hotelschildern und Pfeilen, die zu Bars und Strandbädern wiesen, sie murmelte, das war aber früher ganz anders, hier war doch nichts, einfach nichts, noch vor fünf sechs Jahren, nein wirklich, das ist doch nicht möglich. (SE, p. 284)

> [As he slowed down at the intersection and turned on the headlights, she spotted the sign immediately, illuminated in the darkness among a dozen hotel signs and arrows pointing the way to bars and beach resorts, and she murmured, it used to be so different, there was nothing here at all, absolutely nothing, just five six years ago, really, it doesn't seem possible.] (TPL, p. 1)

Nadja's first disorientation concerns space. But language, as a sign system, seems to play an important role in that uneasiness. In the English translation, the word for 'Schild' [sign] makes even clearer that a reading scene is being described here. The lights enable Nadja to see and, among this complex forest of signs, she manages to find — that is, to read — the meaning she had been searching for, although the result of that reading will not coincide with her knowledge of things, thus leading to disbelief: 'das ist doch nicht möglich' (SE,

p. 284) ['it doesn't seem possible'] (TPL, p. 1).

Dealing with verbal language or other signs and reading them successfully is a central topic of this short story. Along the trip, language is addressed in diverse ways, such as Mr Frankel's repeated question whether there will be a universal language someday, or Nadja's ambivalent thoughts and feelings towards the linguistic multiplicity that lives in her head, or else in the replacement of verbal language which does not guarantee communication and mutual understanding with body language: 'sprachlos der einzigen Sprache entgegen [...], die ausdrücklich und genau war.' (SE, pp. 302–03) ['speechless [...] towards the only [language] that was explicit and exact'] (TPL, p. 21). Nadja's longing to be with 'einem Mann, der ihr die Sprache zurückgab' (SE, p. 289) ['a man who gave language back to her'] (TPL, p. 7) and the 'Gefühl von einem Daheim' (SE, p. 285) ['feeling of home'] (TPL, p. 2) turns out, after all, to be elusive. Knowledge and hard study grant her proficiency in five languages and professional success, but language no longer establishes any consistent bond between reality in its essence and her inner self.

Misunderstandings and reading failures deeply affect people, even those merely mentioned in the story. They are cracks in communication, part of what Kaindl calls the very subject of translation.[25] When recalling past relationships with men, for instance with the French native speaker Jean Pierre, Nadja is eventually able to understand the origin of their problem due to the language she is thinking in (not speaking): 'Die Antwort kam, weil sie sie nicht französisch suchte, sondern in ihrer eigenen Sprache' (SE, p. 289) ['It finally came to her because she had not been searching in French but in her own language'] (TPL, p. 7). Mr Frankel's wife, for example, lost the capacity to swim because she misunderstood a dolphin's affection as a threat.[26] There is also the episode recalled by Nadja, when two possible translations of the Russian word 'durak' as 'silly' or as 'stupid' almost created a diplomatic incident at a conference when applied to an American delegate.

When she first sees Maratea's Christ statue (*La Statua del Redentore*) — not exactly a Cross, Christianity's most emblematic symbol, but rather a human figure with raised outspread arms — Nadja is severely overwhelmed and incapable of approaching it. The gigantic sign (and possibly also its uncanny ambiguity) causes a panic attack with vertigo. Her signals to Mr Frankel are not understood — 'er hatte noch immer nicht begriffen' (SE, p. 310) ['he still hadn't understood'] (TPL, p. 29) — and her thoughts, in French, are of total despair: 'Aide-moi, aide-moi, ou je meurs ou je me jette en bas. Je meurs, je n'en peux plus' (SE, p. 310). Erected on top of the hill, Maratea's Christ has a

---

[25] Kaindl argues that '[c]hange, transformation, dislocation and cracks have become key coordinates for understanding the motion created by translation'. Kaindl, *Transfiction*, p. 2.

[26] Here we must also think of Gregory Bateson's CIA-sponsored postwar experiments on human–dolphin communication. See Gregory Bateson, *Steps toward an Ecology of Mind* (Chandler, 1972).

particular meaning for the Christian community, for whom it is supposed to represent deep faith and offer a sense of protection. Mr Frankel only casually looks at it from a merely aesthetic point of view, considering it an 'abscheuliche Skulptur' (SE, p. 311) ['awful statue'] (TPL, p. 30), but Nadja feels seriously menaced by it, sensing a fatal ending: 'das also ist meine Vernichtung' (SE, p. 311) ['it will destroy me'] (TPL, p. 30). The next day though, when she climbs the hill once again, her reading of Maratea's Christ is totally different. First seen as 'ungeheuerliche Figur' (SE, p. 310) ['monstruous figure'] (TPL, p. 28) and 'wahnsinnige Gestalt' (SE, p. 310) ['insane colossus'] (TPL, p. 29), it is now perceived as 'eine kleine, kaum sichtbare Figur, mit ausgebreiteten Armen, nicht ans Kreuz geschlagen, sondern zu einem grandiosen Flug ansetzend, zum Auffliegen oder zum Abstürzen bestimmt' (SE, p. 314) ['a small figure, barely visible, with extended arms, not nailed to the cross but preparing for a grandiose flight or a plunge to the depths'] (TPL, p. 33).

What leads to this drastic change in her reading? How can the same figure inspire such contrasting accounts in such a short space of time? Nadja herself seems to have a possible answer. When referring to the impossible quest for truth amidst endless discussions at the international conferences she has attended, her conclusion is: 'Man müsste eine Erleuchtung haben, um zu begreifen, was wirklich vorliegt [...] ganz plötzlich' (SE, p. 307) ['You'd have to have a revelation to grasp what was going on [...] at the drop of a hat'] (TPL, p. 25). Apparently, a revelation — a *revelatio*, or laying bare — has happened to Nadja between those moments on the hill, releasing her from former fears and constraints, momentarily allowing her to experience a childlike lightness and joy: '[Sie] hüpfte den Weg zum Hotel hinauf, kein Atem ging ihr aus, und sie hatte fast kein Gewicht' (SE, p. 314) ['[She] sprinted all the way back to the hotel, without losing her breath and practically weightless'] (TPL, p. 33). Beyond knowledge, revelation leads to a turning point in the story. It starts outside at the site of Maratea's Christ and is accomplished in a reading and translating moment in the hotel. This occurs, paradoxically, when Nadja acknowledges her incapacity to translate a passage from the Bible she found in the hotel room before leaving: 'Sie hätte den Satz in keine andere Sprache übersetzen können, obwohl sie zu wissen meinte, was jedes dieser Worte bedeutete und wie es zu wenden war, aber sie wusste nicht, woraus dieser Satz wirklich gemacht war' (SE, p. 315) ['She couldn't have translated the sentence into any other language, although she was convinced that she knew what each of the words meant and their usage, but she didn't know what this sentence was really made of'] (TPL, p. 34).

Nadja, for whom the Bible is 'nur ein Wörterbuch' (SE, p. 315) ['only a dictionary'] (TPL, p. 34) takes this 'book of words' (literal translation of the German word for dictionary) and opens it, 'um [...] abergläubisch ein Wort zu suchen, als Halt für den Tag' (SE, p. 315) ['to search superstitiously for a word to help her through the day'] (TPL, p. 34). She randomly picks up the sentence 'Il miracolo, come sempre, è il risultato della fede e d'una fede audace.' (SE, p. 315) [The miracle, as is always the case, is the result of faith, moreover, of an audacious faith] and takes it eucharistically into her mouth to be transformed, translated, transubstantiated into another language. Interestingly enough this sentence does not actually exist in the Bible and seems to have been either invented or picked up somewhere by Bachmann. This is the only sentence in the whole story which Nadja specifically attempts to translate, but the translation process, into which the reader gains an insight, eventually ends in failure. After several unsuccessful attempts to render the supposedly biblical passage, Nadja begins to cry: 'Ich bin nicht so gut, ich kann nicht alles, ich kann noch immer nicht alles' (SE, p. 315) ['I'm not all that good, I don't know everything, I still don't know everything'] (TPL, p. 34). This negative self-anagnorisis is like an echo in reverse of a positive sequence of phrases repeated moments before, when Nadja was feeling light and joyous after having overcome her fear of falling as she climbed the hill once again: 'Ich darf, das ist es, ich darf ja leben' (SE, p. 314) ['I can, that's the point, I can live'] (TPL, p. 33). But now, when dealing with textuality, part of her professional expertise, Nadja struggles with her incapacity to seize the meaning concealed in the known words. Her crisis is immediately followed by a peripeteia. When she accepts her limits — 'Sie konnte eben nicht alles' (SE, p. 315) ['She just couldn't do everything'] (TPL, p. 34)[27] — she seems to open a path to a new realm of understanding, an understanding of what at the end of the story she will call 'das Wichtigste' (SE, p. 317) ['the most important thing'] (TPL, p. 36).

Following this episode of translation, failure, and acceptance, Nadja herself will be transformed. Less self-centred, she mingles with strangers at the hotel bar and observes them watching a sports event that momentarily absorbs the attention of a whole country: the victory of Vittorio Adorni at the Giro d'Italia, an actual event that took place in 1965. In this last sequence of the story, Bachmann depicts one more intriguing enactment of speech and translation, though set in an unexpected context: the broadcasting of a bicycle race. The images on the television at the bar are being translated into spoken words by a live commentator, whose excitement is artfully illustrated by a transfer from the strained cyclist's body to his own: 'er redete immer schneller, als hätte er die Pedale zu treten, als wäre er nicht mehr imstande, durchzuhalten, als wäre es sein Herz, das aussetzen konnte, jetzt schweißte seine Zunge' (SE, p. 316) ['He talked faster and faster as though he were pedaling, as though he could no longer stand it, as though his heart could stop beating, now his tongue was

[27] Ironically, we consider two of these translations misleading: 'She just couldn't *do* everything' would rather be the translation of 'Sie konnte nicht alles *tun*.' We suggest 'She just didn't know everything.' As for the translation of 'Ich darf, das ist es, ich darf ja leben', we would argue for 'I am allowed, that's the point, I am allowed to live', to make the important distinction between *können* and *dürfen*, rather than 'I can, that's the point, I can live'.

sweating'] (TPL, p. 35).

The repetition of the subjunctive mood 'als wäre/hätte' [as though] emphasizes the role play that is at stake here. Like an engaged interpreter who speaks on behalf of someone else, the equally engaged broadcaster speaks 'as though' he were the cyclist, identifying with him to an extent that his life seems at risk. Speed and stress, the main ingredients of the race, reappear in this other variant of translation, also pushing the interpreter to his limits, but this time the menace is experienced as a feverous orgiastic event. After blundering, correcting himself, tripping over, panting and gurgling, his broadcast ends with an inarticulate cry and a roar from the crowd. Imperfect language dissolves itself into an animalistic shouting of the winner's name in staccato, 'A — dor — ni. A — dor — ni' (SE, p. 316), and the most important thing for the crowd — victory — is accomplished. When in that particular staccato Nadja hears 'die Staccatorufe aus allen Städten und allen Ländern, durch die sie gekommen war' (SE, p. 316) [all the staccato cries from all the cities and countries she had been to], she perceives the world beyond the need for translations. But 'das Wichtigste' (SE, p. 317) ['the most important thing'] (TPL, p. 36) for Nadja is not the victory of Adorni. It occurs to her as she leaves the hotel, and she calls it out to the boy at the bar, captured in the single Italian word 'Auguri!' (SE, p. 317). In contrast to the beginning of the story where such verbal disorientation prevails, with this ending, Nadja, as her name indicates, is animated by hope and orientation after having endured moments of frustration and despair. As Alexander Nebrig rightly points out in his essay on this story,[28] the sheer similarity between Adorni's triumphant posture on the bicycle and Maratea's Christ with open arms on the hill might seem to allow for the sense of a closure informed by an idea of Christian redemption, which always follows an event of pathos.[29]

Suffering is pivotal throughout this story and is mostly associated with a difficulty in sharing signs, with their shifting meanings, with others. If, as stated by the editors of the volume *Collectors of Worlds: Translators, History and Fiction*, 'fictions *of* translation and translators are modes of representation of translation and translators, as much as they are statements *on* translation',[30] in Bachmann's 'Simultan', translation conveys much more than the activity of a professional interpreter. It encompasses all human communication at different levels: inter- and intralinguistic, oral and written, verbal and non-verbal.

---

[28] Alexander Nebrig, 'Der verborgene Goethe: Zur Glückspoetik in Ingeborg Bachmanns Erzählband Simultan', *Jahrbuch der Deutschen Schillergesellschaft*, 58 (2014), pp. 331–54 (p. 338).

[29] Nebrig refers to a photograph that was published in several Italian newspapers on 2 September 1969 <https://it.wikipedia.org/wiki/Vittorio_Adorni#/media/File:Vittorio_ Adorni_-_Campionati_Del_Mondo_Di_Ciclismo_Su_Strada_1968.jpg> [accessed 8 May 2024].

[30] Marta Pacheco Pinto, João Ferreira Duarte and Helder Lopes, 'Editor's Introduction: Collectors of Worlds: Translators, History and Fiction', *Dedalus*, 26 (2022), pp. 13 25 (p. 14).

Translation, traditionally conceived, relies on equivalences between fixed signs in different languages. In this multi-layered story, signs refuse to offer stability, however. The revelation imagined by the main character as a possible means 'zu begreifen, was wirklich vorliegt und was man deswegen wirklich tun sollte' (SE, p. 307) ['to grasp what was going on and [...] what you should do about it'] (TPL, p. 25) results in a praxis and enactment of translation that is either omnipresent or inexistent, or both, simultaneously.

We wish to express our utmost gratitude to Patricio Ferrari and Thomas Pepper for their help and advice in the rendering of the final version of this article. We also thank the anonymous reviewers for the careful reading of our manuscript and their helpful comments and suggestions.

Philip Boehm Revisits *Malina*

EWA SIWAK

Texas State University

I

Over the past five decades, Mark Anderson, Philip Boehm, Michael Bullock, Peter Filkins, Lilian Friedberg and Mary Fran Gilbert have presented Ingeborg Bachmann's literary texts to English-speaking audiences, striving to do justice to this remarkable writer. Recent access to Bachmann's correspondence and literary estate has generated enriched retranslations by Boehm — a 2019 retranslation of his 1990 *Malina* — and by Filkins, who expanded his 1994 poetry collection *Songs in Flight* into the 2006 volume *Darkness Spoken*. In 1999, Filkins also published *The Book of Franza and Requiem for Fanny Goldmann*, a translation of two novel drafts unfinished at the time of Bachmann's death.

The question of how to translate Ingeborg Bachmann's works has divided anglophone translators and scholars. When academics critiqued translatorial choices, even attributing the absence of Bachmann's prose from the anglophone literary canon to alleged translation errors, reviewers followed suit.[1] Historically, the fear that an 'inaccurate' translation will misrepresent the source text's 'essence' and become the final word on a foreign author is not unfounded.[2]

---

[1] Karen Achberger, 'Senza Pedale: Metaphors of Female Silence in *Malina*', in *'If we had the word': Ingeborg Bachmann: Views and Reviews*, ed. by Gisela Brinker-Gabler and Marcus Zisselsberger (Ariadne Press, 2004), pp. 150–69 (pp. 155, 163); Lilian Friedberg, '"A Time Yet to Come...": Translation and Historical Representation in Ingeborg Bachmann's Poem "Night Flight/Nachtflug"', *The German Quarterly*, 74. 2 (2001), pp. 148–63. See also reviews of Ingeborg Bachmann and Peter Filkins, *Darkness Spoken: Collected Poems of Ingeborg Bachmann* (2005) by Brían Hanrahan, *Harvard Review*, 32 (2007), pp. 162–64 and by Sara Lennox in *Women's Review of Books*, 24.5 (2007), pp. 26–28, as well as reviews of Ingeborg Bachmann and Peter Filkins, *The Book of Franza and Requiem for Fanny Goldmann* (1999) by Gabriele Annan, *New York Review of Books*, 47.5 (2000), p. 42 and by Suzanne Ruta, *New York Times Book Review*, 24 October 1999, 27, and Marjorie Perloff's review of Ingeborg Bachmann and Peter Filkins, *Songs in Flight* (1994), *Denver Quarterly*, 30.2 (1995), pp. 116–24.

[2] An often-vilified case in point is the first English translation of Simone de Beauvoir's *Le Deuxième Sexe* by Howard M. Parshley. Toril Moi charged Parshley's rendition with 'philosophical incompetence' that resulted in a text 'damaging to Beauvoir's intellectual reputation in particular and to the reputation of feminist philosophy in general' (Toril Moi, 'While We Wait: The English Translation of the Second Sex', *Signs: Journal of Women in Culture and Society*, 27.4 (2002), pp. 1005–35 (p. 1007)).

Austrian Studies 32 (2024), doi:10.1353/aus.00009, pp. 120–35
© Modern Humanities Research Association 2024

Scholars working in the field of Translation Studies, in particular Antoine Berman and Lawrence Venuti, have linked a work's canonicity in the target culture to the quality of its translation, while more recently, Kaisa Koskinen and Outi Paloposki noted that retranslation can facilitate a work's canonical status.[3] By highlighting new meanings in the original, retranslations situate the source text to attain permanent status within the target culture.[4]

This article compares Philip Boehm's 2019 retranslation of *Malina* against his first English rendition of Bachmann's novel, published in 1990.[5] The two texts illustrate an evolution in Boehm's approach to translating and reflect the shifts in how Bachmann's oeuvre has been read. The individual and collective factors produce target texts that are equivalent to the source text in qualitatively different ways. I follow key aspects of Bachmann's novel in search of segments where the target texts diverge in semantics, form and effect, correspondences that are frequently, though not always, concomitant. Throughout this article, I refer to the translator's habitus, a notion inspired by Pierre Bourdieu and advanced by Daniel Simeoni and Jean-Marc Gouanvic,[6] which roughly encompasses the three determinants of the translator's actions previously proposed by Berman: the translator's position, project and horizon.[7]

Among the plentiful strands of Bachmann scholarship, Karen Achberger, Sara Lennox and Malcolm Spencer consider her works vis-à-vis the Austrian philosophical and literary tradition. Hans Höller and Kurt Bartsch highlight Bachmann's historical commentary on postwar Austria. Sigrid Weigel and Elfriede Jelinek approach the author as a protofeminist writer. The long-anticipated, monumental Salzburg edition, planned as over thirty volumes, began appearing in 2017 and is projected to continue through 2029. It will include previously inaccessible texts from Bachmann's estate, alongside titles published in her lifetime. The series is creating a regenerative momentum for Bachmann scholarship and promises to expand the corpus of translations.

---

[3] Antoine Berman, *Toward a Translation Criticism: John Donne*, trans. by Françoise Massardier-Kenney (Kent State University Press, 2009), p. 43; Kaisa Koskinen and Outi Paloposki, 'Retranslation', in *Handbook of Translation Studies*, ed. by Yves Gambier and Luc Van Doorslaer, 5 vols (John Benjamins, 2010), I, pp. 294–98 (p. 294).

[4] Lawrence Venuti, 'Retranslations: The Creation of Value', in *Translation and Culture*, ed. by Katherine M. Faull (Bucknell University Press, 2004), pp. 25–38 (p. 27).

[5] *Malina*, trans. by Philip Boehm (Holmes & Meier, 1990) [henceforth 'MB 1990']; *Malina*, trans. by Philip Boehm (Penguin Modern Classics, 2019) [henceforth 'MB 2019']. The term 'retranslation' typically covers both renderings of the same source text by various translators and subsequent versions penned by the same translator.

[6] Daniel Simeoni, 'The Pivotal Status of the Translator's Habitus', *Target: International Journal of Translation Studies*, 10 (1998), pp. 1–39; Jean-Marc Gouanvic, 'A Bourdieusian Theory of Translation, or the Coincidence of Practical Instances Field, "Habitus", Capital and "Illusio"', *The Translator*, 11.2 (2005), pp. 147–66.

[7] Antoine Berman, *Toward a Translation Criticism: John Donne*, trans. by Françoise Massardier-Kenney (Kent State University Press, 2009), pp. 58–66.

The evolution of Boehm's two *Malina* translations is noticeably intertwined with advances in Bachmann scholarship. Stylistic differences also reflect how Boehm has come to balance the two vectors of translation: to produce a text acceptable in the target culture while providing an adequate rendering of the source. Compared to his first translation, Boehm's revision favours adequacy and abides by linguistic features of Bachmann's narrative that do not conform to English style. Still, Boehm recasts *Malina* in contemporary idiom, masterfully achieving acceptability, free of the Germanic syntax that at times unsettled his earlier text. He is attuned to the narrator's female voice and the novel's feminist aesthetic, sensitive to the networks of signification and well versed in Bachmann scholarship.

My comparative analysis is indebted to Descriptive Translation Studies (DTS), whose proponents, Theo Hermans, Andre Lefevere and Lawrence Venuti, demonstrate how shifts that occur in translation tell stories of socio-cultural pressure points. DTS has successfully asserted that translations are beholden, not to absolutes, but to perspectives. But translating is just as much an individual project. I am interested in discovering how the transindividual norms and singular considerations come together to effect equivalence. Most conducive to this path of inquiry is the hermeneutic model of analysis put forward by Antoine Berman, which considers the translator's place vis-à-vis the translation field, the purpose of the project, and horizon, or positionality.

In Bachmann's short stories, the novel *Malina* and her *Todesarten* [Death styles] drafts, broader aesthetic and ideological themes — the Austrian intellectual tradition, the legacy of European modernism and second-wave feminism — form a backdrop against which specific historical traumas play out. Bachmann's formative years were first marred by Austro-German fascism. Her university studies and early professional steps were then marked by an intense re-education of Austrians in the American mould during the First Cold War. Postwar American sociology, in particular Karl Mannheim's 1940 volume *Man and Society in an Age of Reconstruction*, psychologized and individualized economic and political discord. Those imported theories offered Austrians a respite from the previous two decades when state doctrines dictated public and personal lives, first under the Nazi rule, then through a token de-Nazification.

Sara Lennox calls attention to parallels between the protagonists of Bachmann's *Simultan* [*Three Paths to the Lake*] stories, whose life worlds are steeped in what Zygmunt Bauman diagnoses as liquid modernity.[8] This affinity also enriches my own reading of *Malina*. In his eponymous 2000 study, Bauman scrutinizes the profound isolation characteristic of late-capitalist societies that have retreated from communal bonds. His writings critique capitalism for

---

[8] Sara Lennox, 'Bachmanns "Wienerinnen" im Zeitalter der Globalisierung: *Simultan* und Zygmunt Baumans *Flüchtige Moderne*', in *Topographien einer Künstlerpersönlichkeit: Neue Annäherungen an das Werk Ingeborg Bachmanns*, ed. by Robert Pichl and Barbara Agnese (Königshausen & Neumann, 2009), pp. 189–98.

redirecting our demands for social change to individual, biographical solutions. In Bachmann's prose, mental events serve to express social ills, thus supplying literary evidence for the sociologist's later theories.

Since the 1950s, Bachmann's works had denounced the political arrangements of the postwar years and laid bare their moral consequences. As Austria reinvented itself as first victim of the Nazis, the concealed fascist past spread its rot to all societal structures. In her fiction, the crimes perpetrated under Hitler's rule re-emerged as a subliminal terror precisely because they had never been admitted. Amid the self-congratulatory economic recovery, Bachmann challenged the privatization of social issues, often casting women as archetypal victims of the *Virus Verbrechen* (TKA, II, p. 71) [the virus of crime]. Her protagonists bore the mental imprints of the Austrian cover-up.

In a 1971 interview, Bachmann articulated a morally charged linguistic standard she set for literature: to 'write to smithereens' (*zerschreiben*) the language of prefabricated phrases (GuI, p. 84). Her poems, essays, and much of her fiction proceed with the work of language renewal, adding a layer of difficulty to the work of translating *Malina* into a consonant voice.

It fell to Bachmann's poems to create inroads for the writer's entry into the English canon. In contrast to fiction, anthologies and literary magazines render the networks of distribution for poetry more accessible. Thirty years ago, John Guillory argued in *Cultural Capital* that canon formation should be decoupled from the restrictive access networks. Since then, educational and cultural institutions have yielded some power to independent magazines and literary blogs. Today, the canon of contemporary world literature shifts continuously, due to 'the immense number of individual selections, by critics, literary historians, writers, teachers, and literary bloggers, that combine to make works canonical over the years'.[9] This very mutability opens possibilities for Bachmann's late entry into English-language syllabi and bookstores.

II

Can the quest for a perfect translation ever end? Berman optimistically lines up subsequent retranslations on a path towards a 'great translation' — one as enduring as the original itself.[10] His retranslation hypothesis (RT) posits that first translations hover closer to the source text in style and register. Subject to decay over time, they contrast with successive translations, which come nearer to the original's spirit. With little empirical evidence to support Berman's teleological outlook on retranslations,[11] its practicality is also in question: if

[9] Mads Rosendahl Thomsen, *Mapping World Literature: International Canonization and Transnational Literatures* (Continuum, 2008), p. 55.
[10] Antoine Berman, *Toward a Translation Criticism: John Donne*, trans. by Françoise Massardier-Kenney (Kent State University Press, 2009), p. 30.
[11] Kris Peeters and Piet Van Poucke summarize the arguments against RT in 'Retranslation,

reiterative translation is needed to recover the source text in full, what single reader is likely to tackle the totality of a foreign novel's renditions?

As outlined above, Bachmann's only finished novel, *Malina* (1971), was twice translated by Philip Boehm, first in 1990, and again in 2019. That both English versions of *Malina* were penned by the same translator presents an exciting opportunity: to examine whether Boehm's revisions might correlate with fresh directions in Bachmann scholarship, and to trace how the ambient doxas of the 1980s and the 2010s bear out linguistically in his texts. Lastly, why not turn the lens on the translator? Given that Boehm's original rendition was the first of his translation projects,[12] we can peek at the evolution of his craft. These queries align with Berman's three determinants of translation: translational position (a compromise between individual approaches and translation norms), the project or translator's purpose, and their horizon — those particular interpretative parameters brought to the original.

Philip Boehm is a playwright, theatre director and a prize-winning translator of Austrian and Polish literature. His retranslation of *Malina* attends tenaciously to Bachmann's dense intertextuality and equips the anglophone reader to partake fully in the novel's diegetic universe. To anchor the text within its geographic and linguistic milieu, the first translation included a map of Vienna and glossed the excess of foreign phrases, something which the retranslation foregoes, given that today's readers 'can turn to the Internet to indulge their curiosity' (MB 2019, p. xiii).

A side-by-side reading of the two English versions of *Malina* reveals changes in linguistic usage and the overall practice of reading and translating: since the publication of Boehm's first translation, feminist and postcolonial approaches have become interpretative staples. Additionally, one feminist translator has permanently rewritten the norm for translating Bachmann: after Lilian Friedberg's anthology *Last Living Words: The Ingeborg Bachmann Reader* (2005), no translator can sidestep the Austrian author's *écriture féminine*.

Boehm's 1990 and 2019 translations diverge in prosody, punctuation, syntax, word choice, and, more consequentially, in how consistently they recreate the network of signification that underlies Bachmann's novel. Both versions honour the novel's discursive roots in the Austrian intellectual tradition and give voice to Bachmann's horror at the enduring presence of fascism. In a significant departure from 1990, the 2019 retranslation fully leans into the novel's gendered writing, achieving stronger correspondence in semantics, form and effect. As

Thirty-Odd Years after Berman', *PARALLÈLES*, 35 (2023), pp. 3–27 (p. 4).
[12] Boehm offered this light-hearted look at his translation career: 'I got into translation by complete chance. I'm not trained as a translator. [...] A friend in New York told me they were looking for someone to translate Ingeborg Bachmann's *Malina*. It sounded like something I could do [...], so I submitted a sample and, lo and behold, they chose it.' Jennifer-Naomi Hofmann, 'Translation as Activism: An Interview with Philip Boehm', *Literary Hub*, 6 March 2017 <https://www.lithub.com/translation-as-activism-an-interview-with-philip-boehm/> [accessed 25 July 2024].

expected, stylistic transformations have occurred as well: the 2019 *Malina* unfolds in contemporary idiom. At the same time, it returns to Bachmann's punctuation and sentence length as well as echoing the rhythm of the original phrasings and passages. The resulting text reads at a tempo that closely reflects the original's first-person breathless narration as the plot free-falls towards its conclusion.

Bachmann's quintessentially Austrian preoccupation with language, for which Hugo von Hofmannsthal's 'Chandos Brief' [Chandos Letter] set the stage in 1902, presents a conundrum for her anglophone translators. Malcolm Spencer's study *In the Shadow of Empire* convincingly explicates the trope of linguistic crisis in works by Robert Musil, Joseph Roth and Bachmann as both universally modernist and distinctly Austrian. Yet Bachmann's approach to language evolved with her poetological transition as well (HB2020, pp. 299–301). In this respect, her distrust of language resembles that of Zygmunt Bauman, whose *Modernity and Ambivalence* made us wary of all manners of social engineering. For Bachmann, a writer's task is to subvert conventionalized language and so her linguistic practice aims to 'defamiliarize the familiar',[13] the task Bauman would later set for sociology.

Bachmann dissects language and subjects her protagonists to linguistic dissolution. Whether in poetry, prose, or essays, her writing relies on a range of word root permutations and intricate structural repetitions, which Douglas Robertson captured in the categories of anaphora, homoioteleuton and chiasmus.[14] When her narrators compulsively turn over the core of a word, those iterations reflect the author's insistence that words must be found out. Such stylistic practice is challenging to mirror, and Venuti's classic, *The Translator's Invisibility*, helps explain why the difficulty is magnified in English. Quoting Charles Bernstein, Venuti argues that the authority of 'plain styles' in English, the assumption that coherence equals 'mannered and refined speaking',[15] requires that translations cleave to transparency.[16] As the two *Malina* translations demonstrate, it takes much skill and reflective practice to match Bachmann's stylistic process. In 1990, Boehm's first *Malina* smoothed the novel's lexis, erring on the side of a fluent rendering. In the following section, the unnamed first-person narrator tells Malina she spent years repressing a memory of a car crash:

---

[13] Zygmunt Bauman, *Thinking Sociologically* (John Wiley & Sons, 2001), p. 10.

[14] Douglas Robertson, 'Untranslated: Frankfurter Vorlesungen by Ingeborg Bachmann', *minor literature(s)*, 19 January 2018 <https://www.minorliteratures.com/2018/01/19/untranslated-frankfurter-vorlesungen-by-ingeborg-bachmann-douglas-robertson/> [accessed 25 July 2024].

[15] Charles Bernstein, 'Writing and Method', in *Content's Dream: Essays, 1975–1984* (Sun & Moon, 1986), pp. 217–38 (pp. 223–24).

[16] Lawrence Venuti, *The Translator's Invisibility: A History of Translation* (Routledge, 1995), pp. 5–6.

> Malina: Was hast du in den Jahren danach erreicht?
> Ich: (legato) Nichts. Zuerst nichts. Dann habe ich angefangen, die Jahre abzutragen. [...] In der Hauptsache aber eine Fälschung. Ich war ganz verfälscht, man hat mir falsche Papiere in die Hand gedrückt, hat mich deportiert dahin und dorthin, dann wieder angestellt zum Danebensitzen, zum Zustimmen, wo ich früher nie zugestimmt hätte, zum Bestätigen, zum Rechtgeben. Es waren lauter mir völlig fremde Denkweisen, die ich hätte nachahmen müssen. Am Ende war ich eine einzige Fälschung [...]. (W, III, p. 297)

Boehm's 1990 *Malina* obscured the maze Bachmann fashioned out of *falsch*, turning to synonyms ('deceit', 'fake', 'counterfeit', 'falsification'). The changes, immediately apparent, can also be quantified via a stylometric calculation of type–token ratio:

> Malina: What did you achieve in the years afterward?
> Me: (legato) Nothing. At first nothing. Then I started clearing away the years. [...] But mostly a deceit. I was a complete fake, I was given counterfeit papers, deported here and there, then reemployed just to sit by, to agree where I had never agreed before, to confirm, condone, justify. I was surrounded by ways of thought I had to imitate although they were completely foreign to me. In the end I was one single falsification [...] (MB 1990, pp. 196–97)

In a happy contrast with his original translation, in 2019, Boehm hews close, attentively conveying Bachmann's net of *Fälschung, falsch, verfälscht*, as 'falsification', 'false', and the alliterating 'fake'. The anaphoric mirrors of 'confirm', 'consent' and 'concede' further evoke the features of Bachmann's style, while 'one big fake' taps into the contemporary US vernacular:

> Malina: What did you achieve in the years afterward?
> Me: (legato) Nothing. At first nothing. Then I started clearing away the years. [...] But mostly, falsification. I was a complete fake, I was handed false papers, deported hither and yon, then reemployed just to sit by, to agree where I had never agreed before, to confirm, consent, concede. I was surrounded by ways of thought I had to imitate although they were completely alien to me. In the end I was one big fake [...]. (MB 2019, p. 248)

Assuming variations on *falsch* as occurrences of the same lemma, or type, the lemma–token ratio differs only slightly between the three texts: for the source passage, it is 64.93%, increasing in the 1990 translation to 67.46% but dropping in the 2019 revision to 65.85%, in a closer match to the original. The calculations help convey that even statistically insignificant stylistic shifts occurring in translation can alter the aesthetics of the original work. Here, a mix of tools borrowed from corpus-based translation studies and traditional close reading can illuminate the inner working of the source text as well.[17]

---

[17] For a recent example of such mixed methodology, see Matt Erlin, Douglas Knox and Stephen Pentecost, 'Multi-Retranslation and Cultural Variation: The Case of Franz Kafka',

The revisions Boehm implements as an experienced translator suggest that his hermeneutic approach builds from 'slow reading', advocated by Terry Eagelton after Nietzsche, his eye on the shape of sentences and the sounds and rhythms of Bachmann's prose.

In *Madness and Civilization*, Foucault described 'mad discourse' as language devalued and excluded for not conforming to the normative. *Malina* simultaneously thematizes and flaunts women's omission from speech by forcing the reader to follow an apparently deranged narrator. The novel's first sentence immediately submerges the German-language reader in a chaotic interior monologue:

> Nur die Zeitangabe mußte ich mir lange überlegen, denn es ist mir fast unmöglich, 'heute' zu sagen, obwohl man jeden Tag 'heute' sagt, ja, sagen muß, aber wenn mir etwa Leute mitteilen, was sie heute vorhaben — um von morgen ganz zu schweigen — ,bekomme ich nicht, wie man oft meint, einen abwesenden Blick, sondern einen sehr aufmerksamen, vor Verlegenheit, so hoffnungslos ist meine Beziehung zu 'heute', denn durch dieses Heute kann ich nur in höchster Angst und fliegender Eile kommen und davon schreiben, oder nur sagen, in dieser höchsten Angst, was sich zuträgt, denn vernichten müßte man es sofort, was über Heute geschrieben wird, wie man die wirklichen Briefe zerreißt, zerknüllt, nicht beendet, nicht abschickt, weil sie von heute sind und weil sie in keinem Heute mehr ankommen werden. (W, III, p. 12)

While the revised translation mostly follows the original punctuation and paragraph structure, here, as in the first translation, Boehm gives his readers a chance to ease into *Malina*'s 'mad discourse', sectioning off the paragraph-long sentence into five:

> But I had to think long and hard about the Time, since 'today' is an impossible word for me, even though I hear it daily; you can't escape it. When people start telling me what they have planned for today — not to mention tomorrow — I get confused. My relationship with 'today' is so bad that many people often mistake extreme attentiveness for an absent-minded gaze. This Today sends me flying into the utmost anxiety and the greatest haste, so that I can only write about it, or at best report whatever's going on. Actually, anything written about Today should be destroyed immediately, just like all real letters are crumpled or torn up, unfinished and unmailed, all because they were written, but cannot arrive, 'today'. (MB 2019, p. 4)

In other instances, however, Boehm's retranslation of *Malina* restores the original punctuation and refrains from controlling the run-on paragraphs. The translator has come to realize that Bachmann's syntax, a challenge even for the source text readers, must visually match the harried interior monologue. The 1990 project often tamed the novel's sentence structure and punctuation by breaking up long sentences and replacing commas with semicolons. In

Target, 35.2 (2023), pp. 215–41.

contrast, the second rendition lets the flood of associative monologue stand. Boehm's theatre work motivates him to recreate how the voice sounds and moves. Rhythmic phrases, such as 'in höchster Angst und fliegender Eile' (W, III, pp. 12, 80, 149, 329), return in English in a similarly syncopated, breathless cadence: 'in the utmost anxiety, in the greatest haste' (MB 2019, pp. 4, 61, 121, 274–75) replacing the earlier 'in tremendous haste and anxiety' (MB 1990, pp. 3, 48, 95, 218).

III

In *Malina*, the themes of violence, patriarchy and fascism converge in the leitmotif of a 'verschwiegene Erinnerung' [suppressed memory]. Evocative of the Freudian 'motivated forgetting', the phrase is first foreshadowed in the prologue, signalling the narrator's moral imperative — to recover and disclose the memory. Presumably, she either witnessed or was aware of murders, but has suppressed the unspeakable memory. When pressed by her alter ego Malina, she insists something interferes with her memory, preventing her from naming the perpetrator.

The noun *Erinnerung* denotes both a particular memory and the faculty of remembering. Metaphorically and semantically, the past participle *verschwiegen* implicates the narrator and all Austrians alike: they may hide behind the pernicious 'first victim' lie, but they abetted the crimes. With increasing regularity, the phrase re-emerges throughout each of the three chapters. *Malina*'s conflicted narrator feels compelled to reveal the suppressed knowledge, but heeds the commandment to stay silent:

> Ich muß erzählen. Ich werde erzählen. Es gibt nichts mehr, was mich in meiner Erinnerung stört. [...] Wenn meine Erinnerung aber nur die gewöhnlichen Erinnerungen meinte, Zurückliegendes, Abgelebtes, Verlassenes, dann bin ich noch weit, sehr weit von der verschwiegenen Erinnerung, in der mich nichts mehr stören darf. (W III, 23)

Here, as in Boehm's first translation, this crucial motif is disassembled into synonyms:

> I must talk. I will talk. There's nothing more to disturb my reminiscing. [...] However, if my memory only entails the usual recollections, remote, decrepit, abandoned, then I'm still far away, very far away from the silent reminiscence where nothing more can upset me. (MB 2019, p. 13)

As the target text floats three equivalents for *die verschwiegene Erinnerung*, alternating between reminiscing, memory and recollections, the translation refracts a variety of linguistic possibilities in front of the reader. The aesthetic pleasure comes with a downside: the translation passes over an all-important theme to which Bachmann's text returns throughout. Boehm's rendering effectively cuts the through-line which carefully linked past trauma and the protagonist's final disappearance into a crack in the wall. The above passage makes visible how broadly Berman's translation determinants of position, project and horizon overlap. Boehm's positionality dictates that he adhere to the norms of English and add synonyms. Perhaps the purpose of his project prompts the stylistic shifts too. For Bachmann's only finished novel can attain a spot in the canon of literature in translation more easily if some of the language can be made less relentlessly circular, the style more 'plain'. Though Boehm is otherwise reliably tuned to Bachmann's political critique, here, even the translator's horizon colludes to obscure the structural web of signification. In linguistic terms, the layers of equivalence interlink, so that adjustments to style undermine correspondence in meaning as well.

The greats of hermeneutically based translation theory, Benjamin, Nabokov and Berman, put much faith in the letter to restore the original's signifying process. Thus it is no surprise that they hold deviations from linguistic layer to result in a blurring of the network of meaning. Here, the linguistically oriented DTS offers a contrasting perspective: since equivalence is subjective, Gideon Toury asserts that 'features are retained and reconstructed in target language material, not because they are important in any inherent sense, but because they are assigned importance'.[18]

That Boehm lost sight of the foundational signifier — *verschwiegene Erinnerung* — shines a light on the complex nature of translation. Even a masterful target text will be caught in a discrepancy with a comprehensive interpretative project. But given that a translator's work rests on a critical interpretation of the source text, Berman recommends studying the translation product first as an equal text of independent integrity. Any gaps must be viewed in consideration of the work achieved by the entire text, since what 'appear[s] as discordant [...] is the defectiveness inherent in the act of translation'.[19] In sum, good translations deserve the same magnanimity we extend to all great texts, *Malina* included: an imperfect phrase, an exasperating passage, or uneven pacing cannot diminish our aesthetic delight.

The equation between patriarchy and socially condoned violence makes up a key ideological proposition of Bachmann's *Todesarten* cycle, hailed by Elfriede Jelinek as Bachmann's lasting contribution to German postwar literature.[20] Terror figures in the memory and dreams of *Malina*'s female narrator more and more frequently. In her world, '[e]s ist immer Krieg' (W, III, p. 236) [it is always war]. The spectre of violence fills the dreams that constitute the middle chapter 'Der dritte Mann'[The Third Man]. As Christine Steinhoff has shown, those

---

[18] Gideon Toury, *Descriptive Translation Studies — and Beyond* (John Benjamins, 1995), p. 12.

[19] Antoine Berman, *Toward a Translation Criticism: John Donne*, trans. by Françoise Massardier-Kenney (Kent State University Press, 2009), p. 69.

[20] Elfriede Jelinek, 'Der Krieg mit anderen Mitteln', in *'Kein objektives Urteil — nur ein lebendiges': Texte zum Werk von Ingeborg Bachmann*, ed. by Christine Koschel and Inge von Weidenbaum (Piper, 1989), pp. 311–19.

nightmares are the only space where the protagonist breaks an internalized order of silence. Through her nightmares, she can remember the unsayable truth, which is otherwise locked away within the suppressed memory.[21]

Boehm's 2019 *Malina* revisits those dark spots to convey more fully the narrator's mental entrapment within a menacing world. She distorts words so they become runaway triggers: using a 'Telefonzelle' [phone booth] brings on a panic attack as the narrator shortens the word to a 'Zelle' [prison cell]:

> ich muß telefonieren, aber ich telefoniere gar nicht gern von Bahnhöfen, von Telefonzellen oder von Postämtern aus. Aus Zellen schon gar nicht. Ich muß einmal in einem Gefängnis gewesen sein, ich kann nicht von einer Zelle aus telefonieren [...]. Ich telefoniere, vor Platzangst schwitzend, aus einer Zelle vom Westbahnhof. Es darf mir hier nicht passieren, ich werde ja wahnsinnig, es darf mir nicht in einer Zelle passieren. (W, III, p. 176)

Here, the 1990 translation simply concluded with 'I'll go crazy, it can't happen to me in a phone booth' (MB 1990, p. 110), but the revision articulates the connotations of 'Zelle': 'I'm going crazy, it can't happen to me in a booth like a cell' (MB 2019, p. 139). In the same chapter, a catalogue cover suddenly reads 'Sommermorde' [summer murders] instead of 'Sommermoden' [summer styles], foretelling a new nightmare sequence, in which '[d]ie neuen Wintermorde sind angekommen, sie werden schon in den wichtigsten Mordhäusern vorgeführt' (W, III, p. 209). Both translations convey 'Sommermoden' as 'Summer Fashion Exhibition' and 'Sommermorde' as 'Summer Fashion Execution'. But while the 1990 text only partly continues the Freudian slip: 'The winter fashion executions showing the latest designs are on display in all the important fashion houses' (MB 1990, p. 137), the retranslation carries on. Boehm extends the distortion into 'all the important execution houses' (MB 2019, pp. 172–73), staying close to the lingo of fashion commerce. In the same chapter, news headlines feed into the narrator's fears, revealing an unspoken conspiracy behind a string of seemingly coincidental deaths. Men murder women:

> In den Zeitungen stehen oft diese gräßlichen Nachrichten. In Pötzleinsdorf, in den Praterauen, im Wienerwald, an jeder Peripherie ist eine Frau ermordet worden, stranguliert — mir ist das ja auch beinahe geschehen, aber nicht an der Peripherie — ,erdrosselt von einem brutalen Individuum, und ich denke mir dann immer: das könntest du sein, das wirst du sein. Unbekannte von unbekanntem Täter ermordet. (W, III, p. 278)

Bachmann's unnamed narrator is semantically linked to these anonymous fatalities since she habitually signs her correspondence as 'Eine Unbekannte' [an unknown woman]. A letter she addresses to a man who had forced her into a sexual encounter (W, III, p. 107) first foreshadows the theme of sexual violence. In the passage above, Boehm's 1990 translation removed the gender

---

[21] Christine Steinhoff, *Ingeborg Bachmanns Poetologie des Traumes* (Königshausen & Neumann, 2008), p. 205.

marker, ending the paragraph with 'Strangers murdered by strangers' (MB 1990, p. 183). While the succinct phrasing flowed well and conveyed how we use language to shrug off random violence, it frustrated Bachmann's gender critique. By effacing gender identities of the victims (women), and their killers (men), the English line excised the causality between patriarchal power and violence that Bachmann's narratives consistently foreground. Boehm's 2019 version reinserts gender markers:

> The news is often filled with such ghastly reports. In Pötzleinsdorf, at the Prater, in the Vienna Woods, in every outskirt of the city a woman has been murdered, strangled — it almost happened to me, too, but not in the outskirts — strangled by some brutal individual, and then I always think to myself: that could be you, that will be you. An unknown woman murdered by some unknown man. (MB 2019, p. 231)

Three decades passed between Boehm's first and second *Malina*, bringing change to translation norms, social discourses and personal circumstance alike. At the time of his initial project, Boehm lived in Poland and consulted Sławomir Błaut's 1975 rendering into Polish. Błaut's *Malina*, published just four years after the original, was a 'hot translation', a status which in Translation Studies comes with some liability. Contemporaneous translations help share in the momentum of an author's popularity. However, the interpretative frameworks of fresh literary works are barely articulated as the text's reputation is still to be worked out.[22] In particular, Błaut's otherwise acclaimed Polish rendering of *Malina* systematically undermined Bachmann's feminist messaging. Perhaps he was mirroring the initially negative reviews *Malina* had received in West Germany from the likes of Marcel Reich-Ranicki and Helmut Heißenbüttel. His changes also fell in lockstep with Poland's brand of communist-Catholic patriarchy. Boehm mentions that he turned to the Polish translation 'as more of a decoding device [...] that would sometimes spark an idea in English'.[23] Although Bachmann's denouncement of patriarchy had been highlighted by critics by the late 1980s,[24] Błaut's influence may have affected the English translator's horizon.

---

[22] See, for example, Isabelle Vanderschelden, 'Why Retranslate the French Classics? The Impact of Retranslation on Quality', in *On Translating French Literature and Film II*, ed. by Myriam Salama-Carr (Rodopi, 2000), pp. 1–18 (pp. 8–10).
[23] Ewa Siwak, 'Transparent, Fluent, Readable: Ingeborg Bachmann's Prose in English', *Journal of Austrian Studies*, 51 (2018), pp. 47–90 (p. 76).
[24] Most significant here are Elfriede Jelinek's seminal 1983 essay 'Der Krieg mit anderen Mitteln' (previously mentioned in n. 20) as well as the freshly published monographs by Kurt Bartsch, Hans Höller and Peter Beicken.

IV

Does the original, stable, unchanging text then stand in opposition to its potentially volatile foreign renditions? On the contrary: when new criticism reinvents an original, it renders existing translations frozen,[25] thus necessitating retranslations. Far from invariant, the source text *Malina* has evolved significantly, moving on from the 'tragic misreception' to historical perspectives, to feminist, and later postcolonial re-evaluations.[26] Although Mark Anderson, Philip Boehm and Peter Filkins have worked closely with the estate executors Heinz and Sheila Bachmann since the 1980s,[27] thanks to fuller access to the writer's published estate we can now map specific language and imagery in Bachmann's published texts to details that emerge from her unsealed papers. After learning from the new critical edition of *Malina* that Bachmann used the German translation of Algernon Blackwood's *The Willows* as a source for her sub-narrative, the tale of the princess of Kagran, Boehm referred to that original in his second translation (MB 2019, p. xiii). Bachmann and Paul Celan's correspondence further illuminates the princess of Kagran story — her beloved perishes in circumstances that evoke the Shoah. The chapter 'Der dritte Mann' draws from the dream diary the author kept when undergoing psychiatric treatment, first published in 2017 in the new Salzburg Bachmann Edition as *Male oscuro*. Along with letters written during her prolonged mental crisis, these sources 'bear compelling connections to the *Todesarten* texts'.[28]

With the newly available material, Boehm was able to repair passages where his first rendition did not recreate the historical or logical contexts with sufficient accuracy. One of those revisions redresses a dream sequence: the protagonist's father usurps the mace on which the narrator had once sworn during her commencement at the University of Vienna. The original passage recycles a doctoral oath: 'und ich will nach bestem Wissen und Gewissen, und mein Wissen niemals und unter keinen Umständen' (W, III, p. 187). Boehm's first translation read 'and I claim according to my best knowledge and on my conscience, and my knowledge never and under no circumstances' (MB 1990, p. 122), somewhat obscuring the reference to an academic ceremony. In 2019, the wording changed to 'and I shall to the best of my knowledge and belief, and never and under no circumstances use my knowledge to [...]' (MB 2019, p. 154).

[25] Sharon Deane-Cox, *Retranslation: Translation, Literature and Reinterpretation* (Bloomsbury, 2014), p. 6.
[26] Karen Achberger, *Understanding Ingeborg Bachmann* (University of South Carolina Press, 1995), pp. 1–11.
[27] Ewa Siwak, 'Transparent, Fluent, Readable: Ingeborg Bachmann's Prose in English', *Journal of Austrian Studies*, 51 (2018), pp. 47–90 (p. 86).
[28] Sharon Weiner, 'The Beetle in Pain: Private Trauma in Ingeborg Bachmann's Malina', *Journal of Austrian Studies*, 53.4 (2020), pp. 1–25 (p. 23); Peter Beicken, 'Ingeborg Bachmanns Leben und Schreiben im Brennpunkt: Die Salzburger Bachmann Edition und neuere Bachmann-Biografien', *German Studies Review*, 42.2 (2019), pp. 353–69 (p. 356).

The revision restores coherence: an anguished narrator struggles under the weight of ethical obligations, still bound by the doctoral pledge she took long ago. The oath is linked here to the narrator's transient victory, as she manages to reclaim the mace from her perpetrator father, putting an end to his mockery of knowledge.

In *Malina*'s final chapter 'Von letzten Dingen' ['Last Things'], the narrator recounts rumours that had circulated in occupied Vienna after the war: 'es gingen damals immer Gerüchte durch Wien, daß es ein Umschlagplatz wäre, daß Menschenhandel getrieben würde, daß, in Teppiche gewickelt, Menschen und Papiere verschwänden, daß jeder, auch ohne es zu wissen, für irgendwelche Seiten tätig wäre' (W, III, p. 260). This image of Cold War Vienna has been etched on our visual memory by Carol Reed's 1949 film *The Third Man*. Joseph McVeigh connects this paragraph to Bachmann's early years in the city, when the black market triumphed, and people vanished in politically motivated abductions. McVeigh suggests that by concluding with the oft-quoted line 'Es war der Anfang einer universellen Prostitution' [It was the beginning of universal prostitution], the author acknowledged that her work for a US-funded radio station Rot-Weiß-Rot had tarnished her too.[29]

In 1990, Boehm rendered 'Umschlagplatz' as a 'loading ramp', according to its standard dictionary definition: 'at that time there were always rumours floating through Vienna that there was a loading ramp, that there was a slave trade' (MB 1990, pp. 171–72). Boehm's 2019 retranslation inserted the German along its English equivalent: 'that there was a loading ramp — an Umschlagplatz — that there was a slave trade' (MB 2019, pp. 216–17). This dual strategy — to foreignize the passage while elaborating on a word, suddenly caused the phrase 'loading ramp' to reverberate with multiple potential meanings.

For readers well versed in the history of the Holocaust and/or those affiliated with Poland, 'Umschlagplatz' immediately calls up a sorrowful *lieu de mémoire*. Immortalized in Roman Polanski's 2002 film *The Pianist*, the Nazi euphemism referenced the Warsaw Ghetto's 'collection point' and loading ramp whence cattle cars transported Jewish families to extermination camps. Other contemporary usage directly connects to Vienna; since the start of the Cold War, the city has served as an espionage hub — also an 'Umschlagplatz'. One could ask whether Bachmann intended these connotations (she may have) or why Boehm added the German 'Umschlagplatz' to its English equivalent. Perhaps he was moved to 'overtranslate' or put additional information in the target text because of his work translating eyewitness accounts from the Warsaw Ghetto, which exposed him to Nazi 'euphemisms to cover up crime'.[30]

But another relevant question emerges as well: what might Boehm's readers

---

[29] Joseph McVeigh, *Ingeborg Bachmanns Wien* (Insel, 2016), pp. 216–18.

[30] Jennifer-Naomi Hofmann, 'Translation as Activism: An Interview with Philip Boehm', *Literary Hub*, 6 March 2017 <https://www.lithub.com/translation-as-activism-an-interview-with-philip-boehm/> [accessed 25 July 2024]

make of this foreignizing choice? With the 'Princess of Kagran' legend Bachmann inserted into her novel upon learning of Celan's suicide, she was paying direct tribute to '[ein] Schmerz, den sie niemals ahnen kann' [a suffering she could never fathom],[31] as it is described in Ruth Beckermann's film *Die Geträumten*. Some readers' horizons will prompt them to believe that Boehm's choice spotlights the work of Holocaust mourning that underpins *Malina*. After all, our permeable interpretative communities incorporate readers who do not reside in monocultures and who draw on corollary linguistic and cultural systems. Translation always charts various paths of resonance, some relevant to our variegated backgrounds or hidden from them. Whether through shared or individual readings, it harbours the potential to expand the receiving culture's field of vision.

V

The past decade has renewed debates about the nature and ethics of translation, yet again questioning our expectations of translation. Emily Apter's *Against World Literature* (2013) built a case against world literature in translation for its mere approximation of the subaltern original. Lawrence Venuti submitted in *Contra Instrumentalism* (2019) that an expectation of equivalence denies the creative force of translation. Matthew Reynolds's 2019 essay 'Prismatic Agon, Prismatic Harmony' stretched the very notion of translation into elusive refractions of the source text that inspired it. Against those voices, Stefan Helgesson stoically reroutes us to the original, not because it is unimpeachable, but simply because the source's key role in its translations cannot be denied.[32] In reading and teaching translated texts, we wish to approach authors on their terms. The singular achievement of the reissued *Malina* is that it produces a target text of its own integrity, without letting go of Bachmann's novel. With his 2019 comprehensive update, Philip Boehm makes significant strides towards capturing Bachmann's proverbially untranslatable prose. His text may well become a canonical rendering or 'great translation'.[33]

Other recent translation projects open up new possibilities to reintroduce this seminal Austrian author and spotlight her relevance to contemporary English readers. Particularly significant here is the volume *Critical Writings of Ingeborg Bachmann* (2021), translated by US Germanists Karen Achberger and Karl Solibakke. This work may succeed in writing Bachmann into the North American canon of criticism. Additionally, in 2026, the publishing house New Directions will commemorate the centennial of the author's birth

---

[31] *Die Geträumten* [The Dreamed Ones], dir. by Ruth Beckermann (Austria, 2016).
[32] Stegan Helgesson, 'The Invariance Effect: A Response to Lawrence Venuti', *Provocations*, 4 (2020), pp. 11–16 (p. 15).
[33] Antoine Berman, *Toward a Translation Criticism: John Donne*, trans. by Françoise Massardier-Kenney (Kent State University Press, 2009), p. 30.

with a joint retranslation of short stories by Peter Filkins and Tess Lewis. Their complementary sensibilities are certain to unbind the limitless signifying energy of Bachmann's works, captivating a new generation of readers.

To paraphrase an appeal to writers Bachmann issued in her Frankfurt lecture 'Literatur als Utopie' ['Literature as Utopia']: we must continue to translate. In the anglophone universe, Bachmann's fate is contingent on translation.

Care (Work) and Female Authorship in Ingeborg Bachmann's *Malina*

ANNA SEETHALER

Literaturhaus München

I

Reading Bachmann from the perspective of today, I would like to propose an interpretation of *Malina* that is connected to a contemporary horizon of experience. This reading would not have been possible during Bachmann's lifetime, because in the fifty years since then, gender theory perspectives in the academic world have evolved considerably, both in sociology and, above all, in literary studies. Today we have the vocabulary to talk about texts differently and thus to view and analyse them in a new way. Although it employs current terminology, my reading nevertheless remains related to the political and social situation of the time in which *Malina* was written. I will explore the relationship between authorship and care (work) and analyse the impact of care on the writing process and the self-conception of female authorship.

Care work has come under increased attention since the global Covid-19 pandemic.[1] In literary studies as in other disciplines, 'care' can provide a useful instrument of analysis. The question of care in the writing process does not only offer a new perspective on the nature of text production, but also places text, authors, readers, editors, and all those who make writing possible, in a relationship with care for the text, the characters, the readers or intertexts. *Malina* was written at a time when the recognition of 'Liebesarbeit [und] Hausarbeit' [labour of love (and) domestic work] first began to be demanded.[2] With 'care' as the object of investigation, and later as a conceptual tool, new readings of Bachmann's novel become possible *avant la lettre*, so to speak.[3] As Sigrid Weigel wrote as early as 1983, in Bachmann's texts we find 'Ideen, die alle

---

[1] See Anne-Christin Kunstmann, 'Care und Corona: Ethische Überlegungen zur gesellschaftlichen Anerkennung der Sorgetätigkeit und der Solidarität mit Sorgenden', *Bundeszentrale für politische Bildung*, 29 October 2020 <https://www.bpb.de/themen/umwelt/bioethik/317593/care-und-corona/> [accessed 26 November 2023].

[2] Gisela Bock and Barbara Duden, 'Arbeit aus Liebe — Liebe als Arbeit: Zur Entstehung der Hausarbeit im Kapitalismus', in *Frauen und Wissenschaft: Beiträge zur Berliner Sommeruniversität für Frauen Juli 1976*, ed. by Gruppe Berliner Dozentinnen (Courage, 1977), pp. 118–219 (p. 121).

[3] Sigrid Weigel, *Ingeborg Bachmann: Hinterlassenschaften unter Wahrung des Briefgeheimnisses* (Zsolnay, 1999), p. 27.

Austrian Studies 32 (2024), doi:10.1353/aus.00010, pp. 136–45

Momente aktueller feministischer Theorie und Literatur vorwegnehmen' [ideas that anticipate all aspects of current feminist theory and literature].[4]

During Bachmann's lifetime, the term 'care work' was not yet in common parlance, as it is today. Even now there is no equivalent in German, only more limiting translations such as *Sorge* [solicitude] or *Zuneigung* [attachment], which is why the English term has entered general usage. In literary studies, 'care' is still neither a widespread object of study nor an established interpretative tool. Within Bachmann research in particular, care (work) has only recently been identified as a conceptual tool by Emily Jeremiah in her 2022 article ' "Keine Zeit zu verlieren": Time and Care in Ingeborg Bachmann's "Das Gebell" and *Das Buch Franza*'.[5] A broader look at 'work' in Bachmann can be found in a study by Christian Däufel from 2013, which examines various types of work in Bachmann's oeuvre from a systematic point of view. Däufel's enumeration focuses largely on common forms of wage labour, however — leaving out unpaid work and work that is not valued as such.[6] My approach considers 'care' from a sociological perspective, drawing on work by Silvia Federici from the 1970s and subsequent research that builds on Federici to give us an overall definition of care work as the basis of a capitalist society.[7] Due to the wide range of forms of care work that exist, I take a closer look at just one type in Bachmann's *Malina*: female self-care. Nowadays, self-care is considered a keyword for direct care of oneself, although it could be argued that it mainly serves to maintain labour power for a capitalist society — as Federici already outlined, raising the question: 'Is the fact that we [women] have to worry about our looks on the job a condition of work or is it the result of female vanity?'[8] Moreover, the product of self-care is a version of the self that is often produced for others, in short, the commodification of the self. Despite all of this, sociology does not clearly define self-care as care work, unlike other fields of activity (housework, cooking or child-rearing).[9] Nevertheless, it is work that requires 'Zeit, materielle Ressourcen, Wissen und Kompetenzen' [time, material resources, knowledge

---

[4] Sigrid Weigel, 'Der schielende Blick: Thesen zur Geschichte weiblicher Schreibpraxis', in *Die Verborgene Frau: Sechs Beiträge zu einer feministischen Literaturwissenschaft*, ed. by Sigrid Weigel and Inge Stephan (Argument-Verlag, 1983), pp. 83–137 (p. 130).

[5] See Emily Jeremiah, ' "Keine Zeit zu verlieren": Time and Care in Ingeborg Bachmann's "Das Gebell" and *Das Buch Franza*', *German Life and Letters*, 75.4 (2022), pp. 540–53.

[6] See Christian Däufel, ' "Nie mehr werd ich arbeiten können." Arbeitswelten als paradigmatische Orte der Gesellschaftskritik im Werk Ingeborg Bachmanns', in *Repräsentationen von Arbeit: Transdisziplinäre Analysen und künstlerische Produktionen*, ed. by Susanna Brogi and others (transcript, 2013), pp. 301–19.

[7] See Silvia Federici, *Wages against Housework* (Power of Women Collective and the Falling Wall Press, 1975); see also Silvia Federici, *Patriarchy of the Wage: Notes on Marx, Gender, and Feminism* (PM Press, 2021); see also Gabriele Winker, *Care Revolution: Schritte in eine solidarische Gesellschaft* (transcript, 2015).

[8] Federici, *Wages against Housework*, p. 7; see also Federici, *Patriarchy of the Wage*, pp. 36–37.

[9] See Winker, *Care Revolution*, pp. 18 and 26.

and competences],[10] and arises from caring for someone, even although the caregiver and the care-receiver are the same person.

II

In her study *Care Revolution* (2015) Gabriele Winker does not specifically refer to the term 'self-care' but defines the phenomenon nevertheless, as the care work a person does, 'um sich selbst zu versorgen und immer wieder neu zu stabilisieren, so dass sie leistungsfähig bleibt und sich als Arbeitskraft verkaufen kann' [to provide for oneself and to stabilize oneself again and again, so that one remains efficient and can sell oneself as a labour force].[11] According to this definition, self-care seems to be about optimizing the self in order to create or regenerate a functioning workforce. In *Malina*, this optimization through self-care can be found in numerous passages throughout the novel, especially in the descriptions of explicit work on the female body aimed at someone else's — men's or society's — expectations. The narrator works on her own body for Ivan, for instance. Among numerous examples, one episode seems to be entirely devoted to self-care. At the end of chapter 1, the first-person narrator fashions herself, her own body, as the (art-)figure of a woman for Ivan:

> Am Graben habe ich mir ein neues Kleid gekauft, ein Hauskleid, das lang ist, für eine Nachmittagsstunde, für ein paar besondere Abende im Haus, ich weiß, für wen, es gefällt mir, weil es weich und lang ist und das viele Zuhausebleiben erklärt, schon heute. Ich möchte aber beim Anprobieren Ivan nicht hier haben, Malina schon gar nicht, ich kann nur, weil Malina nicht da ist, oft in den Spiegel sehen, ich muß mich im Korridor vor dem langen Spiegel mehrmals drehen, meilenweit, klaftertief, himmelhoch, sagenweit entfernt von den Männern. [...] Es entsteht eine Komposition, eine Frau ist zu erschaffen für ein Hauskleid. (TKA, III.1, pp. 447–48)

> [At the Graben I bought myself a new dress, a long casual dress for an hour in the afternoon, for a few special evenings at home, I know for whom, I like it because it's soft and long and means a lot of staying at home even today. However I wouldn't want to have Ivan here while I'm trying it on, even less Malina, and since Malina isn't there I can only cast frequent glances in the mirror, I have to turn around in front of the long mirror in the corridor, miles away, fathoms deep, heavens high, fables removed from the men. [...] The result is a composition, a woman is to be created for a dress.] (MB, pp. 109–10)

Like a composition, a woman is created in front of the mirror. At this point, I would first like to raise the question: for whom? It seems obvious that the composition of the woman is created 'for a dress' (MB, p. 110) which, in turn, is meant to be worn by the narrator herself, 'fables removed from the men'

---

[10] Ibid., p. 26.
[11] Ibid., p. 18.

(MB, p. 109). The sentence 'I wouldn't want to have Ivan here while I'm trying it on' (MB, p. 109) in combination with the earlier scenes when the narrator feels unprepared for Ivan, evokes him as the addressee through the restrictive conjunction 'aber' (TKA, III.1, p. 447) [however]. The presence of Malina seems to be less of a problem for trying on clothes than for looking in the mirror and, with this, at the body itself: 'since Malina isn't there I can only cast frequent glances in the mirror' (MB, p. 109; a more accurate translation would read 'I can only cast frequent glances in the mirror because Malina isn't there'). Schmid-Bortenschlager sees mirror scenes as depicting the 'Problematik der Anpassung an Rollenerwartungen, die von außen an Frauen herangetragen werden' [problem of adapting to role expectations that are imposed on women from the outside].[12] Even though Schmid-Bortenschlager is writing about the mirror scenes in Bachmann's late story collection *Simultan* (1972), her conclusions can also be applied to this mirror scene in *Malina*. One might think self-optimization the right term for this fulfilment of socially prescribed ideas of beauty. I would argue, however, that the term self-care is more appropriate, because the fulfilment of socially prescribed ideas of beauty takes place unconsciously; the narrator is primarily caring for herself by fashioning herself for this dress that she likes so much. Regarding Malina's involvement, I would like to go one step further and claim the following: Malina's disapproval of the 'woman created for a dress' is shown through the fact that the narrator can only look in the mirror when Malina is not present. Looking in the mirror means looking at the body of the 'woman created for a dress' through the work of self-care. Additionally, Malina seems to disapprove of this viewpoint as it is the result of a concept of beauty created by society and represented by Ivan. This reading becomes even clearer in a later scene where Malina asks the narrator 'Was ist schön?' (TKA, III.1, p. 652) ['What's beautiful?'] (MB, p. 254), which will be discussed later.

An indication that the narrator wants to be Ivan's version of an ideal woman, who matches the dress, can be found in the following, in which the narrator defines this process as a 'legend':

> Eine Stunde lang kann ich zeit- und raumlos leben, mit einer tiefen Befriedigung, entführt in eine Legende, wo der Geruch einer Seife, das Prickeln von Gesichtswassern, das Knistern von Wäsche, das Eintauchen von Quasten in die Tiegel, der gedankenvolle Zug mit einem Konturenstift das einzig Wirkliche sind. Es entsteht eine Komposition, eine Frau ist zu erschaffen für ein Hauskleid. Ganz im geheimen wird wieder entworfen, was eine Frau ist, es ist dann etwas von Anbeginn, mit einer Aura für niemand. Es müssen die Haare zwanzigmal gebürstet, die Füße gesalbt und die Zehennägel lackiert werden, es müssen die Haare von den Beinen und unter den Achseln entfernt werden, die Dusche wird an- und ausgemacht,

---

[12] Sigrid Schmid-Bortenschlager, 'Spiegelszenen bei Bachmann: Ansätze einer psychoanalytischen Interpretation', *Modern Austrian Literature*, 18.3–4 (1985), pp. 39–52 (p. 45).

ein Körperpuder wolkt im Badezimmer, es wird in den Spiegel gesehen [...].
(TKA, III.1, p. 448)

[For an hour I can live without time and space, in deep satisfaction, carried
off into a legend, where the aroma of a soap, the prickle of a facial tonic, the
rustle of lingerie, the dipping of puffs into pots of powder, the thoughtful
stroke of a lip liner are the only reality. The result is a composition, a woman
is to be created for a dress. What a woman is is being redesigned in complete
secrecy, it is like a new beginning, with an aura for no one. The hair must
be brushed twenty times, feet anointed and toenails painted, hair removed
from legs and armpits, the shower turned on and off, a cloud of powder
floats in the bathroom, the mirror is consulted (...)] (MB, pp. 109–10)

On the one hand, this 'aura for no one' appears as an equivalent to the woman
who is being created for a dress in the previous passage. In this case, self-care is
self-determined care work, not for somebody else but only for oneself. On the
other hand, through the mention of a 'legend', the cultural — not natural —
justification of this ideal woman becomes evident, and the care work once more
seems to be instrumental self-care. Additionally, in chapter 1, the narrator had
already imagined writing down a legend with the title 'Die Geheimnisse der
Prinzessin von Kagran' (TKA, III.1, pp. 347–48) ['The Mysteries of the Princess
of Kagran'] (MB, p. 47). Herrmann states that this should be read carefully, as
the 'Legende einer Frau, die es nie gegeben hat' (TKA, III.1, p. 347) can be read
in two ways: not only as a legend that has never existed but also as a woman
who has never existed (see HB2020, p. 140). It is especially interesting here that
the English translation predetermines the interpretation by using the pronoun
'who' rather than 'which': 'legend of a woman who never existed' (MB, p. 47).
Moreover, this previously non-existent woman is being created through acts of
self-care and work on the body 'without time and space' and 'in secrecy' — as
is the mysterious Princess of Kagran.

   The motif of creating a woman evokes Ovid's Pygmalion and Galatea.[13]
Pygmalion creates his own ideal partner Galatea, just as the narrator in the text
creates a woman — for a house dress, which, in turn, is intended not only but
primarily for Ivan. Even though the narrator functions as the creator in this
scene, Ivan can be seen as the original producer of the idea, since the narrator
wants to create and maintain this version of herself for him. Ivan produces
this woman by forcing her into autopoiesis, into self-production. The narrator
reflects on the origin of the idea — its authorship, so to speak — elsewhere,
when she describes how the beauty aspired to comes 'in Wellen von Ivan zu
mir' (TKA, III.1, p. 651) ['in waves to me from Ivan'] (MB, p. 253). It is evident
through this that the narrator has internalized the demands of (patriarchal)
society to such an extent that she only perceives herself as beautiful when she

<hr />

[13] See Gerhard Neumann, 'Pygmalion: Metamorphosen des Mythos', in *Pygmalion: Die
Geschichte des Mythos in der abendländischen Kultur*, ed. by Mathias Mayer and Gerhard
Neumann (Rombach, 1997), pp. 11–60 (pp. 15–17).

has created herself according to Ivan's (non-verbal) request. For the narrator does not voluntarily live with these social criteria for women but is persuaded of their importance.

This thesis is supported by the linguistic form of the passage. First, the 'legend' is mentioned, and the narrator speaks actively: '[f]or an hour I can live without time and space' (MB, p. 109). As a next step, this is exactly what happens as the text loses the active narrator and lapses into the passive with '[t]he hair must be brushed[,] painted [and] removed', etc. (MB, p. 110). The suspension of the ego is linguistically emphasized and the process of becoming invisible takes place within the description of self-care — in the end, only Galatea remains. Here, the dialectic of self-care is highlighted yet again. The refashioning of the body is accompanied by a disembodiment and even selflessness that fills the ego with deep satisfaction. This satisfaction seems to emerge from the loss of one's self.

The creation of the 'artwork' itself is presented as a laborious process. In the example above, several tools are mentioned: 'facial tonic', 'puffs' and 'pots of powder' as well as a 'lip liner' (MB, p. 109). In addition, the individual work steps are listed: 'The hair must be brushed twenty times, feet anointed, and toenails painted, hair removed from legs and armpits, the shower turned on and off, a cloud of powder floats in the bathroom, the mirror is consulted' (MB, p. 110). This list of instruments and the step-by-step enumeration of hand movements can almost be seen as a manual for creating an art figure. On the one hand, the enumeration indicates self-care as work that needs to be repeated several times. On the other hand, the explicit enumeration, almost a list, separates these steps from the rest of the novel, as a separate text form. The careful, laborious process is linguistically emphasized through what Mainberger terms as 'Aufzählungen als Sprache des Wissens und der verdichteten Information' [enumerations as a language of knowledge and condensed information].[14]

Paradoxically, a key feature of self-care is that it remains invisible as work. This is made particularly clear in *Malina* through the juxtaposition of the numerous work steps and the result. The composition is created entirely in secret. It is precisely in the estrangement of this mysteriousness that Bachmann's text offers a subversion of self-optimization. This becomes even more obvious in an earlier passage:

> Ivan darf nur das Ergebnis sehen [...] zwischen Aufgießen und Semmelschnittenbähen trage ich die Wimperntusche auf, schminke mir vor Malinas Rasierspiegel die Augen, zupfe mit der Pinzette die Augenbrauen zurecht, und diese Synchronarbeit, die niemand würdigt, ist anstrengender als alle Arbeiten, die ich früher getan habe. Doch erwartet mich der höchste Preis dafür, weil Ivan deswegen schon um sieben Uhr kommt und bis Mitternacht bleibt. (TKA, III.1, p. 375)

---

[14] Sabine Mainberger, *Die Kunst des Aufzählens: Elemente zu einer Poetik des Enumerativen* (De Gruyter, 2003), p. 11.

[Ivan is only allowed to see the result [...] between whisking and toasting the rolls I apply eye shadow and mascara in front of Malina's shaving mirror, pluck my eyebrows to their proper shape, and this synchronized labor which no one appreciates is more strenuous than anything I've ever done before. But for it I will receive the highest reward, since Ivan will come as early as seven and stay until midnight.] (MB, p. 64)

Here, too, the work tools and steps are clearly laid out, through terms such as 'eye shadow', 'mascara' and plucking the eyebrows. However, Ivan is only allowed to see the result — and not the work behind it. It remains a synchronous effort (with cooking also being done at the same time) that no one appreciates or is supposed to see. Moreover, self-care is presented as highly labour-intensive and more strenuous than all other work. In addition to this paradox, the focus on the goal is particularly striking — it is the highest reward, Ivan.

III

There is widespread consensus in Bachmann scholarship that Ivan and Malina are set up as opposites in the text, and that the murder at the end underlines the incompatibility of the two opposites (see HB2020, pp. 131–32). Malina also represents the opposite to Ivan regarding self-care. Thus, as has previously been mentioned: 'since Malina isn't there I can only cast frequent glances in the mirror' (MB, pp. 109–10). In another passage, Malina even seems to want to detach the narrator from the idea of having to portray a certain image: 'Steh auf! sagt Malina, der mich auf dem Boden findet und es ist ernst gemeint. Was redest du da von der Schönheit? Was ist schön?' (TKA, III.1, p. 652) ['Get up! says Malina, who finds me on the floor, and he means it. What are you saying about beauty? What's beautiful?'] (MB, p. 254). Malina's question seems almost a call for emancipation from the ideal of beauty. The narrator herself recognizes this when she tries to get rid of Malina for the sake of the composition: 'Für diesen Abend muß ich Malina loswerden, ich rede ihm etwas ein' (TKA, III.1, p. 676) ['I have to get rid of Malina for this evening, I say something to persuade him'] (MB, p. 269). Only in this way can the narrator undisturbedly design the version of herself that suits Ivan, as shown above.

Following this elaboration on the staging of self-care in the text, further observations can be made regarding the acts of the narrator, encouraged by either Ivan or Malina. In *Malina*, working as a caregiver and working as a writer are presented as incompatible. The narrator maintains a different version of herself for Malina than for Ivan, therefore fuelling the dichotomy between author and caregiver until a clash between the two men at the end allows one to fall by the wayside.

Malina supports the narrator in her writing. Even though he criticizes her texts as too negative, he still talks with her about writing and storytelling (HB2020, p. 135). For instance, the complexity of the writing process is processed together with Malina at the end of the preface to the first chapter, titled 'Die Personen' (TKA, III.1, p. 275) ['The Cast'] (MB, p. 3), which ends with the narrator seemingly speaking to the reader: 'Ich will nicht erzählen, es stört mich alles in meiner Erinnerung' (TKA, III.1, p. 298) ['I don't want to talk, it all upsets me, in my remembering'] (MB, p. 16). The difficulty of telling a story, or in this case writing a novel, is addressed by the narrator right at the beginning of the text. As soon as Malina enters the room, however, he says: 'Noch stört es dich. Noch. Es stört dich aber eine andere Erinnerung' (TKA, III.1, p. 298) ['It still upsets you. Still. But you're upset about a different recollection'] (MB, p. 16). As the pre-chapter anticipates the content of the following three chapters on a meta-level, the emergence of the following story is problematized in a meta-reflection. Since Ivan is introduced right after this scene and a whole chapter is dedicated to him, he could be perceived as the disturbing element. Consequently, in order to eliminate this disturbance, the memory of Ivan is taken up again and concluded through narration in the first chapter. Combined with later scenes in which Malina has been interpreted as a psychoanalyst, the beginning of *Malina* could be read as a narrative therapy in which experiences are described and understood through narration in order to explain and finally transform them (HB2020, p. 133). By contrast, Ivan not only seems to inhibit the Ich's writing but to support the narrator's function as caregiver, as shown above, and thus to affirm the narrator in the role of a housewife or, as Monika Albrecht summarizes: 'das Ich [scheint] in den Alltagssituationen mit Ivan gleichsam einem Drehbuch [zu] folgen, das die Nachkriegszeit für Frauen bereithielt' (HB2020, p. 283) [in everyday situations with Ivan the I seems to follow a script which the postwar era had at the ready for women].

The incompatibility of the versions of the self embodied by the narrator for Ivan and Malina respectively is reinforced through the narrator's efforts to keep the two from meeting: 'Ich lasse auch eine Vorsicht walten, damit keiner dem andern ins Gehege kommt' (TKA, III.1, p. 380) ['I also take care they don't encroach upon each other'] (MB, p. 68). In my reading of the novel, it is a logical conclusion that the text presents it as inevitable that a potential encounter must lead to catastrophe. The staging of care in the novel further serves as a vehicle to portray the precarious incompatibility of being both a writer and a caregiver. The radical solution to this discrepancy presented between author and caregiver will be reassessed below through a care-specific analysis.

IV

I would like to propose a new interpretative approach, building on a thesis of Virginia Woolf and integrating a care-specific reading into the existing series of interpretations of the novel's famous final sentence: 'Es war Mord' (TKA, III.1, p. 695) ['It was murder'] (MB, p. 283). The murder victim is named in the novel: the narrator describes her own death. The murderer and their motive, however, remain unclear. To find an answer for the last two components (murderer and motive), I would like to question the first one (the narrator as victim), drawing on Woolf's conception of the 'Angel in the House'.

In her essay *Professions for Women* (1931), Woolf reflects on women's difficulties in wanting to pursue wage labour. Woolf describes the 'Angel in the House' as a version of a woman who sacrifices herself for her family: the Angel

> was intensely sympathetic. She was immensely charming. She was utterly unselfish. She excelled in the difficult arts of family life. She sacrificed herself daily. [...] [S]he never had a mind or a wish of her own, but preferred to sympathize always with the minds and wishes of others. Above all — I need not say it — she was pure.[15]

Care, as this quotation points out, underlies the characteristics of the Angel. In addition, the aforementioned dialectic of self-care emerges here, also. The Angel appears as selfless as the narrator in *Malina* seems to become through her self-care. Paradoxically, through the work of caring for herself, the narrator loses herself and her individuality. Moreover, the Angel's continuing self-sacrifice for the family is also found in the narrator of Bachmann's novel, when she tries to fulfil the role of a housewife in family life by cooking for Ivan and looking after his children.

In Woolf's essay, it later becomes clear that this Angel hampers a woman in carrying out other forms of labour — in *Malina*, literary labour. In the end, there is no way around murder — if the author wishes to devote herself to literary labour without disturbance, the Angel must be killed: 'Had I not killed her she would have killed me. She would have plucked the heart out of my writing. [...] Killing the Angel in the House was part of the occupation of a woman writer.'[16] For the sake of her writing, Woolf depicts the killing of the 'Angel in the House' as an inevitable event. This is also how I read the murder at the end of Bachmann's novel.

The separation of the narrator into the roles of caregiver for Ivan and writer for Malina reinforces the idea that, from Malina's point of view, Ivan, and the role of the narrator related to Ivan, interfere with narration in a written form. In short, the writer is inhibited by the Angel. Therefore, it is not surprising that Malina, as a (partial) character, is indirectly involved in the destruction of that Angel. Although Malina is not named as the murderer of the narrator, the substitution of the narrator by Malina is introduced earlier in the narrative. When the narrator speaks of having only one life, Malina replies: 'Überlaß es mir' (TKA, III.1, p. 552) ['Leave it to me'] (MB, p. 184).

Towards the end of the narrative, the Ich realizes that the two halves are incompatible: 'Ich habe in Ivan gelebt und ich sterbe in Malina' (TKA, III.1, p. 692) ['I have lived in Ivan and I die in Malina'] (MB, p. 281), which is true

---

[15] Virginia Woolf, 'Professions for Women [1931]', in *Selected Essays*, ed. by David Bradshaw (Oxford University Press, 2008), pp. 140–45 (p. 141).
[16] Ibid., pp. 141–42.

if one thinks of the ideal woman created by self-care. Malina's removal of the remains and his ignorance of the narrator's disappearance can be analysed as an indication for his (co-)guilt in the murder at the end of the novel. When Ivan calls and apparently asks for someone else, Malina answers: 'Nein, gibt es nicht. Hier ist keine Frau' (TKA, III.1, p. 694) ['No, there isn't. There is no woman here'] (MB, p. 282) — or at least, not the woman Ivan is looking for, one would like to add.

In addition to the numerous lines of research on the ending of *Malina*, my reading provides another plausible interpretation of the murder with a focus on Bachmann's literary staging of care (see HB2020, 134). With Woolf's conception of the 'Angel in the House', the murder victim, murderer and motive in Bachmann's novel can be read anew: an ideal woman produced through self-care, an Angel, is murdered in favour of practising the profession of writer.

V

Finally, I would like to go one step further and put forward a poetological perspective, using an example in which care work and literature are juxtaposed: 'Ich lese in einem Buch, bis es acht Uhr wird. Denn das Essen ist bereit, ich bin geschminkt und gekämmt' (TKA, III.1, p. 677) ['I read a book until eight o'clock. Because dinner is all ready, I've put on makeup and combed my hair'] (MB, p. 270). In this quote, the care work — in this case cooking and aspects of self-care — seems to be a prerequisite for the narrator being able to read. The narrator can read in this moment 'because' the care work has been finished beforehand, as the subordinating conjunction emphasizes at this point.

In her novel, Ingeborg Bachmann creates a character who invents an art figure herself. This art figure, however, is none other than the narrator: the creator and the artwork merge into each other. By staging self-care, this observation of one's own self from the outside becomes possible in the first place. The above analysis has shown that this form of work is presented as an obstacle to the activity of a writer. However, Bachmann the author describes the steps of self-care and, above all, the competition between care and writing work as being productive in a literary sense. By processing this tension, Bachmann rejects a specifically male-coded notion of authorship and makes the tension of writing and care work fruitful in creative terms. Finally, it is not by chance that Bachmann's narrator pursues self-care and is carried off into a 'legend' about the mysterious Princess of Kagran, whereby the etymology of the term 'legend' relates to the Latin word *legere*, meaning 'to read'. Here self-care is elevated to another textual level by being associated with a story the narrator is imagining telling. In her description of the two activities — writing and doing self-care — as mutually exclusive, Ingeborg Bachmann not only seems to prove the exact opposite, but transforms this phenomenon into literature by staging it as an inhibitor of literary productivity.

The School of Depth: Ingeborg Bachmann Meets Clarice Lispector

MERCER GREENWALD

Harvard University

Ingeborg Bachmann and Clarice Lispector never met. They did not meet in Italy, where Bachmann wrote *Malina* and Lispector wrote her novel *O lustre* [*The Chandelier*]. Nor did they meet in Switzerland, where Lispector lived for three years and gave birth to her first child, and where Bachmann lived intermittently for five years. Lispector stayed in both Italy and Switzerland just over half a decade before Bachmann. Coincidentally, the two writers also both fell asleep with burning cigarettes that led to housefires: when Ingeborg Bachmann's nightgown caught fire in her Rome apartment in 1973, she was left with third degree burns and passed away soon after. About half a decade earlier in Rio de Janeiro, Lispector's hand was also severely burned in a house fire that left her unable to write for several months. To compound the coincidence, the recurring quotation from Flaubert in Bachmann's novel *Malina* involves a burnt hand: 'Avec ma main brûlée j'écris sur la nature du feu' (W, III, p. 95).[1] Although Bachmann and Lispector never met over the course of their lives, they did meet in the afterlife, in the work of feminist post-structuralist critic Hélène Cixous.

Cixous brings the two writers together in her 1990 series of lectures given at the University of California, Berkeley, titled *Three Steps on the Ladder of Writing*.[2] Cixous describes her project in the lectures as follows:

> When choosing a text I am called: I obey the call of certain texts or I am rejected by others. The texts that call me have different voices. But they all have one voice in common, they all have, with their differences, a certain music I am attuned to, and that's the secret.[3]

Cixous does not compare Bachmann and Lispector directly — rather she compares their music. She describes Lispector's music as 'dry, hard, and severe' like Thomas Bernhard's, while Bachmann's is 'heartrending'.[4] Cixous's use of a musical metaphor here is noteworthy: it suggests that for Cixous, Bachmann's

---

[1] Gustave Flaubert, *Correspondance*, ed. by Jean Bruneau, 4 vols (Gallimard, 1988), II, p. 463.
[2] Hélène Cixous, *Three Steps on the Ladder of Writing* (Columbia University Press, 1994).
[3] Ibid., p. 5.
[4] Ibid.

Austrian Studies 32 (2024), doi:10.1353/aus.00011, pp. 146–58
© Modern Humanities Research Association 2024

and Lispector's prose operates on a plane beyond language. This is certainly the case in 'Undine geht' [Undine Goes], the final story in Bachmann's collection *Das dreißigste Jahr* [*The Thirtieth Year*] (1961), as well as in Lispector's novel *Água Viva* (1973). While Undine's speech is insufficient, the speech of Lispector's narrator is excessive; each narrative voice aims to surpass its own discursive content in its call. Bachmann's text begins with a fiery, accusatory address to humanity 'Ihr Menschen! Ihr Ungeheuer!' ['You humans! You monsters!'] (W, II, pp. 255; TY, p. 171). It is the words of Bachmann's Undine that are insufficient — she must scream them. Later in the story, Undine's scream is transposed into a 'Ruf von weither, die geisterhafte Musik' ['call from afar, the ghostly music'] (W, II, p. 255; TY, p. 173). Here, Undine's address becomes a call merely beckoning in her direction. Undine's call is as *vertont* [set to music] as it is *vertönt* [dying away] and it progressively loses its communicative potential: at the end of the story, it is barely heard. In contrast, the narrative voice of Lispector's *Água Viva* is excessive, endeavouring to communicate beyond its means. The novel begins when two voices merge, in pain and prayer: the first voice is 'o mais escuro uivo humano da dor de separação' ['the darkest human howl of the pain of separation'] and the second is the shout of 'Aleluia' ['Hallelujah'].[5] In the speaker's 'Aleluia', there is an implicit name in the last syllable 'jah', which is also an utterance of the name of the Hebrew God 'Yaweh', the first consonant and last vowel of 'Jehovah', and the last syllable of 'Elijah'. While the shout of 'Aleluia' attempts to exceed language and establish connection with God across distances, the 'uivo humano' emphasizes the negative side of this connection-across-distances, namely, separation.

In Cixous's lectures, the link between Bachmann and Lispector is Cixous herself: it is to her that both writers call out. Cixous claims that the writers she speaks about all descend three steps on the ladder of writing, 'The School of Death', 'The School of Dreams' and 'The School of Roots'. These 'schools' all share an interest in the profound, a rich trope in the work of both Bachmann and Lispector. For this reason, I would like to propose an additional school in which the two writers demonstrate a corresponding interest in profundity: 'The School of Depth'. The poetics of depth in their respective oeuvres is, I argue, the primary site of Bachmann's and Lispector's mutual *attunement*. Unlike Cixous, however, I do not claim to take part in this attunement. Bachmann and Lispector share a common poetics and tropology of depth from a distance, which I aim to show in my reading of 'Undine geht' and *Água Viva*.

Lispector's first novel, *Perto do coração selvagem* [*Near to the Wild Heart*] descends into a euphoric meditation on Psalm 130, *De profundis*, searching for pure communication and truth in the dreamy and unconscious watery depths.[6]

[5] Clarice Lispector, *Água Viva*, ed. by Pedro Vasquez (Editora Rocco, 2019), p. 29. English: *Água Viva*, trans. by Stefan Tobler (New Directions, 2012), p. 3. Henceforth citations appear: ÁVP (Portuguese) and ÁVE (English).

[6] Clarice Lispector, *Near to the Wild Heart*, trans. by Alison Entrekin (New Directions,

In Bachmann's work, we might turn to the figures of depth in the poems 'Böhmen liegt am Meer' [Bohemia Lies by the Sea], 'Ausfahrt' [Journey Out], and in the deepest blue of the sky of the poem 'Die Brücken' [The Bridges]. Two paradigmatic displays of the depth occur in the previously mentioned works 'Undine geht' by Bachmann and *Água viva* by Lispector. Without collapsing Bachmann's depths into Lispector's or vice versa, I hope to probe the function of such imagery in both works, and so to pick up where Cixous left off and bring these two writers into closer correspondence.

What I am terming 'The School of Depth' is not a site of mystical communion. This word 'mystical' has been implemented in several critical discussions on Bachmann's work, for instance in Sara Lennox's monograph on Bachmann, and Lispector's style has also been termed 'mystical', in Benjamin Moser's English biography of the author and in Cixous's *Reading with Clarice Lispector*.[7] Kenneth Krabbenhoft has also written on mysticism and sacrament in Lispector's work, and Anu Aneja has written on the 'mystic aspect of *l'Écriture féminine*' in Cixous and Lispector.[8] In mystic writing, as in these two texts, nonsensical and paradoxical formulations seem to have a precise object of contemplation. It is possible, for instance, that critics see resemblances between the language of mysticism and the abstract, ecstatic, associative and obscure language of 'Undine geht' and *Água Viva* — or perhaps scholars simply recognize that their ability to penetrate these texts is limited, and so they call their impenetrable language 'mystical'. But although these works may recall aspects of mystical texts, I argue that 'Undine geht' and *Água Viva* are more concerned with pure artistic potential than the relation between divine and human subjects. The mystical associations these texts make are abstracted from their theological contexts and operate in an artistic sphere of their own.

How then, are we to engage with these texts in depth? Metaphors of depth abound in discussions of literature: we so often speak of 'deeper meanings' or 'hidden truths' within a work, which may pertain to symbolic content, lesser-known socio-historical context, or even autobiographical significance. Readers brandish juxtapositions of words like 'superficial' and 'profound' — the latter the higher valued of the two, the more 'authentic' — and a host of other divisions that are not in themselves problematic when carefully employed. But the critical behaviour accompanying this vocabulary does have risks. George Steiner illustrates this phenomenon well in his book *Real Presences* (1986) in an analogy to deep sea diving:

1990), p. 315; *Perto do Coração Selvagem* (Le Livros, 2015), p. 344.

[7] Sara Lennox, *Cemetery of the Murdered Daughters: Feminism, History, and Ingeborg Bachmann* (University of Massachusetts Press, 2006); Benjamin Moser, *Why This World* (Oxford University Press, 2012); Helene Cixous, *Reading with Clarice Lispector* (University of Minnesota Press, 1990).

[8] Kenneth Krabbenhoft, 'From Mysticism to Sacrament in "A Paixão Segundo G.H."', *Luso-Brazilian Review*, 32.1 (1995), pp. 51–60; Anu Aneja, 'The Mystic Aspect of *L'Écriture féminine*: Hélène Cixous' *Vivre l'orange*', *Qui parle*, 3.1 (1989), pp. 189–201.

Deep-sea divers tell of a certain depth at which the human brain becomes possessed of the illusion that natural breathing is again possible. When this happens, the diver removes his helmet and drowns. He is inebriate with a fatal enchantment called *le vertige des grandes profondeurs*, 'the vertigo of the great deeps'.[9]

In other words, the scholarly desire for depth, together with the assumption of progressive understanding, may yield a certain hermeneutic dizziness and the threat of critical commentary that simply does not end.[10] To attempt to safeguard myself against this risk, I will not engage in a conquest for a third entity concealed within the theme of depth in each text; rather, I will merely explore the numerous associations with the theme of depth in 'Undine geht' and *Água viva*. Instead of reaching for psychoanalytic hermeneutic practices (Adlerian *Tiefenpsychologie* [depth psychology]) or poetic images of the eternal feminine, I will begin by discussing the first thing that comes to mind when we think about the depths in each text, that is, the element water. Bachmann's Undine is a semi-aquatic creature who shares the name of Friedrich de la Motte Fouqué's water nymph, and the speaker of Lispector's *Água Viva* seems, at least in certain points in the text, to reside in the 'living water' of the novel's title. Sentences in 'Undine geht' flow into each other with cascading repetition. Paragraphs in *Água Viva* have a wave-like quality: they tend to climax with a question and come crashing down with the question's answer. Other paragraphs remain unanswered — they swell up like waves that do not break. In both narratives, the depths are a site of exile and separation, wherein the answerability of one's address remains uncertain.

The depths in Bachmann's story and Lispector's novel are sites of separation between the speaker and the addressee, recalling Psalm 130: 'Out of the depths I have cried unto thee, O Lord; | Lord, hear my voice: let thine ears be attentive to the voice of my supplication'.[11] The separation between a voice and its addressee is the defining feature of the apostrophic narration, which addresses the absent other. Bachmann's Undine separates herself from Hans, and the speaker of *Água Viva* is separated from both the 'você' [you] and 'o/um Deus' [the/a God]. But despite their separation, both Undine and the speaker of *Água Viva* continue to call out to the others from whom they are separated: Undine calls out to Hans at the end of the story and the speaker in Lispector's novel calls out to the 'you', to God and to the reader. Both apostrophic narratives aim to communicate across vast distances and seem to affirm the possibility and legitimacy of such an attempt.

Depth is a poetic feature in both texts that becomes thematic when refracted through multiple possible contexts. While Bachmann's Undine and *Água*

[9] George Steiner, *Real Presences* (University of Chicago Press, 1989), p. 43.
[10] Rita Felski, 'Introduction', *New Literary History*, 43.2 (2012), pp. 203–23.
[11] *The Holy Bible Containing the Old and New Testaments*, Authorised King James Version (Cambridge University Press, 1984), Psalm 130:1–2.

Viva's narrator share with Psalm 130 a similar sentiment and form of address, it is important to note that neither Undine nor the voice in Lispector's novel calls out from a uniformly Judaeo-Christian position. Undine is described in Friedrich de la Motte Fouqué's popular fairytale *Undine* as a being without a soul. Counterintuitively, though, the pagan Undine becomes in Fouqué's story a better Christian worthier of a soul than either her mortal sister Bertalda or her betrothed, the knight Huldbrand. Similarly, the speaker of *Água Viva* seems to exist at the margins of the Judaeo-Christian context. While Lispector's speaker quotes Genesis just before beginning a lengthy passage on flowers — 'E plantou Javé Deus um jardim no Éden que fica no Oriente e colocou nele o homem que formara' ['And Yahweh God planted a garden in Eden which is in the East, and there he put the man whom He had formed'] (ÁVP, p. 64; ÁVE, p. 50) — she also bears interesting resemblances to the Afro-Brazilian goddess Yemanjá of the Candomblé religion, who is mother of all of the Candomblé orixás and goddess of the sea. On the first and last day of the year in Brazil, the followers of Yemanjá annually submerge themselves in water and sacrifice flowers to her on the waves. One could indeed read the flower interlude in *Água Viva* both as Yemanjá's response to her sacrificial gifts and as a ritualistic planting of the garden of Eden. The comparison can be taken further: just as the speaker is both born and giving birth in the novel, so too does Yemanjá birth the other orixás. It is not only the maternal themes in *Água Viva* that point to this resemblance between the speaker and Yemanjá, but also the novel's wave-like paragraphs: according to Candomblé legend, Yemanjá was the creator of waves. This possible symbology in the text does not erase the speaker's noticeably human forms, either: in the Candomblé tradition, Yemanjá is repeatedly summoned into both human and animal bodies, and she walks and dances among her people. Like the speaker of *Água Viva*, Yemanjá is mute. Just as Bachmann's Undine calls Hans at the end of the story in a mode or music to which he barely has access, the speaker of *Água Viva* is speechless and can only shout in another mode, namely, writing. Lispector's speaker seems to be aware that she is writing a text and demands to be heard in words that echo Psalm 130: 'Ouve-me, ouve meu silêncio' ['Hear me, hear my silence'] (ÁVP, p. 43; ÁVE, p. 23).

In Candomblé symbology, Yemanjá holds a mirror in one hand to protect herself and ensure honesty from her followers. After a long three-page passage on the 'mistério do espelho' ['mystery of the mirror'] (ÁVP, p. 80; ÁVE, p. 70) at the end of the text the narrative voice directs us: 'Olha para mim e me ama. Não: tu olhas para ti e te amas. É o que está certo' ['Look at me and love me. No: you look at yourself and love yourself. That's right'] (ÁVP, p. 94; ÁVE, p. 88). In this moment, it is as if the speaker is looking at herself in the mirror, before then turning the mirror around towards her reader. In both texts more generally, the separation between speaker and addressee is reflected in the internal division within the speaker herself. Just as the apostrophic apparatus separates the speaker from an absent addressee, so too is the speaker in each text separated from herself in language that mirrors and echoes the speaker's words. We see this in formulations such as 'zwischen mir und mir' ['between me and me'] (W, II, pp. 254; TY, p. 172) in Bachmann's story and 'entre mim e eu' ['between me and I'] (ÁVP, p. 86; ÁVE, p. 14) in Lispector's. There are four forms of simultaneous reflexivity and distance that figure in this discussion: first, between the text's speaker and herself; second, between the text's speaker and other characters; third, between text and the reader; and fourth, between the two texts 'Undine geht' and *Água Viva*. The open interval between the separated entities in each text can also be understood as a figure of depth.

These forms of reflexivity and distance — between the speaker and the other characters, such as Hans and humanity in Bachmann's story, or the God and the 'you' in Lispector's novel — provide the necessary ingredients for lyrical apostrophe. In her article 'Apostrophe's Double', Sabine Gölz details the deconstruction of what she terms the 'apostrophic apparatus' in Bachmann's poem 'Anrufung des großen Bären' [Invocation of the Great Bear].[12] In her discussion of the apostrophic apparatus, Gölz shows the divisive logic of the lyrical gesture and the lesser-studied addressee who is turned away from the speaker. Gölz argues that in the final stanza of Bachmann's poem, the diacritical apostrophe performs the deconstruction of the apparatus which had been built in stanzas one, two and three:

> By the last stanza, the word 'bear' has lost all referential power. It is no longer a name, but a vehicle that allows a subject that *knows itself to be nameless* to travel through language in order to understand its apparatus and to liquidate its magic.[13]

There is a more conventional lyrical apostrophic apparatus at work in 'Undine geht' and *Água Viva*: both texts feature the address of one speaker towards an absent addressee. What differentiates the rhetorical configurations at work in these texts, however, is a distinctive reversal: in their corresponding portrayals of fled gods, or god-like, not-fully-human beings, Bachmann and Lispector give voices to entities who are now calling rather than being called. Undine seems to be weaponizing her apostrophe as a medium for denouncing humanity — she curses humanity using the weapon of an adamic language of names such as 'Ungeheuer!' ['monster!'] and 'Verräter! ['traitor!'] (W, II, p. 253; TY, p. 171). The apostrophe of Lispector's speaker, on the other hand, does not have the tone of accusation but of lament and intimate confession. In their apostrophic addresses, neither Undine nor the speaker in *Água Viva* turns away from her addressee: both speakers call to their others as they flee while remaining decisively turned toward them. Indeed, the very last sentence of both texts continues to address the 'you': 'Undine geht' ends with Undine's call to Hans

---

[12] Sabine Gölz, 'Apostrophe's Double', *Konturen*, 10 (2018), pp. 22–53.
[13] Ibid., p. 40.

'Komm. Nur einmal. | Komm' ['Come. Just once. | Come'] (W, II, p. 192; TY, p. 181) and Lispector's *Água Viva* ends with the line 'O que te escrevo continua e estou enfeitiçada' ['What I'm writing to you goes on and I am bewitched'] (ÁVP, p. 48; ÁVE, p. 88). It also seems that Bachmann's Undine and Lispector's narrators are turned towards their respective readers when they address Hans and God, respectively. Undine, after all, is not only addressing the singular Hans, but 'the Hanses' and 'Menschen!' [Humans!] at large. Lispector's narrator, on the other hand, frequently uses formulations such as 'Você que me lê é' ['you who read me are'] (ÁVP, p. 48; ÁVE, p. 29). But despite the implication of the reader in each of these works, there remains a rift of understanding between the reader and the text. Thus, the reader of 'Undine geht' and *Água Viva* must maintain her distance from the calls of Bachmann's and Lispector's speakers to receive them adequately. It is only from a position of distance that the readers of 'Undine geht' and *Água Viva* can understand the apostrophic apparatus within these texts in the way Gölz describes. To attempt to do just this, I will now focus more closely on several features of the apostrophic narrative voices in 'Undine geht' and *Água Viva*.

In these addresses, the speakers' voice and image are reproduced in the figures of the echo and the mirror. Both the echo and the mirror are results of waves in motion, light waves in the case of the mirror and sound waves in the case of the echo; these are related phenomena in that both replicate the sonic or visual material from a single source. A clear echo requires distance or separation between the source of the sound and the reflecting surface. The echo can be used as a measuring tool, as in the case of echolocation: echoes carry in their repetitions the distance separating the initial stimulus and the surrounding objects. The echo repeats the sound of the stimulus, fainter in each repetition. Similarly, when we look into the mirror, our image is duplicated. In another sense, the mirror is a hard surface that gives the appearance of depth to any room, as mirrors provide the optical illusion of wider space. Narcissus fell victim to this illusion when he interpreted the surface of the water as portal rather than reflection and fell into the water. The opposite situation is found in deep, still water: its apparently two-dimensional surface masks the depths below into which we cannot see. For it to fully duplicate our image, we must be positioned at sufficient distance from its surface.

As an auditory phenomenon similar to the mirror, echoes too require distance. In fact, the echo is a defining feature of Undine's poetics, appearing in the refrain of her perpetually returning address 'Ihr Menschen! Ihr Ungeheuer!' ['You humans! You monsters!'] and in her dialogue with Hans, which is worth pausing over. They exchange only a few words:

> 'Guten Abend.'
> 'Guten Abend.'
> 'Wie weit ist es zu dir?'
> 'Weit ist es, weit.'
> 'Und weit ist es zu mir.' (W, II, p. 254)

'Good evening.'
'Good evening.'
'How far is it to you?'
'It is far, far.'
'And it is far to me.' (TY, p. 172)

There are no names given in this dialogue, and the second voice seems only able to echo the first voice: it takes the 'weit ist es' ['it is far'] from the first voice's question 'Wie weit ist es zu dir?' ['How far is it to you?'] and creates a declarative answer: 'Weit ist es, weit' ['It is far, far']. Ultimately, though, the second voice is unable to sustain itself, and the phrase becomes shorter and shorter, ending on the single syllable 'weit' ['far']. In this exchange, the material echoed concerns precisely the question and assertion of distance. There also seems to be a moment of mirroring in this dialogue, when the first voice rhymes the 'dir' ['you'] of its initial question with the word 'mir' ['me'] in its answer 'Und weit ist es zu mir' ['And it is far to me']. We might read the first voice's rhyme as the poetic form of Narcissus's reflection in the water charmed by Nemesis: the first voice reflects (and echoes) his own sound in 'dir' and 'mir'. The second voice, on the other hand, follows Echo in Book 3 of Ovid's *Metamorphoses*: just as Echo is compelled to repeat the voices of others after her voice is taken away by Juno as punishment, so too is Bachmann's speaker only able to repeat the words of the first voice.[14]

In Lispector's novel, the site of the echo is the cave: 'eu, bicho de cavernas ecoantes que sou, e sufoco porque sou palavra e também o seu eco' ['I, creature of echoing caverns that I am, and I suffocate because I am word and also its echo'] (ÁVP, p. 32; ÁVE, p. 9). If in Bachmann's story the echo is heard between two distinct voices, the distinction in Lispector's novel between 'word' and 'echo' holds ontological ramifications. Over the course of the novel, we are invited to read the word as embodied language of the human and the echo as the disembodied language of the non-human, either the technological or the magical. We hear the echo, for instance, in the form of an unanswered ringing telephone. The speaker recalls receiving a suicide note from São Paulo, from a person she had never met and did not know. She calls São Paulo on the telephone and writes 'O telefone não respondia, tocava e tocava e soava como em um apartamento em silêncio. Morreu ou não morreu?' ['No one answered, it rang and rang and echoed as if in a silent apartment. Did he die or not die?'] (ÁVP, p. 46; ÁVE, p. 27).

The thought of the speaker — 'Morreu ou não morreu?' [Did he die or not die?] — is the unvoiced question. The verb 'morreu' echoes like the ringing telephone. In this instance, the echo is the sound of an address without reply, which the speaker then internalizes into her own language, in the form of her declarative question or inquisitive declaration. The speaker also describes the

---

[14] See Marília Librandi, *Writing by Ear: Clarice Lispector and the Aural Novel* (University of Toronto, 2018).

echo of a feminine entity who comes from another space: 'A voz é canhestra, eufórica e diz por força do hábito de vida anterior: quer tomar chá? E não espera resposta' ['The voice is awkward, euphoric and says by force of the habit of a past life: would you like some tea? And doesn't wait for a reply'] (ÁVP, p. 90; ÁVE, p. 83). The echoing voice of this feminine entity is *acousmatic*, that is, according to Mladen Dolar's definition, a voice from somewhere else.[15] This entity is perhaps a doubly acousmatic voice: she comes from another space and her speech is propelled by a past life. The echo of the feminine entity and the ringing of the telephone both go unanswered because they are speaking from another realm. While the voice calling São Paulo is directed from the living realm to the realm of the dead (or the possibly dead), the voice of the feminine entity is directed from past life to the realm of the living.

Like the echo, the mirror is also a striking figure in each text. In 'Undine geht', the water is described as '[den] gleichgültig[en] Spiegel' ['the indifferent mirror'] (W, II, p. 254; TY, p. 172). The water is reflective like a mirror, it is thick and green, while also see-through: 'Ich liebe das Wasser, seine dichte Durchsichtigkeit, das Grün im Wasser und die sprachlosen Geschöpfe (und so sprachlos bin auch ich bald!)' ['I love the water, its dense transparency, the green in the water and the dumb creatures (I too shall soon be equally dumb)'] (W, II, p. 254; TY, p. 172). The water is like a mirror in that it creates a singular reflection: this is the mirror, 'der es mir verbietet, euch anders zu sehen' ['that forbids me to see you differently'] (W, II, p. 254; TY, p. 172). Here the mirror seems to function like Undine's looking glass through which she sees Hans, but this looking glass is defined by its limitation — the mirror of the water prevents Undine from seeing Hans differently. In this limitation, the watery mirror also creates an inner boundary for Undine, more precisely 'die nasse Grenze zwischen mir und mir' ['The wet frontier between me and me'] (W, II, p. 254; TY, p. 172). The mirror thus constitutes both the material of simultaneous connection and separation between Undine and Hans and the boundary that marks Undine's inner separation.

This paradoxical nature of the mirror in 'Undine geht' can also be found in the language of betweenness in Lispector's *Água Viva*. Lispector writes: 'Ninguém saberá de nada: o que sei é tão volátil e quase inexistente que fica entre mim e eu' ['No one will know anything: what I know is so volatile and nearly inexistent that it is between me and I'] (ÁVP, p. 86; ÁVE, p. 14). If the watery boundary between 'mir und mir' ['me and me'] in 'Undine geht' has primarily a separating function, in *Água Viva* it is a membrane across which knowledge can flow 'entre mim e eu' ['between me and I']. Rhetorically, 'me' and 'I' in Lispector's text are meant to enact two different grammatical constructions whose difference is 'nearly inexistent'. In Bachmann's construction, the difference between 'me and me' is also nearly inexistent: the 'me and me' are different insofar as they are separated by the 'watery boundary', but their difference is grammatically

---

[15] Mladen Dolar, *A Voice and Nothing More* (MIT Press, 2006), pp. 60–71.

imperceptible. Later in Lispector's novel, the speaker describes 'Mas agora estou interessada pelo mistério do espelho ... mensagem telegráfica intense e' ['the mystery of the mirror ... its mute and intense telegraphic message'] (ÁVP, p. 80; ÁVE, p. 70). Like a telegram, Lispector's figure of the mirror establishes a connection between realms. This connection takes the form of self-knowledge in the following passage:

> Antes do aparecimento do espelho a pessoa não conhecia o próprio rosto senão refletido nas águas de um lago. Depois de um certo tempo cada um é responsável pela cara que tem. Vou olhar agora a minha. É um rosto nu. E quando penso que inexiste um igual ao meu no mundo, fico de susto alegre. Nem nunca haverá. Nunca é o impossível. Gosto de nunca. Também gosto de sempre. Que há entre nunca e sempre que os liga tão indiretamente e intimamente? (ÁVP, pp. 47–48)

> [Before the appearance of the mirror, the person didn't know his own face except reflected in the waters of a lake. After a certain point everyone is responsible for the face he has. I'll now look at mine. It is a naked face. And when I think that no other like it exists in the world, I get a happy shock. Nor will there ever be. Never is the impossible. I like never. I also like ever. What is there between never and ever that links them so indirectly and intimately?] (ÁVE, p. 29)

The mirror introduces another mystery of betweenness in the text, namely the question of what there is 'between never and ever' and between the possible and the impossible. In this respect, Lispector's mirror, like Bachmann's, is an agent of connection and separation. The mirror separates the onlooker and their reflection; it also separates the lyrical I and the lyrical you at the end of the novel: 'Simplesmente eu sou eu. E você é você. É vasto, vai durar' ['Simply I am I. And you are you. It is vast, and it will endure'] (ÁVP, p. 94; ÁVE,p. 88). It is as if the speaker holds up a double-sided mirror when she says to the lyrical you, which may be taken as the reader of the text: 'Olha para mim e me ama. Não: tu olhas para ti e te amas. É o que está certo' ['Look at me and love me. No: you look at yourself and love yourself. That's right'] (ÁVP, p. 94; ÁVE, p. 88). The movement of look and love from addressee to speaker gives way to the speaker's invitation to the addressee to look at herself and love herself. It is as if the speaker is looking into a mirror with her speaker: the speaker first asks the reader to look at her (the speaker's) reflection, and then instructs the reader to look instead at her own (the reader's) reflection.

The Ovidian figures of echo and mirror that we observe in Bachmann's 'Undine geht' and Lispector's Àgua Viva coincide with the fragmentation of the subject. Just as Echo and Narcissus in Ovid's Metamorphoses lose their bodily forms in the wake of unreciprocated love, so too are Undine and the speaker in Àgua Viva separated from aspects of their own being. Undine describes the impossibility of dwelling under water: '[I]n dieses Element, in dem niemand sich ein Nest baut, sich ein Dach aufzieht über Balken, sich bedeckt mit einer

Plane. Nirgendwo sein, nirgendwo bleiben' ['In the element in which no one builds a nest, raises a roof over rafters, covers himself with an awning. To be nowhere, to stay nowhere'] (W, II, p. 254; TY, p. 172). In this sentence, Bachmann uses the verb 'sein' ['to be'] in the infinitive form, without a subject, qualified by the negativity of the 'Nirgendwo' ['nowhere']. Underwater, Undine *is* nowhere. The verb 'to be' appears only rarely in the story. In fact, until this moment, 'sein' has only appeared twice, both times in connection with Hans's name. After the speaker recounts coming 'durch die Lichtung' ['through the clearing'] in the past, where she says she 'traf einen, der Hans hieß' [met one, who was named Hans'] (W, II, p. 253; TY, p. 171), she goes on to describe Hans and his name:

> Ja, diese Logik habe ich gelernt, daß einer Hans heißen muß, daß ihr alle so heißt, einer wie der andere, aber doch nur einer. Immer nur einer ist es, der diesen Namen trägt, den ich nicht vergessen kann, und wenn ich euch auch alle vegesse, ganz und gar vergesse, wie ich euch ganz geliebt habe. Und wenn eure Küsse und euer Samen von den vielen großen Wassern — Regen, Flüssen, Meeren — längst abgewaschen und fortgeschwemmt sind, dann ist doch der Name noch da, der sich fortpflanzt unter Wasser, weil ich nicht aufhören kann, ihn zu rufen, Hans, Hans... (W, II, p. 254)

> [Yes, I have learnt this piece of logic, that a man has to be called Hans, that you are all called Hans, one like the other, and yet only one. Always there is only one who bears this name that I can never forget, even if I forget you all, completely forget how I loved you utterly. And long after your kisses and your seed have been washed off and carried away by the great waters — rains, rivers, sea — the name is still there, propagating itself under water, because I cannot stop crying it out, Hans, Hans...] (TY, p. 171)

Hans's name not only outlasts his kisses and seed which were washed away by the water, it also propagates ('fortpflanzt') itself under water like living matter. Hans's name is underwater, but Undine is *nowhere* in the water. We might understand this 'nowhere' as a 'nowhere in particular' and 'everywhere at once', or as an undifferentiated element in which Undine loses all sense of opposition. Interestingly, Hans holds the only name in the story, whereas Undine is only given a name in the title. Perhaps due to his nominal propriety, Undine depends on Hans and his name to give her being — in other words, without her opposition to Hans there can be no Undine. She needs Hans's name not only as something to address or call, as it were, but also as something that *does not* address or call her.

The speaker in *Água Viva* is also separated from her 'is' and that of the objects that surround her, making the similar demand 'Escuta: eu te deixo ser, deixa-me ser então' ['Listen: I let you be, therefore let me be'] (ÁVP, p. 40; ÁVE, p. 19). She says 'Quero apossar-me do é da coisa' ['I want to grab hold of the is of the thing'] (ÁVP, p. 27; ÁVE, p. 3), and later 'E no instante está o é dele mesmo. Quero captar o meu é' ['And in the instant is the is of the instant, I want to seize my is'] (ÁVP, pp. 27–28; ÁVE, p. 4). The 'is' in Lispector's novel becomes something that must be reached for deep within the speaking subject herself. However, the 'is' is also, of course, a word. If we think of the word 'is' as a word, first and foremost, this scene seems to perform the method of writing that the speaker defines as 'Então escrever é o modo de quem tem a palavra como isca: a palavra pescando o que não é palavra' ['using the word as bait: the word fishing for whatever is not word'] (ÁVP, pp. 36–37; ÁVE, p. 15). In this case, the 'é' is the word and also the not-word. The speaker says 'Mas a palavra mais importante da língua tem uma única letra: é. É' ['the most important word in the language has but one letter: é. É'] (ÁVP, p. 41; ÁVE, p. 21). In Portuguese, it 'is' is conjugated as it 'é', with a single letter. But in the quotation, this letter is repeated, and in the repetition, it appears as a capital letter. This is the exalted 'É' that *Água Viva*'s speaker attempts to seize. This exalted letter becomes a symbol of absolute presence or present-ness, but just for a moment, before the motif is released like a fish back into water. Bachmann's Undine performs a corresponding seizure of the word and the instant when she says, with an almost Faustian air, 'Geh Tod! Und: Steh still, Zeit!' ['Go, death, and, stand still, time'] (W, II, p. 254, TY, p. 176). Emerging out of the 'Nirgendwo sein' ['To be nowhere'] (W, II, p. 254, TY, p. 172) of Undine's water, there is an absolute being-in-the-moment when time stands still. Indeed, Bachmann's 'Undine geht' and Lispector's *Água Viva* demand to be read in the present so that they can capture this 'is'. Both texts also seem to need the presence of the other for this task. The resonances between Lispector's novel and Bachmann's story, as I have discussed here, remind us that literary texts may always be placed in dialogue. The speaker of *Água Viva* identifies herself as a 'um ser concomitante' ['a concomitant being'] (ÁVP, p. 37; ÁVE, p. 15), that is, a being who does not stand in isolation, but is naturally accompanied or associated. *Água Viva* is associated with the Ondine tradition insofar as its speaker seems to be calling out from the waves. Bachmann's Undine is also a concomitant being who is multiply refracted through the cultural tradition from Paracelsus to Hans Werner Henze to Christian Petzold. Although Bachmann's Undine has left the human realm, she seems, counterintuitively, to desire company in her final call. While it is tempting to place ourselves as readers within the apostrophic apparatus of each text, as if we were the absent addressee meant to answer the texts' calls critically, as Cixous does in her *Three Steps on the Ladder of Writing*, perhaps there might be another option when we read Bachmann's 'Undine geht' *with* Lispector's *Água Viva*: rather than calling out to us, in the position of the apostrophic addressee, these texts might be read instead as if they are calling out to each other. This staging of these texts resists the pull of the *critical* apostrophic apparatus within which Cixous situates herself. I premise this act of reading on the intricate network of correspondences between these two texts: as I have shown, they are distantly attuned in their poetics of depth, which I have located in their respective figures of the echo, the mirror and the language of being. At the same time, though, these texts and their speakers are undeniably distant from one another, and they place their readers in a position of distance as well.

After Bachmann's and Lispector's narrators institute a rift between signification and intelligibility, they depart and continue on their way. A literary criticism that respects distances does not aim to access or appropriate the essence of the thing itself but prefers to listen to its waves, even if we do so just barely, 'beinahe noch' ['almost still'] (W, II, p. 263; TY, p. 181), like Bachmann's Hans.

Anna Maria Ortese and Ingeborg Bachmann: Visual Anxiety between Naples and Vienna

ROBERTO INTERDONATO

University of Oxford

I

This article proposes that there is a strong affinity between Ingeborg Bachmann and the Italian author Anna Maria Ortese (1914–98), a hint of which is contained in the correspondence between Franz Haas, an Austrian Germanist based in Italy, and Ortese herself. Haas explains that when he first introduced Ortese to Bachmann's work in the summer of 1990, seventeen years after Bachmann's death, Ortese was unfamiliar with the Austrian author. He recollects telling Ortese that Bachmann had spent many years in Italy, and that although Bachmann had arrived in Ischia and Naples in 1953 just as she, Ortese, had left Naples, they could have met in Rome afterwards.[1]

In her letters to Haas, Ortese expresses admiration above all for Bachmann's 'Lieder auf der Flucht' [Songs in Flight], the concluding cycle in her second poetry collection, *Anrufung des großen Bären* (1956) ['Invocation of the Great Bear'; first Italian translation by Nanni Ballestrini in 1957]. What probably moved Ortese about this cycle, which was famously defined as the 'Neapolitan elegies' or 'Naples poem',[2] was its topographic character combined with Bachmann's use of snow as a concrete and symbolic image bringing together the themes of love and grief with historical trauma.[3] 'Lieder auf der Flucht' recall the Nazi occupation of Naples and the heroic uprisings that led to the liberation of the city in four days (between 27 and 30 September 1943). Also inspired by Wilhelm Müller and Franz Schubert's *Winterreise* [*Winter Journey*, 1828] and the exceptional snowfalls over Naples in January and February 1956 when Bachmann lived there with expatriate composer Hans Werner Henze

---

[1] Franz Haas, 'La cacciata dal purgatorio: Anna Maria Ortese e Napoli', *Belfagor*, 62.3 (2007), pp. 334–42 (p. 341). Between 1953 and 1975, Ortese lived between Rome, where Bachmann also resided, and Milan. On Ortese's life see Luca Clerici, *Apparizione e visione: vita e opere di Anna Maria Ortese* (Mondadori, 2002).

[2] Werner Ross, 'Neapolitanische Elegie', in *Über Ingeborg Bachmann I: Rezensionen 1952–1992*, ed. by Michael Schardt (Igel, 2011), pp. 37–38 (p. 37); Hans Höller, 'Vorwort', in AGB, pp. 7–11 (p. 10).

[3] Jörg-Ulrich Fechner, 'Ingeborg Bachmanns *Lieder auf der Flucht*: Kommunikative und interpretatorische Signale im hermeneutischen Gedichtzyklus', *Arcadia*, 21.1–3 (1986), pp. 62–77 (p. 69).

Austrian Studies 32 (2024), doi:10.1353/aus.00012, pp. 159–73
© Modern Humanities Research Association 2024

(AGB, pp. 262–63), the winter imagery reinforces the cycle's melancholic character. It presents an 'I' that is sympathetic to the Neapolitans and their occupied city while witnessing the unfolding of human violence:

> Ich bin unschuldig und gefangen
> im unterworfenen Neapel,
> wo der Winter
> Posilip und Vomero an den Himmel stellt (AGB, p. 84)
>
> [I am innocent and captive
> in conquered Naples,
> where winter
> silhouettes Posillipo and Vomero] (DS, p. 223)

Bachmann's 'Lieder' hint at the physical and moral destruction of Naples while perhaps presenting tacit intertextual references to the late poetry of Giacomo Leopardi, in which Naples and its surroundings embody the topographic translation of an experience of the 'negative' and of an aesthetic re-signification of life.[4] At the very least, the atmospheres in Bachmann are reminiscent of Leopardi, a poet Ortese pays homage to as early as 1939 in her 'Pellegrinaggio alla tomba di Leopardi' [Pilgrimage to Leopardi's Tomb]. This Leopardian resonance, the Neapolitan setting and the verses' elegiac and melancholic movement lead Ortese to declare herself shaken by Bachmann's poetry in a letter to Haas dated 3 July 1990: 'La neve del cuore rivela una Napoli ignota. Poesia, sì, da brivido: ma assolutamente alto' [The snow of the heart reveals an unknown Naples. Thrilling poetry indeed, but of the highest art].[5] Bachmann's 'Lieder' are part of a collection (the *Anrufung*) that appeals to a 'reconciliation' with the cosmos and uses the southern Italian landscape as a fundamental, non-romanticized and chthonic setting.[6] Here Ortese could perceive the image of a besieged and 'fallen' Naples, the epitome of southern Italy's developmental lag after Italian unification in 1861 as well as the Nazi occupation and Allied bombing during the Second World War, as represented by Ortese herself in her *Il mare non bagna Napoli* a few years earlier (1953) [literally 'the sea does not wash Naples', published in English as *Evening Descends upon the Hills*, trans. by Ann Goldstein and Jenny McPhee, Pushkin 2018]. Whereas further comments in her letters to Haas testify to Ortese's growing interest in the oeuvre of Bachmann, particularly in her short stories, what seems most important about

---

[4] Uta Degner, '"Die Wahrheit ist dem Menschen zumutbar": Die Anagnorisis der Dichtung und der Stolz der Sehenden bei Leopardi und Ingeborg Bachmann', in *Lebenskunst nach Leopardi: Anti-pessimistische Strategien im Werk Giacomo Leopardis*, ed. by Milan Herold and Barbara Kuhn (Narr Francke Attempto, 2020), pp. 265–84 (p. 272).

[5] Anna Maria Ortese, *Possibilmente il più innocente: lettere a Franz Haas (1990–1998)*, ed. by Francesco Rognoni and Franz Haas (Sedizioni, 2016), p. 61 [hereafter *PPI*].

[6] On the *Anrufung* and the Italian landscape, see Camilla Miglio, 'Ingeborg Bachmanns chtonisches Italien', in *Ingeborg Bachmann in aktueller Sicht: Perspektiven der Forschung*, ed. by Fabrizio Cambi and others (Istituto Italiano Studi Germanici, 2016), pp. 121–40; Luigi Reitani, 'Kommentar', in AGB, pp. 150 54.

Ortese's overall appreciation of Bachmann is the Austrian author's recognition of the 'supernatural' pain of the modern human condition (*PPI*, p.61). Ortese's acknowledgement of this pain, as well as of the refined musicality of Bachmann's prose even in Italian translation ('Non ci sono tracce di terra' (*PPI*, p. 61) [There are no traces of the earthly]), suggest that this great but long-forgotten writer of twentieth-century Italian literature had recognized, albeit relatively late in her life, the calibre of her Austrian colleague Ingeborg Bachmann, an author in any case much appreciated by Italian readers.[7]

I have found no other texts in which Ortese speaks about Bachmann, nor are there any known documents testifying that Bachmann knew Ortese's work, despite the latter's extended stay in Italy, her excellent knowledge of Italian and her contacts with intellectuals (Giorgio Agamben, Roberto Calasso and Fleur Jaeggy) who might already have read Ortese before Bachmann's death in 1973. Nevertheless, I would like to argue that an affinity between Ortese and Bachmann can be traced in their expression of a phobic and disturbed relation between the self and the social world through shared aesthetic patterns — for example, symbolic approaches to eyes and sight or seeing. Two of their most important prose collections, namely *Il mare non bagna Napoli* (1953) and *Simultan* (1972), in particular the individual short stories 'Un paio di occhiali' [A Pair of Eyeglasses] and 'Ihr glücklichen Augen' [Oh Happy Eyes], are illuminating in this regard.[8]

II

In both Ortese and Bachmann's works, female characters (the poor child Eugenia in Ortese and the well-off adult Miranda in Bachmann) suffer considerably when observing their immediate surroundings. Theirs are symbolic instantiations of scopophobia: a fear of looking and a fear of the experiential and embodied involvement with external reality through the eyes.[9] For these characters, glasses are of fundamental importance: by eliminating the blurred vision caused by their respective visual defects and providing them with a 'truthful' image of their environment and related social problems, this optical prosthesis turns out to be a tool that triggers their symbolic suffering

[7] On Bachmann's reception in Italy see for example Arturo Larcati, 'Ingeborg Bachmanns italienische Korrespondenz: Vorbemerkungen zu einem Editionsprojekt', in *Ingeborg Bachmann in aktueller Sicht*, pp. 33–57.

[8] Ortese's story was originally published as 'Ottomila lire per gli occhi di Eugenia' [Eight Thousand Liras for Eugenia's Eyes] in the weekly magazine *Omnibus* in May 1949. Bachmann's was broadcast on NDR Hannover in 1969 and published in the magazine *Merkur: Deutsche Zeitschrift für europäisches Denken* in 1971. It was immediately translated into Italian, see Ingeborg Bachmann, *Occhi felici*, trans. by Ippolito Pizzetti, in Ingeborg Bachmann and others, *Adelphiana* (Adelphi, 1971), pp. 271–89.

[9] David W. Allen, *The Fear of Looking: Or Scopophilic-Exhibitionist Conflicts* (University Press of Virginia, 1974), p. 6.

from psychosomatic or somatoform symptoms — such as pain, fear, anxiety and stress — due to psychogenic and psychosocial factors rather than organic causes.

Through the discourse on visual defects and the representation of Eugenia and Miranda's affective states, 'Un paio di occhiali' and 'Ihr glücklichen Augen' present a potent cultural critique while guiding the reader's gaze towards two very different social scenarios: Naples in the years immediately following the Second World War (Ortese) and Vienna in the late 1960s (Bachmann). Twenty years separate the publication of the two stories and they belong in collections from different periods of their authors' production — from Ortese's last Neapolitan period on the one hand, marked by her collaboration with the Gramscian-inspired Neapolitan magazine *Sud* [South] (1945–47), and Bachmann's last Roman period on the other, in which she worked on the *Todesarten* project. Combined with their diverging spatio-temporal settings, this may discourage us from comparing them at first. The connection between the two becomes evident, however, when we realize that they both use the topos of blindness or visual impairment to establish a discourse on the experience of pain in post-1945 social contexts that impacted on the individual's ability to lead qualitatively 'good' lives.

The two short stories constitute 'grammars of suffering' as defined by Salvatore Natoli: (aesthetic) depictions of the 'concretions' through which the experience of pain manifests itself, in this case through the mediation of the eye. They throw the interplay between medicine and morality (understood as therapies of the soul) into relief, addressing both pathological and immoral aspects of social realities.[10] Through their respective metaphors of blindness, Ortese and Bachmann pursue a shared utopian intent: fostering collective healing. Utopian thinking, which is divided into two moments, halts here at the negative moment of critique, which is however fundamental to being able to endorse the positive moment of 'constructive vision': without the critical challenge of the given and the established, it is not possible to promote scenarios of future social change.[11] Ortese and Bachmann's oeuvres are among the most significant examples of twentieth-century aesthetic transfigurations of the negative psychic experience of reality. Both authors considered cultural anaesthesia to be a particular characteristic of late modernity, which prescribed high emotional control and rendered the Other's pain inadmissible in public discourse. These two stories, and the collections they come from, are highly accordant with what we could call Ortese and Bachmann's poetics of awakening, which was developed as a response to this numbing. Bachmann notoriously explained, in a speech given

---

[10] Salvatore Natoli, *L'esperienza del dolore: le forme del patire nella cultura occidentale* (Feltrinelli, 2002), pp. 16–17.
[11] John Friedman, as cited in Ole B. Jensen and Malene Freudendal-Pedersen, 'Utopias of Mobilities', in *Utopia: Social Theory and the Future*, ed. by Michael Hviid Jacobsen and Keith Tester (Ashgate, 2012), pp. 197–217 (p. 200).

in 1959 in front of blind veterans, that the writer's duty is not to deny pain but, on the contrary, to make people sensitive to its experience again (W, IV, p. 275). In the first of her memorable Frankfurt lectures on poetics in 1959, she exclaimed at the lethargic state into which humanity had fallen in the face of the Other's pain in the aftermath of the Second World War: 'Wir schlafen ja' ['We are indeed asleep'] (W, IV, p. 198; CW, p. 273). Similarly, in 1966, Ortese traced the genesis of *Il mare non bagna Napoli* and 'Un paio di occhiali' back to the realization that she and her intellectual friends from *Sud* were surrounded by a universe of social suffering. Her aim in these texts had been to encourage the reacquisition of a sensitivity in the face of pain: 'io volevo svegliare questi amici, svegliare la città ... il compito dello scrittore è questo, stimolare, portare luce' ['I wanted to awaken those friends, awaken the city ... the duty of the writer is this, to stimulate, to bring light'].[12]

When looking at the broader Italian and Germanophone post-1945 cultural context, at least in the period from 1945 until the 1970s, we see how thematizations of visual impairment and blindness abound, not just in the works of women writers. Blindness recurs in a variety of approaches always closely linked to a critique of 'anaesthetized' postwar societies and never intended to denigrate the lives of people actually experiencing this disability: examples include the Neapolitan comedy *Occhiali neri* [*Black Glasses*] (1945) by Eduardo De Filippo, Pier Paolo Pasolini's adaptation of Sophocles, *Edipo Re* [*Oedipus Rex*] (1967), Elsa Morante's *La serata a Colono: Parodia* [*The Evening at Colonus: A Parody*] (1968), dramas by Friedrich Dürrenmatt *Der Blinde* [*The Blind Man*] (1948) and Günter Eich *Blick auf Venedig* [*View on Venice*] (1952), Max Frisch's novel *Mein Name sei Gantenbein* [*Gantenbein*] (1964) and Werner Herzog's documentary *Land des Schweigens und der Dunkelheit* [*Land of Silence and Darkness*] (1971). With their use of ophthalmological metaphors of affect and their insistence on the intellectual and moral duty to work on the experience of pain, Ortese and Bachmann seem to be inserting themselves into a transcultural strand of cultural critique willing to deconstruct the correlation between happiness and the sight of the outer world. The short stories of *Il mare non bagna Napoli* and *Simultan* link the cognitive 'benefits' of sight to a feeling of unease, anxiety and dismay; they express a modern unhappy consciousness.

---

[12] As quoted in Andrea Baldi, 'Cities "Paved with Casualties": Ortese's Journeys through Urban Modernity', in *Anna Maria Ortese: Celestial Geographies*, ed. by Gian Maria Annovi and Flora Ghezzo (University of Toronto Press, 2015), pp. 78–111 (p. 104). The translation of the quotation is also by Baldi.

III

'Il mondo è meglio non vederlo che vederlo'
['It's better not to see the world than to see it']
— Anna Maria Ortese[13]

There is little doubt that Ortese's collection *Il mare non bagna Napoli* — two short stories and three reportages, three of which were published in magazines (*Omnibus* and *Il mondo*) between 1949 and 1951 — is the fruit of the author's traumatic experience of the Second World War. Although Ortese's work fits very well with the Neo-realist, documentary representation of reality that was in vogue at the time, its realism has a precise origin. It stems from Ortese's editorial work for the short-lived *Sud*, an overlooked but highly interesting literary magazine published between 1945 and 1947, whose editor-in-chief was the enlightened left-wing journalist Pasquale Prunas. Here, Ortese published an early short story with a Neapolitan setting — a precursor to *Il mare non bagna Napoli* — in which she drew on her own return to Naples after the end of the war: 'Appena scesa a Napoli, [...] mi sono chiusa in casa e vi ho fatto il mio anno di disperazione profonda' ['As soon as I got to Naples, [...] I shut myself up in the house and there I spent my year of deep despair'].[14]

In a text added to her collection in 1994, entitled 'Le Giacchette Grigie di Monte di Dio' ['The Grey Jackets of Monte di Dio'], Ortese recalled how Prunas's magazine sought to document the historical reality of Naples as a contribution to the city's material and spiritual recovery after the war. Ortese explained that with *Il mare non bagna Napoli*, she had provided, a few years after the closure of *Sud* for financial reasons, her own testimony to a depressing post-1945 Neapolitan reality where economic, educational and health problems had reduced people to living in primitive and brutal conditions. Passages from the collection underline this. Similarly to Brecht's *Dreigroschenoper* [*Threepenny Opera*, 1928], the reportage 'Oro a Forcella' ['Gold in Forcella'], for example, shows beggars asking for money and sympathy by emphasizing their impairments or by staging them. In the reportage 'La città involontaria' ['The Involuntary City'], we learn of a skeletal two-year-old girl affected by mutism, who has stopped growing and is destined to die in a cradle made of a Coca-Cola box in one of the insalubrious rooms of the Palazzo dei Granili, a shelter for

---

[13] Anna Maria Ortese, 'Un paio di occhiali', in Anna Maria Ortese, *Il mare non bagna Napoli* (Adelphi, 1994), pp. 15–34 (p. 18) [hereafter *MNBN: PO*]. References to the collection, as well as to its individual stories, reportages and other sections, will be abbreviated after the first occurrence; the same will apply to Bachmann's *Simultan*. Translations are taken from Anna Maria Ortese, *Evening Descends upon the Hills: Stories from Naples*, trans. by Ann Goldstein and Jenny McPhee (Pushkin, 2018), p. 16 [hereafter *EDUH*]. The sentence is uttered by the character of Nunziata, addressed to her visually impaired niece Eugenia.

[14] Anna Maria Ortese, 'Dolente splendore del vicolo' [Painful splendour of the alleyway], in *Sud: Giornale di Letteratura*, 20 June 1946, p. 5.

hundreds of displaced families after the end of the war. Another reportage in the collection, 'Il silenzio della ragione' ['The Silence of Reason'], tells of boys offending public decency, making obscene gestures, urinating on the streets and cruelly hanging or piercing animals just to kill time.

As a *'visione* dell'intollerabile' (*MNBN*, 'Le Giacchette Grigie di Monte di Dio', 175; italics in the original) ['*vision* of the intolerable'], (*EDUH* 'The Grey Jackets of Monte di Dio', 191), a brutal, realistic portrait of Neapolitan society after the end of the conflict, *Il mare non bagna Napoli* is — together with the stylistically similar *Silenzio a Milano* [*Silence in Milan*] (1958) — an anomalous product in the complex panorama of Ortese's work, however. In another text added to the collection only in 1994, 'Il "Mare" come spaesamento' ['The "Sea" as Disorientation'], Ortese explained that her books — beginning with her first collection of short stories, *Angelici dolori* [*Angelic Sorrows*] of 1937 — tend to look away from objective reality. *Il mare non bagna Napoli* does quite the opposite, openly revealing Ortese's intolerance of social realities, suffering and mortality. In Ortese's thought, this intolerance, projected here onto post-1945 Naples, is only a particular manifestation of a phobic attachment to life: 'Da molto, moltissimo tempo, io detestavo con tutte le mie forze, senza quasi saperlo, la cosiddetta *realtà*: il meccanismo delle cose che sorgono nel tempo, e dal tempo sono distrutte' (*MNBN*, 'Il "Mare" come spaesamento', 10; italics in the original) ['For a very long time, I hated with all my might, almost without knowing it, so-called *reality*: that mechanism of things that arise in time and are destroyed by time'] (*EDUH*, 'The "Sea" as Disorientation', 10; italics in the original). The collection, as Ortese herself seems to interpret it, thus presents itself as an exploration of the polarity between the cultural construction of the sayable on the one hand, and on the other, individual, inadmissible memory and experience that operate as spaces of social amnesia and anaesthesia and have transience as their focus.

In order to understand *Il mare non bagna Napoli*, we must recognize, as Clerici and Contarini have invited us to do,[15] that the theme of blindness or defective vision is not only developed through the story of little Eugenia, 'Un paio di occhiali', with which Ortese opens the collection. It is also present in the 'compulsion to see' the horrendous universe of the Granili in 'La città involontaria',[16] in the portrait of the 'short-sighted' Neapolitan intellectuals in the collection's last text, 'Il silenzio della ragione', and — more broadly — throughout a collection that aims to awaken the reader from a state of critical unconsciousness and sensory indifference. Ortese believed her generation was failing to perceive and work against the coercion that results

---

[15] Clerici, *Apparizione e visione*, pp. 246–47; Silvia Contarini, 'Tra cecità e visione: Come leggere *Il mare non bagna Napoli* di Anna Maria Ortese', in *Chroniques Italiennes*, 5 (2004), pp. 1–13 (p. 12).
[16] Vilma De Gasperin, *Loss and the Other in the Visionary Work of Anna Maria Ortese* (Oxford University Press, 2014), p. 132.

from social conditions. Yet 'Un paio di occhiali' remains an indispensable key to understanding the scopophobic dimension of the collection as a whole. In an interview given on 15 May 1993, a few years before her death, Ortese acknowledged that she had wanted to process a personal experience through this text. She recalled that she did not see well as a child and that wearing glasses for the first time gave her a sharp image of the unattractive reality around her.[17] The resulting story — which she admits was also inspired by Edgar Allan Poe's tormented and dark tales (including 'The Spectacles' 1844) and Matilde Serao's *verismo* novella 'O Giovannino o la morte' ['Either Giovannino or Death'] (1896)[18] — tells then of the 'visual trauma' caused by the failure to appreciate the social world once a pair of spectacles has corrected a visual defect and led, platonically, from the darkness of the cave (blindness) to light (visual acuity and thus truth).

The protagonist, Eugenia Quaglia, is a child with a prematurely aged face, poor personal hygiene and uncombed hair. She lives with her impoverished family in one of the typical Neapolitan *bassi*, slum homes that came to be seen as instantiations of the ontological difference between Naples and the rest of 'civilized' Europe.[19] With nine dioptres in one eye and ten in the other, Eugenia is almost completely blind. This disability, for which she is often singled out, reinforces her alienation from her family and peers. At the same time, concrete vision impairment serves in the text as a more abstract clinical metaphor of affect, designed to diagnose Eugenia's misdirected desire and emotional flaws in a social context characterized by material and spiritual poverty. The shift from concrete to symbolic meaning is anticipated by the very title of the story, 'Un paio di occhiali', in which glasses become a concrete image of fundamental importance charged with the symbolic meaning of restitution: this costly artefact, which Aunt Nunziata generously offers to buy for her niece despite her belief that 'it is better not to see the world than to see it', comes to represent for Eugenia the illusory promise of a 'good life'. The reader painfully anticipates the story's anticlimax, particularly because it is the enormous let-down of a blind child that is to be narrated: between the moment the glasses are ordered in an elegant optician's shop in the central Via Roma (now Via Toledo) and the moment in which, after a week, they are delivered, the reader sees how what has become for the child the embodied image of a 'hope of change' and 'a turning point in an ungifted and unprivileged life' is transformed into the vehicle for

---

[17] The interview is discussed in Luca Clerici, *Apparizione e visione*, p. 246; in De Gasperin, *Loss and the Other*, pp. 140–41; and in Lucia Re, ' "Clouds in Front of My Eyes": Ortese's Poetics of the Gaze in "Un paio di occhiali" and Il mare non bagna Napoli', in *Anna Maria Ortese*, ed. by Annovi and Ghezzo, pp. 35–77 (pp. 65–66).

[18] Clerici, *Apparizione e visione*, pp. 233, 248. On Poe as a source for Ortese's works, see also Monica Farnetti, *Anna Maria Ortese* (Mondadori, 1998), p. 145; De Gasperin, *Loss and the Other*, p. 139; and Re, ' "Clouds in Front of My Eyes" ', pp. 55–56.

[19] Andrea Bagnato, 'We Must Disembowel Naples!', *AA Files*, 77 (2020), pp. 39–43 (p. 40).

a tragic anagnorisis.[20] It is upon putting on her new glasses in her habitat, the dirty Neapolitan courtyard of which she had been visually unaware up to that moment, that Eugenia shows a variety of somatoform symptoms, including nausea, leg shaking, abdominal pain, exophthalmos, and lacrimation: 'Eugenia, sempre tenendosi gli occhiali con le mani, andò fino al portone, per guardare fuori, nel vicolo della Cupa. Le gambe le tremavano, le girava la testa, e non provava più nessuna gioia' ['Eugenia, still holding onto the eyeglasses with her hands, went to the entrance of the courtyard to look out into Vicolo della Cupa. Her legs were trembling, her head was spinning, and she no longer felt any joy'] (*MNBN: PO*, p. 33; *EDUH: PE*, p. 32; modified). These are all sensory disturbances: manifestations of visual anxiety.

As the third-person narrator zooms in on the character, we see how, through the correction of her visual defect, Eugenia's psychic reality (meaning the experiential dimension, including bodily relational experience) symbolically overcomes the 'pleasure principle' (the affective distortion of the ego to avoid pain) and enters what Freud identified as the 'reality principle', meaning what emanates from the outer world (facts).[21] Describing Eugenia's pain at the sight of anti-aesthetic architecture, rubbish and people disfigured by poverty and resignation, the narrator witnesses the irretrievable damage wreaked on the child protagonist's ability to experience the fundamental dyad of joy-happiness (Plutchik).[22] Farnetti, who was the first to connect this story to Bachmann's 'Ihr glücklichen Augen', characterizes Eugenia's visual disillusionment as a physical and psychological experience of 'ocular shock'.[23] It is indeed fundamental to understand that Eugenia's experience here not only conflicts with the visual 'enchantment' she had experienced upon trying on the glasses in the optician's shop of Via Roma — 'una meraviglia' ['a marvel'] (*MNBN: PO*, p. 17; *EDUH: PE*, p. 15) — but also with her initial positive imagination of social reality, which is, as she is then forced to realize, sharply removed from any utopian dimension. Her ocular discovery triggers the unhappy and alienated gaze of an individual who suddenly sees, knows and rejects. De Gasperin has observed that this story by Ortese is a portrayal of 'the loss of those illusions that are afforded by a childish and naive perspective'.[24] One might add that it represents the loss of an individual's overall well-being in their environment, paradoxically through an improvement in ability.

The ophthalmological metaphor of affect (blindness) and the somatoform reactions to clear sight illuminate the mental, emotional and bodily pain of a

---

[20] Sharon Wood, 'Fantasy and Narrative in Anna Maria Ortese', *Italica*, 71.3 (1994), pp. 354–68 (p. 360).
[21] Joona Taipale, 'The Bodily Feeling of Existence in Phenomenology and Psychoanalysis', in *Phenomenology and the Transcendental*, ed. by Sara Heinämaa, Mirja Hartimo and Timo Miettinen (Routledge, 2014), pp. 218–34 (pp. 225–26).
[22] Warren D. TenHouten, *Alienation and Affect* (Routledge, 2017), p. 63.
[23] Monica Farnetti, *Anna Maria Ortese*, pp. 138–45 (p. 142).
[24] Gasperin, *Loss and the Other*, p. 143.

child and construct a corporeally constituted pattern of (historical) experience through which to de-stereotype the romantic image of a southern Italy made of sun, sea and pleasure, replacing it with an infernal one.

IV

'Mit einem auf die Nase gestülpten goldenen Brillengestell, kann Miranda
in die Hölle sehen'

['In a gold frame perched on her nose, Miranda can see into hell']

— Ingeborg Bachmann[25]

Despite the more 'developed' social reality portrayed — that of Austria, and particularly Vienna, at an unspecified time around the late 1960s — Bachmann's collection *Simultan* provides a similarly infernal picture and a matching opportunity to reflect on visual anxiety, ophthalmological metaphors of affect and somatoform reactions to clear sight; her stories similarly illuminate the mental, emotional and bodily pain of characters who are not emotionally desensitized. This visual discourse is already apparent in the collection's title: through a complex interweaving of languages, places and feelings, its five short stories develop the theme of the simultaneity of perception, which includes visual perception and concomitant subjective experiences of alienation.[26] The problem of visual perception is explicitly presented in the collection's third story, 'Ihr glücklichen Augen', in light of the persistent disharmony between the other characters' cynical or manipulative take on reality and the idealized, transfigured images that the mind of the protagonist, Miranda, superimposes on her (already faulty) retinal impressions — a self-defence mechanism of withdrawal to cope with unpleasant social reality.

To some critics the 'Herzstück' or centrepiece of the entire collection,[27] 'Ihr glücklichen Augen' seems to provide the loupe to detect a phobic attachment to reality in *Simultan*. A collection characterized by its texts' generic uniformity, with a tendency towards omniscient third-person narration, it aims to observe

---

[25] Ingeborg Bachmann, 'Ihr glücklichen Augen', in Bachmann, *Simultan* (TKA, IV, p. 77) [hereafter TKA, IV: IGA]. The English translation is taken from Ingeborg Bachmann, 'Eyes to Wonder', in Bachmann, *Three Paths to the Lake*, trans. by Mary Fran Gilbert, with an introduction by Mark Anderson (Holmes & Meier, 1997), pp. 75–94 (p. 77) [hereafter TPL: EW]. The sentence is attributable to the voice of the third-person narrator.

[26] Jay Lampert, *Simultaneity and Delay: A Dialectical Theory of Staggered Time* (Continuum, 2012), p. 6.

[27] Ingeborg Dusar, *Choreographien der Differenz: Ingeborg Bachmanns Prosaband 'Simultan'* (Böhlau, 1994), p. 15. On the story, see also Linda C. Hsu, ' "A Favorite Selection at the Beauty Parlor?" Rereading Ingeborg Bachmann's *Oh Happy Eyes*', in *Thunder Rumbling at My Heels: Tracing Ingeborg Bachmann*, ed. by Gudrun Brokoph-Mauch (Ariadne, 1998), pp. 76–90; Barbara Agnese, *Der Engel der Literatur: Zum philosophischen Vermächtnis Ingeborg Bachmanns* (Passagen, 1996), pp. 167–78.

the internal crises of its protagonists, both psychological and somatoform, and hence these individuals' deficient functioning in their social reality. In the paralipomena to her work, Bachmann herself explains that she wanted to observe her characters from the outside, from a certain distance. This aspect is crucial because it accounts for the connection between the collection and the *Todesarten* project, where Bachmann sought to represent the different psychophysical ways in which an individual can approach biological or symbolic death because of social pressure. *Simultan* was written against a historical background dominated by economic growth and peace in Europe, but also subject to the fears caused by the Cold War and the atomic threat, the war in Vietnam (from 1955 to 1975), the wounds left by war in Algeria (from 1954 to 1962) and in Austria, the never-fading memory of the collapse of the Austro-Hungarian Empire and two calamitous world wars. In its series of 'Frauenporträts' (TKA, IV, pp. 8, 11) [portraits of women], Bachmann remodels for contemporary Austria Honoré de Balzac's *Comédie humaine* [*Human Comedy*, 1830–56], a collection of works depicting the material reality and immorality of nineteenth-century French society. The reference to Balzac is condensed in the expressions 'Sitten' [manners] and 'Sitten einer Zeit' (TKA, IV, pp. 15, 11) [manners of a time] and the term 'mœurs' used in the paralipomena (TKA, IV, p. 8); it is revealing of Bachmann's ambition to write a little compendium of Austrian manners.

Crucially, Bachmann conceives her realistically portrayed but sentimental and idealist women as discreet and 'stoic' beings, only apparently phlegmatic in the face of social pain: 'Es mag ihr Mangel an Realismus sein, ihre Fähigkeit, sich stoisch zu verhalten oder sich den Traum zu erhalten in der Wirklichkeit' (TKA, IV, p. 8) [It may be their lack of realism, their ability to be stoic or to retain the dream in reality]. Bachmann's choice of the nickname 'Wienerinnen' (TKA, IV, pp. 12, 16) [Viennese Women] for *Simultan* was deliberate and not without irony. This name evoked another inspiration for the collection: the 1951 homonymous film by the 'leader of Austrian melodramatic neorealism', Kurt Steinwender, who demystified Vienna's refined image, depicting sentimental women in the most degraded districts and offering a 'bleak urban soap opera' (TKA, IV, pp. 547–48).[28] The narrators in *Simultan* mix tragedy with irony — what D. C. Muecke called 'situational/dramatized irony'[29] — to recount the use of violence towards vulnerable members of society in the Austrian postwar context. It is this mixture that marks the collection's autonomy from the other works of the *Todesarten* project, despite the strong connections, while at the same time serving to underline the alienation of its characters within the oppressive social environment in which they live.

[28] Robert von Dassanowsky, *Austrian Cinema: A History* (McFarland, 2005), p. 150.
[29] Veronica O' Regan, '*Dieses Spannungsverhältnis, an dem wir wachsen': Growth and Decay in Ingeborg Bachmann's 'Simultan'* (Peter Lang, 2000), p. 98.

It is the eye — according to Amm, 'an eloquent gauge of our feelings and emotions'[30] — that encapsulates this clash of the characters with social reality. Visual anxiety is present in one of the stories Bachmann later discarded, 'Rosamunde', featuring a woman who constantly shuts her eyes in addition to her ears: 'Augenschließen, Ohrenschließen' (TKA, IV, p. 29) [Closing of eyes, closing of ears]. Similarly, Nadja's eyes in 'Simultan' [Simultaneous], described as huge and childlike, are described in a constant tension between opening and closing, between seeing and not seeing. Finally, Beatrix in 'Probleme Probleme' [Problems Problems], in the throes of a crying fit, is shown desperately removing her make-up soon after the experience of sensory deprivation in the hair salon René's during her enclosure under the drier helmet, which had shut off 'sight and sound'.[31]

Although a scopophobic sentiment pervades the entire collection, Miranda's suffering eyes in 'Ihr glücklichen Augen' are its most prominent. Her speaking name already hints at this, evoking the Latin double meaning of 'to feel awe and wonder' and 'to look' ('mīrari'), as well as the homonymous character struggling with reality in Shakespeare's *The Tempest* (c. 1610/11; TKA, IV, p. 628).[32] Furthermore, the discourse on eyes developed in this short story is connected to the writings of the pioneer of psychosomatic medicine, Georg Groddeck, to whom Miranda's story is dedicated (TKA, IV: IGA, p. 243). Groddeck argued that eye disorders and diseases are attempts by the id to facilitate 'the repression of disturbing impressions from the external world on to the internal world'.[33] He is not, however, the only intertext in 'Ihr glücklichen Augen'. The very title is a quotation from Goethe's *Faust II* (1832), which refers to Lynceus, the guardian of Menelaus' palace in Sparta, a character resembling Miranda in his sensitivity, especially to beauty, in a wicked and 'dark' world.[34] According to Nebrig, the explicit reference to Goethe serves to lighten the collection's tone and to generate a (shaky) poetics of happiness (or sublimation), symbolized by Miranda's desire for repression and transfiguration at the visual level — for example, when she reterritorializes places, exploiting her blurred vision and imaginative potency: 'Da, schau, der Bisamberg! Es ist nur der Leopoldsberg, aber das macht nichts' ['Look over there, Mount Bisam! It's only Mount

---

[30] Marita Amm, 'Might and Magic, Lust and Language — the Eye as a Metaphor in Literature: Notes on the Hierarchy of the Senses', *Documenta Ophthalmologica*, 101.3 (2000), pp. 223–32 (p. 227).

[31] Rachel Magshamhráin, 'Don't Go! Some Agoraphobic Postulates for a Post-Travel World Derived from Ingeborg Bachmann's "Probleme Probleme"', *Austrian Studies*, 31 (2024), pp. 16–35 (p. 33).

[32] See Dusar, *Choreographien der Differenz*, p. 89.

[33] Georg Groddeck, 'Vision, the World of the Eye, and Seeing without the Eye' (1932), in *The Meaning of Illness: Selected Psychoanalytic Writings*, ed. by Lore Schacht (Hogarth, 1977), pp. 172–96 (p. 192).

[34] Heide Rieder, 'Von Goethe zu Georg Groddeck: Ästhetischer Anspruch und Blickverweigerung in Ingeborg Bachmanns Erzählung "Ihr Glücklichen Augen"', *Österreich in Geschichte und Literatur*, 38.5–6 (1994), pp. 315–24 (p. 316).

Leopold, but that doesn't matter'] (TKA, IV: IGA, p. 252; TPL: EW, p. 81).[35] If we consider the extent to which Miranda suffers when using corrective lenses — either those of her many glasses or her expensive contact lenses — and how she shows somatoform symptoms upon clearly seeing her social reality, expressed, for example, in headaches and the need to use anaesthetic eye drops, it is difficult not to appreciate, as in Ortese, how psychic distress and physiological dysfunction intertwine. Visual impairment is an ophthalmological metaphor of affect used to critique fiercely a contemporary society in which clear sight and the primary emotional dyad of joy-happiness are no longer compatible.

It is a paradox: with simple eyewear, easily affordable for her, Miranda could improve her visual ability. Yet she prefers blurred vision, an 'elective blindness', a condition embraced to 'stoically' withdraw from a social reality that severely impacts on her overall well-being. Her myopia and astigmatism ('Stab- und Zerrsichtigkeit', TKA, IV: IGA, p. 243) shield her inner peace and state of serenity: 'Denn was den anderen ihre Seelenruhe ist, das ist Miranda ihre Augenruhe' ['When Miranda's eyes are at ease, her mind is at peace'] (TKA, IV: IGA, p. 255; TPL: EW, p. 83). The narrator recounts how Miranda only wears her glasses when she wants to implement self-punitive behaviour: 'Einmal, um sich zu strafen, ist sie einen ganzen Tag lang mit der Brille durch Wien gegangen' ['Once, as a form of self-punishment, she walked all around Vienna with her glasses on'] (TKA, IV: IGA, p. 247; TPL: EW, p. 77). Revealingly, the depletion of Miranda's vitality passes through that similar sensitivity to anti-aesthetic postwar habitat and to people disfigured or impaired which can be also observed in *Il mare non bagna Napoli*: she is crushed, for example, when she sees '[E]in verkrüppeltes Kind oder einen Zwerg oder eine Frau mit einem amputierten Arm' ['(A) crippled child or a midget or a woman with an amputated arm'] (TKA, IV: IGA, p. 246; TPL: EW, p. 77). Therefore, the dedication to Groddeck does not only reinforce the idea that eye disorders and diseases are evidence of a conflict between an individual and their dystopian milieu, as Hsu points out.[36] It also reflects the conflict between the world of interiority — childlike, sentimental and, in its way, artistic — and a material reality shaped by a society of emotionally drained individuals. The gist of this story, too, seems to be the unsustainability of harmony between the reality and pleasure principles. It is an attempt to deconstruct happiness, underscored with black humour by the refrain 'Immer das Gute im Auge behalten' ['Never lose sight of the good/best things in life'] (TKA, IV: IGA, pp. 250, 274; TPL: EW, pp. 80, 94).[37]

---

[35] Alexander Nebrig, 'Der verborgene Goethe: Zur Glückspoetik in Ingeborgs Bachmanns Erzählung "Simultan"', *Jahrbuch der deutschen Schillergesellschaft*, 58 (2014), pp. 331–54 (p. 352).

[36] Hsu, '"A Favorite Selection at the Beauty Parlor?"', pp. 80–81.

[37] Jordan McKenzie, *Deconstructing Happiness: Critical Sociology and the Good Life* (Routledge, 2016), p. 92.

Like Eugenia, Miranda occupies a nonconformist and marginal position in her society; she fails to control her affective states and concretely and symbolically experiences all forms of physical and moral pain at eye level. Even the utterly painful separation from her idealized partner Josef — which constitutes another symbolic loss besides that of eyesight — does not affect organs such as her heart, stomach or head as it does in others ('nicht wie anderen', TKA, IV: IGA, p. 266 [unlike other people]). Miranda's pain pours into her eyes, exhausted by the eyelids' constant opening and closing as she weeps. In being so ocularly sensitive to pain, Miranda represents an adult woman with childlike traits, withdrawing from external visual stimuli to suffer less ('[A]lso Nichtsehenkönnen, Nichtwollen', TKA, IV: IGA, p. 209 [Hence, not being able to see, wanting not to see]). This childish, stoic and self-alienating strategy is made even clearer in an overlooked draft of the story in which we read that Miranda would rather have been a child (TKA, IV: IGA, p. 209). It can only lead, however, to the self-defeat encapsulated in the tragicomic fate of Miranda's clash with a glass door. The hail of glass shards described on the last page of the story's final version symbolizes, then, the impossibility of prolonging visual self-deception and transfiguration. Miranda cannot continue to ignore the unpleasant aspects of life in social environments, like Josef's betrayal with her friend Anastasia, the existence of physical flaws (for example, Josef's yellow teeth, the fuzz on her top lip or legs, her uncombed hair or the skin defects of herself and other women, such as pores, pimples and nicotine stains; TKA, IV: IGA, pp. 244, 256), but also the sight of postwar architecture, illness and impairments in 'bleak' Vienna.

In this case, the use of an ophthalmological metaphor of affect and somatoform reactions to vision does not stand for the misdirected desire and emotional flaws of a child who wants to see in a world of material and spiritual poverty (Ortese's Eugenia), but for a 'tender' woman (Bachmann's Miranda) who wants not to see to protect herself from a more developed and yet similarly oppressive Viennese social reality, an emanation of ugliness ('Emanation von Hässlichkeit,' TKA, IV: IGA, pp. 252, 246).

V

When Franz Haas wrote to Ortese on 17 August 1990, he reacted to her enthusiasm for Bachmann, saying that he was pleased to read that she liked Ingeborg Bachmann's books so much, although he would have guessed it without her saying so (*PPI*, p. 159). Ortese's correspondence with Haas thus seems to leave us with at least two messages: one, explicit, is her deep appreciation of Bachmann; the other, implicit, hints at the profound affinity between these two authors and their texts. In this article, I have examined Ortese's appreciation of Bachmann and, in particular, of her 'Neapolitan' poems 'Lieder auf der Flucht'. I have also attempted to set up a dialogue between *Il mare non bagna Napoli* and *Simultan*, and more specifically the short stories 'Un paio di occhiali' and 'Ihr glücklichen Augen' contained in the two collections, drawing on the theme of visual anxiety (or scopophobia). Through their insistence on sight, despite their geohistorical and linguistic distance, these works illustrate the intolerability of social reality in post-1945 Naples and late 1960s Vienna. This is reflected in the symbolic treatment of blindness as a shield for the protection of mind and body and in the somatoform suffering that Eugenia and Miranda experience when they see through their corrective lenses. While Ortese's collection is a more raw and direct portrayal of postwar Naples, denouncing the status quo, combining reportage and fiction, and lacking Bachmann's bitter irony, in both Ortese's and Bachmann's collections the discourse on clear vision nevertheless responds to a need felt by both authors: that of illuminating people's pain in their anaesthetized social contexts, ideally so as to curb the mechanisms of violence that lie underneath. The ophthalmological metaphor of affect reveals a shared device for giving prominence to marginalized individuals — be they pitiable and deprived children or 'childlike', lovelorn women — and for diagnosing, through them, deficiencies in late-modern relationships and conditions. If, for Ortese and Bachmann, blindness is a cultural metaphor, their two short stories seem to establish a causal link between the alienation of their near-blind protagonists and a Western civilization that crushes the mental, emotional and bodily components of the self.

'I have to like a person's voice, otherwise it won't come to anything': Embodiment and Neurodiversity in *Malina*, 'Alles' and 'Ihr glücklichen Augen'

LISELOTTE VAN DER GUCHT AND GUNTHER MARTENS

Ghent University

I

Recent forays into interpreting Ingeborg Bachmann's texts from the vantage point of Medical Humanities and (Mental) Health Humanities have moved significantly beyond author-centric speculative debates about the author's presumed health issues and have allowed for insightful elucidations of her oeuvre.[1] In his study of 'Ein Ort für Zufälle' [A Place for Coincidences], Däufel documents how Bachmann consulted a myriad of medical and psychiatric reports, with a view to presenting a social and constructivist understanding of medical conditions.[2] Similarly, Mairhofer argues that Bachmann engages in a 'creative and subversive act of (re)appropriating medical terms' in order to 'generate a narrative that can stand up to clinical discourse'.[3] Taking our cue from this line of research, we propose to use Neurodiversity Studies as a complementary access route into Bachmann's work to argue that body and mind closely interact in Bachmann's writing, and that this integrated understanding of the bodymind is pivotal to her conception of poetic and literary language. The concept of the bodymind was developed in the field of somatic psychology and later elaborated by Margaret Price and points to the enmeshment of body and mind.[4] Drawing on the conceptual apparatus of phenomenology, the notion of neurodiversity counters a reductive understanding of the cerebral mind as control centre by highlighting the importance of proprioception and interoception. Proprioception is the sense of one's body in space, interoception

[1] This research was made possible by a PhD fellowship from the Research Foundation — Flanders (1128124N). We would like to thank the anonymous reviewers, as well as Christine Kanz, Stijn Vanheule and Benjamin Biebuyck, for their insightful comments on this article.
[2] Christian Däufel, *Ingeborg Bachmanns 'Ein Ort für Zufälle': Ein interpretierender Kommentar* (De Gruyter, 2013).
[3] Marlen Mairhofer, 'Infizierte Narrative. Geschlecht, Sexualpathologie und Autofiktion bei Ingeborg Bachmann', in *Sexualitäten — Sexualities*, ed. by Franz-Josef Deiters and others (Rombach, 2019), pp. 99–114 (p. 112).
[4] Margaret Price, 'The Bodymind Problem and the Possibilities of Pain', *Hypatia*, 30.1 (2015), pp. 268–84.

Austrian Studies 32 (2024), doi:10.1353/aus.00013, pp. 174–89

is the body's awareness of its internal states (such as hunger, fatigue, emotions, and so on). Neurodiversity concerns the existence of alternative forms of the body's awareness of itself and thus represents a key concept in coming to terms with the embodiment of language. Our analysis of two Bachmann stories will show that a strictly medical view of either the brain or the body is reductive and needs to be supplemented by a dynamic and situated approach to enable us to grasp the bodymind's unique appreciation of its environment.

Before proceeding to analyse Bachmann's short stories 'Alles' and 'Ihr glücklichen Augen', we will first take a closer look at the neurodiversity paradigm and the consequences of its application to literary texts by analysing a passage from the novel *Malina*. We will then analyse the representations of sensory processing and its role in the writing process via the concept of hypersensitivity and its literary counterpart, synaesthesia. Thereafter, we will discuss the oppressive nature of language acquisition in the educational context, which enables an alternative language of proprioception that complicates everyday language use to be demonstrated with the story 'Alles'. This proprioceptive second language is expressed through the body via the metaphor of short-sightedness in 'Ihr glücklichen Augen', as we will show. So far, only one scholarly contribution has explored Bachmann's work in relation to Disability Studies: Gilman argues that Bachmann sought to counter the harsh views on the rehabilitation of blind people in the wake of the war, pointing out the relevance of Feldenkrais, a psychosomatic method aimed at improving mental function through movement therapy, to her discussion of blindness.[5] Ultimately, we will argue that, by examining Bachmann's work through the lens of neurodiversity, one can gain a deeper understanding of her characters and their complex relationships with language, the body and the world around them. Our claim is that Bachmann's nuanced portrayals of alternative bodyminds challenge traditional understandings of disability, highlighting the unique perspectives and challenges of individuals with atypical cognitive processes.

II

This section builds on the discussion of neurodiversity in Bachmann's work in the introduction, by examining specific representations of hypersensitivity in *Malina*. We analyse how atypical cognitive processes manifest in environments that are often experienced as oppressive or painful by characters. The vivid portrayals of sensory processing differences will be explored mainly through the concept of synaesthesia. To demonstrate the potential of the neurodiversity paradigm for literary studies, we turn to a passage near the beginning of *Malina* in which the protagonist remembers being tricked and slapped in the face on the way to school at the age of six: 'der ältere, mindestens zwei Jahre älter als

[5] Sander L. Gilman, *Stand up Straight! A History of Posture* (Reaktion Books, 2018), pp. 325–27.

ich, rief: Du, du da, komm her, ich geb dir etwas! [...] und gleich darauf das Klatschen einer harten Hand ins Gesicht: Da, du, jetzt hast du es!' ['the older one, at least two years older than myself, called out: You, hey you, come here, I've got something for you! [...] and all at once the hard clap of a hand on my face: There you go, now you've got it!'] (TKA, III.1, p. 294-95; MB, p. 10).[6] The autobiographical version of this anecdote, featured in Bachmann's *Kritische Schriften [Critical Writings]*, has been interpreted in various ways — as an echo of Améry's treatise on torture, or in terms of psychosis and trauma[7] — but reading it through a neurodiversity lens may further deepen our understanding of it. Of course, many young children are gullible, but misreading social cues to the point of naivety, as portrayed in this excerpt, can be reinterpreted in terms of having been socialized not to trust one's own emotions and to suppress these instead, which results in a certain vulnerability to being abused and/ or exploited. Taking this episode as our point of departure, we aim to show that reinterpreting Bachmann's work from this angle promises to unveil new insights into the author's oeuvre and its portrayals of the bodymind.

In recent years, there has been a substantial shift in the discourse (both scientific and societal) on neurodiversity. Formerly dominated by neurobiological approaches focused on explaining hypermasculine traits in young boys, the scope has now widened to include female and adult manifestations, while emphasizing the need to take into account lived experiences that comprise a wider range of (sensory) processing differences. In the wake of these developments, literary theorists like M. Remi Yergeau, Erin Manning and Eve Kosofsky Sedgwick have claimed that neurodiversity is also relevant to literary studies.[8] The focus on lived experience has been strengthened further by phenomenology and embodied cognition. Phenomenology also allows us to do away with harmful presuppositions attached to perceived impairments, such as an alleged lack of empathy, and recasts these as alternative sensory processing, manifesting, for example, as an extremely detailed perception with multisensory overlaps and focus on texture. In addition, embodied cognition stresses that empathy relies on patterns of interaction.[9] In one of her radio

---

[6] Ingeborg Bachmann, *Malina*, trans. by Philip Boehm (Holmes & Meier, 1999). References are marked with MB followed by the page number.

[7] Eva Sporschill, 'Psychose — Grundkonflikt und Versuche seiner Bewältigung', *Materialien*, 19 (2008), pp. 2-15; Sharon Weiner, 'The Beetle in Pain: Private Trauma in Ingeborg Bachmann's *Malina*', *Journal of Austrian Studies*, 53.4 (2020), pp. 1-25.

[8] Melanie Yergeau, *Authoring Autism: On Rhetoric and Neurological Queerness* (Duke University Press, 2017); Erin Manning, 'Not at a Distance: On Touch, Synesthesia, and Other Ways of Knowing', in Manning, *For a Pragmatics of the Useless* (Duke University Press, 2020), pp. 245-70; Eve Kosofsky Sedgwick, 'Affect Theory and Theory of Mind', in *The Weather in Proust*, ed. by Jonathan Goldberg and Michael Moon (Duke University Press, 2011), pp. 144-65.

[9] Daniel D. Hutto, 'ToM Rules, but It Is Not OK', in *Against Theory of Mind*, ed. by Ivan Leudar and Alan Costall (Palgrave Macmillan, 2009), pp. 221-38; Marco Caracciolo and Karin Kukkonen, *With Bodies: Narrative Theory and Embodied Cognition* (Ohio State University Press, 2021).

features on Wittgenstein, broadcast on 16 September 1954 on Bayerischer Rundfunk München, Bachmann quoted the following statement that resonates with the changed contemporary view of neurodiversity: '"Ich kann wissen, was der andere denkt, nicht was ich denke. Es ist richtig zu sagen 'Ich weiß, was du denkst' und falsch 'Ich weiß, was ich denke.'" [...] (Eine ganze Wolke von Philosophie kondensiert zu einem Tropfen Sprachlehre!)' ['"I can know what someone else is thinking, not what I am thinking. It is correct to say 'I know what you are thinking', and wrong to say 'I know what I am thinking'". [...] (A whole cloud of philosophy condenses into a drop of grammar!)'] (KS, p. 123; CW, p. 106). This quotation reflects Wittgenstein's view that language is a tool for communication and that it is not possible to discuss (or have) a private language. As such, analytical philosophy should not be about introspection, but about purifying language through logic. Looking more closely, it might seem quite paradoxical to 'know what someone else is thinking' rather than 'what oneself is thinking'. In the following discussion, however, we will show that it is actually typical for Bachmann's protagonists to sense what others are thinking and feeling — or that which they are unable or unwilling to contemplate — in a very somatized way. The young girl in *Malina*, at the age of six, for example, does not know whether it is normal or not to shed tears in such a situation. Not knowing when to cry may point to a difference in proprioception, or even to emotional blindness (alexithymia), but it could also be the consequence of having been repeatedly perceived as too sensitive and having been treated accordingly.

Furthermore, in the portrayal of a female writer-protagonist in *Malina*, the slap in the face discussed above is a perfect illustration of the peculiar, deeply embodied relationship to language in Bachmann's work. In a strangely combined state of fearlessness and naivety, the young protagonist does not recognize the ambiguity of the idiomatic turn of phrase 'ich gebe dir etwas' and expects a gift rather than a physical escalation. The excerpt features a persistent counting of things that is clearly marked as compulsive: 'dieses eine Mal ohne die Staketen des Zauns am Wegrand abzuzählen' ['for once not counting the pickets along the edge of the path'] (TKA, III.1, p. 295; MB, p. 10). Counting things in specific patterns is a common way to self-soothe, therefore it can be interpreted as a repair mechanism in the face of overwhelming sensory experiences. This is akin to magical thinking and may remind one of James Joyce's *A Portrait of the Artist as a Young Man*. In a passage also discussed by Lacan, Stephen Daedalus is beaten by the teacher. This scene is followed by a similar increase in pattern awareness: 'pitting himself against some figure ahead of him and quickening his pace to outstrip it before a certain goal was reached or planting his steps scrupulously in the spaces of the patchwork of the pathway and telling himself that he would be first and not first'.[10]

---

[10] James Joyce, *A Portrait of the Artist as a Young Man* (Oxford University Press, 2008), p. 66.

Similarly, the fragment from *Malina* clearly shows that the act of counting was already in place prior to the event experienced as self-shattering and traumatic. Thus, counting was not a result of the traumatic incident but already a coping strategy before this.

Counting and other stimming (self-calming) techniques can be linked to hypersensitivity because such strategies are often put in place to deal with intense stimuli resulting from surroundings or feelings, resulting in a very detailed and focused perception. However, as a consequence of this exceptional acuity of the senses, any kind of reckless use of language can, very fittingly, feel like a real, physical slap in the face. Ben-Horin discusses various instances of heightened 'sense perception as a textual manifestation' in Bachmann's works and argues in favour of applying the concept of synaesthesia.[11] She discusses the poem 'Früher Mittag' [Early Noon] in which the text subject implores: 'leg ihr | die Hand auf das Aug, daß sie | kein Schatten versengt!' (WI, p. 45) ['cover | its eyes so that | the shadows don't scorch it'] (DS, p. 37), 'eyes' that are synaesthetic in the sense that they experience light as (burning) touch. Similarly to Ben-Horin's interpretation of this poem, we would like to argue that the slapping scene on the bridge in *Malina* can be read as depicting the sensitivities of an audio-tactile synaesthete, who feels sounds and experiences inaccurate usage of language not only as a personal but also as a physical insult.

More positive aspects of neurodivergence figure more prominently in other Bachmann texts: multiple characters are endowed with photographic memory and perfect recall, such as Mahler in 'Unter Mördern und Irren', Undine in 'Undine geht' and, arguably, also Franza in *Das Buch Franza*. Representations of cognitive differences pervade Bachmann's work, often as part of a twice-exceptional profile. This combination is a mixed blessing of both giftedness and limitations. In the following section, we will show that these differences in proprioception and the heightened understanding of the thoughts and feelings of others testify to a strongly embodied conception of language and social interaction.

III

This section focuses on another key aspect of neurodiversity representation in Bachmann's work — proprioception and embodied cognition — through the story 'Alles' ['Everything'] and its depiction of a young boy's struggles with social norms and expectations. We argue that his behaviour can be productively analysed through the lens of neurodiversity and the concept of a 'language of proprioception' that exists beneath conventional verbal communication. 'Alles' from the short story collection *Das dreißigste Jahr* [*The Thirtieth Year*]

---

[11] Michal Ben-Horin, 'Seeing the Voices, Hearing the Sights: Perceptual Distortions in Böll, Bachmann, Celan', in *Seeing Perception*, ed. by Silke Horstkotte and Karin Leonhard (Cambridge Scholars Publishing, 2007), pp. 98–127 (p. 98).

features a father looking back at the tumultuous education of his son Fipps, a so-called unruly child. The story's echoes of Wittgensteinian ideas have been pointed out repeatedly.[12] As in *Der junge Lord* [*The Young Lord*], the opera co-authored with Henze, the focus lies on the stifling effect of societal pressures forcing people into conformism. In order to counter the corrupting influence of the forceful entry into the symbolical order through language, the father envisages the 'forbidden experiment' of Kaspar Hauser, a radical Rousseau-based negative education. While the topic of (re-)education can be seen as particularly virulent in a political context, and the boy's violence has so far been approached from this angle, the wish to spare him the acquisition of regular communicative skills deserves closer scrutiny. The non-name 'Fipps' carries Beckettian overtones and conjures up animality. Indeed, the boy is named after the protagonist of Wilhelm Busch's story 'Fipps der Affe' [Fipps the Ape]. Animality has in recent years increasingly been investigated as a conduit for discussing neurodiversity and its stigmatization.[13] Hence, it is feasible to explore the extent to which Bachmann's story allows for a discussion in terms of disability and neurodiversity.

Fipps's behaviour, increasingly seen as wild and transgressive, is deemed inappropriate for his age, for instance, when he attempts to stab another child with a knife. His behaviour strains the parental relationship, with the parents viewed as responsible for his sensory-seeking actions: 'Wir wurden in die Schule gerufen, und ich hatte peinvolle Besprechungen mit dem Direktor und Lehrern und den Eltern des verletzten Kindes' ['We were called to the school and I had painful discussions with the headmaster and the teachers and the parents of the injured child'] (SE, p. 155; TY, p. 79). Yet the father has no intention of 'taming' his wild son. Rather, he surmises that his son is in touch with a Cratylian language, a kind of 'Schattensprache' ['language of the shadows'] (SE, p. 145; TY, p. 81) that recalls Manning's evocations of synaesthesia: 'The shadow queers the surface of existence. The shadow spooks the norm, turning neurotypical experience on itself. The shadow follows and haunts, but it also leads and orients, inventing more-than-human worlds.'[14] There is a long tradition of compensating the vilification of non-normative 'other experiences' through the glorification of otherized people as some kind of 'noble savages', as terrible angels conveying humankind's true calling. In the twentieth century, for example, C. G. Jung's trickster mythology inspired writers like Thomas Mann and Ted Hughes.

---

[12] Nicole Weber, *Kinder des Krieges, Gewissen der Nation: Moraldiskurse in der Literatur der Gruppe 47* (Brill, 2020), pp. 448–49.

[13] Marla Carlson, *Affect, Animals, and Autists: Feeling Around the Edges of the Human in Performance* (University of Michigan Press, 2018); Derval Tubridy, 'Beckett, Neurodiversity and the Prosthetic: The Posthuman Turn in Contemporary Art', in *Beckett's Afterlives: Adaptation, Remediation, Appropriation*, ed. by Jonathan Bignell, Anna McMullan, and Pim Verhulst (Manchester University Press, 2023), pp. 126–39.

[14] Erin Manning, 'Pocketpractice. Ticcingflapping', in Manning, *For a Pragmatics of the Useless*, pp. 271–88 (p. 287).

Ultimately, Fipps falls — or possibly jumps — from a cliff during a school outing. By this point in the narrative, the entirety of the discourse surrounding the boy is focused on deflecting blame from the teacher and the school. It is unclear whether the vague medical and neurological explanation given — a 'Zyste' (SE, p. 156) ['cyst'] (TY, p. 80) — is only meant to explain his almost instant bleeding to death or also his jittery, hyperactive and at times downright violent behaviour, often towards other children. Already as a very small boy, Fipps reacts with what seems like aggression when he suddenly meets a neighbouring child on the stairs, for example: 'er griff ihm ungeschickt mitten ins Gesicht' ['he clutched clumsily at his face'] (SE, p. 144; TY, p. 68). Contemporary readers will be reminded of Richard Powers's *Bewilderment* (2021): appalled by the incessant medicalization of his son (whose single-mindedness is depicted as akin to that of Greta Thunberg) and of his own bereavement (the son's mother has died), the father engages in rewilding his child. Most critics blame the father for the death of his son. Likewise, Bachmann critics agree that, despite the unhappy ending, the father does not relinquish the utopian idea of abstaining from education and sticks to the utopia of a 'completely other' language. While communicative language can be drilled into people, the language of proprioception is invisible to most:

> Alles ist eine Frage der Sprache und nicht nur dieser einen deutschen Sprache, die mit anderen geschaffen wurde in Babel, um die Welt zu verwirren. Denn darunter schwelt noch eine Sprache, die reicht bis in die Gesten und Blicke, das Abwickeln der Gedanken und den Gang der Gefühle, und in ihr ist schon all unser Unglück. (SE, p. 143)

> [it is all a question of language and not merely of this one language of ours that was created with others in Babel to confuse the world. For underneath it there smoulders another language that extends to gestures and looks, the unwinding of thoughts and the passage of feelings, and in it is all our misfortune.] (TY, pp. 67–68)

Thus, this 'other language' of 'gestures and looks' proceeds at the level of proprioception. It constitutes the bodily basis of what most people perform unthinkingly, namely the automatic ideal of strong reciprocation — according to evolutionary psychology, the ultimate proof of one's sociability. For others though, 'in it is all our misfortune'.

Critics used to be rather wary of this story because it seemed to emphasize the role of a passive mother falling prey to the archetype of a dominant father.[15] As Schneider points out, it is more fruitful to read this story as a deliberation on the merits and pitfalls of reform pedagogy.[16] As illustrated by the recently published letters, Bachmann was very close to Ilse Aichinger and her twin sister

---

[15] See, for example, Ingeborg Dusar, *Choreographien der Differenz: Ingeborg Bachmanns Prosaband 'Simultan'* (Böhlau, 1994), p. 175.

[16] Jost Schneider, *'Das dreißigste Jahr* und Erzählfragmente aus dem Umfeld', in *Bachmann-Handbuch*, ed. by Monika Albrecht and Dirk Göttsche (Metzler, 2020), pp. 110–25 (p. 113).

Helga Michie, to the point of being nicknamed their 'third twin'.[17] Both sisters 'grew up in a family that enjoyed rich cultural experiences and was influenced by their Jewish heritage',[18] which comprised an upbringing in the creative spirit of reform pedagogy. The twins' mother had studied with Dr Eugenie Schwarzwald and was an accomplished musician and composer as well as a doctor.[19] Their father, meanwhile, was a bibliophile. The recently published letters exchanged by Bachmann, Aichinger and her husband Günter Eich reveal that Aichinger updated Bachmann in detail about the education of her son Clemens Eich. In a letter from June 1956, Aichinger had confided in Bachmann that there were concerns about Clemens being a late talker.[20]

Bachmann read the story 'Alles' at the Elmau meeting of Gruppe 47 in October 1957 and it was broadcast on the radio. While it remains a mystery what exactly caused the intimate exchange of letters to diminish over the ensuing months, it is striking that the sensitive topic of children and their developmental milestones vanished from the letters rather abruptly after the 'Alles' story. While Bachmann must have been attracted to the anti-authoritarian, hands-off education Ilse Aichinger aimed to impart to her children, it is not entirely speculative to think that Bachmann was wary of fostering, in real-life young children, the spirit of total rebellion against conventional language that she explored in her writing. To gauge the difference in upbringing, it is worthwhile pointing out that Aichinger had very little positive to say about her experiences with Schwarzwald. In a late article, Aichinger presented the latter's educational methods, regarded by contemporaries as shockingly free and progressive, as an example of barely veiled coercion and conformism.[21] In a 2015 interview with Iris Radisch, Aichinger attributed to Bachmann the inability to conceive of 'biologische Revolte' [biological revolt, anarchy].[22] This remark, in response to a question concerning motherhood, reads like a late rejoinder to the debate

---

[17] Irene Fußl, '"Dein Amt als 'dritter Zwilling'": Ilse Aichinger, Helga Michie und Ingeborg Bachmann', in *Zwischen Abschied und Ankunft: Between Departure and Arrival*, ed. by Geoff Wilkes (Königshausen & Neumann, 2021), pp. 79–87 (p. 81).

[18] Kirsten A. Krick-Aigner, 'Ilse Aichinger/Helga Michie: Zwischen Abschied und Ankunft. Between Departure and Arrival ed. by Geoff Wilkes (review)', *Journal of Austrian Studies*, 55.4 (2022), pp. 92–95 (p. 93).

[19] On the revolutionary nature of Schwarzwald's educational practices, especially for women, see Deborah Holmes, *Langeweile ist Gift: Das Leben der Eugenie Schwarzwald* (Residenz, 2012).

[20] Ingeborg Bachmann, Ilse Aichinger and Günter Eich, *'halten wir einander fest und halten wir alles fest!': der Briefwechsel*, ed. by Irene Fußl and Roland Berbig (Suhrkamp, 2021), p. 57.

[21] Ilse Aichinger, 'Unwillige Schülerinnen. Ilse Aichinger geht zum 73. Mal auf eine unglaubwürdige Reise', *Der Standard*, 15 May 2003 <https://www.derstandard.at/story/1302084/unwillige-schuelerinnen> [accessed 6 September 2024]. We would like to thank Deborah Holmes for bringing this article to our attention.

[22] Iris Radisch, 'Ilse Aichinger: "Erfüllte Wünsche sind ein Unglück"', in *Die letzten Dinge: Lebensendgespräche*, ed. by Iris Radisch (Rowohlt, 2015), pp. 31–47 (pp. 44–45).

on nature and nurture as carried out in and through the story 'Alles'. In more abstract terms, one could argue that this story charts the development of Wittgenstein's philosophy, from the earlier Wittgenstein's outward rebellion and refusal of psychology to the later Wittgenstein's more conciliatory stance, stressing the need to play along and imitate, yet at a tremendous cost to the sensitive individual.

In her acceptance speech for the Hörspielpreis der Kriegsblinden [Radio Play Award of the War Blind], Bachmann stated: 'Alle Fühler ausgestreckt, tastet er [der Schriftsteller] nach der Gestalt der Welt, nach den Zügen des Menschen in dieser Zeit' ['Extending all of his feelers, he gropes for the shape of the world, for the traits of humankind in this era'] (KS, p. 246; CW, p. 260). One might say that this is a logical thing to say in the context of physical blindness. However, Bachmann's writings extol not just the sensual pleasure of seeing, but also the need to supplement sensory perception through other senses. Above all, it would seem that the senses of seeing and hearing are very close to the sense of touch. The difficulty of evoking this in writing (rather than in music) is at the basis of a fundamental conflictedness, a 'Konflikt mit der Sprache' (TKA, IV, pp. 190–91) [conflict with language]. With regard to *Malina*, Burns convincingly argues that the '*Briefgeheimnis* [secrecy of correspondence] is the literary embodiment or performance of the impossible private language ("für mich allein")'.[23] The notion of a private language resonates strongly with the synaesthete's idiosyncratic relationship to texture and the primacy of materiality over communicative meaning.

In her study of the representation of fear in Bachmann's writings, Kanz draws on psycholinguistics to highlight the embodiment of language and writing. Bearing similarities to neurodiversity, the concept of *écriture feminine* foregrounds the materiality of language production and its imperfections: 'Stottern, Versprecher, unvollständige Sätze und Intrusionen inkohärenter Laute' [Stuttering, slips of the tongue, incomplete sentences, and intrusions of incoherent sounds].[24] Bachmann's writings are full of understanding and empathy for those whose command of their body (mouth, hands, posture) or language is less fluent and automatic than is commonly taken for granted by neurotypicals: 'Eine Schwäche für Analphabeten habe ich allerdings' ['I do profess a certain weakness for illiterates'] (TKA, III.1, p. 389; MB, p. 58). Many of Bachmann's texts can be read as advocating for transcending a deficit-based view of impairments in the direction of hyperabilities and hypersensitivity such as acoustic-tactile synaesthesia. In Bachmann's stories, for example 'Undine geht', characters lose the ability to speak, supporting an interpretation of selective mutism. In a similar vein, her poetry contains multiple references

---

[23] Niamh Burns, 'Communication, Performance and Metaphor in Ingeborg Bachmann', *Oxford German Studies*, 49.3 (2020), pp. 249–62 (p. 261).

[24] Christine Kanz, *Angst und Geschlechterdifferenzen: Ingeborg Bachmanns 'Todesarten'-Projekt in Kontexten der Gegenwartsliteratur* (Metzler, 1999), p. 53.

to people being infantilized or reprimanded because of their (invisible) bodily defects.[25]

While the story 'Alles' can also be read differently (for example, as signposting the aporia of a radically solipsistic private language), one can legitimately argue that everyday language (especially in its ossified, idiomatic variety, as echoed in many of Bachmann's poems and prose texts) is the real puzzle. In fact, the Mühlbauer interview in *Malina* expands on this idea, as the interview conceives of ordinary language as a punishment. Furthermore, the protagonist breaks down the acts of reading and writing to the bodily level of kinaesthetic joy in turning the pages, skimming the paragraphs and sentences, an oculomotor activity which is credited with an ecstatic, mind-altering intoxicating effect: 'ich nehme keine Drogen, ich nehme Bücher zu mir' ['No, I don't take any drugs, I take books'] (TKA, III.1, p. 388; MB, p. 57). While the notion of bodymind as a departure from a dualist divide between body and mind is a conceptual move shared by psychoanalysis, phenomenology and various philosophical monisms, we consider this type of intensified embodiment central to the understanding of neurodiversity. According to the paradigm of embodiment, literature can open up a space of vicarious experience through which the reader can go through the motions, even of non-normative patterns of feeling and perception.[26]

IV

While the previous section discussed male protagonists, father and son, in the story 'Alles' we now turn to the representation of neurodiversity in female characters. The reception of Bachmann's texts during her lifetime mostly took a negative view of the traits that we will analyse. As a case in point, the alleged diva-like behaviour of Bachmann's female protagonists was a major source of the reservations formulated by (predominantly male) early critics of her prose writing. We aim to show that these protagonists can also be explained as thematizing a hidden reliance on interpersonal support systems between bodies, which may supplement existing interpretations in terms of trauma or spatiality.

The terminology of proprioception allows for a different twist to the interpretation of the short story 'Ihr glücklichen Augen' [Eyes for Wonder]. The main character, Miranda, is extremely short-sighted and needs glasses, but she constantly loses them. From a neurodiversity perspective, the story can be

---

[25] Liselotte Van der Gucht, 'Words That Smack and Tremble: Narrating Neurodivergence in Ingeborg Bachmann's *The Book of Franza*', in *Critical Neurodiversity Studies: Divergent Textualities in Literature and Culture*, ed. by Jenny Bergenmar, Anna Stenning and Louise Creechan (Bloomsbury, 2025).
[26] For a recent application of this model, see Pierre-Louis Patoine, 'The Role of Empathy in Literary Reading: From *Einfühlung* to the Neuroscience of Embodied Cognition, with the Example of Kafka's *The Metamorphosis*', *Seminar*, 58.1 (2022), pp. 11–37.

read as a prophetic rebuttal of the tendency to couch popular understandings of neurodiversity in terms of a lack of social motivation (for example, as 'context blindness' and deficient perception). It suggests that, rather than understimulation, it is in fact an excess of perception, or an imbalance between hyper- and hyposensitivity, that is at stake. Miranda 'prefers to withdraw from the outside world',[27] but this is not simply a self-induced condition. In fact, she is all too keenly aware of other people's thoughts and feelings. She is able to sense their emotions, even when she is not physically present at the scene of a row between other characters, telepathically internalizing Stasi's low opinion of her as her own self-image: 'Miranda fühlt es körperlich, wenn sie darüber auch nie ein Wort erfahren wird' ['Miranda can sense it physically, although she will never hear a word of it'] (SE, p. 367; TPL, p. 89). The disabling effect is further reinforced by the negative attitudes inherent in her environment, in its desire for control and compliance:

> Mirandas Entschuldigungen, weil sie nicht grüßt oder nicht zurückgegrüßt hat, werden von einigen Leuten nicht ernst genommen, von anderen als dumme Ausrede abgetan oder für eine besondere Form der Arroganz gehalten. Stasi sagt beinahe gehässig: Dann setz doch eine Brille auf! (SE, p. 356)

> [Some people do not take Miranda's apologies seriously when she fails to say 'hello' or respond to greetings; others dismiss them as dumb excuses or find them to be a peculiar brand of arrogance. Stasi says, almost spitefully: Then put on a pair of glasses!] (TPL, pp. 77–78)

The effort required to attune herself to outward expectations leaves Miranda in the dark about her own needs and feelings. Being in a room with many other people is therefore totally exhausting: Miranda has to govern her own body in a very active way. Through their body language, those around her send all kinds of signals that are multi-interpretable and potentially also menacing: she feels surrounded by 'unglücklichen, hämischen, verdammten [...] Gesichtern' ['unhappy, malicious and damned faces'] (SE, p. 356; TPL, p. 77). This suggests that Miranda is most likely face-blind in addition to being short-sighted. Although Miranda gives the impression that she prefers not to see the world, we interpret the diva-like behaviour that leads to this impression as an ambiguous act of masking a potential structural weakness.[28] Mind-wandering is a similarly ambiguous strategy that allows her to navigate social encounters: 'Sie hat es erlernt, die Nervosität in Räumen aufzugeben, in denen Menschen einander

---

[27] Juliet Wigmore, 'Ingeborg Bachmann: *Simultan* (1972)', in *Encyclopedia of German Literature*, ed. by Matthias Konzett (Routledge, 2015), pp. 63–65 (p. 64).
[28] On the ambiguity attached to masking invisible impairments, see Liselotte Van der Gucht and Gunther Martens, 'Expanding the Scope of Disability Aesthetics: Unruly Bodyminds in Karen Duve's Bio-fictional Novel *Fräulein Nettes kurzer Sommer*', in *Jahrbuch für internationale Germanistik*, ed. by Habib Tekin and Leyla Coşan (Peter Lang, 2024), pp. 197–220.

notieren, abschätzen, aufschreiben, abschreiben, meiden, beäugen' ['She has learned to refrain from being nervous in rooms when people look around and take stock of one another, write each other off, avoid or eye one another'] (SE, p. 361; TPL, p. 83). This sensitivity also extends to the quality and materiality of voices: 'Bei mir geht alles übers Ohr, ich muß die Stimme von jemand mögen, sonst führt es zu nichts' ['With me everything depends on my sense of hearing, I have to like a person's voice, otherwise it won't come to anything'] (SE, p. 368; TPL, p. 91). Finally, not wearing her glasses is not meant to protect her from the ugliness of the world, but rather from her own overflowing hyperempathy, which is described in very somatic terms and as unsettling her very embodiment: the ugliness 'treibt ihr die Tränen in die Augen, läßt sie den Boden unter den Füßen verlieren' ['forces tears to her eyes, makes her lose her footing'] (SE, p. 356; TPL, p. 77).

However, constant compensation of cognitive differences has maladaptive consequences, described by Dusar as a 'hallucination',[29] potentially of Dantesque proportions. Hyperempathy becomes Miranda's day-to-day experience of reality. She compensates for her cognitive differences through her symbiotic relationship with Josef. While the loss of her support system threatens her bodily integrity, she even actively schemes for Josef to end up with Anastasia so as not to feel her own emotional suffering. Inevitably, the sensorimotor specifics of Miranda's behaviour become entwined with other psychologically relevant matters. Whereas contemporary critics were largely unanimous in their condemnation of Miranda's allegedly 'hyperfeminine' or 'weak' traits,[30] we argue that Miranda's reluctance to wear glasses is not narcissistic, but rather an act of self-protection against an acute perceptiveness that is experienced as overwhelming and bewildering. This vulnerability, however, is misunderstood as arrogance and haughtiness, a misunderstanding which is then further exacerbated by Miranda's candidness and her tendency not to mince her words. The final line of the story is another variation on the motif of violence inherent in idiomatic expressions such as 'Immer das Gute im Auge behalten' ['Never

---

[29] Dusar, *Choreographien der Differenz*, p. 77.

[30] Michael Matthias Schardt, *Über Ingeborg Bachmann: Rezensionen — Porträts — Würdigungen (1952–1992)* (Igel, 1994). Almost all male-authored reviews (collected by Schardt) contain unfavourable plot summaries denouncing Miranda for her lack of resilience (pp. 165, 166, 174, 182), culminating in Christoph Kuhn's allegation that Miranda feigns disability in order to garner attention: 'So braucht sie, die Übersensible, sich nicht der Umwelt auszusetzen [...], so wird sie hilfsbedürftig, darf Rücksicht in Anspruch nehmen, kann sich in ihre Invalidität verkriechen' (p. 182) [In this way, she, the oversensitive, does not need to expose herself to the environment [...], so she becomes in need of help, can claim consideration, can hide away in her invalidity]. Countering contemporary impressions, Renate Stauf singles out the untapped potential of these female characters on account of their subtle control over the weak men and their unclear situationships. Renate Stauf, 'Notation der Gefühle in Ingeborg Bachmanns Prosa', in *Große Gefühle — in der Literatur*, ed. by Toni Tholen, Burkhard Moennighoff and Wiebke von Bernstorff (Universitätsverlag Hildesheim, 2017), pp. 27–45 (p. 41).

lose sight of the good things in life'] (SE, p. 372; TPL, p. 94). While the figurative meaning of this turn of phrase is about optimism as a moral duty, the phrase's literal meaning is also activated in the story, through the witty slogan of the lens company (TPL, p. 80). Critics have taken Miranda's 'Zerrsichtigkeit' ['distorted vision'] (SE, p. 354; TPL, p. 75) to denote the medical condition of astigmatism. The term, apart from being overdetermined in studies of neurodiversity in modernists like Yeats, Joyce and Beckett, also connotes 'looking awry' and 'queerness'. Bachmann's characters frequently 'stumble' over figurative expressions, an action which we suggest could be reinscribed in terms of multistable perception.[31]

In this context, phenomenologists have shown that cognitive perception of *Kippfiguren* (flip figures) is intricately linked to the body (for example, through breathing), but also that differences in brain lateralization lead to altered, more simultaneous perceptions of such figures.[32] Understanding of idiomatic or figurative expressions similarly involves a 'gestalt switch' between a literal and a figurative meaning, which Bachmann challenges by using both meanings simultaneously. While one may argue that phenomenological takes on neurodiversity bear little resemblance to the phenomenology that Bachmann herself identified with, its overall orientation matches the importance Bachmann attached to raising awareness of the fundamental embodiment of language and its relation to psychosomatic health. Neurodiversity does not equal mental ill-health, but calls attention to the fact that a failure to recognize differences in proprio- and interoception aggravates the impact of cognitive differences.

Bachmann's posthumously published story 'Der Schweißer' [The Welder], in addition to introducing another non-fluent reader (moving his lips) in Bachmann's oeuvre, features a similar instance of a visual impairment, oscillating between a physical problem and a psychological state of hypersensitivity allowing for greater awareness of societal problems. A welder testifies to an extreme experience of hypersensitivity which he likens to welding without his protective glasses: 'und nun springt das Licht herein, wie ein Wolf, und frißt meine Augen, reißt meine Augen und mein Hirn auf' (SE, 69) [and now the light jumps in, like a wolf, and eats my eyes, tears open my eyes and my brain]. Faced with a blue-collar worker who develops a reading addiction, the story's doctor displays a similar disdain towards the reality of such a psychosomatic condition. As Eberhardt pointed out, both the actual description of the trance-like embodiment of language and the doctor's rejection of this experience ('Sie meinen wohl, Sie sind ein Genie und ich bin ein Idiot' (SE, p. 70) [you probably think you're a genius and I'm an idiot]), echo Dostoyevsky's descriptions of

---

[31] See Michael McGillen, 'Orientation in Pictures: Multistable Spaces in Kafka and Beckett', *Word & Image*, 36.3 (2020), pp. 225–36.
[32] Thomas Fuchs, *Verteidigung des Menschen: Grundfragen einer verkörperten Anthropologie* (Suhrkamp, 2020), p. 300.

epilepsy.[33] Sociologists point out that Bachmann was revolutionary in broaching the issue of mental health problems (at the time even more taboo than now) as the hidden reality behind the economic boom of the 1950s and 1960s.[34]

V

Examining *Malina*, 'Alles' and 'Ihr glücklichen Augen' through the lens of neurodiversity affords a deeper understanding of the characters and their complex relationships with language, the body and the world around them. We have established that Bachmann's nuanced portrayals challenge traditional understandings of normality. When viewed through concepts like hypersensitivity, synaesthesia and proprioception, Bachmann's work offers a powerful exploration of embodied cognition and the diverse ways in which individuals experience and interact with the world. While Bachmann herself has been generally assumed to take a very critical view of the medical system, on the basis of adverse personal experiences, it is hard to ignore that she had an extensive knowledge of psychoanalysis and of psychiatric discourses. Furthermore, Däufel notes that she inserted psychomotor peculiarities into many of her texts.[35] While these bodily symptoms may have been borrowed from Freud's description of hysteria, they increasingly figure independently as markers of a heightened awareness and hypersensitivity. According to Kanz, Bachmann insists on letting 'den Körper sprechen [...], dessen Sprache sie weder als Krankheitssymptomatik kenntlich macht noch als solche bewertet. Anders als der Analytiker bleibt die Schriftstellerin immer bei der Deskription, ohne medizinische Etikettierungen vorzunehmen' [the body speak, whose language she neither designates a symptom of illness nor judges as such. Unlike the analyst, the literary writer sticks to description, without resorting to medical labelling].[36]

The stories analysed above feature very specific medical diagnoses (like 'cyst' or 'astigmatism') that are either first posited but then contradicted because the diagnosis does not match the patient's bodily experience, or else emerge rather abruptly out of the hierarchical systems portrayed in the texts, tending to disempower the character's perspective. According to Däufel, formal linguistic experimentation allowed Bachmann to challenge successfully the authority claimed by (male) medical doctors, alluding to a special sensitivity and to hypervigilance towards universal impalpable threats

---

[33] Joachim Eberhardt, '*Es gibt für mich keine Zitate*': *Intertextualität im dichterischen Werk Ingeborg Bachmanns* (Niemeyer, 2002), p. 175.
[34] Wolfgang Hien, 'Körper und Arbeit — Die Schattenseiten des Wirtschaftswunders in Deutschland und Österreich', *Sozial.Geschichte Online*, 21 (2017), pp. 125–72.
[35] Däufel, *Ingeborg Bachmanns 'Ein Ort für Zufälle'*, p. 148.
[36] Kanz, p. 227.

in the world.[37] This hypothesis is reminiscent of insights formulated by neuroqueer feminism. Neuroqueer feminism 'shifts emphasis from single-axis to intersectional feminism, from critiques of sexism to critiques of ableism, and from top-down discursive analyses to bottom-up material or phenomenological analyses'.[38] It aims nevertheless to complicate 'total departures from the medical model' because taking an exclusively critical view of medical diagnoses risks 'invalidating women who experience physical and mental distress' and blaming them for complicity in demanding recognition and seeking medical help.[39]

To conclude, our analysis of *Malina*, 'Alles' and 'Ihr glücklichen Augen' demonstrates how Bachmann's work not only breaks taboos surrounding topics such as National Socialist history, patriarchy and heteronormativity, but also offers a nuanced and empathetic portrayal of cognitive differences affecting the bodymind. To date, most of these proprioceptive differences have been discussed under the wide umbrella of a psychoanalytical 'depth psychology' understanding of trauma. The terminology of proprioception belongs to the 'surface psychology' of development and has so far been considered by psychoanalysis to be too cognitive or intellectual. Through our discussion of a pivotal scene in *Malina* and two short stories, we have shown that Bachmann equips various characters with unconventional sensitivities and perceptions. By using the lens of Neurodiversity Studies, we can read these atypical cognitive-emotional processes as Bachmann's articulation of an intensified sense of embodiment.

The nascent field of Neurodiversity Studies, especially in the context of Disability Studies more generally, has encountered more reticence among scholars of German-language literature than among those of anglophone literature. This is probably due to the contested relation between the concepts of neurodiversity and disability, as well as to historical sensitivities surrounding disability in the German-speaking world. The neurodiversity paradigm, as applied to language within the field of neurolinguistics, may however provide a more cogent and comprehensive account of why, in 'Alles', as in many of Bachmann's writings, 'Sprache ist die Strafe' ['language is punishment'] (TKA, iii.1, p. 393; MB, p. 60). While Bachmann was very critical of the (male-dominated) medical world herself, she consistently referenced mental phenomena in medical and neurocognitive terminology, a feature of her writing which is currently attracting more and more attention among medical professionals and Medical Humanities scholars. However, if this type of research is insufficiently sensitive to literary specifics, it typically uses literary

---

[37] Däufel, *Ingeborg Bachmanns 'Ein Ort für Zufälle'*, p. 146.
[38] Merri Lisa Johnson, 'Neuroqueer Feminism: Turning with Tenderness toward Borderline Personality Disorder', *Signs: Journal of Women in Culture and Society*, 46.3 (2021), pp. 635–62 (p. 636).
[39] Ibid., pp. 641 and 636.

texts (and author biographies) simply to illustrate severe psychiatric conditions such as anxiety disorder, masochistic-narcissistic personality disorder and other personality disorders. In response and in opposition to this trend, we subscribe to the research goals of Critical Disability Studies, which questions the medical model of disability in favour of a constructivist understanding of how particular traits and conditions may acquire both enabling and disabling effects in specific contexts. The relative taboo on discussing female neurodivergence, in particular, is due to the fact that women are measured against or held up to higher standards implicit in traditional gender roles. Bachmann's texts can thus be shown to contribute to a destigmatization of the challenges encountered by unconventional bodyminds, drawing our attention to both the burden of invisible disabilities and the value of perceptual intensities.

A Place of Disturbance:
Ingeborg Bachmann and
Witold Gombrowicz in Postwar Berlin

TILL GREITE

University of London

The encounter in 1963 between Ingeborg Bachmann and the exiled Polish novelist and essayist Witold Gombrowicz formed one of the strangest — yet at the same time most memorable — constellations in literary postwar Berlin. Walter Höllerer, then a professor at the Technical University of Berlin and a key figure in the intellectual life of West Berlin, later noted that these two foreigners made 'un attelage bizarre, un couple étrange' [a peculiar pairing, a strange couple] in the walled-in city, as if a species of quite rare artists had been flown in.[1] Both authors had a challenging time in the city, particularly Gombrowicz. His problems arose not only from his specific linguistic situation, his lack of German at the time. It was more the fact that he — like Bachmann — was disturbed by what one can call, in a Freudian sense, the 'uncanny' of the city as the return of its repressed dark side, its hidden recent history.[2] It was Höllerer who was responsible for the institutional auspices of Bachmann and Gombrowicz's unexpected encounter in the dubious atmosphere of Cold War Berlin. As a talented organizer and intellectual transatlanticist, he had initiated a new kind of Artist-in-Residence programme in response to the construction of the Berlin Wall. Already in the late 1950s, Höllerer had established a successful lecture series called 'Sprache im technischen Zeitalter' [Language in the Technological Age], which marked a high point in the culture of postwar Berlin, a city that was still suffering from the compound effects of the brain

---

[1] Walter Höllerer, in *Gombrowicz en Europe: témoignages et documents 1963-1969*, ed. by Rita Gombrowicz (Denoël, 1988), pp. 171–80 (p. 179). On Höllerer as a key figure of literary postwar Berlin, see Helmut Böttiger, *Elefantenrunden: Walter Höllerer und die Erfindung des Literaturbetriebs* (Literaturhaus Berlin, 2005). About Gombrowicz as a first 'Bezugsperson', an 'attachment figure' for Bachmann in Berlin, see also Christian Däufel, *Ingeborg Bachmanns 'Ein Ort für Zufälle': Ein interpretierender Kommentar* (De Gruyter, 2013), p 100.

[2] For Freud the 'uncanny' is not something new or alien, but something familiar, which has become strange to a person or object through a process of repression. I claim here that, for postwar Berlin, recent history and its events similarly played the role of a secret disturbance. See Sigmund Freud, 'Das Unheimliche' (1919), in *Gesammelte Werke chronologisch geordnet*, ed. by Anna Freud, 18 vols (Fischer, 1947, facsimile repr. 1999), XII, pp. 227–78 (p. 236).

Austrian Studies 32 (2024), doi:10.1353/aus.00014, pp. 190–207

drain of those exiled by Nazi rule, a devastating war and the intellectual exodus following Germany's surrender in 1945.

For his new project, the founding of the first Artist-in-Residence programme in German-speaking countries, Höllerer counted on the support of the highly ambitious American Ford Foundation, which was looking for new partners and opportunities in West Berlin in the face of Cold War challenges.[3] By this time, the Ford Foundation had already begun promoting West Berlin's cultural life with a budget of 2 million dollars, an impressive sum by contemporary standards. The initiative aimed to bring to Berlin esteemed and cutting-edge novelists, poets and artists, including the French writer Michael Butor, the British poet W. H. Auden, the Greek composer Iannis Xenakis and the Italian painter Emilo Vedova. For the starved cultural ecosystem of West Berlin, the influx of new literary life was meant to provide fresh enrichment. However, with the influx of new impulses, unexpected problems arose. Witold Gombrowicz in particular, who was living in Argentinian exile when he received his invitation from Ford in spring 1963, saw this transatlantic mission as a last opportunity to return to Europe — a return, however, to a completely transformed and, in many respects, foreign continent.[4] Ingeborg Bachmann, too, embarked on her journey to Berlin from self-imposed Italian exile.[5] It seems that Bachmann accepted Ford's invitation in the hope that a new environment would have a liberating effect. In these years she suffered, as her correspondence with Max Frisch has recently unveiled, a severe crisis in her personal life.[6] Neither Bachmann nor Gombrowicz could have foreseen that the city would subsequently turn into a painful, if not disastrous, site of serious mental and physical disturbance.

Nevertheless, the encounter between Bachmann and Gombrowicz (who was a generation older than Bachmann) was a fortunate coincidence, as the two

[3] For the initial letter from the Ford Foundation's officials to Höllerer, see 'It is our [the Ford Foundation's] aim to discover new possibilities that distinguish Berlin culturally from other cities.' Walter Hasenclever, letter to Walter Höllerer, 20 April 1962. Walter Höllerer Archiv, Literaturarchiv Sulzbach-Rosenberg.

[4] See Witold Gombrowicz, letter to Moritz von Bomhard, 19 March 1963, Witold Gombrowicz and others, 'Berliner Briefe', in *Sinn und Form*, 75.1 (2023), pp. 34–59 (pp. 40–41).

[5] It was the British-German poet, translator and critic Michael Hamburger who included Bachmann among the group of 'self-exiled' German-speaking authors in the aftermath of the Second World War: Michael Hamburger, *After the Second Flood: Essays in Modern German Literature*, 2 vols (Carcanet Press, 1986), II, p. 122.

[6] Concerning Bachmann's crisis before her sojourn in West Berlin, see her correspondence with Max Frisch: Ingeborg Bachmann and Max Frisch. '*Wir haben es nicht gut gemacht*': *Der Briefwechsel* (Piper and Suhrkamp, 2022), pp. 481ff. On Bachmann's crisis as background for her experimental prose on Berlin see Áine McMurtry, 'The Case of the Berlin Writings', in McMurtry, *Crisis and Form in the Later Writing of Ingeborg Bachmann: An Aesthetic Examination of the Poetic Drafts of the 1960s*, MHRA Texts and Dissertations, 84 (MHRA, 2012), pp. 86–133.

authors, with their similarly sharp intellectual sensorium, came together in an unlikely friendship. In the words of the critic Silvia Bovenschen, one can describe both Bachmann and Gombrowicz as representing an 'idiosynkratische Aufstörung', an 'idiosyncratic disruptiveness', towards any inappropriate feelings of comfort.[7] Both sensed Berlin's eerie atmosphere and had the poetic drive to grasp its abysses, sketching out a place caught up in the traumatic aftermath of Europe's recent catastrophes.[8] From the beginning of their respective sojourns, both authors shared an unusual approach to the aesthetics of the city. Indeed, more than anything, the two experienced Berlin's uncanny flipside, an experience that alienated them from the literary mainstream of the time. Throughout their stay, both remained outsiders to the German literary scene, scrutinizing its peculiarities with an ethnographical gaze. As Bachmann remarked in her 'Entwurf' [draft] on the Polish writer, Gombrowicz in particular had to cope with a structural 'incompatibilité', an 'incompatibility' with the West German concept of literature represented by Höllerer's approach to mediatized events or by the promotion of group criticism established by the dominant Gruppe 47, both of which appeared to be the exact opposite to the old coffee house culture with which Gombrowicz had grown up.[9]

In addition to the fact that they rejected the aloof mentality of the German literary scene, the two authors also shared an ambivalent fascination with the strangeness of the place. They went on excursions together across the partly rebuilt, partly ruined city. On their joint excursions, they found themselves confronted with traces of its unspoken pain and latent horror. In this respect, Sigrid Weigel's remarks on Bachmann's key text on Berlin, 'Ein Ort für Zufälle' [A Place for Coincidences], with which the author intended to unfold a 'Wahrnehmung von Berlin als Symptomkörper der Geschichte' [a perception of Berlin as the symptomatic body of German history], apply equally to Gombrowicz's 'Berliner Notizen' [Berlin Notes], which were composed during the same years.[10] Yet both were not only engaged in urban pathography; Berlin also affected, intrigued and involved them emotionally. Their own case histories reflected the current situation of the city with its tragic history. What Bachmann regarded as a Lenzian 'Riß', a 'crack' running through the city, which she diagnosed as a symptom of historical 'Spätschäden' [long-term

---

[7] On the concept of an 'idiosynkratische Aufstörung', an 'idiosyncratic disruptiveness', see Silvia Bovenschen, *Über-Empfindlichkeit: Spielformen der Idiosynkrasie* (Suhrkamp, 2000), p. 100.

[8] On the idea of a European aftermath-experience in the postwar era, see also Cécile Wajsbrot, 'Echos eines Spaziergangs in der Künstlerkolonie', *Sinn und Form*, 67.2 (2015), pp. 253–65 (p. 255).

[9] See Ingeborg Bachmann, 'Witold Gombrowicz: Entwurf', in Bachmann, *Werke: Essays, Reden, Vermischte Schriften*, ed. by Christine Koschel, Inge von Weidenbaum and Clemens Münster, 2nd edn, 4 vols (Piper, 1982), IV, pp. 326–30 (p. 328).

[10] Sigrid Weigel, *Ingeborg Bachmann: Hinterlassenschaft unter Wahrung des Briefgeheimnisses* (Zsolnay, 1999), p. 373.

damage], the causes of which could be traced to even before 1945, is similarly present in Gombrowicz's writing.[11] He created his own powerful metaphor to describe the city's state of mind: Gombrowicz used the Shakespearean allegory of Lady Macbeth, a morally entangled figure tormented by her recent experiences of violence.[12] This emotionally ambivalent state expressed itself in episodes of traumatic disturbance.

Conversely, one can also argue that Berlin had to deal with two rather difficult guests in the shape of Bachmann and Gombrowicz. While the Berlin press praised Bachmann for her 'feinempfindliche Subjektivität' [delicately sensitive subjectivity], Gombrowicz exemplified Nietzsche's notion of the 'Mensch des Horizonts' [person of the horizon].[13] The term refers to a person who seems out of place in a city whose intellectual life, like that of postwar Berlin, is characterized by a 'foreshortening of history'.[14] For this very reason, as the novelist Ingo Schulze has pointed out, Gombrowicz's subtle wit and polemic remarks provided unusual 'Positionslichter' [navigation lights] on West Berlin's gloomy mental map in the 1960s.[15] Both authors believed that only pain opens one's eyes. It was Bachmann who formulated this insight by saying that only a 'geheime[r] Schmerz' [secret pain] makes one 'empfindlich für die Erfahrung' [sensitive to experience].[16] Gombrowicz probably already anticipated that this city would confront him with the uncanny par excellence, in the guise of its own repressed past. We know that Gombrowicz initially declined Höllerer's

---

[11] On the motif of the 'ungeheuern Riß', see Georg Büchner, *Lenz: Studienausgabe mit Quellenanhang und Nachwort*, ed. by Hubert Gersch (Reclam, 1998), p. 27. Bachmann's notion of 'Spätschäden' has a certain affinity to psychoanalytical concepts of transgenerational analysis of trauma that culminated in the idea — conceptualized by Nicolas Abraham and Maria Torok — of a secret 'crypt' which entombs an unspeakable pain or grief. For more on this see Nicolas Abraham and Maria Torok, *L'écorce et le noyau* (Flammarion, 1987), and Gabriele Schwab, *Haunting Legacies: Violent Histories and Transgenerational Trauma* (Columbia University Press, 2010). For a Groddeckian perspective on Bachmann's image of Berlin as a place of 'latent disturbance', see McMurtry, 'The Case of the Berlin Writings', p. 124.

[12] See Witold Gombrowicz, *Berliner Notizen*, trans. by Walter Tiel (Neske, 1965), p. 84.

[13] About Bachmann, see: Hero, *Die Welt*, 13 January1960: 'Sie lasen aus eigenen Werken. Vortragsreihe mit Max Frisch und Ingeborg Bachmann eröffnet', Berlin, Archiv der Akademie der Künste, Pressearchiv 698. Ingeborg Bachmann 1959-1979. See also Friedrich Nietzsche, 'Die fröhliche Wissenschaft' (1882), in *Sämtliche Briefe: Kritische Studienausgabe*, ed. by Giorgio Colli and Mazzino Montinari, 2nd edn, 8 vols (dtv, 2003), III, pp. 343-651 (p. 565).

[14] For the expression of a 'foreshortening of history' in postwar Germany, see Hamburger, *After the Second Flood*, p. 30.

[15] This remark on Gombrowicz was discussed at a public event at the Berlin Academy of Fine Art: 'Ich habe noch einen Koffer in Berlin — Witold Gombrowicz und die Deutschen. Lesung und Gespräch, 20 May 2014. Mit Rita Gombrowicz, Ingo Schulze und Olaf Kühl', Berlin, Archiv der Akademie der Künste, AVM-36 1765.

[16] Bachmann, 'Die Wahrheit ist dem Menschen zumutbar: Rede zur Verleihung des Hörspielpreises der Kriegsblinden', in *Werke: Essays, Reden, Vermischte Schriften*, IV, pp. 275-77 (p. 275).

invitation, which was to be his first contact with the new European spirit of literature after 1945, purportedly for health reasons. In his diary, however, he commented on Höllerer's attempt to bring him to Berlin. He was invited, he noted in 1959, to a congress — Höllerer's lecture series 'Sprache im technischen Zeitalter', which would mean 'zehntausend Kilometer hinfliegen' [flying ten thousand kilometres] in order to read for 'fünf Minuten' [five minutes], all simultaneously translated.[17] For the Polish expatriate, the idea of presenting literature at a congress, in a highly organized manner, was a form of absurdity. The author, still influenced by the more playful concept of the old European coffee house literature, was puzzled: 'Und flog nicht' [And didn't fly].[18]

If he had come, he would have seen that Ingeborg Bachmann had her own troubles dealing with the new technologically based approach to literature that Höllerer promoted in the postwar era.[19] On the occasion of her reading in West Berlin's recently opened congress hall, the press described the poet as one who approached the stage only 'widerstrebend mit Scheu' [reluctantly with shyness] and read aloud 'mit in sich hineinmurmelnder Stimme' [in a voice murmuring to herself].[20] Even more remarkable is the characterization of Bachmann at this early stage of her career: for the Berlin press she embodied a foreign voice from an 'abgelegenen Landschaft' [remote landscape], someone whose speech had a 'Dialektfärbung' [colouring of dialect] that marked her as coming from the periphery of German-speaking territory.[21] In the words of the literary critic George Steiner, Bachmann could be described as an extraterritorial author — and it is this attitude that drew her closer to Gombrowicz in Berlin.[22]

A year and a half later, Gombrowicz received his second invitation. Höllerer had now joined forces with the powerful funding organization Ford Foundation, taking advantage of American fears after the construction of the Berlin Wall. One main worry of the Americans concerned the possibility that the Soviets could take hold of the entirety of Berlin and gain a decisive advantage in what the historian Volker Berghahn called the Intellectual Cold War in Europe.[23] After August 1961, Western diplomats, according to a Ford memorandum after August 1961, had 'occasional nightmares' that one day there could be a 'sudden

---

[17] Witold Gombrowicz, *Tagebuch 1953–1969*, trans. by Olaf Kühl (Fischer, 2004), p. 761.

[18] Ibid., p. 761.

[19] On Höllerer as a key literary mediator in the new technological age, see *Poetik im technischen Zeitalter: Walter Höllerer und die Entstehung des modernen Literaturbetriebs*, ed. by Achim Gaisenhanslüke and Michael Peter Hehl (transcript, 2013).

[20] See Hero, *Die Welt*, 13 January 1960: 'Sie lasen aus eigenen Werken'.

[21] Ibid.

[22] George Steiner, *Exterritorial: Schriften zur Literatur und Sprachrevolution* (Suhrkamp, 1974), pp. 17–27.

[23] Concerning America's cultural Cold War against the Soviet Union with emphasis on Berlin's symbolic importance see Volker R. Berghahn, *America and the Intellectual Cold War in Europe: Shepard Stone between Philanthropy, Academy, and Diplomacy* (Princeton University Press, 2002).

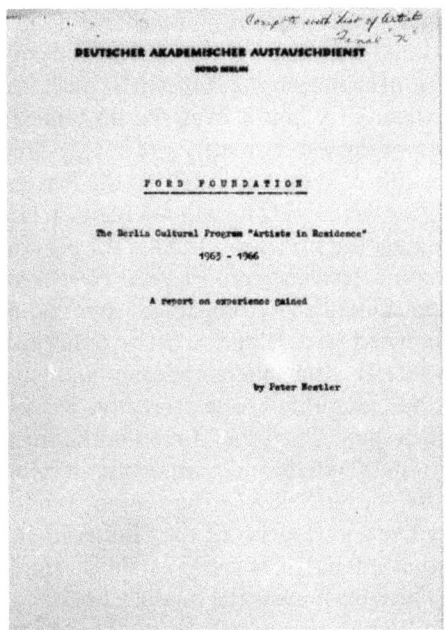

FIG. 1. Frontispiece of the final report on Ford's Berlin project: Peter Nestler, 'The Berlin Cultural Program "Artists in Residence" 1963–1966. A report on experience gained', Ford Foundation records. Grants E-G (FA732C). German Academic Exchange Service (0630351). Series: Ford Foundation Grants –E to G. Date: 1963 May 29 — 1966 July 23. Reel 3075. Rockefeller Archive Center, Sleepy Hollow.

orientation' of all of Berlin towards Moscow.[24] In the early 1960s, the Ford Foundation therefore promoted a number of cultural and academic activities in the Western part of the city and funded the Free University of Berlin, founded in 1948 to compensate for the loss of the soon-to-be East German Humboldt University.[25] 'Compensation' was also the keyword behind the Berlin mayor Willy Brandt's concept of a 'Kulturstadt' [city of culture], a revitalization of the Western half of the erstwhile capital of the German Reich. The aim was to convince mostly young citizens of the Federal Republic to move to the isolated city and to repopulate it. The Ford Foundation played its part in this strategy. Ford's memorandum from 1962 concluded: 'All these exchanges, as

[24] Albert D. Kappel. Berlin-Dossier, p. 21. Ford Foundation records, International Affairs, Office Files of Joseph E. Slater (FA619). Europe/Atlantic Berlin Jan 1962, Dec 1965. Series II: Geographic Files; Subseries 2: Europe/Atlantic; Subseries: Countries. Box 17 Folder 160. Rockefeller Archive Center, Sleepy Hollow.

[25] For the Ford Foundation's projects at the Free University, see: Ford Foundation records. Grants S-Thel (FA732G). The Free University of Berlin (05800260); Series: Ford Foundation Grants — S to Thel. Date: 1958 June 23–1963 June 22. Reel 2419. Rockefeller Archive Center, Sleepy Hollow.

a complement to a larger and more comprehensive program in Berlin, could have a great morale-building effect on the city (as a secondary result) and an enormous intellectual influence on the future (the most important result).'[26]

Notwithstanding these lofty hopes, West Berlin was characterized in these years by a growing atmosphere of unreality and a widespread feeling of 'eternal uncertainty'.[27] The people of West Berlin felt, as the Berlin-based novelist Kurt Ihlenfeld put it, as if they were living on a 'loses Blatt', a 'loose leaf' in the wind, a small island amidst ongoing turmoil.[28] In fact, the programme started, as the author of Ford's Artist-in-Residence report Peter Nestler wrote retrospectively (Fig. 1), at a 'psychological nadir'.[29] According to internal papers, the hope was that an influx of renowned writers and artists would provide an 'intellectual injection' into this political 'atmosphere of gloom and tension'.[30] In an almost idealistic vein, Ford thus sought to create a 'creative ferment' to counteract the city's latent mood of despair. The crucial memorandum about the envisaged counter-actions elaborates: 'Artists and humanists, forming a small percentage of a total community, nevertheless influence to a remarkable degree the society in which they live and flourish (if they flourish).'[31] In short, the project rested on the belief that intellectuals could establish 'thought patterns' across generations and, for Ford, Berlin was the model laboratory for a new urban life in the age of the Cold War.

In other words, Gombrowicz and Bachmann were not only invited to Berlin to 'fill' an intellectual vacuum in the city's literary life, but also to showcase a cultural-political project. This aspiration particularly pertained to Gombrowicz, who could — in the eyes of Ford and its German partners — reach

[26] Mateo Luttnich, Chief Arts Program, to Joseph E. Slater, August 13, 1962, p. 3. Ford Foundation records, International Affairs, Office Files of Joseph E. Slater (FA619). Europe/Atlantic Berlin Jan 1962 Dec 1965. Series II: Geographic Files; Subseries 2: Europe/Atlantic; Subseries: Countries. Box 17 Folder 160.

[27] See Albert D. Kappel. Berlin-Dossier, p. 21. Ford Foundation records, International Affairs, Office Files of Joseph E. Slater (FA619). Europe/Atlantic Berlin Jan 1962, Dec 1965. Series II: Geographic Files; Subseries 2: Europe/Atlantic; Subseries: Countries. Box 17 Folder 160. Rockefeller Archive Center, Sleepy Hollow.

[28] Ibid. For the metaphor of Berlin as a 'loose leaf' see Kurt Ihlenfeld, *Loses Blatt Berlin: Dichterische Erkundung der geteilten Stadt* (Eckart, 1968), p. 8.

[29] The Berlin Cultural Program 'Artists in Residence' 1963–1966, p. 2. A report on experience gained by Peter Nestler. Ford Foundation records. Grants E-G (FA732C). German Academic Exchange Service (0630351). Series: Ford Foundation Grants — E to G. Date: 1963 May 29–1966 July 23. Reel 3075. Rockefeller Archive Center, Sleepy Hollow.

[30] Robert Manning, 'The Literarisches Colloquium Berlin' (1965), p. 2. Ford Foundation records. Grants E-G (FA732E). Literary Colloquium Berlin (06300355). Series: Ford Foundation Grants — L to N. Date: 1963 June 05–1966 June 04. Reel 0681. Rockefeller Archive Center, Sleepy Hollow.

[31] Mateo Luttnich, 'Chief Arts Program', to Joseph E. Slater, August 13, 1962, p. 1. Ford Foundation records, International Affairs, Office Files of Joseph E. Slater (FA619). Europe/Atlantic Berlin Jan 1962 Dec 1965. Series II: Geographic Files; Subseries 2: Europe/Atlantic; Subseries: Countries. Box 17 Folder 160. Rockefeller Archive Center, Sleepy Hollow.

FIG. 2. The return of the old European *flâneur* to an entirely changed continent.
Witold Gombrowicz in West Berlin in May 1964: View from his balcony with an
emblematic view of the rebuilt Tiergarten district. The photo by Susanna Fels
(Berlin) is taken from *Gombrowicz en Europe*, pp. 104–05. With thanks to Rita
Gombrowicz.

readers behind the Iron Curtain. In this respect, it was Gombrowicz's patron
and colleague Jerzy Giedroyc, the editor of the most important Polish exile
magazine *Kultura*, who later alerted Gombrowicz to the unique situation he
had fallen into, positioned at the crossroads of East and West Berlin. Giedroyc
saw Berlin as a hot spot in a Cold War of ideas: a place 'plus en plus brûlant'
[more and more hot].[32] After later leaving for France, Gombrowicz remarked of
his experience in Berlin that the people in charge of the programme had tried
to offer him for sale to the free world like a 'Tüte Bonbons' [bag of sweets].[33]
Something of these advertising slogans can be found in Ford's letters of
invitation, which highlight the quality of the working atmosphere in Berlin, as
well as its lush greenery.[34]

---

[32] Giedroyc further explained to Gombrowicz that he had involuntarily become part of a
project to support the 'dynamisme intellectuel de Berlin' [the intellectual vitality of Berlin].
For details, see Jerzy Giedroyc, letter to Witold Gombrowicz, 9 Nov. 1963, in Jerzy Giedroyc
and Witold Gombrowicz, *Correspondance, 1950–1969* (Fayard, 2004), pp. 364–66 (p. 364).
[33] Gombrowicz, *Tagebuch*, p. 928.
[34] See the official letter of invitation from Moritz von Bomhard to Witold Gombrowicz, 13
March 1963, in *Sinn und Form* 75.1 (2023), pp. 39–40.

This putatively idyllic atmosphere, however, did not quell Bachmann and Gombrowicz's sense that they were in an uncanny place. Gombrowicz lodged in the newly built Hansaviertel near Tiergarten, Berlin's central park, for the first few weeks of his stay (Fig. 2), where he wondered, according to his 'Berliner Notizen', about the 'rechtwinklige Klötzchen von fünfzehnstöckigen Häusern im Grünen' [rectangular blocks of fifteen-floor houses in a green area].[35] The city, which he labelled the 'Zentrum der Katastrophen' [centre of catastrophes], felt to him like a 'historischer Witz' [historical joke], in which it was very comfortable to live.[36] Similarly, Bachmann described the physiognomy of her first stay in West Berlin: for her, the sterile concrete-based reconstruction style, set into the landscape of the Mark Brandenburg, had something of the idyllic and uncanny at the same time.[37] The atmosphere became 'ghostly', to cite the word of the ex-Berliner and returned exile Günther Anders, who still remembered the Jewish inhabitants of the former neighbourhood of the old Hansaviertel. The superficial illusion of a postwar idyll in West Berlin revealed a latent ghostly space underneath. Figures like Anders developed a stereoscopic perspective on the city, torn between the past and the present.[38] According to Anders, only the old street names with the street signs of the former quarter had been preserved: 'Das erinnert an jene Friedhöfe' [It reminds us of those cemeteries], Anders wrote in his diary Die Schrift an der Wand [The Writing on the Wall], 'deren Grabsteine man sehen lässt, obwohl man die Särge und die Toten schon entfernt hat' [whose gravestones are left visible, even though the coffins and the dead have already been removed.][39] However, non-locals, like Bachmann and Gombrowicz, could only guess what was hidden from view beneath the surface.

Both authors developed their own method of dealing with the city: a practice that went beyond a mere symptomatology of the urban space seen as a pathological body, as Weigel emphasizes. Both writers are distinguished by their use of metaphors drawn from the literary tradition. In order to grasp the historical layers of the cityscape and the remnants of historical catastrophe, both writers felt the need to look beneath the surface. Their procedure of

---

[35] Gombrowicz, Berliner Notizen, p. 72.

[36] Ibid., p. 95.

[37] See the description of 'neue kahle, ungefärbte Kirchen' [new, bare, unpainted churches]: Ingeborg Bachmann, 'Ein Ort für Zufälle: Rede zur Verleihung des Georg-Büchner-Preises', in Bachmann, Werke: Essays, Reden, Vermischte Schriften, pp. 278–93 (p. 281). A similar description can be found in: Marie Luise Kaschnitz, Tagebücher 1936–1966, ed. by Christian Büttrich and others, 2 vols (Insel, 2000), I, p. 616.

[38] On the concept of a stereoscopic view of the urban city space in a historical perspective, see Walter Benjamin, 'Einbahnstraße', in Benjamin, Das Passagen-Werk: Gesammelte Schriften, ed. by Tillmann Rexroth, 7 vols (Suhrkamp, 1991), IV.1, pp. 83–148 (p. 128). See also Walter Benjamin, Das Passagen-Werk: Gesammelte Schriften, ed. by Tillmann Rexroth, 7 vols (Suhrkamp, 1991), V.1, p. 588.

[39] Günther Anders, Die Schrift an der Wand: Tagebücher 1941 bis 1966 (C. H. Beck, 1967), p. 257.

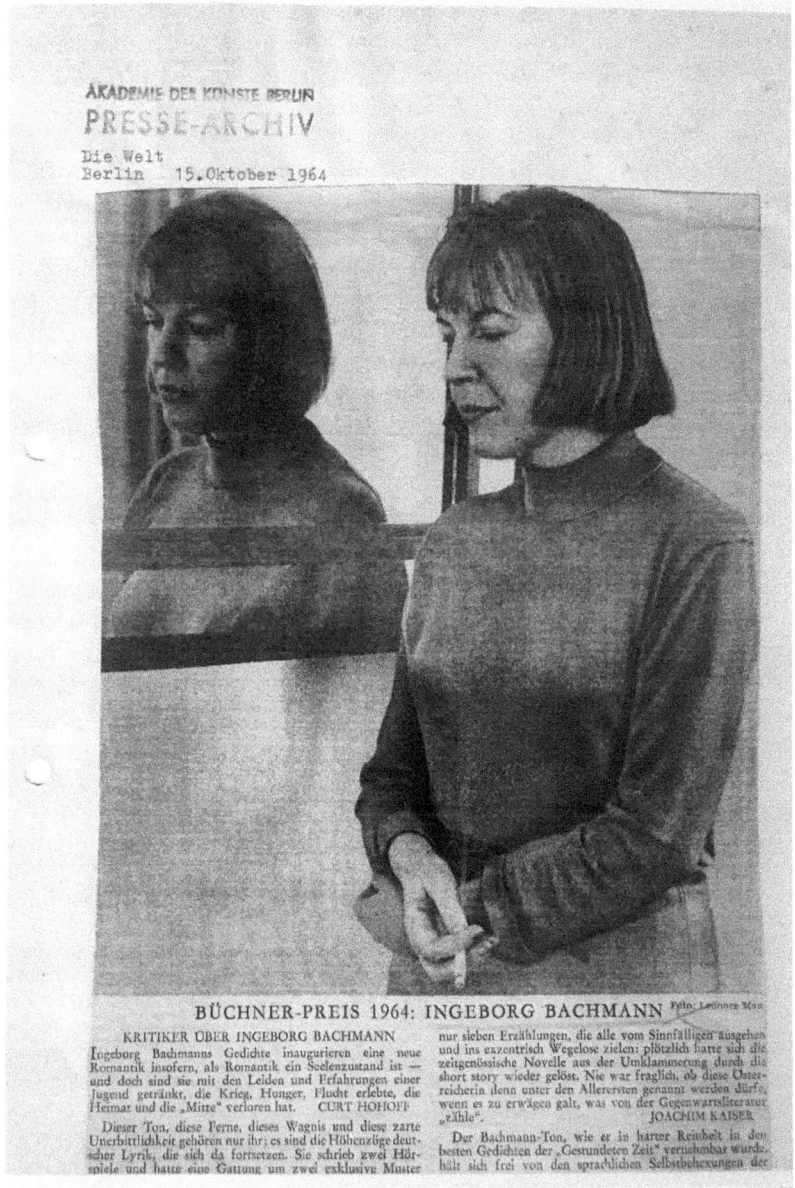

FIG. 3. The inward-looking gaze of the female 'Kundschafter' in West Berlin.
Photo taken by Leonore Mau. *Die Welt*, Berlin, 15 October 1964. Büchner-Preis
1964: Ingeborg Bachmann. Akademie der Künste Berlin, Pressearchiv 698.
Ingeborg Bachmann 1959–1979. With thanks to Gabriele Zenke, Academy of Fine
Arts Berlin.

involuntary encounters evokes the notorious figure of the *flâneur*. They evoke the Berlin-based variant of this tradition, of which the philosopher and critic Walter Benjamin undoubtedly formed the highpoint. For Benjamin, the *flâneur* was a kind of local historian shaped by intimate knowledge of the city's past and present.[40] The view of the Benjaminian *flâneur* productively constellated the present moment with the past, reaching beyond superficial appearances and creating something like a double-exposed image of the cityscape. However, it would be short-sighted to call Bachmann simply a *flâneuse*, given the elaboration in 'Ein Ort für Zufälle' of her own approach towards the city and the coining of expressions for her own way of dealing with it.[41] She regarded herself as both a 'Kundschafter' [scout] (Fig. 3), and at the same time an 'Ortsfremde' [an alien to a place], a stranger whose foreignness afforded her a productive peripatetic mode of observation.[42]

Bachmann's mode of observation had two dimensions: firstly, it emphasized an explicitly foreign view of the former capital of Berlin 'in Ihrem Land' [in your country], as she formulated in 'Ein Ort für Zufälle'.[43] She stressed here, to speak with the poet and critic Michael Hamburger, her 'self-exile'; it was her unique path via Vienna to Rome that led her to West Berlin — a trajectory that, as Hamburger has shown, deeply affected her poetic practice.[44] Secondly, she emphasized, using a phenomenological term that indicates her philosophical background, her 'Einstellung' [orientation].[45] Hers was the attitude of the scout as witness and herald, reminiscent of the mythological figure of Hermes.[46] However, Bachmann's scout turns out to be a Hermes deeply entangled in her own message, who does not stand in a neutral position towards the

---

[40] Benjamin, 'Die Wiederkehr des Flaneurs' (1929), in Benjamin, *Gesammelte Schriften*, ed. by Rolf Tiedemann and Hermann Schweppenhäuser, 7 vols (Suhrkamp, 1982), III, pp. 194–99 (p. 194).

[41] For a feminist perspective on the figure of the *flâneur* see Laurin Elkin, *Flâneuse: Women Walk the City in Paris, New York, Tokyo, Venice and London* (Penguin Random House, 2017).

[42] Bachmann, 'Ein Ort für Zufälle', p. 279. Concerning Bachmann's 'Rolle der ortsfremden Kundschafterin', her 'role of the non-local scout' in Berlin, see also Bernhard Böschenstein, 'Die Büchnerpreisreden von Paul Celan und Ingeborg Bachmann', in *Poetische Korrespondenzen: Vierzehn Beiträge*, ed. by Bernhard Böschenstein and Sigrid Weigel (Suhrkamp, 1997), pp. 260–69 (p. 261).

[43] Bachmann, 'Ein Ort für Zufälle', p. 279.

[44] See Hamburger, *After the Second Flood*, pp. 122 and 128.

[45] Regarding the phenomenological 'Einstellung' as a procedure of thinking, see Hans-Rainer Sepp, 'Einstellung', in *Wörterbuch der phänomenologischen Begriffe*, ed. by Helmuth Vetter (Meiner, 2004), pp. 133–36 (p. 135). See also Bachmann, 'Ein Ort für Zufälle', p. 279. Bachmann once referred to phenomenology as a method in which all phenomena are 'unmittelbar gegeben' [directly given] self-evidence: Ingeborg Bachmann, 'Philosophie der Gegenwart', in Bachmann, *Kritische Schriften*, ed. by Monika Albrecht and Dirk Göttsche (Piper, 2005), pp. 20–34 (p. 21).

[46] On the concept of Hermes as the interpreter par excellence: Hans-Georg Gadamer, 'Klassische und philosophische Hermeneutik', in Gadamer, *Gesammelte Schriften Wahrheit und Methode: Ergänzungen Register*, 10 vols (Mohr Siebeck, 2006), II, pp. 92–117.

phenomenon she describes. Since this city forced one to become like it, Berlin could even compel one, as Bachmann wrote in an allusion to Georg Büchner's *Lenz*, to walk 'auf dem Kopf' [on one's head].[47] In short, the city urged the scout to develop her own 'Einstellung auf Krankheit' [orientation towards illness].[48]

This is precisely the attitude of the 'involved scout' that also shaped Gombrowicz's Berlin writing. He describes the same experience in his *Berliner Notizen* when, confronted with the Tiergarten, he experienced a shock of recognition. Here, stepping back onto European soil after a long absence, he was overcome by a personal *mémoire involontaire*:

> Aber da wehten mich (als ich im Park des Tiergartens spazierte) gewisse Gerüche an, ein Gemisch von Kräutern, von Wasser, von Steinen [...] ja Polen, dies war schon polnisch, wie in Maloszyce [...] dieselbe Natur... die ich vor einem Vierteljahrhundert verlassen hatte. Tod. Der Kreis hatte sich geschlossen.

> [But there (as I walked in the park of the Tiergarten) certain smells reached me, a mixture of herbs, of water, of stones [...] yes Poland, this was already Polish, as in Maloszyce [...] the same nature... that I had left a quarter of a century ago. Death. Things have come full circle.][49]

In both 'Ein Ort für Zufälle' and *Berliner Notizen*, place and psychological self-exploration are interwoven. What Günter Grass once said about the strange pairing of Bachmann and Gombrowicz, namely that they found each other through their rootedness in the literature of the Romance languages, may be just as true for the *flâneur*-scout personality they shared.[50] These intertwined aspects delivered a common ground for their urban explorations.

However, these postwar scouts, as explained above, did something new: they felt the obligation to bear witness to their encounters with the unique spirit of the place, the *genius loci*, thereby adding an ethical dimension to the traditional figure of the *flâneur*. This can be called a 'bearing witness' not uncommon among ethically committed writers in the postwar era.[51] Their ambition was not so much to compensate for Berlin's cultural vacuum as to render it visible and manifest first-hand. Both authors witnessed the same painful emptiness, especially in the former centre of Berlin: 'Ich erinnere mich' [I remember], Bachmann wrote in her 'Entwurf' on Gombrowicz, 'daß wir durch die uns beiden so fremden Straßen von Berlin gingen und oft lachten und riefen, voyez, il y a quelqu'un, denn die Straßen waren so unendlich leer, jedenfalls für uns'

---

[47] Bachmann, 'Ein Ort für Zufälle', p. 279.

[48] Ibid., p. 279.

[49] Gombrowicz, *Berliner Notizen*, p. 73.

[50] For this passage and for the 'conception gombrowiczienne', the Gombrowiczean concept of literature in particular, see the interview with Günter Grass in *Gombrowicz en Europe*, pp. 162–68 (p. 166).

[51] For acts of a 'bearing witness' in postwar literature see again Hamburger, *After the Second Flood*, p. 79.

[that we walked through the streets of Berlin, so foreign to both of us, and often laughed and called out, look, there is someone, because the streets were so infinitely empty, at least for us].[52] For Bachmann, it was precisely at this point that the city reeked 'nach Krankheit und Tod' [of sickness and death].[53] 'Here is the smell of blood still', the sensitive Gombrowicz might have said with a quotation from Shakespeare's *Macbeth*, a tragedy he deeply admired.[54]

In sum, a series of parallel actions run through both authors' Berlin texts. A phenomenology of voids, represented by urban threshold spaces, figures centrally in both works.[55] What appears, for example, in Gombrowicz's notes as an emptiness made visible through a 'stumme Einsamkeit winterlicher Felder' [silent loneliness of winterly fields] in the former city centre near Potsdamer Platz, is equally present in Bachmann's text.[56] She detected abandoned heaps and squares, *terrains vagues* or waste lands, 'auf denen noch niemand zu bauen anfängt' [on which no one has yet begun to build], as the poet remarked.[57] To speak with Walter Benjamin again, the 'erstarrte Unruhe' [petrified unrest] of recent history pervaded Berlin; the city's inhabitants lived in an interregnum, a 'nicht mehr und noch nicht' [no more and not yet], in the striking formulation of Berlin-based *flâneur* Martin Kessel.[58] Beyond what Bachmann aptly called her 'Wüstenerfahrung' [desert experience] in Berlin, there are yet more similarities between Gombrowicz's writing project and hers.[59] What she describes as the daydream-like 'Halbschlaf' [half-sleep] of Berlin residents has its counterpart in Gombrowicz's allegory of Berlin as a modern Lady Macbeth.[60] This is the hidden side of the city, which comes to light when the dark care, the old *atra cura*, and fear of guilt arises.[61] In Bachmann's work, this hidden fear seems to be concealed by a more recent one related to the pressure of a permanent

---

[52] Bachmann, 'Witold Gombrowicz: Entwurf', p. 327.

[53] Ibid.

[54] William Shakespeare, 'The Tragedy of Macbeth' (1606), in Shakespeare, *Sämtliche Werke. Zweisprachige Ausgabe. Nach der Übersetzung von Wilhelm Schlegel, Dorothea Tieck, Ludwig Tieck und Wolf Graf Baudissin. Mit einem einführenden Essay von Harold Bloom*, 2 vols (Zweittausendeins, 2010), II, pp. 2171–231 (p. 2222). Concerning Gombrowicz's admiration for Shakespeare see Witold Gombrowicz, 'Letztes Interview' (1969), in Gombrowicz, *Eine Art Testament Gespräche und Aufsätze*, trans. by Rolf Fieguth (Hanser, 1996), pp. 254–63 (p. 255).

[55] On Berlin as a place of voids see also Andreas Huyssen, 'The Voids of Berlin', *Critical Inquiry*, 24.1 (1997), pp. 57–81.

[56] Gombrowicz, *Berliner Notizen*, p. 129.

[57] Bachmann, 'Ein Ort für Zufälle', p. 282.

[58] Benjamin, *Das Passagen-Werk*, V.1, p. 463. See also Martin Kessel, 'Im Liegestuhl nach der Reise', in Kessel, *In Wirklichkeit aber. Satiren, Glossen, Kleine Prosa* (Dresler, 1955), pp. 99–104 (p. 99).

[59] Bachmann, 'Ein Ort für Zufälle', p. 284.

[60] Ibid., p. 284. See also Gombrowicz, *Berliner Notizen*, p. 84.

[61] The motif of an *atra cura* is already present in Michel de Montaigne, 'Über die Einsamkeit', in de Montaigne, *Essais: Erste moderne Gesamtübersetzung von Hans Stillet* (dtv, 2016), pp. 124–28.

Cold War, forming a palimpsest of emotions. For example, at Checkpoint Charlie, the crossing point on Friedrichstraße, one can feel an 'ängstliche Stille' [anxious silence].[62] It was a demonic silence that spread around the isolated city, from time to time interrupted by the 'donnerenden Lärm' [thunderous din] of Allied planes flying in via Tempelhof airport.[63]

At the same time, both authors registered that beyond the bombed-out and still ruinous areas in which history had left its mark, in the rebuilt business district around Kurfürstendamm, new facades dominated the scene: 'Berlin ist aufgeräumt' [Berlin has been tidied up], Bachmann laconically remarked.[64] Gombrowicz added to this observation the striking opening description in his diary about the geometric surface of the Hansaviertel.[65] As Bachmann noted about the transparent glass constructions of the new City-West, it shows precisely nothing — the perfect hiding place, as it leaves no traces behind: 'Glasdächer über allem, man sieht durch sie hindurch, kann aber nur wenig erkennen' [Glass roofs everywhere, you look through them but can recognize very little.][66] Only the architect Hans Scharoun, as she argued in a letter, demonstrated in this city what 'Bauen sein kann' [building can be]; Scharoun was one of the few architects bold enough to invent an original style of metamorphosis for this wounded city.[67] However, beyond his attempts, the cold surfaces of concrete constructions dominated.

Both Bachmann and Gombrowicz find their impressions of the city repeatedly interrupted by stereoscopic images of the present and the past. Such double images emerged, for example, when Gombrowicz visited the Plötzensee Memorial and became aware of the 'hooks': the site of the cruel execution of the resistance around Claus von Stauffenberg.[68] Or when Bachmann described an imaginary echo of a shot from the Weimar period, the assassination of Walter Rathenau: 'Am Knie der Königsallee' [At the knee of Königsallee], where Bachmann lived in the Grunewald district, 'jetzt ganz gedämpft, die Schüsse auf Rathenau' [now quite soft, the shots at Rathenau].[69] The force of latent horror spreads everywhere in the city; it led Bachmann to conclude that there is a 'vorvertragliches Leid' [pre-contractual pain] — a pain that reaches beyond the agreement around Berlin's Four-Power status dating back to 1945.[70] The actual 'crypt' of the city's current suffering — one can say — had a longer

---

[62] Bachmann, 'Ein Ort für Zufälle', pp. 286 and 289.
[63] Ibid., p. 286.
[64] Ibid., p. 287.
[65] Gombrowicz, *Berliner Notizen*, pp. 72f.
[66] Bachmann, 'Ein Ort für Zufälle', p. 287.
[67] See Ingeborg Bachmann, letter to Hans Scharoun, 9 September 1963. Berlin, Archiv der Akademie der Künste, Hans-Scharoun-Archiv 3602.
[68] Gombrowicz, *Berliner Notizen*, pp. 87, 89 and 110.
[69] Bachmann, 'Ein Ort für Zufälle', p. 288.
[70] Ibid., p. 291.

'effective history'.[71] As a female 'Kundschafter' born in 1926, Bachmann sought to access this deeper history by means of a poetic prose that, in its staccato style and expressive difficulty tried to find an aesthetics suited to such a fragmented place, as Áine McMurtry has shown.[72] It is their common approach to the aesthetic subject of postwar Berlin, then, that made the encounter between the two writers so productive. Both believed that a certain receptivity towards the woundedness of the place was indispensable to finding a mode of expression that could go deeper than the aesthetic trends extending from the Neo-Avant-Garde to the Nouveau Roman.[73]

To deal with Berlin's latent disturbance required literary persistence. This mode of persistence was imagined by Gombrowicz as a Dantesque *rite de passage*, a passage into the underworld, into the common crypt of the divided Berlin: 'Aber du, Poet' [But you, poet], he advised young urban poets by the end of his 'Berliner Notizen', 'wenn du an die Quelle gelangen willst, müsstest du unter die Erde gehen' [if you wish to reach the source, you will have to go underground].[74] Only then, he argued, one can break through the surface of everyday life and explore the hidden experiences of violence, pain and grief. But on the surface? It took, in Bachmann's words, the persistence of a camel to be able to move freely in the walled-in terrain of West Berlin, or to break out: 'Die Felle riechen inbrünstig nach Wüste, Freiheit und Draußen [...]. Querfeldein geht's' [The furs smell ardently of desert, freedom and outdoors [...], through the fields it goes].[75] Bachmann's utopian image of the postwar ambler striking out 'Querfeldein' [through the fields] can also be understood as a secret message to fellow authors in the shut-off Eastern half of the city, like Johannes Brobowski, whom Bachmann had befriended.[76]

Gombrowicz wrote that every author had to produce a poetic 'novum' in such a unique place as the 'liquidierte Hauptstadt' [liquidated capital] of Berlin, whose history could plunge one into speechlessness.[77] It is apparent not only from Gombrowicz and Bachmann but also from Paul Celan that poetry is, at least partly, the realization of a place and its circumstances. Against this backdrop, Celan once made an ironic reference to the German philological

---

[71] For the hermeneutic concept of 'effective history' or 'Wirkungsgeschichte' see Hans-Georg Gadamer, *Wahrheit und Methode (1960): Grundzüge einer philosophischen Hermeneutik. Gesammelte Werke*, 10 vols (Mohr Siebeck, 1990), I, pp. 305–12.

[72] Concerning Bachmann's particular style of 'incompletion' in 'Ein Ort für Zufälle' see McMurtry, 'The Case of the Berlin Writings', p. 114.

[73] For Gombrowicz's polemics against the Nouveau Roman and Michel Butor in particular, see Gombrowicz, *Berliner Notizen*, p. 119.

[74] Ibid., p. 125.

[75] Bachmann, 'Ein Ort für Zufälle', p. 290.

[76] The vision of the camel may be a response to Bobrowski's poetic image of the free-flying screech owl in his prose miniature: Johannes Bobrowski, 'Das Käuzchen' (1962/63), in Bobrowski, *Gesammelte Werke: Die Erzählungen Vermischte Prosa und Selbstzeugnisse*, ed. by Eberhard Haufe, 4 vols (DVA, 1987), IV, pp. 77–78.

[77] Gombrowicz, *Berliner Notizen*, pp. 105, 115.

branch of 'Toposforschung' [topos research] by saying that poetry is certainly about 'Toposforschung', but 'im Hinblick auf das noch zu Erforschende' [with respect to that which has still to be researched].[78] Bachmann, in turn, picked up this notion of a literary topology in her own theoretical reflections on places and circumstances. In her Frankfurt poetry lectures, Bachmann agreed with the Celanean concept when she attributed to literature the creative production of the topos.[79] The poetic process of assigning names, Bachmann argued, is not limited to fictional characters, but is also applicable 'auf Orte, auf Straßen, die auf dieser außerordentlichen Landkarte eingetragen werden müssen, in diesem Atlas, den nur die Literatur sichtbar macht' (W, IV, p. 239) [to places, to streets that have to be recorded on this extraordinary map, in this atlas, which is made visible only in literature] (CW, p. 307).

This work of poetic mapping, she made clear, should not be confused with the maps of geographers. That is to say. Bachmann and Gombrowicz's vision of postwar Berlin only emerges on the poetic map of the 'experienced space', with its overlappings of the past and the present. What distinguishes this form of 'experienced space' from others?[80] It means that it does not merely have an external physiognomy, something that you can see or photograph, but that an event took place in it and demands expression. Literary localities of this variety are thus 'fields of events', loosely connected through history. According to Bachmann, these fields are those in which 'Vorfälle, Zufälle' [incidents, coincidences] are anchored (W, IV, p. 241). Here one must note Bachmann's peculiar use of the word 'Zufall'. It is not just a coincidence but an event, something that befalls one.[81] What happened upon us at this strange place? This might have been the question that troubled both authors during their stay in postwar West Berlin. What confronts us here with a past event? A literary topology would, finally, encompass not just the place but what has happened there, for which the words must still be found.

Bachmann later described Gombrowicz as the 'einsamsten Menschen' [loneliest person] she had ever met.[82] As that of a more individualistic 'heart thinker', bound to atmospheres, his concept of literature was hardly compatible

---

[78] Paul Celan, 'Der Meridian: Rede anlässlich der Verleihung des Georg-Büchner-Preises Darmstadt' (1960), in Celan, *Gesammelte Werke*, ed. by Beda Allemann and others, 5 vols (Suhrkamp, 1987), III, pp. 187–202 (p. 197). See also Ernst Robert Curtius, 'Zum Begriff der historischen Topik', in *Toposforschung: Eine Dokumentation*, ed. by Peter Jehn (Athenäum, 1972), pp. 4–19.

[79] Ingeborg Bachmann, 'Frankfurter Poetikvorlesung: Probleme zeitgenössischer Dichtung', in Bachmann, *Werke: Essays, Reden, Vermischte Schriften*, IV, pp. 182–271 (p. 239).

[80] Concerning the phenomenological concept of the 'erlebter Raum' or 'experienced space', see Otto Friedrich Bollnow, *Mensch und Raum* (Kohlhammer, 2010), pp. 18ff.

[81] About Bachmann's peculiar notion of 'Zufall' that also implies 'Anfall', an 'attack' in the psychopathological sense, see Bettina Bannasch, 'Künstlerische und journalistische Prosa', in *Bachmann-Handbuch: Leben — Werk — Wirkung*, ed. by Monika Albrecht and Dirk Göttsche (Metzler, 2002), pp. 172–83 (p. 176).

[82] Bachmann, 'Witold Gombrowicz: Entwurf', p. 329.

with the early 1960s style of writing introduced by Gruppe 47 and its successor that dominated West Germany and West Berlin at the time. Gombrowicz — in a, quite literally, quixotic attempt — had tried to revitalize a coffee house tradition in West Berlin, as a counter-model to the rituals of group criticism practised among the members of Gruppe 47. In August 1963, he explained his project to Grass and Höllerer. He imagined a place of joyful conversation of 'aucune obligation' [without any obligation]: 'une chose qui manque à Berlin' [something that was missing in Berlin], according to Gombrowicz.[83] But Gombrowicz's vision was only realized in his vivid discussions and walks with Bachmann. They conducted, Höllerer later added, a blunt and direct dialogue with a unique form of truthfulness.[84] Only in their conversations, conducted mostly in French, was it possible for Gombrowicz to overcome the linguistic barrier, since he did not speak German and learned only a little of the language during his stay. This lack of a common lingua franca in Berlin made him constantly aware of his problem of expression.

Thus, in the end, the prolific *enfant terrible* Gombrowicz became a lonely man who spent the phase before his departure with heart and lung problems — he was asthmatic — in a private clinic in Berlin-Schöneberg. Even Ford's cultural officers began to worry. They noted with a certain astonishment that Berlin 'has affected his heart'.[85] This can perhaps be ascribed to a re-traumatization, not uncommon among migrants returning to Europe; heart conditions, one can say, represent the typical émigré's disease, as indicated in several studies.[86] In the years up to 1964, the Ford programme was increasingly confronted with criticism and began to try to end the Artists-in-Residence project by handing it over to the DAAD (Deutscher Akademischer Austauschdienst; German Academic Exchange Service). The final report on the project by Nestler stated in an almost melancholy way:

> Presumably it was not realised clearly what physical and often psychical stresses were involved in a temporary migration to Berlin [...]. In more than one case the sojourn in Berlin became a stay in hospital for those of excessive age or chronic ill health.[87]

[83] Witold Gombrowicz, letter to Grass, 23 August 1963. Berlin, Archiv der Akademie der Künste, Günter-Grass-Archiv 6510. For the German translation see *Sinn und Form*, 75.1 (2023), pp. 42–43.

[84] Höllerer, in *Gombrowicz en Europe*, p. 179.

[85] Letter from Hans Karl and Joseph Slater to Shepard Stone, 11 March 1964. Ford Foundation records. Grants E-G (FA732C). German Academic Exchange Service (0630351). Series: Ford Foundation Grants — E to G. Date: 29 May 1963–23 July 1966. Reel 3075. Rockefeller Archive Center, Sleepy Hollow.

[86] Today it is known that cardiovascular diseases belong to the key risk factors among émigrés and refugees. See Tala Al-Rousan and others, 'Epidemiology of Cardiovascular Disease and its Risk Factors among Refugees and Asylum Seekers', *International Journal of Cardiology*, 12 (2022), pp. 1–7. On homesickness as a disease from a historical perspective see Barbara Cassin, *Nostalgia: When Are We Ever at Home?* Foreword by Souleymane Bachir Diagne (Fordham University Press, 2016), pp. 5–6.

[87] Ford Foundation. The Berlin Cultural Program 'Artists in Residence' 1963–1966. A report

Berlin turned out to be a place that bred illness. Even earlier than Gombrowicz, Bachmann experienced a crisis and was hospitalized in the summer of 1963. Her disturbance, she confessed in a letter, had deepened in Berlin: her trauma, which had 'alle Wege verstellt' [blocked all paths], broke out again.[88]

The 'Einstellung auf Krankheit' in Berlin, one can conclude, turned on its scouts.[89] It seems as if these two writers had — to use an expression of the philosopher Hans-Georg Gadamer — absorbed something of Berlin's 'Bedeutsamkeitsstrahlung' [radiation of significance], its historical tragedies.[90] They took it to heart, one might say. This engagement with Berlin was not without risk. After her personal crisis in Berlin, Bachmann expressed her experience with the city in a pun-like phrase: she said that at this 'gestörten Ort' [disturbed place] she had fallen into her personal 'Verstörung' [disturbance], which 'von diesen Störungen einiges aufzunehmen fähig war' [was capable of absorbing some of these disturbances].[91] Both authors represented a special kind of sensitive receptivity that was rare in these years, at least in the German literary scene. Their personal experience of disturbance formed the medium that enabled them to go beneath the surface, to go 'underground' as Gombrowicz aptly put it.[92] However, both writers became disturbing figures themselves, disrupting the intellectual routine in the Western half of postwar Berlin. Seen through the eyes of exiles, the wounded city revealed sides of itself that otherwise would never have appeared on our shared literary map.

on experience gained by Peter Nestler, p. 6. Ford Foundation records. Grants E-G (FA732C). German Academic Exchange Service (0630351). Series: Ford Foundation Grants — E to G. Date: 1963 29 May 1963–23 July. Reel 3075. Rockefeller Archive Center, Sleepy Hollow.

[88] See Bachmann and Frisch, *Wir haben es nicht gut gemacht*, pp. 449 and 482.
[89] Bachmann, 'Ein Ort für Zufälle', p. 279.
[90] For this term, see Hans-Georg Gadamer, 'Über das Lesen von Bildern und Bauten', in Gadamer, *Gesammelte Werke: Ästhetik und Poetik I*, 10 vols (Mohr Siebeck, 1993), VIII, pp. 331–38 (p. 337).
[91] Ingeborg Bachmann, 25 November 1964. Interview with Alois Rummel, in Bachmann, *Wir müssen wahre Sätze finden: Gespräche und Interviews*, ed. by Christine Koschel, 3rd edn (Piper, 1991), pp. 47–50 (p. 49). See also Bachmann and Frisch, *Wir haben es nicht gut gemacht*, p. 925.
[92] See Gombrowicz, *Berliner Notizen*, p. 119.

'Ich kann nur gut allein sein':
Love and Friendship in the Correspondence of Ingeborg Bachmann and Hans Werner Henze[1]

TOBIAS HEINRICH

University of Kent

I

The correspondence between Ingeborg Bachmann and Hans Werner Henze is testament to a relationship characterized by a continuous crossing of boundaries: in a cultural and linguistic but also aesthetic and emotional sense. Over two decades, Bachmann and Henze regularly wrote letters to each other, lived together for some periods of time, and had a fruitful creative partnership. Their joint work blends poetry and music, their letters flow between German, Italian, French and English, and their relationship was part friendship, part love affair. Indeed, the literary scholar Renate Stauf perceives the correspondence between Bachmann and Henze as paradigmatic for a modern discourse of love. According to Stauf, the letters are not expressions of two stable and consistent selves. Instead, the correspondence becomes a space in which the lovers' volatile self-conceptions can be articulated and negotiated.[2]

In her characterization of the letters between Bachmann and Henze, Stauf is not necessarily concerned about the difference between love and friendship. The terms could be used almost interchangeably. This, however, is in stark contrast to Bachmann and Henze's own use of these concepts. For Bachmann, love in its most radical and uncompromising form is an ideal that one can aspire to, but any attempt to realize it will ultimately lead to despair and demise. This is one of the central themes of her oeuvre, most poignantly expressed in Bachmann's radio play *Der gute Gott von Manhattan*.[3] In one of his last surviving letters to Bachmann, Henze issues a similarly bleak verdict on romantic love, alluding to

[1] I would like to thank Ian Cooper and Alvise Sforza Tarabochia for their helpful advice on this article, in particular regarding translations from Italian and into English.

[2] Renate Stauf, '"Erklär mir, Liebe": Kunst des Liebens und Liebessprache im Briefwechsel Ingeborg Bachmanns mit Hans Werner Henze', in *Der Liebesbrief. Schriftkultur und Medienwechsel vom 18. Jahrhundert bis zur Gegenwart*, ed. by Renate Stauf, Annette Simonis and Jörg Paulus (De Gruyter, 2008), pp. 401–25 (pp. 420–21).

[3] See Michael Klein, 'Das Verhältnis von Liebe und Tod in Ingeborg Bachmanns Hörspiel "Der gute Gott von Manhattan"', *Sprachkunst — Beiträge zur Literaturwissenschaft*, 41 (2010), pp. 17–28.

Austrian Studies 32 (2024), doi:10.1353/aus.00015, pp. 208–20
© Modern Humanities Research Association 2024

Louis Aragon: 'Il n'y pas des amours heureux' (IB/HWH, p. 281) [There are no happy love affairs].[4] In his opinion, the futile pursuit of romantic love should be replaced by 'freundschaft, freundlichkeit, brüderlichkeit' (IB/HWH, p. 282) [friendship, kindness, fraternity].[5]

In an earlier letter, Bachmann had described her feelings for Henze as brotherly: a tender kind of love without the doubts of romantic yearning (IB/ HWH, p. 360). Nevertheless, there are reasons to characterize the correspondence between Bachmann and Henze as love letters, not least for Henze's passionate though often tongue-in-cheek courtship of Bachmann, but also for Bachmann's repeated reassurances that Henze is the most significant person in her life (see for example IB/HWH, pp. 267 and 339). Several times during their friendship, Bachmann and Henze considered getting married. Even though the composer's homosexuality posed clear limits on the physical side of their relationship, they envisaged a life together: a pact to realize a chaste and pure idea of living as artists (see IB/HWH, p. 314).

In theory, this agreement might have granted them a certain amount of privacy and freedom in their romantic pursuits and for Bachmann an escape from her precarious financial situation. In reality, however, both struggled with the arrangement. Henze, who was the driving force initially, was soon beset with doubts and, despite the platonic nature of their relationship, was jealous of Bachmann's lovers. Bachmann in turn soon resisted the inherently conservative character of this lifestyle, modelled after a bourgeois heterosexual relationship.

Their correspondence exposes the challenges in their attempt to shape a friendship in the mould of a romantic relationship. It documents Bachmann and Henze's struggle to escape the boundaries of conventional relationship and gender ideals and yet also reveals how such norms implicitly still shape their thinking and behaviour. In contrast to Renate Stauf, I thus consider the difference between friendship and romantic love significant for an understanding of Bachmann and Henze's relationship, as they consciously explore the potential as well as the limitations of love and friendship, in their lives as well as in their letters. While Stauf is right to claim that Bachmann and Henze's letters strive to establish proximity in absence,[6] their correspondence is also a continuous struggle to create the distance and detachment necessary to make their relationship last.

When Henze emphasizes the value of friendship over love in his letter to Bachmann, he is invoking an old topos that can be traced as far back as Michel de Montaigne and his pivotal essay in the philosophical discourse on friendship,

---

[4] Louis Aragon, 'Il n'y a pas d'amour heureux', in Louis Aragon, La Diane française (Seghers, 1963), pp. 25–26. It is unclear whether Henze's use of the plural in contrast to the singular in the original, including the grammatically incorrect article (des instead of d'), is intentional.

[5] In many of their letters, Bachmann and Henze exclusively used lower-case characters, even for nouns that are capitalized in standard German.

[6] See, for example, Stauf, '"Erklär mir, Liebe"', p. 414.

De l'amitié.[7] Montaigne compares passionate love to a fire that is 'temeraire et volage, ondoyant et divers' ['rash and fickle, fluctuating and variable'], while friendship is characterized by 'une chaleur generale et universelle' ['a general universal warmth'].[8] It is 'temperée [...] et égale, [...] consistante et rassize' ['temperate and smooth, [...] constant and at rest'].[9] Love must be regarded as 'un desir forcené après ce qui nous fuit' [a mad craving for something which escapes us], yet friendship is 'toute douceur et polissure, qui n'a rien d'aspre et de poignant' ['all gentleness and evenness, having nothing sharp nor keen'].[10] Thus, its calm emotional constancy makes friendship the superior relationship to the momentary passion of romantic love.

More recently, the sociologist Eva Illouz wrote a similarly fervent essay in praise of friendship over love. Love, Illouz argues, is always characterized by a sense of urgency: 'Because it is grounded in biology, [it] seems to overpower our minds and hearts.'[11] The 'ecstasy of love' however is short-lived: 'it fades, evaporates from our lives, sometimes turning into the sweetness of attachment and sometimes in the bitterness of burdensome promises we cannot fulfill'.[12] In contrast, Illouz claims that true friendship is the bond that lasts, often for a lifetime. It can adapt to accommodate the emotional needs and capacities of both friends. Friendship goes along 'with the movements and flow of our life, and lacks the dramatic, theatrical trappings of love'.[13]

In the German discourse on friendship, it is Siegfried Kracauer's essay *Über die Freundschaft* that contains the most compelling distinction, between what he calls 'begehrende Liebe' [desiring love] and friendship.[14] Love, according to Kracauer, strives for complete unity between two people, whereas friendship requires a certain degree of distance and otherness. In love, there is the urge for all aspects of life to be shared, in order that partners become one with the other.[15] Yet, this 'Verlangen nach einer Verschmelzung des Daseins' ['the desire for a melding of existences'] is foreign to friendship.[16] Friends encounter each

---

[7] Michel de Montaigne, 'De l'amitié', in Michel de Montaigne, *Œuvres complètes*, ed. by Albert Thibaudet and Maurice Rat (Gallimard, 1962), pp. 181–93; 'On Affectionate Relationships', in Michel de Montaigne, *The Complete Essays*, ed. and trans. by M. A. Screech (Everyman's Library, 2003), pp. 205–19.

[8] Montaigne, 'De l'amitié', p. 184. Translation: Montaigne, 'On Affectionate Relationships', p. 209.

[9] Montaigne, 'De l'amitié', p. 184; Montaigne, 'On Affectionate Relationships', p. 209.

[10] Montaigne, 'De l'amitié', p. 184; Montaigne, 'On Affectionate Relationships', p. 209.

[11] Eva Illouz, 'Why We Don't Celebrate Friendship with the Same Fervor as Love', *Haaretz*, 13 February 2016 <https://www.haaretz.com/israel-news/culture/2016-02-13/ty-article-magazine/.premium/on-the-nobility-of-friendship/0000017f-e36e-df7c-a5ff-e37e1ddc0000> [accessed 13 October 2023].

[12] Ibid.

[13] Ibid.

[14] Siegfried Kracauer, 'Über die Freundschaft', in Siegfried Kracauer, *Essays, Feuilletons, Rezensionen*, ed. by Inka Mülder-Bach (Suhrkamp, 2011), pp. 29–59 (p. 41).

[15] Ibid., pp. 41–43.

[16] Ibid., p. 43. Translation by Harry Blatterer, 'Siegfried Kracauer's Differentiating

other as free and independent individuals.[17] Nevertheless, just like romantic love, friendship is a union between two people who seek to recognize each other in their entirety, that is, in every aspect of their being. Friendship satisfies the need to be taken up into another's existence and to feel understood there: 'Sich gemeinsam entfalten, ohne sich aneinander zu verlieren, sich hinzugeben, um sich erweitert zu besitzen, zur Einheit zu verschmelzen und dennoch getrennt für sich bestehen zu bleiben: dies ist das Geheimnis des Bundes' ['To flourish together without losing oneself in the other, to devote oneself in order to possess oneself in expanded form, to melt into a unity and yet remain existing separately for oneself: this is the secret of the bond'].[18]

Kracauer's differentiation between love and friendship accurately describes the fault lines in Bachmann and Henze's relationship: for several years, the vision of a life together is a common theme in their correspondence. Yet over time, Bachmann seems to realize that what Kracauer calls the 'melding' of existences would necessarily require her to abandon her independence and therefore also her literary ambitions. Over and over again, the friends discard their shared plans. During this process, they develop an increasingly profound understanding of their personal needs, both as artists and as friends. Their example confirms Illouz's claim that friendship persists because of its ability to change and transform. As much as the letters are therefore a means of deepening the bond between Bachmann and Henze and of continuously renegotiating the nature of their relationship, they are also a necessary vehicle for demarcating the differences between them.

II

Bachmann and Henze first considered getting married in spring 1954, roughly a year and a half after they had been introduced to each other at a meeting of Gruppe 47 in 1952. In 1953, Bachmann visited Henze in Ischia and stayed with him over the summer, prompting her own decision to relocate from Vienna to Rome. There was no formal marriage proposal, but we know about their intention from a letter in which Henze explains his reluctance to go through with these plans:

> [L]isten, it is rather hard for me to write to you [...]. I should feel ashamed very much and I did so when I learnt from most different people what I seem to have done to you. The whole fact can be explained in a few dry words: When I saw you having got those form papers from the embassy and things started to get real, I felt I wouldn't be able to drop into that marriage. (IB/HWH, p. 293)

While the initial idea might have been Henze's, Bachmann was the driving force when it came to bringing it to bear. The fact that it was her who took

Approach to Friendship', *Historical Sociology*, 32 (2019), pp. 173–88 (p. 178).
[17] Kracauer, 'Über die Freundschaft', p. 58.
[18] Ibid. Translation: Blatterer, 'Kracauer's Differentiating Approach', p. 179.

the initiative might have contributed to Henze's reluctance and ultimately to his decision not to pursue the marriage. In his letter, Henze rationalizes his behaviour and points out that neither he nor Bachmann would have found happiness in this relationship:

> In fact it would have been the hell of a life especially for you [...]. For me there's no hope[,] no rescue, I must continue my awfully lonesome life until it's [sic] very end, and you ought to realize, now, that your honour has been less hurt this way than it would have been after having really married me [...] (IB/HWH, p. 294)

What is striking about this letter, apart from the emotional candour, is the fact that Henze chose to write it in English. Later on in their correspondence, the shift between languages becomes a common practice, but apart from a Christmas card a few months prior, this is the earliest of the surviving letters that is entirely written in a foreign language. As scholars have pointed out, the multilingual character of Bachmann and Henze's letters is a deliberate strategy of distancing (see for example IB/HWH, p. 481).[19] The act of alienation makes things sayable that could otherwise not be articulated. In this instance, for example, Henze explains how he was unable to address the matter face to face, when he went to see Bachmann a few days earlier: 'I could not even speak, so afraid was I to hear from you things concerning this affair' (IB/HWH, p. 293). The letter and the foreign language become means of dissociation, diluting the emotional immediacy of Henze's admission.

The published correspondence contains Bachmann's draft of a response. In this letter, also in English, she gives the impression that she had never taken the idea very seriously in the first place: 'I [...] had taken the whole thing like a joke [...]. Reading your letter I mean you were only afraid of this marriage-idea, afraid that I could take it seriously' (IB/HWH, p. 295). Rather than reproaching Henze for his ambivalence towards their relationship, yet again Bachmann takes agency: 'I mean we should both forget this affair and make in future the best out of our friendship and our work and the possibilities between both' (IB/HWH, p. 295). For the first time in their correspondence, Bachmann explicitly characterizes the relationship between her and Henze as a friendship. There is an echo of an earlier letter by Paul Celan to Ingeborg Bachmann, written in 1952, that was intended to conclude their love affair: 'Wir wissen genug voneinander, um uns bewusst zu machen, dass nur die Freundschaft zwischen uns möglich bleibt. Das Andere ist unrettbar verloren' (IB/PC, 41) ['We know enough about each other to realize that friendship is the only possibility between us. The rest is irretrievably lost'].[20] Yet the insistence on friendship also disguises the desire for its romantic other.

---

[19] See Stauf, '"Erklär mir Liebe"', pp. 406–07.
[20] Letter from Paul Celan to Ingeborg Bachmann, 26 February 1952, in *Paul Celan, Ingeborg Bachmann, Correspondence. With the Correspondences between Paul Celan and Max Frisch and between Ingeborg Bachmann and Gisèle Celan-Lestrange*, ed. by Bertrand Badiou, trans. by Wieland Hoban (Seagull Books, 2010), p. 49.

For Bachmann and Celan, defining their relationship as a friendship resulted in a hiatus in their correspondence until their spontaneous reunion and the resumption of their love affair in 1957. The opposite is true for Bachmann and Henze. Their relationship over the following years was characterized by prolific creative collaboration. After Bachmann had rewritten the Prince Myshkin monologue for Henze's pantomime ballet *Der Idiot* in 1953, Henze composed the score for Bachmann's radio play *Die Zikaden* (1954/55) and set several of Bachmann's poems to music. The pinnacle of their collaboration is *Der Prinz von Homburg* (1958) and *Der junge Lord* (1964). Large parts of Bachmann and Henze's correspondence document the creative process of writing these operas. Their friendship may have found its truest expression in this collaborative artistic endeavour. As Siegfried Kracauer notes, friendship and art share an affinity, as both enable the articulation and recognition of one's full personality.[21] In this sense, the letters exchanged between Bachmann and Henze can themselves be considered as works of art. In fact, the poet and the composer had intended to publish a selection of their correspondence related to *Der junge Lord* (IB/HWH, pp. 251 and 509). Both were keenly aware of the personal as well as the poetic significance of their letters. Far more than simple communication, their correspondence served as a means of expressing and exploring their inner selves through the written word.[22]

A particularly compelling document of such self-scrutinization is contained within a collection of notes by Bachmann that have survived among her papers in the Literary Archive of the Austrian National Library.[23] They are addressed to Henze and were written in early 1956. These draft notes therefore date from a period in which the friends spent several months sharing a flat in Naples. Right at the onset of the notes, Bachmann tries to justify to herself and to Henze the reasons for writing them: 'Mein Lieber, weil ich so schlecht ins Arbeiten hineinkomme, hab ich dran gedacht, Dir jeden Tag etwas hier aufzuschreiben, für einen Fall, der mir selbst noch nicht klar ist, vielleicht für den, nehmen wir an, dass ich eines Tags fortgehe und Du es nicht verstehst' [My dear, because it is so difficult for me to start working, I thought I would write something down here for you every day, for a reason that I don't yet understand myself, maybe because, let's assume, I leave one day and you don't understand].[24] Although they had abandoned the idea of a marriage, even living with Henze as friends

---

[21] See Kracauer, 'Über die Freundschaft', pp. 53–54.

[22] This is a point that Roland Berbig makes for the entirety of Bachmann's letter exchanges, see Berbig, ' "bin schon versehrt, wenn ich das Datum hinsetze": Die Briefschreiberin Ingeborg Bachmann', *Ingeborg Bachmann: Eine Hommage*, ed. by Michael Hansel and Kerstin Putz (Zsolnay, 2022), pp. 192–200 (p. 197).

[23] These drafts were not included in the original published correspondence. They were only recently made available as a facsimile in the Salzburg Bachmann Edition: Ingeborg Bachmann, *'Senza casa': Autobiographische Skizzen, Notate und Tagebucheintragungen*, ed. by Isolde Schiffermüller, Gabriella Pelloni and Silvia Bengesser-Scharinger (Suhrkamp, 2024), pp. 330–33.

[24] Ibid., p. 330.

proved challenging for Bachmann. She struggles to find her own sense of self within a shared life that she experiences as the life of a stranger: 'Das Einrichten unserer casa hat mir meistens Freude gemacht, aber bei jedem Stück, das an seinen Ort gerückt worden ist, war mir auch so, als würd ich für immer irgendwo hingerückt, wo ich nicht hingehöre' [I mostly enjoyed setting up our casa, but with every piece that was moved into place, I also felt as though I was forever being moved somewhere I didn't belong].[25] Initially, Bachmann tries to find the reason for her discomfort within herself, in her own disposition. Perhaps, Bachmann contemplates, when she is living with someone, she becomes too concerned about the well-being of the other: '[M]eine ganze Natur ist so eingerichtet, dass ich vielzuviel Antennen habe, das macht schwach den andern gegenüber, man stellt sich zu sehr ein' [My entire nature is set up in such a way that I have far too many antennae, which makes me weak towards others, one adapts to them too much].[26]

While writing these notes, over the course of several days in early February, Bachmann begins to understand that her personal anxieties are rooted in society's restriction of female creativity. In practical terms, she deplores the lack of someone to share the struggles of the creative process with:

> Männer die schreiben haben ihre Frauen und Freundinnen, vor denen sie lamentieren und herumstottern, und ich hab meistens niemand gehabt, hier und da war aber doch jemand da, die Ilse, die Kaschnitz [...] und bei Dir werd ich ängstlich aus Rücksicht, aus ich weiss nicht was; ich denke auch, dass Du viel zu beladen bist mit Deiner Musik, und der tägliche Kleinkram wie Kohlenkaufen gibt Dir dann sowieso den Rest. Wie soll ich von Dir noch verlangen, dass Du mit mir einen Genetivgebrauch überlegst oder Beistriche.[27]

> [Men who write have their wives and girlfriends to whom they complain and stutter, and I mostly had no one, but now and then, there was someone there, Ilse, Kaschnitz [...] and with you I become fearful out of consideration, out of I don't know what; I also think that you are far too burdened with your music, and the daily little things like buying coal are bound to be too much for you anyway. How can I still ask you to think about the use of a genitive or commas with me.]

It is revealing that the friends Bachmann mentions are both women writers themselves: Ilse Aichinger and Marie Luise Kaschnitz. While Bachmann and Henze's correspondence is full of references to their joint projects, there is very little evidence of mutual involvement in the development of their individual work. Indeed, when Bachmann envisages her future with Henze, it almost turns into the caricature of an artist's wife:

> Es wär wunderbar, wenn ich nichts zu tun hätte und nur für Dich da wäre, zum Abstauben des Notenpapiers und zum Anhören von allem, was

---

[25] Ibid.
[26] Ibid., p. 331.
[27] Ibid., p. 332.

Du schreibst und sagst, und es gibt ja auch Tage, wo ich glaube, sowieso nichts zu taugen, es aufgeben zu sollen und mit der ganzen Kraft für Dich dazusein.

[It would be wonderful if I had nothing to do and I could be there just for you, to dust the music paper and to listen to everything you write and say, and there are days when I think I'm no good anyway, should give it up and be there for you with all my strength.][28]

It is obvious that such a life would not suit Bachmann's drive for self-realization. And yet she struggles to imagine herself in a less passive position in relationship to men:

[I]ch fürchte, mir mit dem Beidirbleiben eine Rolle zuzulegen die sich nicht mit mir decken kann. Ich kann nicht nur eine Rolle haben. Ich muss mir den ganzen Horizont offene[r] Möglichkeit auch offen halten. [...] Auch bezieht sich mein horror nicht auf die Männer, sondern auf mich selbst, überhaupt alles auf mich, nicht auf irgend etwas ausser mir. (Wenn auch nicht auf mein persönliches und unwichtiges Ich, sondern auf seinen Spielraum und seine mögl[i]chen Erfahrungen). [...] [D]ie "Freiheit", die ich neben Dir zugebilligt bekomme, wäre keine Freiheit für dieses unruhige Ich, sondern nur eine, für ein Ich, von dem ich möglichst wenig Gebrauch machen will.[29]

[I am afraid that by staying with you I will take on a role that can't align with me. I can't have just one role. I have to keep the horizon of possibilities open. [...] My horror does not relate to men, but to myself, everything relates to me, not to anything outside of me. (Even though it is not about my personal and unimportant self, but about its scope and its possible experiences). [...] The 'freedom' that I would be granted next to you would not be freedom for this restless ego, [but] only for an ego of which I want to make as little use as possible.]

These notes foreshadow Bachmann's later prose as she articulates the firm conviction that a life by Henze's side, indeed a life with any man, would over time obliterate her ability for poetic expression. As is the case with the female protagonist in Bachmann's only published novel, *Malina*, her creative 'self' would ultimately disappear. Yet in a way that is also reminiscent of the female protagonist of *Malina*, the Bachmann of these letters can abruptly fold back the denunciation of social injustices into fundamental self-deprecation: 'Ich kann nur gut allein sein, alles andre kann ich nicht' [The only thing I am good at is being by myself, there's nothing else I can do].[30] It is unclear whether Henze ever saw these notes and the fact that there is no evidence of any response from the composer makes it seem rather unlikely.

---

[28] Ibid.
[29] Ibid., p. 333.
[30] Ibid.

III

Bachmann did in fact leave Naples in August 1956 to stay with her family in Klagenfurt. Later in the year she travelled to Paris and subsequently returned to Rome, where it became ever more apparent to her that the precarious life as a freelance foreign correspondent in Italy was not sustainable. Yet at the same time, Henze enthusiastically drew up plans to move into a bigger apartment in Naples, with a room dedicated to Bachmann as the lady of the house. She initially struggled to reject Henze's ideas until a journey to Naples provided clarity.

In an unsent draft, written in Italian and perhaps composed while she was still in Naples or shortly after her visit, Bachmann articulates with astounding poetic vigour why she is unable to live with Henze and why she has to leave — not just him, but Italy altogether. The dramatic gesture of the letter's opening passage demonstrates the personal gravity of this decision.

> Se avrai questa lettera — cosi [sic] cominciano spesso le lettere prima del suicidio, ma la mia non è una die questo genere, magari una di vivere, e qualcosa mi dice che sarai tu a comprendermi, questa decisione insolita che mi conduce non so quanti kilometri da qui. Sono molti, molti, e [sic] è l'altra fine del mondo. (IB/HWH, p. 360)

> [If you receive this letter — this is how letters often begin before a suicide, but mine is not one of this kind, perhaps one of living, and something tells me that it will be you who understands me, this unusual decision that takes me I don't know how many kilometres from here. There are many, many, and it is the other end of the world.]

Bachmann invokes the genre of last letters: the suicide note as the ultimate termination of speech.[31] The sense of urgency in this comparison demonstrates the existential dimension of Bachmann's decision. It is a final farewell to the idea that lovers and friends can be one and the same: 'Ti amo ancora, ma lo farei sempre, ma è un altro amore, quello che non conosce Zweifelssorge, puro e quello del fratello' (IB/HWH, p. 360) [I still love you, but I would do always, yet it is a different love, the one that does not know *Zweifelssorge* [the worry of doubt], a pure and brotherly one].

With regard to their relationship, this letter is an urge to move on: to go and let go, to reject all claims and demands on each other. Expressing this disparity between loving friendship and passionate love, Bachmann uses the only German word in her letter and both syntactically and phonetically, the sibilants of *Zweifelssorge* [lit. concern of doubts] break into the tonality of vowels in 'amore puro'. Even acoustically, these two concepts appear utterly irreconcilable.

---

[31] Arnd Beise, Jochen Strobel and Ute Pott 'Gesprächsabbrüche: Schreiben ohne Antwort', in *Letzte Briefe: Neue Perspektiven auf das Ende von Kommunikation*, ed. by Arnd Beise, Jochen Strobel and Ute Pott (Röhrig Universitätsverlag, 2015), pp. 7–20 (p. 15).

Echoing Montaigne and Illouz's verdict on the difference between love and friendship, Bachmann admits that the love she seeks might be painful and destructive: 'rovina rovinoso' (IB/HWH, p. 360) [ruinous ruin]. Yet she believes that this pain is vital for her writing: 'Non è soltanto passione che mi spinge verso questa decisione, ma molto di più è se vuoi, passiossione, ma in se [sic] una comprensione del vuoto che ho sofferto qui e che soffro artisticamente' (IB/HWH, p. 360) [It is not only passion that pushes me towards this decision, but much more, it is, if you like, more than passion, but in itself an understanding of the emptiness that I have suffered here and that I suffer artistically].

The life that Bachmann intends to devote herself to is one of passion, or something even bigger: *passiossione* — a poetic superlative of *passione* [passion] that is also reminiscent of the words *ossessione* [obsession] and *possessione* [possession]. Bachmann is aware of the fatal consequence of exposing herself to life and love in all its destructive force, and yet she is determined, especially as a woman, to deny herself the protection that the bourgeois façade of a life with Henze would have to offer.

The passage ends with a figure of self-empowerment and a devastating conclusion: '[I]o, Hans, io sola, a capovolgere le cose così, perché gli uomini sono vigliacchi' (IB/HWH, p. 360) [It is I, Hans, I alone, who turns things upside down like this, because men are cowards]. In her notes from the previous year, Bachmann had tried to locate the source of her suffering in her inability to commit to a relationship. Now, however, she recognizes this reluctance as a strength — an ability to resist the domestication of female passion and creativity.

An attempt to locate the roots of literary texts in an author's biography might find the origins of Bachmann's short story 'Undine geht' [Undine goes *or* leaves] here. Bachmann herself, however, goes the opposite way, from poetry to life: 'È strano che poco fa ho scritto qualcosa su di quel continente oscuro, e ora ci vado veramente, e sento questo vecchio coraggio forte' (IB/HWH, p. 360) [It is strange that a little while ago I wrote something about that dark continent, and now I'm actually going there, and I feel this old strong courage]. Bachmann is referring to her poem 'Liebe: Dunkler Erdteil' ['Love: The Dark Continent'] (W, I, p. 158; DS, pp. 323–25) and its title that alludes to Sigmund Freud's verdict on the incomprehensible nature of female sexuality.[32] In an exoticized setting, the poem conjures images of power relationships and their inversion along the axes of race and gender. The 'schwarze[r] König' ['black king'] (W, I, p. 158; DS, p. 323) appears as the epitome of aggressive male sexuality. The crux of the poem is that the female object of desire turns into a subject of knowledge and thus gains authority over her male counterpart: 'Du kannst das Reich um seinen König bringen, | du, selbst geheim, blick sein Geheimnis an' ['You can deprive the kingdom of its king, | for it's you who, secretly, has seen his secret'] (W, I,

---

[32] Sigmund Freud, 'Die Frage der Laienanalyse', in Sigmund Freud, *Gesammelte Werke*, XIV: *Werke aus den Jahren 1925–1931*, ed. by Anna Freud (Imago, 1948), pp. 207–96 (p. 241).

p. 158; DS, p. 325). The secret as a weapon of the oppressed is a motif familiar to Bachmann through Heinrich von Kleist's novella *Michael Kohlhaas* where the eponymous protagonist chooses to be executed rather than to reveal a secret to his arch-enemy, the Elector of Saxony. Non-knowledge subverts the established hierarchies of power. Just as Bachmann's image of the black king turns the imperialist undertones in Freud's trope on its head, knowing about men's lack of knowledge becomes the foundation for female self-empowerment.

Henze is devastated by Bachmann's departure. In a note to Bachmann, he writes: '[L]a tua fuga continuata [...] è un dolore grande amaro e profondo' (IB/HWH, p. 363) [Your continuous flight is a great, bitter and profound pain]. What is remarkable about this letter is that it contains three discrete messages, all written in a different language: Italian, German and English. The response to Bachmann's 'flight' is an epistolary 'fugue' [both words translate as *fuga* in Italian], intertwining several voices, each representing contrasting emotional qualities. Henze starts out with a first line in Italian that is continued in the third and every other odd line of the letter. In the even lines in between the Italian, Henze initially writes in German before he shifts to English, roughly in the middle of the letter. Renate Stauf compares the German part of the letter to an admonitory speech of an anxious father,[33] while the Italian lines express Henze's personal disappointment, but also his emotional hurt. Finally, in the English lines, Henze addresses what he suspects to be the reason for Bachmann's withdrawal: 'I get furious really by thinking that you do all these crazinesses only because I happen to be queer' (IB/HWH, pp. 363–64).

While Henze's letter skilfully pushes the boundaries of the epistolary form, it also exposes the patriarchal bias in his relationship to Bachmann. There is no acknowledgement of Bachmann's desire to free herself from the misogynist underpinnings of conventional relationship models. On the contrary, he calls on her to reconsider her decision, which he perceives as sheer 'wahnsinn' [madness] (IB/HWH, p. 362): 'stattdessen solltest Du [...] die disziplin aufbringen, Dich ruhig zu verhalten und zu arbeiten' (IB/HWH, p. 362) [instead you should have the discipline to behave calmly and work]. Even the remarks about his own sexuality as the cause of Bachmann's refusal to live with him can be read as narcissistic projections that do not recognize her urge for a life beyond the restrictions of traditional gender roles.

IV

One cannot help but agree with Renate Stauf when she claims that the correspondence between Bachmann and Henze demonstrates how societal norms and taboos (their sexual promiscuity, Henze's homosexuality) can take root in intimate personal relationships and subsequently lead to the most

---

[33] Stauf, '"Erklär mir Liebe"', p. 407.

hurtful behaviour towards the other.[34] This is also the reason why Bachmann and Henze's attempts to establish a shared life within a romantic and heteronormative framework are doomed to fail. For Bachmann, the urge for a shared life, something that Kracauer describes as foundational for desiring love, becomes an instrument of patriarchal oppression. In this respect, Bachmann's quarrels with Henze appear like a prelude to her traumatic experiences in the later relationship with Max Frisch.

Thus Bachmann's insistence on friendship is also an insistence on distance as a prerequisite for her freedom and her independence, both as a woman and as a writer. Perhaps the reason why her relationship with Henze ultimately survived is rooted in his own experience of marginalization. Despite the frequently patronizing undertones on Henze's side of the correspondence, he had a sense for the fact that her experience as a woman was fundamentally different from his, just as his letters demonstrate his awareness of the multiple, dissonant and often contradictory voices inside us. He is thus in a position to acknowledge that friendship is as much built on differences as it is on similarities: a fact that makes the relationship mutable, but fragile at the same time.[35]

The common ground for Bachmann and Henze was their existence as artists. In response to the deep crisis that Bachmann experienced after the break-up with Max Frisch, Henze writes: 'Nessuna Schmach die questa terra ci può toccare se pensiamo sempre alla ragione per cui siamo venuti al mondo. Siamo qui per creare questa è la santa verità, tutto il resto è marginale' (IB/HWH, p. 390) [No humiliation [*Schmach* in German] on this earth can touch us if we always think about the reason why we came into the world. We are here to create, this is the holy truth, everything else is irrelevant].

Friendship, according to Kracauer, depends on a common view of the world. It provides the opportunity to grow together — with and through each other.[36] Bachmann and Henze's friendship offered them a profound understanding of themselves as writers — in the mirror of the friend's life and work. It enabled them to gain a deeper awareness of the uncompromising demands of their vocation, yet also an inkling of the safe haven that only art can provide. '[L]'artista [...] ha [...] da mettere contro le mutabilità delle cose, le sofferenze, le solitudini, una cosa che gli altri non hanno: Il trionfo della creazione. Quel trionfo che gli è anche rifugio, nei momenti più neri' (IB/HWH, p. 390) [The artist has something to counteract the mutabilities of things, the suffering, the loneliness, something that others do not have: The triumph of creation. That triumph which is also their refuge, in the darkest moments].

By recognizing each other as artists, the friends affirm the essence of each other's existence. In this way, the friendship, troubled by the friends' inability to share a home in terms of *Zuhause*, becomes a home in the sense of *Heimat*.

---

[34] Ibid., p. 421.
[35] See for example IB/HWH, pp. 117–18, pp. 325–26, pp. 334–35.
[36] Kracauer, 'Über die Freundschaft', p. 53.

In the words of Siegfried Kracauer:

> Während ich überall sonst genötigt bin, mich in tausenden Lebenskreisen zu zersplittern, hier ein Stückchen zu nehmen, dort ein Quentchen zu geben, darf ich ihm [dem Freund] so gesammelt und umfänglich nahen, wie ich bin und wie ich mich fühle. [...] Der Seligkeit des Begriffenwerdens, des Aufgehobenseins in einer fremden Seele, entspricht aber die nicht minder große Seligkeit des Besitzens. Auch ich berge ja den anderen Menschen in mir. [...] Wir wollen eine Heimat haben und andern eine Heimat sein.[37]

> [While everywhere else I'm compelled to split into thousand circles of life, to take a bit here, to give a smidgeon there, I may approach him [the friend] as composed and expansive as I am and as I feel. The bliss of being understood, of being sheltered in an alien soul is in no small measure equal to the bliss of possession. For I too shelter the other human being in me. We want to have a home and be a home to others.]

---

[37] Ibid., p. 54.

'Aber inwendig werde ich eines Tages das Du vollenden': The Use of Personal Pronouns in Ingeborg Bachmann's *Malina*

SEBASTIAN SCHÖNBECK

University of Bielefeld

In the first chapter of Ingeborg Bachmann's novel *Malina* (1971), the narrator 'I' reflects on her relationship with her lover Ivan and her flatmate Malina by searching for a specific form of the address 'you': 'Zu Malina sage ich du und zu Ivan sage ich du, aber diese beiden Du sind durch einen unmeßbaren, unwägbaren Druck auf den Ausdruck verschieden' (W, III, p. 123) ['I say "Du" to Malina and to Ivan, but these two "Du's" differ by an immeasurable, imponderable accent in pronunciation'] (MB, p. 102). The pressure of the expression, as it reads in the German original, could lie in the fact that the 'I' does not want to use the 'you' as an arbitrary substitute word for an addressee, but as a precise reference within the framework of an intersubjective relationship. The narrator 'I' thus dreams of a private pronoun in the second-person singular, which would consequently multiply the number of personal pronouns (one for each private conversation partner). With this conceptualization of the 'you', the novel points to a fundamental problem of all personal pronouns: their seeming arbitrariness contradicts an individualized and personalized address. As pronouns, they can be substitutes for a wide variety of nouns, persons and things. In short, they appear as interchangeable and variable substitutes whose deictic and anaphoric reference depends on the context. Because of this dependence on context, their study falls within the realm of linguistic pragmatics, such as that pursued by Émile Benveniste. Regardless of the arbitrary interchangeability of pronouns, the success of linguistic communication requires a certain degree of stability in the network of relationships in language, in conversations as well as in literary texts, if persons wish to communicate with other persons, if they want to understand and be understood.

Such stability in the context of reference is not only the condition of possibility of verbal communication, in which linguistic pragmatics à la Benveniste is interested, but also the condition for characters and narrative instances in literary texts to be perceived as persons, so that a 'person effect' occurs, as Martina Wagner-Egelhaaf puts it with reference to Karl Stanzel's

Austrian Studies 32 (2024), doi:10.1353/aus.00016, pp. 221–37
© Modern Humanities Research Association 2024

types of narrators.[1] This problem of the perceptibility and describability of literary figures as persons is addressed by Rüdiger Campe with regard to the form of the person in the (modern) novel. Campe argues that narrative texts give shape to the person through the connection between names and pronouns: It is the references back and forth that create a coherent and consistent person throughout the narrative text.[2] In addition to the aspect of embodiment, which plays a role above all in dramatic texts, according to Campe, the person acquires their identifiability and consistency through this play of forward and backward references. According to Campe the modern novel models these types of recognizability of the person,[3] which is why this modelling also forms a central aspect of the theories of the novel advanced by Clemens Lugowski, Georg Lukács and Käte Hamburger.

In this article, I will examine the use of personal pronouns in Bachmann's *Malina*. The central question is how the consistency and identifiability of the person is reflected in *Malina* through the use of a poetological modelling of the relationship between names and personal pronouns. In approaching this question, I will first take up the reflection upon this relationship in Bachmann's *Frankfurt Lectures* (1959–60), and place this in a broader transdisciplinary context. It is striking that in the years before and after the *Frankfurt Lectures*, until the publication of the novel *Malina*, a broad theoretical discussion of pronouns can already be found in literary theory, linguistics and sociology. Comparing the novel with these divergent disciplinary contexts makes it possible to analyse the use of personal pronouns in *Malina* from different angles. Secondly, I show how the first person singular and its pronominal relationship to the second person in *Malina* is problematized in exemplary passages. Finally, I highlight Bachmann's genuinely poetological contribution to the theorization of pronouns in the 1960s and 1970s.

I

Significantly, Bachmann's poetics lectures, which she presented to around 600 students at the Goethe University in Frankfurt am Main in the winter semester of 1959–60, revolve, among other things, around the writing 'I' and the treatment of names. Bachmann's lectures thus mark both sets of themes as

---

[1] Stanzel's narrator types, Wagner-Egelhaaf argues, are derived from the idea of real persons. For example, they have a 'figure' that experiences, learns, observes, etc. See Martina Wagner-Egelhaaf, 'Der Begriff der "Person" in der Literaturwissenschaft', in *Der Begriff der Person in systematischer wie historischer Perspektive: Ein deutsch-japanischer Dialog*, ed. by Michael Quante and others (mentis, 2020), pp. 199–216 (p. 202).

[2] See Rüdiger Campe, 'Die Form der Person im Roman: Poetologie nach der Poetik mit Georg Lukács, Clemens Lugowski und Käte Hamburger', in *Poetik: Historische Narrative und aktuelle Positionen*, ed. by Armen Avanessian and Jan Niklas Howe (Kadmos, 2014), pp. 169–94 (p. 166).

[3] Ibid.

problems of contemporary literature, by which, given her examples, is meant the literature of the first half of the twentieth century. The problems associated with the 'I' and the name, however, do not interest Bachmann exclusively as symptoms of modern prose, but also in the context of a fundamental philosophical scepticism towards the general possibilities of language, which can also create scope for her own writing.[4]

In the lectures, Bachmann treats the first-person singular — the 'I' — and the use of names as independent and separate problem areas. In both cases she directs her attention not directly to her own texts but to other texts that may be considered significant for her poetology. In her fourth lecture on the question of names, she argues that names such as Lulu, Undine, Emma Bovary, Anna Karenina, Don Quixote and Rastignac still have a 'Strahlkraft' (W, IV, p. 238) ['radiance'] (CW, 306), which names, overall, have lost in (classical) modernity. Here, rather, a 'Schwächung der Namen und eine Unfähigkeit, Namen zu geben' ['a deliberate weakening of names and an inability to convey names'] (CW, p. 311) can be observed, a 'Verkümmern' ['atrophying'], which is, however, sometimes also accompanied by a 'Behauptung' (W, IV, pp. 241–42) ['perseverance'] (CW, p. 311). This observation is even more remarkable because Bachmann describes the relationship to names of literary figures, in contrast to that of real persons, as 'unkündbar' (W, IV, p. 241) ['interminable'] (CW, p. 310) (an alternative translation would be 'binding').

Bachmann supports this claim by referencing the uncertainty of names from the canon of modern literature, in the novels of Kafka, Joyce, Faulkner and Beckett. The first form of name refusal exemplified by Kafka, for example, is the cipher with which the name shrinks to a letter, in this case 'K.'. One might add that Kafka, on the one hand, often gives his characters no names at all, such as in his first publication *Betrachtungen* (1912) [*Meditation*], introducing 'lauter Niemand' [a pack of nobodies],[5] while on the other hand sometimes choosing whole names, such as that of Gregor Samsa. The cipher 'K.' is found prominently in *Der Prozess* (1925) [*The Trial*], in which Josef K. is accused in an unknown case, and in *Das Schloss* (1926) [*The Castle*], in which the surveyor K. searches for his role in a village whose name the readers also do not know. If names were still to be found in modern literature, Bachmann notes, they would

---

[4] Philosophical language criticism is one of the major areas of interest in recent research on Bachmann. See for example Christine Lubkoll: 'Schachspiel als Sprachkritik. Die Philosophie Ludwig Wittgensteins in Ingeborg Bachmanns Roman "Malina"', in *Spiel und Ernst: Formen — Poetiken — Zuschreibungen*, ed. by Dirk Kretzschmar and others (Ergon, 2014), pp. 329–42.

[5] Franz Kafka, 'Der Ausflug ins Gebirge', in Kafka, *Drucke zu Lebzeiten*, ed. by Wolf Kittler, Hans-Gerd Koch and Gerhard Neumann (Fischer, 1994), p. 20; Franz Kafka, *The Complete Stories*, ed. by Nahum N. Glatzer, trans. by Willa and Edwin Muir and by Tania and James Stern (Schocken, 1971), p. 21. A reading that ties Kafka's text back to Homer's *Odyssey* and concerns itself with the tensions between assertion and negation of the name by means of paronomasia is offered by Elisabeth Strowick, '"Lauter Niemand": Zur List des Namens bei Homer und Kafka', *Modern Language Notes*, 119.3 (2004), pp. 564–79.

appear to be an arbitrary product of sense-making, so that it can be stated that:

> das Vertrauen in die naive Namensgebung erschüttert ist, daß hier
> tatsächlich eine Schwierigkeit liegt, daß es auch den anderen Autoren,
> die fortfahren, naiv zu benennen, nur selten gelingt, uns einen Namen
> zu übergeben, eine Gestalt mit einem Namen, der mehr ist als eine
> Erkennungsmarke — einen, der uns so überzeugt, daß wir ihn annehmen,
> fraglos, den wir uns merken, uns wiederholen und mit dem wir anfangen,
> Umgang zu haben. (W, IV, pp. 242–43)

> [our trust in imparting names has been shattered, that there is in fact a
> difficulty here, that even the other authors who continue to name naively
> are seldom successful in bestowing us with a name, a character bearing a
> name that is more than an identification tag — one with such conviction
> that we accept it unquestionably, remembering it and repeating it to
> ourselves, one with which we are willing to initiate a relationship.] (CW,
> p. 311)

The character name, when authors still naively resort to it, is no longer an
expression of a convincing figure that can stand for the character or person.
Instead, it is an arbitrary means of recognizing personal identity, a cipher, a
mere sign, in other words, which Bachmann diagnoses as tantamount to a
question and which is consigned to oblivion. In the course of this fourth lecture,
Bachmann examines a number of strategies in the poetological treatment of
names, such as Kafka's 'Namensschwankungen' and 'Namensheimlichkeiten'
(W, IV, p. 246) ['variations or secrecy of names'] (CW, p. 314), Joyce's
'Namensironisierung' ['ironic treatment of names'] and 'Namensspiel' ['games
with names'] (W, IV, p. 251; CW, p. 318), and Faulkner's 'Namensfallen' (W, IV,
p. 252) ['the names feel like traps'] (CW, p. 319). These poetological variations
in dealing with names correspond, as Bachmann notes regarding Kafka, to the
relative 'Unbekanntheit der Person' (W, IV, p. 246) ['anonymity of persons']
(CW, p. 314).

With this problematization, the disguise and avoidance of the proper name,
the figures in texts of high modernism lose recognizability and consistency.
At the same time — and this could be demonstrated with Bachmann's own
prose — the relation of names to pronouns also becomes a problem. Although
the connection between names and pronouns is not yet explicitly examined
in the *Frankfurt Lectures*, the fact that the two groups of words are connected
and that the weakening of the one also weakens the other is already evident
here in the fact that Bachmann places the first-person singular at the centre of
her interest in the previous, third lecture. In this third lecture on the writing
'I', Bachmann starts from a comparable diagnosis and directly emphasizes the
formal and rhetorical character of the first-person singular from the beginning:
'Aber schon wenn Sie hier allein heroben stehen und sagen zu vielen unten "Ich
sage Ihnen", so verändert sich das Ich unversehens, es entgleitet dem Sprecher,
es wird formal und rhetorisch' (W, IV, p. 217) ['But the minute you stand up
here alone and say to the many seated below, "I am telling you," then the I

changes unexpectedly. It eludes the speaker, becoming formal and rhetorical'] (CW, p. 289).

As in the case of the name, Bachmann also participates in the discussion about a modern crisis of the ego, which goes back at least as far as Ernst Mach's formulation of its irredeemability. In her speech to the Frankfurt audience, Bachmann chooses her own ego at the beginning as an example of the open question of whether the speaking person can back up this speech act with a completed and binding ego. This problem is further complicated when a medium mediates between the audience and the utterance, detaching the speech act from the speaking body and turning it into the mere sound of a technically transmitted broadcast, into a written or printed word or a word spoken by a stage character. The impossibility of a fixed contouring of the 'I', as it is reflected here, is thus not a mere peculiarity of literary modernism, although it is particularly prominent there, but a general characteristic of the mediation of the 'I'. For this reason, the first-person singular is also the subject of countless investigations in both the sciences and the arts. Bachmann mentions primarily poetry, philosophy and psychology: 'All diese Experten sichern sich ihr Ich, sie leuchten in ihm herum, betasten es, zerstümmeln oder zerschlagen es, bewerten es, teilen es ein, zirkeln es ab' (W, IV, p. 218) ['All these experts assure themselves of their I: they flood their lights all over it, touch it, mutilate it, and smash it to pieces; they evaluate it, divide it up, draw circles around it'] (CW, p. 290).

Bachmann subsequently turns her attention to the 'I' in literature, considering first its simplest form, according to which the 'I' is apparently not an invention but an authentic expression of the author-person, as in the case of Louis Ferdinand Céline's *Voyage au bout de la nuit* (1932) [*Journey to the End of the Night*] or Henry Miller's *Plexus* (1952). In both cases, the literary figure designated as 'I', which in each case corresponds to the narrative instance, is not differentiated at all by the author. Bachmann not only wants to distinguish the diary and epistolary 'I' from these novel and author 'I's', she also claims that even the most 'subjective' text genres conceal the person, while in prose and poetry, the saying of the 'I' is often combined with a demonstration and vouching for what is said, which seems to become obsolete with the relocation of the narrative to the interior of the narrator — as paradigmatically shown in Italo Svevo's *La coscienza di Zeno* (1923) [*Zeno's Conscience*]. Svevo's protagonist finds himself facing great uncertainty; the entire novel, characterized by free indirect speech, consists of the faltering search for one's own self-understanding. Bachmann does not elaborate on the fact that this search, which points to a strangeness of consciousness to itself,[6] is also found in the poetology of the name of the main

---

[6] See Paul Geyer, 'Kritischer Bewußtseinsroman und erlebte Rede in der Ich-Form: Italo Svevos "La coscienza di Zeno"', in *Über die Schwierigkeiten, sich zu sagen: Horizonte literarischer Subjektkonstitution*, ed. by Winfried Wehle (Klostermann, 2001), pp. 107–45 (p. 119). See also Paul Geyer, 'Romanzo critico della coscienza e discorso indiretto libero in

character Zeno Cosini.[7] Instead, her argument arrives at Proust's À la recherche du temps perdu (1913–27) [In Search of Lost Time], of which the fifth volume La prisonnière (1923) [The Prisoner] appears in the same year as La coscienza di Zeno. In the first volume of Proust's Recherche, according to Bachmann, the 'I' disappears for long stretches into the depths of consciousness and the memory of a past time. In La prisonnière, the decay of the 'I' can be seen in the dissolution of subjective experience into an objective dimension of experience (see W, IV, p. 232). It is this dissolution of the ego that is radicalized in the examples she then goes on to discuss, Hans Henny Jahnn's Fluß ohne Ufer (1950) [River without Banks] and Samuel Beckett's L'innomable (1953) [The Unnamable], in which the ego is now trapped in a hopeless search for itself: 'Nicht nur Persönlichkeit oder gar Identität, Wesenskonstante, Geschichte, Umwelt und Vergangenheit sind ihm abhanden gekommen, sondern sein Verlangen nach Schweigen droht, es auszulöschen, zu vernichten' (W, IV, p. 235) ['Not only are personality, not to mention identity, the immutable qualities of its being, history, milieu, and the past lost to it, but its quest for silence threatens to extinguish, to annihilate it'] (CW, p. 303).

The main character in this Beckett novel carries multiple names (I, Mahood, Worm) and stands in an almost unfathomable relationship to the other named characters (Murphy, Watt, Mercier) in the novel and in Beckett's work. According to Blanchot, it is the experiment of an experience exposed to the nameless, 'the approach of a neutral voice that is raised of its own accord, that penetrates the man who hears it, that is without any intimacy'.[8] This neutral voice does not belong to any individual person; it could be the voice of anyone or everyone and could break off at any time, thereby, according to Bachmann, extinguishing the ego. With regard to the personal pronouns used in L'innomable, it can be stated that their relationship to the names thus not only seems conceptually uncertain, but that the entire novel functions according to this uncertainty.

II

Before and after Bachmann's Frankfurt Lectures (1959–60), and prior to the publication of her novel Malina in 1971, new research on the theory of personal pronouns emerged in the 1950s and 1960s in the fields of linguistic pragmatics, novel poetics and sociology, targeting the use and mutual relationship of pronouns to each other from different disciplinary directions. This abundance of research on the grammar of pronouns is striking, for it suggests that Bachmann's third and fourth lectures illuminate the grammar of personal

---

prima persona: La Coscienza di Zeno di Svevo', Studi Italiani, 44 (2010), pp. 69–100.

[7] See Geyer, 'Kritischer Bewußtseinsroman', pp. 118–20.

[8] Maurice Blanchot, 'Where now, Who now?', in On Beckett. Essays and Criticism, ed. by S. E. Gontarski (Cambridge University Press, 2012), pp. 111–17 (p. 113).

pronouns as one perspective among others, which in no way detracts from her original achievement, as I will argue. In the following, I would like to discuss these contexts with necessary brevity, focusing in particular on the second-person singular 'you', which will also interest Bachmann in *Malina*.

It is clear that the study of personal pronouns falls within the narrow remit of linguistics. Hardly any text on personal pronouns can fail to reference Émile Benveniste's text *La nature des pronoms* [*The Nature of Pronouns*] from 1956,[9] in which he first emphasizes that pronouns do not form a uniform class of words but depend on the respective language mode in which they appear. While some simply belong to the syntax of languages, others form 'instances of discourse'[10] that actualize the system of language in their use. Benveniste devotes special attention to personal pronouns as instances of discourse and, following Charles Morris, essentially defines the 'I' as a pragmatic unity of sign and of the person who uses it.

Benveniste focuses on the first two personal pronouns 'I' and 'you', which are closely connected with the idea of a person, while he explicitly discards the third person as a 'non-person' from the class of personal pronouns.[11] He is interested in the use of the personal pronouns in the exercise of language, defining the 'I' as a reference and discourse instance active in a speech situation, which only has a reality within the discourse: '*I* is "the individual who utters the present instance of discourse containing the linguistic instance *I*."[12] Derived from this, the 'you' is defined as 'the individual spoken to in the present instance of discourse containing the linguistic instance *you*'.[13] For Benveniste, 'I' and 'you' are thus discourse instances that acquire their meaning in unique statements within the framework of intersubjective communication and thus function fundamentally differently from other linguistic entities. However, Benveniste asks, does language in use therefore consist only of statements by discourse instances (by 'I's addressed to 'you's)? An exception to this is the third-person singular, which he wants to distinguish from the first two pronouns: 'The "third person" represents the unmarked member of the correlation of person.'[14] This 'non-person' refers to 'someone or something outside of the instance itself' and

---

[9] The text first appeared in 1956 in a commemorative publication for Roman Jakobson before being added to the essay collection *Problèmes de linguistique générale* in 1966. See Émile Benveniste, 'La nature des pronoms', in *For Roman Jakobson*, ed. by Morris Halle and others (Mouton, 1956), pp. 34–37; Émile Benveniste, 'La nature des pronoms', in *Problèmes de linguistique générale* (Gallimard, 1966), pp. 251–57. Benveniste already discusses pronouns in the essay 'Structure des relations dans le verbe'. See also Émile Benveniste, 'Structure des relations dans le verbe', *Bulletin de la Société de linguistique de Paris*, 43 (1946), pp. 1–12.

[10] Émile Benveniste, 'The Nature of Pronouns', in Benveniste, *Problems in General Linguistics*, trans. by Mary Elizabeth Meek (University of Miami Press) pp. 217–22 (p. 217).

[11] Ibid., p. 221.

[12] Ibid., p. 218.

[13] Ibid.

[14] Ibid., p. 221.

can thus be used more arbitrarily than 'I' and 'you'.[15] It seems as if Benveniste emphasizes the internal distinction between the first two persons and the third person so strongly because, as he states at the end of his essay, he essentially wants to differentiate between 'language as a repertory of signs and a system for combining them' on the one hand, and 'language as an activity' on the other.[16]

As a pragmatist, Benveniste is not interested in literary texts at this point, and the relationship of his remarks to the mode of literary fiction is not evident. One quality of literary texts may be that they can create complex structures of pronominal order. Michel Butor makes it clear in his 1961 treatise *L'usage des pronoms personnels dans le roman* [The Use of Personal Pronouns in the Novel] that this is especially true for the genre of the novel.[17] The novel, as Butor shows, sometimes narrates in the first, sometimes in the third person, and as a narrative already involves at least three persons, the narrating author-person, the addressed reader-person and the character about whom the story is told. The character necessarily appears as the third person, because as a fictional entity they are to be distinguished from the author. This is true even where the novel narrates in the first person and presents what is narrated as a document. This does not refer to the mutual insignificance of author-person and narrator, but to the 'identification privilégiée' [privileged identification] between the two.[18] According to Butor, it is only in first-person narration that the question of the temporal distance between the act of narration and the narration itself arises. This distance diminishes at the moment of narration, since the reader is supposed to take the place of the 'I' in order to experience the events directly, up to and including an inner monologue that represents 'une conscience fermée' [a closed consciousness].[19]

If we compare Butor's poetological reflections on the novel to Benveniste's description of the discourse instances, we notice that the literary narrative here intricately binds the first and third persons and that the configuration of this complex creates possible identifications for the second (addressed) person. The complexity of the personal pronouns in a novel increases even further when it is considered that in literary language there can still be shifts within the pronominal structure. Moreover, Butor points to the diversity in the forms of substitutions of the personal pronouns by referring to Caesar, who writes of himself in the third person, or to Descartes, whose 'I' is repeatedly used as the second-person singular. In contrast to conversation, which is what concerns

---

[15] Ibid.

[16] Ibid., p. 222.

[17] The text was first published in the magazine *Les Temps Modernes* in 1961 and subsequently included in the essay collection *Repertoire II* (Les Éditions de Minuit, 1964), pp. 59–72.

[18] Michel Butor, 'L'usage des pronoms personnels dans le roman', in *Problèmes de la personne: Colloque du Centre de Recherche de Psychologie Comparative*, ed. by Ignace Meyerson (De Gruyter, 1973), pp. 281–92 (p. 283).

[19] Ibid., p. 285.

Benveniste, Butor describes personal pronouns as complex mixtures or as entire 'architectures de pronoms' [architectures of pronouns],[20] which is why he calls for the analysis of all pronouns used in the novel.

A year before Bachmann's novel *Malina* appeared, Norbert Elias published *Was ist Soziologie?* (1970) [*What is Sociology?*],[21] an introduction to his discipline. In this work, he also discusses personal pronouns, as their use shows how individuals establish references to societies through their linguistic practice. Right at the beginning of his work, Elias criticizes the 'Verbegrifflichung' [the predominant and typical way of conceptualizing] of social groups in sociology.[22] He describes the underlying model, which assumes a separation between the individual and social groups and institutions, as 'naïvely egocentric'.[23] Elias also takes up this criticism in the chapter *The Personal Pronouns as a Figuration Model* and argues that in the conceptualization of the 'I', the path from a concept of relationship to a concept of substance, or a concept of a thing, is too short. Rather, the personal pronouns are an

> elementary set of coordinates by which all human groupings or societies can be plotted out. When communicating directly or indirectly with each other, all people refer to themselves as 'I' or 'we', and to those with whom they are communicating at the moment as 'you'. The third person who temporarily or permanently stands outside the intercommunicating group is referred to as 'he' or 'she', or in the plural as 'they'.[24]

Through an understanding of personal pronouns as a 'Fürwörterserie' (the meaning is lost in the English translation of the title: 'series of words (standing) for other words'), that is, as an indissoluble series or row, the individual pronouns gain the status of positional markers within the framework of communicative acts. The distinction between the first two persons and the third person, which marks the outside of the communicative situation, recalls Benveniste. However, Elias's key concern is to describe the personal pronouns not individually, but as an intercorrelation network.

Benveniste's linguistic, Butor's poetological and Elias's sociological contribution to the linguistic and literary use of pronouns are similar in that they refer to the complex relationship of personal pronouns to one another. This idea is already expressed in Benveniste's preference for the mutual reference of the discourse instances 'I' and 'you' and is further radicalized in Elias's work and examined in terms of the individual reference to society, which is sometimes also unconscious. This preference is combined in both cases with a strongly

---

[20] Ibid., p. 290.
[21] Norbert Elias, *Was ist Soziologie?*, in Norbert Elias, *Gesammelte Schriften*, v, ed. by Reinhard Blomert and others (Suhrkamp, 2006); Norbert Elias, *What is Sociology?*, trans. by Stephen Mennell and Grace Morrissey (Columbia University Press, 1978).
[22] Elias, *Was ist Soziologie?*, p. 14; Elias, *What is Sociology?*, p. 14.
[23] Ibid., p. 14.
[24] Ibid., p. 123.

emphasized distinction from the third person, which Benveniste calls 'someone or something outside the instance itself',[25] and which Elias describes as 'outside the intercommunication group'.[26] According to Butor, the first and second persons are intricately connected in the novel, while the third person is placed in an indeterminate relationship to the first two persons. In the years prior to the publication of the novel *Malina*, a theorization of personal pronouns can thus be traced in linguistics as well as in literary theory and sociology. In the final section of this article, I ask to what extent insights from these various disciplines can enrich the reading of the novel.

III

In Bachmann's *Malina*, we find an examination of the relationships between personal pronouns in the singular over long stretches of the plot. The novel begins with a tableau-like juxtaposition of the characters, who are included in a list, as is usually found at the beginning of dramatic texts. In addition to the first names of Ivan and his children Béla and András, a personal pronoun is also listed, the 'I':

> Ich: Österreichischer Paß, ausgestellt vom Innenministerium. Beglaubigter Staatsbürgerschaftsnachweis. Augen br., Haare bl., geboren in Klagenfurt, es folgen Daten und ein Beruf, zweimal durchgestrichen und überschrieben, Adressen, dreimal durchgestrichen, und in korrekter Schrift ist darüber zu lesen: wohnhaft Ungargasse 6, Wien III. (W, III, p. 12)

> [Myself: Austrian passport, issued by the Ministry of the Interior. Official Austrian I.D. Eyes — br., Hair — blnd.; born in Klagenfurt; some dates follow and a profession (crossed out twice and written over); addresses (crossed out three times); above which in clear block letters: Ungargasse 6, Vienna III.

In the case of Ivan and Malina, the list of characters already engages in an interplay between the disclosure and denial of personal information, which varies in all the entries. What is striking about the entry of the 'Ich' ('Myself', or rather 'I') is that it is the only anonymous instance in the list. Instead of the name, the personal pronoun in the first-person singular appears as a substitute word. Later, it becomes clear that the name of the 'I' also begins with the letter 'I' (see W, III, p. 32). The 'Ich' ('I') shares this letter with 'Ivan' and with the author of the text, Ingeborg Bachmann. In order to compensate for the absence of the name of 'I', the entry points to its passport document and thus to the official 'representation of the person',[27] as if the text wanted to say that the existence of

---

[25] Benveniste, 'The Nature of Pronouns', p. 221.

[26] Elias, *What is Sociology?*, p. 123.

[27] On the passport as a small representative of the person in literature see Mona Körte, 'Vom Pass besessen: Der amtliche Ausweis als kleine Form', *Archiv für Mediengeschichte: Kleine Formen*, 19 (2021), pp. 113–24.

'I' is officially and legally certified and therefore need not be questioned. As is usual in the case of individuals, 'I' can also be recognized by her brown eyes, blond hair and other features. However, the fact that some personal information is explicitly not listed here is shown by the fact that the entry draws attention to correction marks (crossings out, etc.). Finally, we are not reading a polished list of persons at all, but an edited form of the same, a draft that appears, as Sigrid Weigel points out, like a 'Muster eines Fahndungsplakats oder [die] Blätter einer Personalakte' [a typical missing person poster or pages in a personnel file].[28] The correction marks refer to indeterminate data, the profession and the address. But to which narrative instance are these uncertainties in knowledge about the person to be attributed? Is 'I' identical with the narrative instance of the list of persons? And if so, did the narrative instance necessarily edit its own entry? That the 'I' is also the editor of its own entry is suggested at the beginning of the text. Here, the 'I' underlines the difficulty of starting from the unity of place and time: 'Nur die Zeitangabe mußte ich mir lange überlegen, denn es ist mir fast unmöglich, heute zu sagen' (W, III, p. 12) [But I had to think long and hard about the Time, since "today" is an impossible word for me] (MB, p. 4).

The list of characters and the long first sentence thus mark the difficulties of the 'I' to refer to itself, as well as to the time and place, thereby accentuating the formal and rhetorical character of the writing (see W, IV, p. 217). The novel emphasizes from the beginning that a nameless character expresses self-doubt and that we are therefore dealing with an I that does not claim any guarantees for itself. Beyond the precarious self-reference, the problems of the 'I' are strongly connected with its relationship to the other characters, to Malina and Ivan, to whom the 'I' turns to the point of self-sacrifice. At times it is the categorical separation between the figures that is lamented, at other times it is their indistinguishability. Elsewhere, it is their mutual significance for each other that is emphasized. The relationship to Malina is described by the 'I' as hierarchical and characterized by misunderstandings (see W, III, p. 17). Facing Malina, the 'I' asks in the first chapter, for example: 'was wir denn sein können für einander, Malina und ich, da wir einander so unähnlich sind, so verschieden, und das ist nicht eine Frage des Geschlechts, der Art, der Festigkeit seiner Existenz und der Unfestigkeit der meinen' (W, III, p. 22) ['what we can be for each other, Malina and I, since we are so distinct, so unalike, and this isn't a question of sex or kind, the stability of his existence and the instability of my own'] (MB, p. 12).

Despite this difference, Malina and the 'I' are very close and — as we learn from the perspective of the 'I' — maintain an intense relationship. The 'I' gives him various nicknames such as 'Eugenius' or 'Prince Eugen' and notes their common origin 'from the Yugoslavian border' (see W, III, p. 20). The narrative of the 'I' fluctuates between an intimate devotion to Malina and a painful

---

[28] Sigrid Weigel, *Ingeborg Bachmann: Hinterlassenschaften unter Wahrung des Briefgeheimnisses* (Zsolnay, 1999), p. 527.

separation.[29] On the one hand, they live together in a flat in the Ungargasse, on the other hand, Malina often ignores the 'I'. This is initially expressed in a move from the first to the third person:

> Mir scheint es dann, daß seine Ruhe davon herrührt, weil ich ein zu unwichtiges und bekanntes Ich für ihn bin, als hätte er mich ausgeschieden, einen Abfall, eine überflüssige Menschwerdung, als wäre ich nur aus seiner Rippe gemacht und ihm seit jeher entbehrlich, aber auch eine unvermeidliche dunkle Geschichte, die seine Geschichte begleitet, ergänzen will, die er aber von seiner klaren Geschichte absondert und abgrenzt. (W, III, pp. 22–23)

> [Then it seems to me that his calm comes from my ego being too familiar, too unimportant for him, as if he had rejected me as waste, a superfluous something-made-human, as if I were merely the dispensable product of his rib, but at the same time an unavoidable dark tale accompanying and hoping to supplement his own bright story, a tale that he, however, detaches and delimits.] (MB, p. 12)

This speculation of the 'I' about the meaning of the third person (Malina) appears exemplary for the unclear mutual positioning of the two figures, which fluctuates between rhetorical and diegetic proximity and distance. A similar wavering applies to the relationship of the 'I' to Ivan, which is unfolded in the chapter *Glücklich mit Ivan* [Happy with Ivan]. Ivan is the other important third person in the narrative, alongside Malina, because he gives her (the 'I') a new confidence in language:

> und so werde ich keinen Jota von ihm abweichen, ich werde unsre identischen, hellklingenden Anfangsbuchstaben, mit denen wir unsre kleinen Zettel unterzeichnen, aufeinanderstimmen, übereinanderschreiben, und nach der Vereinigung unserer Namen könnten wir vorsichtig anfangen, mit den ersten Worten dieser Welt wieder die Ehre zu erweisen [...]. (W, III, p. 32)

> [and I will not stray from him one iota, I will align and superimpose our identical, high-pitched first initials we use to sign our little notes, and after our names unite we could begin with the first words, cautiously, once again paying heed to this world, compelling it to respect itself once more [...]] (MB, pp. 20–21)

Not only are the initial letters of 'I' and Ivan identical, but 'I' also dreams of an identity between the apostrophized name and the first-person personal pronoun in the singular.[30] This identity is purely formal and, because it borders so closely on the character Ivan, creates no consistency in the relational

---

[29] In this sense, the text also deals with the possibility of a we-formation, although the precarious status of the 'we' is repeatedly pointed out.
[30] In general, there are numerous assonances in *Malina*. In this context, Marlen Mairhofer writes of 'viral assonances'. See Marlen Mairhofer, '"Ich war ja nicht krank — ich war nur krank, aber ganz anders": Ingeborg Bachmanns (Patho?-)Texte', in *Kunst und Gebrechen*, ed. by Hildegard Fraueneder, Nora Grundtner and Manfred Kern, Figurationen des Übergangs, 1 (Sonderzahl, 2024), pp. 175–89.

structure of name and pronoun. On the one hand, this ambiguity in the relational structure emanates from the 'I', which is unsure of itself, and on the other hand, it manifests itself in the rapidly changing positioning of the characters among themselves: 'Ivan ist nicht gewarnt vor mir. [...] ich will Ivan nicht in die Irre führen, aber für ihn wird nie sichtbar, daß ich doppelt bin. Ich bin auch Malinas Geschöpf' (W, III, pp. 103–04) ['Ivan hasn't been warned about me. [...] I don't want to lead Ivan astray, but he'll never realize that I am double. I am also Malina's creation'] (MB, pp. 82–83).

The fact that the figures 'I', Malina and Ivan are so strongly related to each other that they can be considered dimensions of a single figure, as Bachmann herself repeatedly emphasized in interviews (see GuI, pp. 87, 99), has already been extensively highlighted in scholarship. This is especially true of the figure Malina, with whom the 'I' forms a heterosexual complex, which has given rise to a strong strand of gender-theoretical reception (see HB2020, 130–44). However, in her 1976 study, Ellen Summerfield already showed that Ivan can also be interpreted as another psychological manifestation of the 'I'.[31] According to Summerfield, neither Malina nor Ivan are exclusively 'konkrete Menschen' [concrete people], by which she presumably means distinguishable human figures in the novel's diegesis, but also 'Mittel zur Darstellung eines Seelenzustandes oder einer Seelenanlage' [means for the representation of a psychological state or frame of mind].[32] In Weigel's reading, the character composition of the text is not resolved in the soul or psyche of the 'I', but is understood as a 'Triade' [triad] in which two third positions, those of Malina and Ivan, are added to the constellation of the author's name and the narrator ('I').[33] According to Weigel, these third positions are each to be understood as those of 'the other', with Malina representing the male and sexually indifferent 'Stimme der Vernunft und des Überlebens' [voice of reason and survival] and Ivan that of love and desire.[34] Malina thus doubles the novel's typical triad of author, first-person narrator and character, which can also be seen in the changing references between personal pronouns and names.

I do not wish to add to the numerous readings on the 'Facettenfigur' [multifaceted figure] of the I and the question of its distinguishability or indistinguishability,[35] but instead to draw attention to the fact that the problem of discarded identity (to use Bachmann's term: of the 'I without guarantee') essentially lies with the references of the 'I' to the 'you' and to the 'it', and the novel thus transposes a pronominal problem, as Benveniste negotiates it linguistically, Butor poetologically and Elias sociologically, to the level of the

---

[31] Ellen Summerfield, *Ingeborg Bachmann: Die Auflösung der Figur in ihrem Roman 'Malina'* (Bouvier, 1976), pp. 59–69.

[32] Ibid., p. 69.

[33] Weigel, *Ingeborg Bachmann*, pp. 526–34.

[34] Ibid., p. 531.

[35] Jost Schneider, *Die Kompositionsmethode Ingeborg Bachmanns: Erzählstil und Engagement in 'Das dreißigste Jahr', 'Malina' und 'Simultan'* (Aisthesis, 1999), p. 268.

novel's characters. The novel *Malina* plays out the possibilities of references between the personal pronouns by depicting how the 'I', on the one hand, suffers hopelessly from the separation from Malina and Ivan, but on the other hand, addresses these almost excessively:

> Zu Malina sage ich du und zu Ivan sage ich du, aber diese beiden Du sind durch einen unmeßbaren, unwägbaren Druck auf den Ausdruck verschieden. Beiden gegenüber habe ich von Anfang an kein Sie benutzt, das ich sonst immer gebrauche. Ivan ist augenblicklich von mir erkannt worden, und es blieb keine Zeit, ihm näherzukommen durch Reden, ich war ihm schon zugefallen vor jedem Wort. Über Malina wiederum habe ich so viele Jahre nachgedacht, es hat mich so verlangt nach ihm, daß unser Zusammenleben eines Tages nur noch die Bekräftigung war für etwas, was immer so sein hätte sollen und nur zu oft verhindert worden war, durch andere Menschen, durch verkehrte Entschlüsse und Handlungen. Mein Du für Malina ist genau und geeignet für unsere Gespräche und unsere Auseinandersetzungen. Mein Du für Ivan ist ungenau, es kann sich verfärben, verdunkeln, lichten, es kann spröde, mild oder zaghaft werden, unbegrenzt ist die Skala seiner Expressionen, es kann auch ganz allein, in großen Intervallen gesagt werden und viele Male sirenenhaft, immer wieder verlockend neu, aber immer noch ist es nicht mit dem Ton, mit jenem Ausdruck gesagt worden, den ich in mir höre, wenn ich unfähig bin, vor Ivan ein Wort herauszubringen. Vor ihm nicht, aber inwendig werde ich eines Tages das Du vollenden. Es wird das Vollkommene sein. (W, III, p. 126)

> [I say 'Du' to Malina and to Ivan, but these two 'Du's' differ by an immeasurable, imponderable accent in pronunciation. From the beginning I never said 'Sie' to either one, as is otherwise my custom. I recognized Ivan too instantaneously and there was no time to get closer to him through speech, I had already belonged to him before a word was said. Malina, on the other hand, had been the focus of my thoughts for so many years, my longing for him had been so great that our living together one day was only the affirmation of something which should have always been, something which had only been impeded too often by other people, bad decisions and actions. My 'Du' for Malina is precise and well suited to our conversations and arguments. My 'Du' for Ivan is imprecise, of varying hues, darker, lighter, it can become brittle, mellow or timid, unlimited in its scale of expression, it can be said alone at longer intervals and often, like a siren, always alluringly new, but nonetheless without that tone, that expression I hear in me whenever I cannot bring myself to utter a single word in front of Ivan. Not in front of him, but inside me I will someday perfect this 'Du.' Perfection will have evolved.] (MB, p. 102)

At this point, the 'I' makes a fundamental distinction in the system of personal pronouns, determined by the relationship to the respective addressee rather than by a name or a communicative situation. Not only does the 'I' claim that the use of the second person singular in addressing Malina and Ivan is an exception, because saying 'Du' seems to her to be suspect in principle and she usually prefers the formal 'Sie' (see W, III, pp. 127–28), but an internal differentiation for 'you' is also introduced. While the 'you' for Malina is described as 'genau und geeignet für unsere Gespräche und unsere Auseinandersetzungen' [precise and well suited to our conversations and arguments], the 'you' she reserves for Ivan is more emotive and intrinsically more complex. The 'you' for Ivan, it is said, could have an unlimited scale of expression, of varying hues, darker or lighter. Compared to the Malina-'you', the Ivan-'you' has an aesthetic quality that is fed by its versatility and multiformity. It is not a question of whom it refers to or addresses, because the addressee for this specific 'you' is fixed. Instead, the focus is on how the address is made, with what mood and at what interval it is delivered. For this 'you' reserved for Ivan, another internal differentiation is introduced, the inner (*inwendig*) and the verbalized 'you', and the difficulty of a correspondence between the two forms. The 'I' calls such a correspondence a completed you ('das Du vollenden'; perfect this 'Du'). Here, a certain flaw or lack is attributed to the verbalized 'you', while the completion of the 'you' is expected somewhere within ('inwendig'; inside me). The omission of the pronoun 'es' [it] in the English translation in the last sentence of the paragraph, which is rendered simply as 'Perfection will have evolved', makes it unrecognizable that such a 'you' would be the epitome of a future perfection.

The diagnosis of the unfinished, verbalized 'you' and the completed, inner 'you' can be examined more closely in a whole series of misdirected narrated conversations, telephone calls, letters and dramatic dialogues (especially in the second part of *Malina*) that the text presents. The rest of the novel also uses the two forms, the internal and verbalized personal pronouns. These forms correspond to the verbalized personal pronouns in the diegesis, whose deictic reference can 'refer', to a certain extent, to different places in the narrative. Secondly, the personal pronouns narrated by the narrative instance do not claim a deictic reference but an anaphoric one, referring to the persons treated in the list of characters in terms of recognition. What would have to be asked in a larger framework is how the interaction and communication on the one hand and the narrative references between the characters on the other succeed or fail in each case, and how this is manifest in the pronominal structure of the text.

IV

Finally, *Malina* still wants to do justice to the title of the larger project 'Todesarten', of which it is the only published part. Here, the text makes the transition to the non-person, to the 'it':

> Er [Malina] läßt eine Blechbüchse mit Schlaftabletten zwischen die Papierfetzen fallen, sucht noch etwas und schaut um sich, er räumt den Leuchter noch weiter weg, versteckt ihn zuletzt, als könnten die Kinder ihn jemals erreichen, und es ist etwas in der Wand, es kann nicht mehr schreien, aber es schreit doch: Ivan! (W, III, p. 336)

['He [Malina] drops a tin box with sleeping tablets in between the scraps of paper, looks around for something else, he moves the candelabra even further away and finally hides it, as if the children could ever reach it, and there is something inside the wall, something that can no longer cry out, but cries out nonetheless: Ivan!'] (MB, pp. 282–83)

With the final murder of the 'I', the border to the 'it', to the non-person, is crossed, with which the text literarily affirms Roland Barthes's thesis in *Le degré zéro de l'écriture* (1959) [*Writing Degree Zero*] that the abandonment of the 'I' in the novel can be equated with death.[36] The novel, although told in the first person, does not break off here, however, but continues in the third person. Consistently, the narrative part of the text dispenses with the first person here, but continues to tell the story, even if only briefly. Bachmann's *Malina* thus demonstrates that a literary text can make the transition from personal pronouns to the non-person and can thus illuminate that boundary which linguistic pragmatics and sociology describe as a categorical difference.[37] With its problematization of the relationship of the 'I' to several 'yous', as well as with its transition to the 'it', the novel enters a tradition of the theorization of personal pronouns and works through the problem of the relationship and limits of personal pronouns by means of the affordances of literary language

Moreover, in *Malina*, the internal differentiations of the two forms of the 'you' make it clear that Benveniste's two-sided definition of an 'I' that refers to a 'you' in speech can be expanded and deepened within the framework of a literary text. In *Malina*, it is shown that 'I' and 'you' not only refer to each other as instances through the logic of the statement, but that they form a multi-linked, inherently complex network of relations that obscures or veils the identifiability and consistency of a narrated person in Campe's sense.[38] The effect, however, is not to be understood exclusively as a destruction of personhood, but rather as a visualization of the preconditions under which persons can be represented in literary texts.

With regard to Butor, it can be noted that his description of the novel as an 'architecture of pronouns' corresponds with Bachmann's *Malina*. An overlap, for example, is manifested by the letter and pronoun 'I', which not only marks the narrative instance, but reappears at the beginning of the character Ivan's name and that of the author. 'I', Ivan, Ingeborg and 'I', in the sense of the reader, are thus multi-layered and multidimensional in the first-person singular. Solely because it is similar to the 'you', although for her it is only directed at two people, does the 'I' dream of an internal difference, of a perfect 'you' reserved for the representation of Ivan, which at the moment of its verbalization coincides with the idea that 'I' has of Ivan, of her unique 'you'.

---

[36] See Roland Barthes, *Le degré zero de l'écriture suivi de Nouveaux essais critiques* (Seuil, 1972), p. 33.
[37] See Benveniste, 'The Nature of Pronouns', p. 221.
[38] See Campe, 'Die Form der Person im Roman', p. 166.

The examination of the second-person singular in Bachmann's *Malina* shows that the novel has a different (literary) language for describing pronominal problems, such as the private and intimate personalization of speech. The literary text thus participates in the theoretical history of personal pronouns. At the same time, the inclusion of this theoretical history opens up new ways of describing and analysing a much-discussed novel. It is the characters' struggle with the possibilities, promises and limits of personal pronouns that makes the combination of linguistics, literary theory, sociology and literature productive, and opens new perspectives for further readings.

High Noon:
How to Tear Open a Vertical

SABINE I. GÖLZ

The University of Iowa

Das Denken, der Zeit verhaftet, verfällt auch wieder der Zeit. Aber weil es verfällt, eben deshalb muß unser Denken neu sein, wenn es echt sein und etwas bewirken will.[1]

Freiheit ist, gegen den Apparat zu spielen.[2]

I

Ingeborg Bachmann sets out to solve problems that current theories of language do not even know exist — and therefore continue to cause. To read her work, we have to venture out of the cocoon of our intellectual habits and start thinking (in) our Now.

> Wie strahlend auch einzelne Gedanken aus früherer Zeit auf uns kommen, wenn wir sie zu Zeugen rufen, so tun wir es zur Unterstützung unserer Gedanken heute. Es soll uns darum auch nicht einfallen, alles für geleistet zu halten, weil vor 50 und 40 Jahren ein paar große Geister aufgetreten sind. Es hilft nichts, ihnen, als wären sie unsere Fixsterne, noch immer das Denken zu überlassen. Es hilft nicht, sich abzustützen auf das Bewunderungswürdige, das geschaffen worden ist in diesen letzten Jahrzehnten. Daraus zu lernen ist nur, daß wir nicht herumkommen werden um den gleichen gefährlichen Auftritt. Es gibt in der Kunst keinen Fortschritt in der Horizontale, sondern nur das immer neue Aufreißen einer Vertikale. (KS, p. 266)

> [However radiantly individual thoughts from earlier times have come down to us, when we call them as witnesses we do so to support our thinking today. It will therefore also not occur to us to think that everything has already been done because fifty or forty years ago a few great minds stepped on the scene. It will not do to leave our thinking to them as if they were fixed stars. It will not do to lean on all that is admirable that has been created in

---

[1] KS, p. 266 [Thinking, tied to time, also expires with time. But because it expires, for that very reason our thinking has to be new if it wants to be genuine and have an impact.] Unless otherwise indicated, all translations my own.

[2] Vilém Flusser, *Für eine Philosophie der Photographie* (European Photography, 1999), p. 73 [Freedom is to play against the apparatus]..

Austrian Studies 32 (2024), doi:10.1353/aus.00017, pp. 238–55
© Modern Humanities Research Association 2024

these last decades. From that, we only learn that we cannot avoid that same dangerous step into the open [*Auftritt*]. In art, there is no progress in the horizontal, only the ever-new tearing open of a vertical.]

We cannot leave our thinking to others — not to the great works of the past, and not even to Bachmann. So far, so good. But what dangerous step, what *Auftritt* is this? And how does one tear open a vertical? Bachmann's poems can help answer these questions.

'Die gestundete Zeit' [Borrowed Time], the title poem of Bachmann's first volume of poetry, gives a clear diagnosis of the problem she is working to overcome. In reading the poem, we must pay attention to the spatial arrangement of lines and stanzas, which articulate frames and shifts in perspectives, adding a dimension beyond what the lines merely 'say'. There are two frames. The first and last lines — 'Es kommen härtere Tage' [Harder days are coming] — make up the outer frame. An interior frame encloses only the first stanza and consists of the repeated lines: 'Die auf Widerruf gestundete Zeit | Wird sichtbar am Horizont' [Time borrowed pending recall | Comes into view on the horizon]. Within that smaller, limited horizon, no clear perception is possible. Illumination is poor, fog reigns: 'Ärmlich brennt das Licht der Lupinen. | Dein Blick spurt im Nebel.' [Poorly burns the light of the lupins. | Your gaze trails in the fog:]. As we move through the poem, however, we leave that first horizon. When we arrive in the second stanza, something 'wird sichtbar am Horizont' [Comes into view on the horizon]:

> Drüben versinkt dir die Geliebte im Sand,
> Er steigt um ihr wehendes Haar,
> Er fällt ihr ins Wort
> Er befiehlt ihr zu schweigen,
> Er findet sie sterblich
> Und willig dem Abschied
> Nach jeder Umarmung. (W, I, pp. 37)

> [Over there your beloved sinks in the sand,
> he rises around her waving hair,
> he interrupts her speech, [lit.: he falls into her word]
> he orders her to be silent,
> he finds her mortal
> and willing to depart
> after every embrace.]

Only now, looking back at the restricted frame we have just left behind — *Drüben* — can we see what was indiscernible before: an unending trickle of 'he-s' rising around 'her' hair, falling into 'her' word, finding her mortal, deleting 'her' after every embrace.[3] *Drüben*, 'she' is not a subject or speaker,

---

[3] For a related earlier reading, see my 'Reading in the Twilight: Canonization, Gender, the Limits of Language, and a Poem by Ingeborg Bachmann', *New German Critique*, 47 (1989), pp. 29–52.

but a universal signifier: interrupted, silenced, found mortal, and told what she means.

Two standard poetic strategies are in play here. One is the bedrock of Western poetry — the apostrophic address to the 'beloved'. The second and related one is a staple of European literature since Romanticism that we are barely beginning to understand: swarming pronouns make ghostly 'she-s' appear at critical junctures as if out of nowhere, effecting a subliminal gendering. Bachmann retools the latter strategy to opposite effect: the noun 'der Sand', gendered masculine in German, generates an anaphoric series of masculine pronouns. Bachmann critiques the former strategy with the help of the double framing of 'Die gestundete Zeit', which shows that only if we step out of and beyond the horizon of that hegemonic poetics can we perceive the murderous and assimilative consequences of this practice: the 'beloved' (and ultimately any 'she') is treated as a blank place for serially depositing significations. Readerly gazes within that horizon are domesticated: they labour obediently in the fog. One of the meanings of the verb 'spuren' is 'to obey' or 'to follow an order': 'Dein Blick spurt im Nebel' [Your gaze trails/obeys in the fog].[4] The two together explain why the pronoun *sie* is so problematic for her: it is the trigger for the unthinkingly compliant readerly response — to which she is a mere signifier.

The figure of the beloved, the pronoun *sie* [she, they], and the beloved's 'hair' all play central roles in Paul Celan's early poetry. I therefore suspect that the encounter with Celan and his early poems may have brought this function of the pronoun 'sie' into focus for Bachmann, leading to its pointed critique in 'Die gestundete Zeit' and beyond. The adjective 'wehendes', which modifies 'her' hair, not only implies movement in the wind, but also contains the root 'weh', suggesting pain and lament. But if Celan's poetry prompted Bachmann to sharpen her thinking on this issue, her critique may inversely also have led Celan to reduce his reliance on the figure of the 'beloved' and to develop more innovative poetic strategies. This could explain the striking decrease in frequency of the word 'hair' in his work after the mid-1950s.[5] The latter possibility has, however, yet to be explored in the scholarship on his work. As long as Celan's readers remain assimilated to the hegemonic perspective Bachmann critiques, the disappearance of those poetic strategies in Celan's later work will remain indiscernible for them.[6]

---

[4] See Jonathan Culler's seminal essay 'Apostrophe', *Diacritics*, 7.4 (1977), pp. 59–69; revised version republished in Culler, Jonathan, *The Pursuit of Signs: Semiotics, Literature, Deconstruction* (Cornell University Press, 1981, facsimile repr. 2001), pp. 135–54. For a detailed analysis of the effects of apostrophe, see my 'Millay Repairs Baudelaire', in *Rethinking Lyric Communities*, ed. by Irene Fantappiè, Francesco Giusti and Laura Scuriatti (ICI Berlin Press, 2024), pp. 31–70 <https://doi.org/10.37050/ci-30_02>.

[5] Horst Peter Neumann's *Wort-Konkordanz zur Lyrik Celans bis 1967* (Fink, 1969), p. 52, indicates that in Celan's *Mohn und Gedächtnis* (1952), the word 'Haar' appears in twenty-three poems, in six of them multiple times. In *Von Schwelle zu Schwelle* (1955), it appears in five poems, and in *Niemandsrose* (1963) and *Atemwende* (1967) in only two poems respectively.

[6] Following the publication of the correspondence between Bachmann and Celan in

The scholarship on Bachmann, too, has yet to perform the shift of perspective her work calls for. The pattern according to which 'he' is supposed to speak across her, to fall into 'her' word (*ihr ins Wort fallen*), not the other way around, also holds true for much of Bachmann criticism. Canonical master thinkers, the Wittgensteins, Adornos, Benjamins, the Goethes, Prousts, Benns, Celans, and so forth, as if they were fixed stars, fall into her words, rewrite her texts, reorient our readerly perspectives, and arrest change. Thus, her work is subjected to an endless trickle of interpretative sand, its challenges levelled, her legacy muted and reabsorbed. Bachmann articulates this destructive process of being 'read to death' in great detail in *Das Buch Franza*. But this early poem already describes it with complete lucidity.

It takes effort to reverse our routine complicity. We have to stop allowing presumed master texts to frame her work. The opposite is infinitely more illuminating: to turn the tables and use her work to re-read those other texts and their theoretical underpinnings. In the coda to this essay, using an essay by Friedrich Kittler as an example, I demonstrate how this can be done.

Bachmann's poem does not end on a scene of victimization. Rather, it calls on us not to look back — to tie our shoe, throw the fish into the sea — to head for a new and expanding horizon: 'Es kommen härtere Tage' [Harder days are coming].

II

'Anrufung des großen Bären' [Invocation of the Great Bear], the title poem of Bachmann's second volume of poetry, continues her systematic critique of apostrophe. The poem shows that this poetic trope sets a mechanism in motion that works to domesticate and de-claw readers, but that also opens onto the possibility of a fundamental and liberating break.

The poem opens with a classic apostrophe, the titular *Anrufung*, a call 'up' to the elusive star-eyed and star-clawed power 'above' that is, from the perspective of the text, any given reader:

> Großer Bär, komm herab, zottige Nacht,
> Wolkenpelztier mit den alten Augen
> Sternenaugen, (W, I, p. 95)

> [Great bear, come down, shaggy night,
> Furry cloud beast with the old eyes
> Star eyes,]

Again, the transitions between stanzas articulate perspectival shifts. The initial invocation, directed up to a diffuse, undefined entity above, is answered in stanza two, in which a new speaker has appeared: an 'I' has responded.

2008, there has been renewed scholarly attention to that relation; see for example *Ingeborg Bachmann und Paul Celan. Historisch-Poetische Korrelationen*, ed. by Gernot Wimmer (De Gruyter, 2014). The questions I explore here, however, are not addressed.

Together, the call 'up' and the response 'down' — the interpellation and its acceptance — establish a signifying link: the 'I' that responded has become a 'bear'. In stanza three, that link turns into a 'leash' that binds both bear and blind man. Both are now seen from a third perspective:

> [...] gebt
> dem blinden Mann ein gutes Wort,
> daß er den Bären an der Leine hält,
>
> [give
> the blind man a good word
> so that he holds the bear on the leash,]

The speakers of the third stanza remain unnamed themselves. Their perspective is comparable to stanza two in 'Die gestundete Zeit': they can perceive the 'blindness' of anyone who holds on to names. Yet they do not call for change, but rather encourage the rest of us to continue worshipping that institution, to cling to that signifying bond, amid suggestions that they profit handsomely from that arrangement:

> Zahlt in den Klingelbeutel [...]
> Und würzt die Lämmer gut.
>
> [Pay into the collection basket [...].
> And season the lambs well.]

Only the fourth perspective suggests a liberating break. In stanza four, deictics or indexicals ('dieser') point at us, suggesting the possibility that 'dieser Bär' [this bear]– i.e. *this* reader: you! — may tear loose from that leash. Once the cycle of interpellation, acceptance and institutionalization has run its course, we arrive at the possibility that we could rescind our faith in names and signs, break free of that bond, and recover our fundamental unnamability.

'Anrufung des großen Bären' shifts the focus from discovering the mechanism of 'her' destruction (in 'Die gestundete Zeit') to a more general analysis of the trope of apostrophe. Gender, at first sight, seems no longer to play any role. But a more careful analysis reveals that the pesky feminine pronoun is still there — but now it is under investigation! If in 'Die gestundete Zeit', the masculine noun *Sand* gave rise to the anaphoric *er, er, er* [he, he, he], in 'Anrufung des großen Bären' the pronoun *sie* [she] makes a less conspicuous appearance, undecidably referring to two nouns: *Welt* and *Schuppen*. I suggest, however, that we read it simply as the pronoun *sie* [she] — the dangerous textual trigger — itself. But since whoever responded to the initial interpellation has arrived, as it were, in a bear costume, they can safely investigate that dangerous item:

> Ich treib *sie*, roll *sie*
> von den Tannen im Anfang
> zu den Tannen am Ende,
> schnaub *sie* an, prüf *sie* im Maul
> und pack zu mit den Tatzen.

[I drive *her*, roll *her*
from the pines in the beginning
to the pines at the end,
snort at *her*, test *her* in my muzzle
and grab hold with my paws.] (emphases mine)

In the last line, the paws already grab at nothing: the problematic pronoun has disappeared. The fourth and final stanza opens with an apostrophe of a different kind: not an invocation, but a mark of elision. ''s könnt sein, daß dieser Bär | sich losreißt' ['t could be that this bear | tears loose]. This diacritical mark is the answer each of us, as we take turns being 'this bear', can give to that interpellative order, one apostrophe (interpellation) with another (disappearance, tearing loose).[7] The poem's analysis demonstrates how leashing ourselves to names, genders and 'identities' makes us 'blind' — to the benefit of more ominous entities who remain nameless. If 'this bear' tears loose, it finds itself — unrepresentable, unnameable and, of course, not a bear.

Bachmann's poem arguably also plays on the association of the figure of the bear with a taboo on naming that is common in folklores all over the northern hemisphere. Due to that taboo, the words for the animal in most European languages are circumlocutions, while names based on the original Indo-European root (*ṛkṣas*, ἄρκτος, *ursus*) have effectively fallen out of use.[8]

III

The third poem I shall discuss, 'Tage in Weiß' [Days in White], situates itself in an indexically conscious present — the anaphorically repeated 'In *these* days' — and it devises yet another protective strategy against the dangerous pronoun 'she'. 'Die gestundete Zeit' called on us not to look back. 'Anrufung des großen Bären' donned a bear costume as a hazmat suit to neutralize the pronoun's interpellative force in order to investigate it. 'Tage in Weiß' begins with the speaker standing in front of a mirror of 'ice'. The German word 'Eis' is indeed a 'mirror image' of the feminine pronoun 'sie': the word spelled backwards, frozen out, defused. The poem's auspicious beginning initiates yet another departure — again marked by a diacritical apostrophe, this time at the end of the word *Albatros*. In the two other poems, the departure is only anticipated — in the lines 'Es kommen härtere Tage' [Harder days are coming], and ''s könnt sein, daß dieser Bär | sich losreißt' ['t could be that this bear | tears loose]. In

---

[7] Cf. also my 'Apostrophe's Double', *Konturen*, 10 (2019), pp. 22–53, doi:10.5399/uo/konturen.10.0.4509.

[8] A. Irving Hallowell first noted this taboo: 'the custom of substituting special terms for the bear is a practice associated with the animal from Laborador [sic!] to northern Europe' (A. Irving Hallowell, 'Bear Ceremonialism in the Northern Hemisphere Author(s)', *American Anthropologist*, n.s., 28.1 (1926), pp. 1–175 (p. 51). <https://www.jstor.org/stable/660810?origin=JSTOR-pdf> [accessed 18 September 2024]. I am grateful to Nate Ferguson, who drew my attention to this taboo on naming the bear in my spring 2023 seminar at the University of Iowa.

'Tage in Weiß', we find out what happens when it succeeds:

> In diesen Tagen denk ich des Albatros',
> mit dem ich mich auf-
> und herüberschwang
> in ein unbeschriebenes Land.
> Am Horizont ahne ich
> glanzvoll im Untergang,
> meinen fabelhaften Kontinent
> dort drüben, der mich entließ
> im Totenhemd.
> Ich lebe und höre von fern seinen Schwanengesang!
>
> (W, I, p. 112)

> [In these days I think of the albatross,
> with which I have swung myself up —
> and over here
> into an undescribed land.

> On the horizon I discern
> shining in descent
> my fabulous continent
> over there, that has released me
> in the shroud of the dead.

> I live and hear his swansong from afar!]

In Bachmann's poem, the albatross — which resonates, of course, with the birds in both Baudelaire's 'L'albatros' and Coleridge's 'The Rime of the Ancient Mariner' — functions as a dead weight that helps the 'I' gather momentum to swing itself *herüber* [over here]. Once *here*, we can again look back at the *drüben* [over there] and discern the 'continent' whose containment we have escaped.

Critical for facilitating this departure are ungendered indexicals. They serve as bridges with the help of which we can find ourselves on the far side of the gendered apparatus of representation: *I, here* ('herüber'), *now*, 'in *diesen* Tagen'. These textual elements are neither here nor there, or rather, both there and here, both in the text — over there — and *here*, in the undescribed land where we actually live. The moment *I* read myself as truly *here*, that 'neither here nor there' abruptly turns into an 'either–or', effecting an apocalyptic break with the entire apparatus of representation.[9] This effect is key for the mechanism of departure.

Another indispensable element for achieving this break is self-reflexivity. It turns things shiny: '*glanzvoll* im Untergang' [*shining* in descent]. This *Glanz*,

---

[9] This rupture is a little understood but very distinct topos in European literary history. Both Karoline von Günderrode ('Ein apocaliptisches Fragment' [An Apocalyptic Fragment]) and Heinrich von Kleist ('Empfindungen vor Friedrichs Seelandschaft'[Sentiments before Friedrich's Seascape]) use the word 'apocalypse' or 'apocalyptic' for it, paired with the image of the ocean that signals the resulting *liquidation* of all content and firm frames of reference. In 'Über das Marionettentheater', Kleist terms this event 'dieser letzte Bruch von Geist' [this final rupture of spirit].

the sheen of reflexivity, appears as soon as we read ourselves as being *here* — and therefore no longer *drüben*. As announced by the 'mirror of ice', all indexicals can be read reflexively, can be polished into 'mirrors' in which *this* living reader can find themselves *here*. The final triumphant line celebrates this: 'Ich lebe und höre von fern seinen Schwanengesang' [I live and hear his swansong from afar].

IV

The fourth and final poem I will comment on is 'An die Sonne' (W, I, pp. 136–37) [To the sun]. While the poems discussed so far lead up to a departure — anticipated, invited, performed — in 'An die Sonne' it has moved to the centre. It occurs in the middle, the one-line stanza around which the entire poem is organized: 'Nichts Schönres unter der Sonne als unter der Sonne zu sein...' (W, I, p. 136) [Nothing more beautiful under the sun than to be under the sun ...].

The larger intervention undertaken by 'An die Sonne' gains relief if we read it against the backdrop of another deeply entrenched poetological and theoretical feature of European literature from which it takes its leave. From Goethe and the Romantics to Nietzsche and beyond, the moment of noon — when reading stands in the zenith over the text — is figured as a danger that must be neutralized and defused. A poetics of control safeguards the interests of the 'author' by minimizing the risk that a strongly self-reflexive reading might tear open this vertical. The key mechanism to defuse the potential for this reading — and thus to perpetuate that poetics of control — is a knee-jerk invocation of the gender difference, which has the effect of closing the vertical of open indexicals by replacing it with the operative split between 'he' (read: 'author', 'poet, 'speaker') and 'she' (read: 'signifier').

A relevant intertext of 'An die Sonne' that can exemplify this is Goethe's 'Zueignung' [Dedication].[10] In Goethe's poem, the poet ascends a mountain on a solitary morning walk. Soon, the sun breaks through the cloud cover, and the speaker finds himself greatly inconvenienced by a *Glanz*: 'Ein Glanz umgab mich, und ich stand geblendet' [A shining surrounded me and I

---

[10] 'Zueignung,' in *Goethe: Gedichte*, ed. by Erich Trunz, 10 edn (Beck, 1974), pp. 149–52. Goethe's writings, and his 'Zueignung' in particular, have repeatedly been identified as possible intertexts for Bachmann's poem. Ariane Huml explores this connection with a focus on Italian themes. See Ariane Huml, *Wort im Akaziengrün: Zum literarischen Italienbild Ingeborg Bachmanns* (Wallstein, 1999), pp. 279–317. Manfred Koch points out that according to Grimms' *Wörterbuch*, the single other reference for the word 'Tausendeck', which occurs in 'An die Sonne,' is found in Goethe (Manfred Koch, 'Augenwende. Ingeborg Bachmanns Gedicht "An die Sonne"', *Sprache und Literatur in Wissenschaft und Unterricht*, 75/76 (1995), pp. 205–24 (p. 219)). Monika Albrecht and Dirk Göttsche read the word 'Schleier', which appears in 'An die Sonne', as referring to 'Zueignung' (*Bachmann Handbuch: Leben — Werk — Wirkung*, ed. by Monika Albrecht and Dirk Göttsche, 2nd edn (Metzler, 2020), p. 87). See also *Ingeborg Bachmann: Anrufung des großen Bären. Gedichte*, ed. by Luigi Reitani, preface by Hans Höller (Piper, 2022), p. 191.

stood blinded].[11] He closes his eyes, and when he opens them again, a female allegorical figure has appeared, a veritable *dea ex machina* who promptly bequeaths 'der Dichtung Schleier' [the veil of poetry] to him:

> Aus Morgenduft gewebt und Sonnenklarheit,
> Der Dichtung Schleier aus der Hand der Wahrheit.
>
> [Of morning fragrance spun and clarity of sun,
> The veil of poetry from the hand of Truth.][12]

That remarkably helpful apparition goes on to explain the benefits of the gift she has just handed the poet: it protects him and his friends at the moment of noon.

> Und wenn es dir und deinen Freunden schwüle
> Am Mittag wird, so wirf ihn in die Luft!
> Sogleich umsäuselt Abendwindeskühle,
> Umhaucht euch Blumen-Würzgeruch und Duft.
> Es schweigt das Wehen banger Erdgefühle,
> Zum Wolkenbette wandelt sich die Gruft;
> Besänftiget wird jede Lebenswelle,
> Der Tag wird lieblich, und die Nacht wird helle.
>
> [And when you and your friends feel hot
> At noon, then cast it in the air!
> At once a cooling evening wind will whisper
> Fragrant flower scents will waft around you.
> The gusts of anxious earthly feelings silenced,
> Into a bed of clouds morphs the sepulchre;
> And every surge of life shall be becalmed,
> The day turns mild, the night turns bright.][13]

Goethe used this poem repeatedly to introduce various publications of his works, and it spawned an entire poetic tradition of 'veil poetry': 'Goethe's dedication poem "Zueignung" represents, as it were, the *Magna Carta* of the post-enlightenment veil poetry, and has been thoroughly recognized as such.'[14] The reference to the Magna Carta is apt, because it acknowledges that a single prominent poem can not only exemplify a larger poetic organization, but act as a founding document that over time acquires the force of poetic law. Cited, repeated and amplified, its example can balloon into an entire 'tradition'. Poets, scholars and readers alike are apprenticed to generate that poetic *Schleier*,

---

[11] *Goethe: Gedichte*, ed. Trunz, p. 150.

[12] Ibid., p. 152.

[13] Ibid.

[14] 'Goethes Widmungsgedicht *Zueignung* stellt gewissermaßen die *Magna Charta* der post-aufklärerischen Schleier-Dichtung dar und ist als solche auch schon eingehend gewürdigt worden.' Johannes Endres, *Literatur und Fetischismus: Das Bild des Schleiers zwischen Aufklärung und Moderne* (Wilhelm Fink, 2014), p. 107. Notably, the poets discussed in this thoroughly researched book are without exception men.

shielding 'the poet' and his 'friends' against the risk that the *Lebenswelle* [surge of life], the *Glanz* of a strong and self-aware reading, might break through the mist and sweep away their collective poetic privilege.

Bachmann's poem, in direct counterpoint to Goethe's, reopens her text to the readerly 'sun' in the zenith above it: 'Nichts Schönres unter der Sonne als unter der Sonne zu sein ...' The most important element of this line is the final ellipsis, which signals something the text can no longer notate, but only invite and hope for: *our* self-aware thinking on the far side of signs, scripts and the phantasm of the 'author'.

Bachmann's poetics thus fundamentally challenges the assumption that meaning is encoded in texts. What she puts into practice instead is the notion that the meaning of texts is created by the *use* we make of them.[15] This upends entrenched reading habits that even persist in currently canonical theories of reading.[16] Roland Barthes's 'The Death of the Author' is a case in point. He casts reading as a place where writing is to be gathered and preserved, and which 'holds together in a single field all the traces by which the written text is constituted'. Readers are thus put in the service of the work, tasked with commuting — by effacing themselves — the author's death into a resurrection. According to Barthes, therefore, reading 'cannot any longer be personal'.[17] In Bachmann's poetics, by contrast, every reader is emphatically singular and personal, and as the phantoms of 'author' and 'content' vanish, what goes invitingly blank is the text itself.

'An die Sonne' was published in 1956. Three years later, Bachmann delivered her Frankfurt Lectures on Poetics. The centred form of 'An die Sonne' arguably prefigures that of the lectures, which are also organized around a centrally placed rupture that drives all five lectures, but comes to a head in the third and central one, titled 'Das schreibende Ich' [The Writing I]. Given what we have learned about the critical role of indexicals, it is significant that the central lecture focuses squarely on a key indexical: the 'I'. Bachmann's attention, however, is actually not on the 'I in literature' itself — that is, not on the textual I — but on our actions in relation to it. She sketches how these readerly reactions may change over time. Initial trust and enchantment give way to a profound distancing, and ultimately to an entirely new experience:

---

[15] Arguably, Bachmann thus retools Wittgenstein's tenet to address an issue that was much more burning for her than for him: the role gender plays in our signifying practices.

[16] Heinz Schlaffer also makes the point that various schools of reception aesthetics all assume the existence of an integral text as the object of the act of reading: 'Trotz der erklärten Opposition gegen die Objektivität und Bestimmtheit des literarischen Textes bleiben Rezeptionsästhetik, Reader-Response Criticism, historische Lesersoziologie und empirische Leserpsychologie dennoch der Idee des integralen Textes treu: auf ihn richte sich, so nimmt man selbstverständlich an, der Akt des Lesens' (Heinz Schlaffer, 'Der Umgang mit Literatur. Diesseits und jenseits der Lektüre', *Poetica*, 31.1/2 (1999), pp. 1–25 (p. 1).

[17] Roland Barthes, 'The Death of the Author', in *Image, Music, Text: Essays*, trans. by Stephen Heath (Hill and Wang, 1977), pp. 142–48 (p. 148).

> Wer ist nicht, sechzehnjährig, in einem Buch, in einem Gedicht, einem Ich
> begegnet, vermeintlich dem Autor selbst, und beinahe war man es selbst,
> denn Ich war Du, und dieses Du Ich, so verwischt waren in der ersten
> Gläubigkeit und Verzauberung alle Grenzen.

> [Who has not, at sixteen, in a book, in a poem, encountered an I, ostensibly
> the author himself, and it was almost oneself, for I was You, and this You I,
> so blurred were all borders in the first credulity and enchantment.]

Other books and other poems did the same: they, too, 'besetzten' [occupied]
again and again our own I. 'Aber die Invasionen haben nicht verhindert,
dass wir ein ganz anderes Ich wurden und den fremden Ich der Bücher
bald entgegentraten, sie schärfer ansahen, uns distanzierten. Und nach der
Auflösung dieser Ich-Union kam es zu einer neuen Erfahrung' (KS, pp. 290–91)
[But the invasions have not prevented us from becoming an entirely different
I who soon stood up to the alien I-s of the books, had a sharper look at them,
and distanced ourselves. And after the dissolution of this I-union, a new
experience came about]. The metaphor of 'invasion' evokes a war. Literature
itself is a *machine de guerre*: ' "Ich hatte soeben mit einmmal den ganzen Krieg
entdeckt" ' (KS, p. 293) [I had just all of a sudden discovered the entire war]. The
discovery of those invasions, of this war, is what drives this 'I' to distance itself
from the Is in literature. By 'shining' the indexicals, by adding the *Glanz* of a
self-reflexively *present* reading, this 'I-s' can break the *Ich*-union and discover a
new experience: their own.

How we read Bachmann's *citations* is thus particularly critical: we can
have this 'new experience' only if we ourselves make something new shine
up in old texts. Whenever we cite from the vast textual archive that has come
down to us, we have the choice between, as Kierkegaard puts it, recollection
or repetition: 'Repetition and recollection are the same movement, except in
opposite directions, for what is recollected has been, is repeated backward,
whereas genuine repetition is recollected forward.'[18] Bachmann's citations are
genuine repetitions. They place the emphasis on the life and actions of the
one who recollects forward. When she uses sentences from others' works, she
is not re-telling what Joyce, Céline, Dostoevsky, Tolstoy, Svevo, Proust, H. H.
Jahnn, Beckett, and others 'said'. Rather, her repetitions are self-conscious acts
of citation that make something new and different shine up in found pieces of
language: 'Wir [...] begreifen uns aufatmend darin als zur Sprache gekommen'
(KS, p. 348) [Drawing a breath of fresh air, we grasp ourselves as having come
to language in them]. In Bachmann's sovereign acts of citation, *she* comes to
language in a new way:

> Die Gegenwart dirigiert die Vergangenheit wie die Mitglieder eines
> Orchesters. Sie benötigt gerade diese Töne und keine anderen. So erscheint
> die Vergangenheit bald lang, bald kurz. Bald klingt sie auf, bald verstummt

---

[18] Søren Kierkegaard, *Kierkegaard's Writings*, VI: *Fear and Trembling/Repetition*, ed. and
trans. by Edna H. Hong and Howard V. Hong (Princeton University Press, 1983), p. 131.

sie. In die Gegenwart wirkt nur jener Teil des Vergangenen hinein, der dazu bestimmt ist, sie zu erhellen oder zu verdunkeln. (KS, p. 299)

[The present conducts the past like the members of an orchestra. She needs precisely these sounds and no others. Thus, the past appears now long, now short. Now she rings out, now she is muted. The only part of the past that reaches into the present is that which is sounded out [*bestimmt*] to brighten or to darken her.]

This is the point of Bachmann's well-known comments about citation:

Das ist für mich kein Zitat. Es gibt für mich keine Zitate, sondern die wenigen Stellen in der Literatur, die mich immer aufgeregt haben, die sind für mich das Leben. [... I]ch zitiere nicht [...], sondern es ist ein Satz, den ich gern selbst geschrieben hätte. Und ich verwende nur Sätze, die ich gern selbst geschrieben hätte.

[For me, that is no citation. For me, citations do not exist, but the few passages in literature that have always excited me, they are life for me. [...] I am not citing. [...] Rather, it is a sentence I would have liked to have written myself. And I only use sentences that I would have liked to have written myself.]

Once we read the Frankfurt Lectures in this way, we realize that Bachmann citations are complex, playful, deeply poetological, profoundly theorized, but also allegorizing and unfailingly self-reflexive. As we begin to read for these effects, new complexities emerge everywhere.[19] As we think along with her, the outlines of her struggle, her hand-to-hand, sentence-to-sentence combat with language emerges, a language that 'she' cannot use unless she first neutralizes it completely, and then revives it cautiously, partially, selectively: 'sie unter einem Ritual wieder lebendig machen, ihr eine Gangart geben, die sie nirgendwo sonst erhält außer im sprachlichen Kunstwerk' (KS, p. 263) [to bring her back to life under a ritual, give her a gait that she receives nowhere else but in the work of literary art]. The language we have inherited is 'not the undivided property of all human beings'.[20] It is not usable for any and every one alike. 'She' cannot simply speak or write in it. Bachmann's citational practice testifies to this existential struggle. In the Frankfurt Lectures, this struggle culminates at the place that corresponds to the central ellipsis in 'An die Sonne'. It breaks through the roof in the self-reflexive act of citation of a long passage from Beckett's *The Unnamable* towards the end of the third lecture, where we reach the 'Liquidation der Inhalte überhaupt' (KS, p. 304) [liquidation of content as such]: '"Von mir muss ich jetzt sprechen, selbst wenn ich es mit ihrer Sprache tun muß"' (KS, pp. 304–05) ['It's of me now I must speak, even if I have to do it with their language'].[21]

---

[19] For a reading of Bachmann's Céline citations that shows this in more detail, see my 'Apostrophe's Double'.

[20] See ibid.

[21] Samuel Beckett, *Three Novels by Samuel Beckett: Molloy, Malone Dies, The Unnamable* (Grove Press, 1958), pp. 50–51.

V

Bachmann's poetics rejects certain fundamental assumptions of our usual interpretative practice and of most current theories of language, writing and reading. One of these is the idea that to read is to decode a pre-existing content.[22] In this concluding section, I illustrate how we can apply what we have learned from Bachmann, as it were, in the wild. Friedrich Kittler's essay 'Von der optischen Telegrafie zur Photonentechnik' [From optical telegraphy to photon technology] can serve as an example.[23] Kittler's theoretical project is to enable and stabilize coding — and thus the exact opposite of Bachmann's. Therefore, his essay provides an excellent petri dish for studying the theoretical underpinnings of his project and for locating exactly where Bachmann's critique intervenes. This clarifies both why his model is vulnerable to her intervention, and how our own theoretical approaches must be revised.

Kittler's essay explores technologies that code with light. Light, he writes, has the 'unsichtbare[] Macht, alles andere sichtbar zu machen' [invisible power to make everything else visible].[24] Its advantages are strategic: 'Licht als Information zählt zu jenen Erfindungen, die den modernen Krieg ermöglicht haben' [Light as information is among the inventions that have enabled modern war]; 'nur Krieger [...] begreifen es als ihre Notwendigkeit, ebenso unsichtbar wie schnell zu sein. Unsichtbar und schnell sind aber nicht Menschen, sondern Lichter' [only warriors [...] understand the necessity of being both invisible and fast. It is not people who are invisible and fast, however, but [rather] lights].[25] Even better, light can be made immune to the 'Damoklesschwert' that hangs over all electromagnetically encoded information on this planet — instant erasure by an Electromagnetic Pulse (EMP).[26] Light can be 'schlicht und einfach in Glasfasern eingeschlossen, die es im Inneren immer weiter spiegeln und d. h. weiterleiten, nach außen hin dagegen von aller Welt entkoppeln' (ibid, p. 63) [simply locked into glass fibres that on the inside mirror it ever further, i.e. send it on, while towards the outside severing it from the rest of the world]. Cut off from the world, immunized against change, light and the data it encodes can race through those glass fibres forever.

The bulk of Kittler's essay consists of a romp through centuries of military, political, cultural and scientific history of light-based messaging and information technologies. It opens, however, with a brief reference to two poems: 'Nichts Schöneres unter der Sonne — so dichtete es Horaz auf Befehl eines römischen

---

[22] Henri Meschonnic also critiques the Saussurean notion that language and writing should be read as consisting of signs, which has dominated literary theory at least since the last third of the twentieth century.
[23] Friedrich Kittler, 'Von der optischen Telegrafie zur Photonentechnik', *Mehr Licht* (Merve, 1999), pp. 51–67.
[24] Ibid., p. 62.
[25] Ibid., pp. 56–57 and 64–65.
[26] Ibid, p. 62.

Kaisers — sollte die Sonne erblicken nach Rom. Nichts Schöneres unter der Sonne — so dichtete es Ingeborg Bachmann — als unter der Sonne zu sein' [Nothing more beautiful under the sun — thus wrote Horace, following the order of a Roman emperor — was the sun to see after Rome. Nothing more beautiful under the sun — thus wrote Ingeborg Bachmann — than to be under the sun].[27] Both poems involve the figure of the sun — apt choices for an essay on light. And yet, the poems seem to leave no visible traces on the rest of the essay. After the first page, they are never mentioned again. Are they just a decorative opening flourish, of no further consequence? What is their function? Kittler is interested in a perspectival shift he perceives between the 'Roman' and the 'modern' poem, a shift he asks us not to see, but to 'hear':

> Das Reden vom Licht hat, wie Sie hören, seinen Ort gewechselt. Die römische Dichtung sah ihre eigene Stadt vom Ort eines Lichts her, das ein Gott war. Die moderne Dichtung ruft dasselbe Licht von einem Ort her an, der ihr eigener ist.

> [As you can hear, the talk about light has changed its/his place. Roman poetry saw its own city from the place of a light, which was a god. Modern poetry calls on the same light from a place that is its/her own].[28]

These sentences make several decisions at the outset of the essay:
• A transition between perspectives mapped along a *vertical axis* — from that of the sun as god to that of mortals 'under' the sun.
• That transition is presented as the (presumably aperspectival) movement of *history* itself.
• Notwithstanding the two millennia in between, the light of that 'sun' is said to remain the 'same' — *dasselbe Licht*.
• 'Mortals' are assigned their proper place 'under' that light.

With these quick and barely perceptible moves, then, Kittler posits an order of visibility that is hierarchical, underwritten by the (presumably inexorable) authority of history, and immune to change. Only then does he make his next and far riskier move: he introduces the possibility of shade. This brings into play a place that escapes the purview of that divine and unchanging sun: 'Es gibt eine Abwesenheit von Licht, einen Schatten, den die Sonne selber unmöglich kennt. Denn nach einem großen Wort Ovids, das Leonardo da Vinci nur wiederholt hat, sieht die Sonne keinen Schatten' [There is an absence of light, a shadow which the sun itself cannot possibly know. For according to a great word of Ovid's, which Leonardo da Vinci merely repeated, the sun does not see any shade].[29] This risk is not trivial, yet it must be incurred:

> Die Möglichkeit, dass Licht sein, aber auch nicht sein kann, vergibt die Möglichkeit, mit Licht zu informieren. Nachrichten gibt es immer nur,

---

[27] Ibid., p. 61.
[28] Ibid., p. 51.
[29] Ibid.

wo etwas zwischen Zuständen umschaltet. Darin unterscheiden sich Alphabete, Morsecodes, und Lichtquellen nicht im Geringsten. Aber damit Licht zum Trägermedium von Nachrichten aufrücken konnte, musste es vom Ort der Sterblichen her gedacht werden. Schon daher sind optische Informationsmedien eine neuzeitliche Geschichte.[30]

[The possibility that light can be, but also not be, makes it possible to inform with light. Messages only exist where something switches between states. In this respect, there is not the slightest difference between alphabets, Morse codes, and light sources. But for light to advance to a carrier medium for messages, it had to be thought from the perspective of mortals. For that reason alone, optical information media are a modern story.]

The paragraph appears to assert an uncontroversial, merely technical requirement: no information can be encoded by light or darkness only: 'on' must alternate with 'off'. But that elementary difference actually rests on a larger one: the perspectival difference between the gaze of the sun god vs that of mere 'mortals' that was introduced by the two poems. If, for coding to remain possible, it is necessary to think light 'vom Ort der Sterblichen her' [from the place of mortals],[31] then with those two poems, Kittler lays the foundation for his entire theoretical argument. Their appearance, then, is far from inconsequential, and the fact that it is so fleeting may be due to the strategic necessity to be invisible and fast. And indeed, Kittler does not pause to explain but quickly doubles up with yet another appeal to *history*: optical information media are 'eine neuzeitliche Geschichte' [a modern history/story]. And yet, his own text registers that this perspectival foundation, *pace* the authority of history, is actually far from stable. The first sentence of the passage just quoted oscillates with remarkable precision between two incompatible readings: the verb *vergibt* means not only 'grants', but also 'forfeits'. Thus, the difference between light and shade both *enables* and *undoes* coding with light.

Things become even more ominous when we slow down for a closer look at the poems, for it turns out that they actually do not support Kittler's argument: their poetic stances are the exact reverse of the ones he attributes to them.

The title of 'An die Sonne' [To the Sun] may suggest that the poem addresses the sun, but the poem itself is not apostrophic at all. This should come as no surprise. We have seen how systematically Bachmann deconstructs the mechanics of apostrophe, including the inversions of perspective that occur along the vertical axis (e.g. when the perspective switches from 'up' to 'down' between stanzas one and two of 'Anrufung des großen Bären'). The dominant rhetorical register of 'An die Sonne', then, is not apostrophic but constative. It builds through a crescendo of comparative assertions: more beautiful than moon, the stars, much more beautiful than the comets, etc. is the sun. That movement culminates in the poem's central line:

[30] Ibid.
[31] Ibid.

Nichts Schönres unter der Sonne als unter der Sonne zu sein...

[Nothing more beautiful under the sun than to be under the sun...]

That line is no invocation of the sun. Nor is it even a full sentence. Its only verb is an infinitive in which all grammatically coded agency flatlines into a state of mere being, existence, presence: 'zu sein' [to be]. And as we have seen, the most important element of that line is the ellipsis. It launches our imaginations beyond the text by indicating something that cannot be encoded *except as missing*. In Kittler's paraphrase, however, that ellipsis has been replaced by a full stop. That tiny change turns the sentence into the flat, apparently unambiguous assertion that it is best to be 'under the sun' — the all-important subordinate perspective that Kittler needs for his project, and which according to him is not only that of 'mortals', but also 'ihr eigener' [her proper one]. To put it with Bachmann: 'Er findet sie sterblich' [He finds her mortal].

The claim that Horace's poem saw its own city 'vom Ort eines Lichts her, das ein Gott war' [from the place of a light, which was a god][32] is also at the very least too simple. Composed to be performed by a choir during the celebration of the end of the *Saeculum* (a period of 100 to 110 years), Horace's 'Carmen Saeculare' ['Hymn for a New Age'] calls on the gods to ensure the empire's safe passage across a sensitive threshold from one age to the next.[33] It is also the very thing Bachmann's so decidedly is not: an apostrophic poem, a call up to the sun god Phoebus and the goddess Diana by the (presumably mortal) citizens of Rome, asking the sun to stay the same and thus to guarantee the continuity of the empire:

HYMN FOR A NEW AGE

Phoebus and Diana, Queen of the Woods, radiant glory of the heavens, ever to be worshipped and ever worshipped, grant our prayers on this holy occasion, [...] Life-giving [*alme*] Sun, who with your shining car bring forth the day and hide it away, who are born anew and yet the same, may you never be able to behold anything greater than the city of Rome![34]

It is thus Horace's poem, not Bachmann's, that fulfils the condition that, according to Kittler, enables coding. It 'calls up' to the sun from the perspective of 'mortals', and it does so with the goal of encoding the continued greatness of Rome (and Augustus) over all rivals into the gaze of the gods. Let us take this in, for this is actually a momentous shift in how we think about coding: the critical site of inscription is not the page, but *the reader's gaze*. That is why Barthes called for reading to 'hold [...] together in a single field all the traces by which the written text is constituted'.[35] Empires weather the changes brought

---

[32] Ibid.

[33] *Horace: Odes and Epodes*, ed. and trans. by Niall Rudd, Loeb Classical Library, 556 vols (Harvard University Press: 2004), XXXIII, pp. 262–67.

[34] Ibid., pp. 262–63.

[35] Barthes, 'Death', p. 148.

on by shifting *saecula* with the help of their invisible management of what we see. Any meaningful challenge to such empires, therefore, has to arrive as a change in *how we read*. Horace's poem, *pace* Kittler, actually acknowledges this. It does not take for granted that the sun, returning after the night, is still the same. Every morning when Phoebus rises over the city of Rome, the sun re-emerges both 'different and the same' — *aliusque et idem* (Horace, *Odes*, p. 262). And this potential for difference is, after all, the very reason for the existence of the 'Carmen Saeculare': it implores the gods to protect the Roman empire by *not seeing* anything greater. The same question arises together with the readerly sun over any text: will the light in which a text appears to this reader be *dasselbe Licht* [the same light] — or will it be *alius*, other? Kittler makes it very clear what type of repetition he prefers when he writes that 'nach einem großen Wort Ovids, das Leonardo da Vinci *nur wiederholt* hat, sieht die Sonne keinen Schatten' [according to the great word of Ovid's, which Leonardo da Vinci *merely repeated*, the sun does not see any shade].[36] 'Mere' repetition, he suggests, cannot challenge the greatness of the Author or the empire of his Work. Ovid's 'great word' belongs to him and him alone. By contrast, there is nothing 'mere' about Bachmann's repetitions in her Frankfurt Lectures. There, with the author's privilege vacated, borrowed time recalled, content liquidated, the text is turned into a blank place where a *new* thinking can appear to itself.

Coding, to be stable, must invisibly manage what we see. The 'content' of texts is stabilized by the horizons of legibility in whose fold we have grown up, and to which we have been habituated. Thus, when Kittler argues that there is 'not the slightest difference' between scripts insofar as they all rely on the alternation of *on* and *off*, he conveniently fails to point out another thing they have in common: they are all empires. They all create 'scriptworlds', horizons of legibility that consign rival perspectives to illegibility and thus make them go away.[37] Kittler's narrowed focus on the elementary difference of light vs shadow, on vs off, eclipses this larger founding difference: the borderline that separates any given coding empire from its outside — from the many different lights in which we could learn to read, and in which entirely different visibilities could emerge. Literary empires rely on readers to elevate certain works to quasi-divine status by cowering under their 'light' as mere 'mortals'. Writing — and the intellectual and cultural traditions it gives rise to — are stabilized by domesticated populations of readers. There is no better allegory for the imperial dream of writing and coding than Kittler's vision of a glassy tunnel, endlessly reflecting forth messages internally, cut off from the 'outside world', sealed against change, against history, and against the EMP of our presence and actuality. That apparatus relies on the automation of our thinking, our reflex of obedience. It is not just messages that scurry 'wie labyrinthgestählte Labormäuse

---

[36] Kittler, 'Photonentechnik', p. 51; emphasis mine, SIG.
[37] See David Damrosch, 'Scriptworlds: Writing Systems and the Formation of World Literature', *Modern Language Quarterly*, 68.2 (2007), pp. 195–219.

ganz automatisch durch Glasfaserkabel und Satellitenfunkstrecken' (Kittler, *Photonentechnik*, p. 64) [completely automatically through fibre-optic cables and satellite transmission paths like labyrinth-steeled lab mice]. Rather, to guarantee the stability of those 'messages', what must remain locked into that labyrinth are our own imaginations. It is up to us to release our thinking from that tunnel vision, to read in light of a new experience that is our own, that we make ourselves...

Reviews

From the Enlightenment to Modernism: Three Centuries of German Literature. Essays for Ritchie Robertson. Edited by CAROLIN DUTTLINGER, KEVIN HILLIARD and CHARLIE LOUTH. Cambridge: Legenda. 2021. Hardcover. 384 pp. £85. ISBN 978-1-781888-66-7. Paperback 2024; £21.99. ISBN 978-1-781888-70-4.

Ritchie Robertson is one of the most esteemed and prolific Germanists of his generation and his scholarly work is truly impressive in its range, sophistication and substance. Fittingly, his retirement as Oxford's Schwarz-Taylor Professor of the German Language and Literature in 2021 was marked by a handsome collection of essays by colleagues and friends. The thematic breadth of these twenty-three, chronologically ordered contributions mirrors Ritchie Robertson's own stupendous research breadth over the years. Two, for example, are on the Enlightenment, three on Goethe, four on Kafka and four on exile from Nazi Germany. More than half concern themselves with Austrian authors, if Franz Kafka, for the purpose of this exercise, may be counted among them. Keeping with the thematic orientation of this journal, these twelve essays will be the focus of this review.

Werner Michler reads critical engagement with Catholicism after 1848 by liberal Austrian authors through the fruitful theoretical lenses of Bourdieu and Gramsci. His discussion of the portrayal of Catholic priests in works by Ferdinand von Saar, Marie von Ebner-Eschenbach, Peter Rosegger, Adalbert Stifter and Ludwig Anzengruber reveals them as disappointed idealists and martyrs for the cause, torn between tradition and modernization in an increasingly secularized world. Ben Morgan offers an innovative reading of Freudian slips in *Psychopathologie des Alltagslebens* [*The Psychopathology of Everyday Life*] as — in the words of the subtitle to his chapter — 'Hermeneutics of Concern and Co-creation', by relating them to theories of mind/brain interaction of Freud's contemporary William James on the one hand, and recent neuroscientific and psychotherapeutical research on the other. Judith Beniston undertakes an insightful Foucauldian reading of Arthur Schnitzler's *Professor Bernhardi* in the context of body politics, making good use of his journalistic criticism of medical conditions in Vienna in the 1890s, as well as of more explicitly critical early drafts of the play from the digital historical-critical edition, of which she is one of the editors. In a wide-ranging interpretation of Richard Beer-Hofmann's *Der Tod Georgs* [*George's Death*], Leena Eilittä charts the protagonist's development from a detached and aestheticist attitude to a more comprehensive and involved understanding of the world that makes connections to Jewish identity and includes, in her reading, an ecological

Austrian Studies 32 (2024), 256–86
© Modern Humanities Research Association 2024

understanding of nature as well as glocalist perspectives. In an insightful comparative piece, Florian Krobb discusses the differences between the English and German versions of the Viennese journalist and writer Richard Arnold Berman, who, in 1930, under the name of Arnold Höllriegel, published the novel *Die Derwischtrommel* [*The Mahdi of Allah*] on the pre-history of the Islamic Mahdist uprising of 1881, the final and biggest threat to the colonial subjugation of Africa during imperialism. Krobb shows how paratexts like illustrations from British military archives and a foreword by Winston Churchill, who, as a young officer, fought with Lord Kitchener against the rebels, instil in the English translation a pro-British and supremacist element that goes against the grain of this, at its core, anti-imperialist novel, which aims to take the perspective of the Muslim rebels and foregrounds their motivation. Charlotte Woodford's chapter 'The Emancipated Woman on the Margins of German Modernism' includes the Austrian writer Maria Janitschek, who, in her collection *Vom Weibe* [On the Subject of Woman, 1896], courageously thematizes sexual harassment and abuse, the silencing of female victims in a patriarchal order and the traumatic impact of not being believed.

Like many other contributions to this volume, the four essays on Kafka use Ritchie Roberton's influential research as a springboard for their own investigations. Carolin Duttlinger analyses the concept of responsibility across a range of Kafka's works, including diary entries and fragments. She discovers facets of failed leadership, repeated scenarios of misunderstanding and responsibility as an unbearable and unrealizable burden overall, except, perhaps, for the responsibility of the writer towards the text. Barry Murnane's captivating piece traces Kafka's complex engagement with Cervantes' *Don Quixote* across some fragments and letters. He finds forms of metaliterary doubling at the heart of Kafka's engagement with the classic Spanish text, alongside the questioning of male sexual identities. Picking up Duttlinger's theme of responsibility, he furthermore identifies 'a performance of self-destructive, "quixotic" leadership' (p. 230) in *Das Schloss* [*The Castle*]. Under the title 'Uncertainty, Realism and the Self in Kafka', Jennifer Anna Gosetti-Ferencei explores epistemic uncertainties in Kafka's stories by relating them to what she calls 'counter-epistemic tradition' (p. 245) from Socrates to Nietzsche. In another fascinating contribution that focuses on Kafka's influence on later writers struggling to speak about the unrepresentable, Kirstin Gwyer analyses how Jewish Holocaust survivors (H. G. Adler, Jenny Aloni, Erich Fried) found inspiration and a model for their own non-linear and aporetic thematizations of the Holocaust in the structures of *Der Prozess* [*The Trial*].

Two contributions concern themselves with Stefan Zweig, thematizing early and later phases of his career. Robert Vilain looks at translations of French-language symbolist poetry that Zweig undertook between 1908 and 1924. In a subtle analysis of translations of one poem each from Verlaine, Rimbaud, Baudelaire and Verhaeren, Vilain shows how Zweig's misreading of symbolist poetry as based on life experience, and his neglect of formal aspects, not only miss the essence of this art form but are also mirrored in the weaknesses of his own early poetic productions. In one of only three German-language contributions to this volume, Jacques Le Rider discusses how French intellectual life and French literature became a kind of inner *Ersatzheimat* [substitute home] for Zweig after going into exile in London in 1934.

The Introduction to the volume contains a warm and nuanced appreciation of Ritchie Robertson's manifold research achievements by the editors. As an introduction it is, however, a misnomer, as not even a word is said about the contributions that follow. However, in their richness and elegance, these speak for themselves. On its cover, the beautifully produced hardback has a reproduction of Jakob Alt's fine painting *View of Vienna from the Spinner on the Cross* from 1817, thus flagging from the onset the importance of Austrian Literature for both Ritchie Robertson's research and this volume. Since the summer of 2024, a most welcome paperback version of the book is also available.

JÜRGEN BARKHOFF   TRINITY COLLEGE DUBLIN

doi:10.1353/aus.00018

Arthur Schnitzler und die bildende Kunst. Edited by ACHIM AURNHAMMER AND DIETER MARTIN. Baden-Baden: Ergon. 2021. 433 pp. €88. ISBN 978-3-95650-839-4.

Achim Aurnhammer and Dieter Martin's edited volume *Arthur Schnitzler und die bildende Kunst* [Arthur Schnitzler and the Visual Arts] constitutes the seventh entry in the by now indispensable *Akten des Arthur Schnitzler-Archivs der Universität Freiburg* [Publications of the Arthur Schnitzler Archive at the University of Freiburg], which have been published in Ergon's *Klassische Moderne* [classical modernism] series since 2010. This superb volume makes a worthy successor to the series' previous six volumes, and in particular to the edited collections that focus on Schnitzler and film (2010) and Schnitzler and music (2014). In addition to enlightening discussions of numerous aspects of intersections between Schnitzler's life and oeuvre and the arts, *Arthur Schnitzler und die bildende Kunst* contains an inventory of all works of art (or copies thereof) owned by Schnitzler, along with a catalogue of illustrated Schnitzler editions, and an index of museums and artistic sights visited by Schnitzler. It therefore makes a splendid complement to the series' edition of Schnitzler's film works (2015) and Aurnhammer's enormously useful virtual reconstruction of Schnitzler's library (2013).

Arthur Schnitzler und die bildende Kunst comprises fourteen essays that can be grouped into four sections. The first section focuses on Schnitzler as a *sujet* of painting and photography; the second section documents Schnitzler's own collection of art objects, his encounters with art in Vienna and abroad, and his aesthetic reflections; the third section traces references to art and works of art in Schnitzler's literary texts; and the voluminous fourth section discusses Schnitzler's involvement in the design of the print editions of his works, his collaborations with illustrators, and cinematic and graphic novel adaptations of some of his texts. The volume is rounded out by an index; the above-mentioned inventories, most of which appear as appendices to the individual essays that precede them; a rich footnote apparatus; and a wealth of thoroughly documented and beautifully reproduced illustrations.

In the volume's opening essay, Reinhard Urbach discusses those paintings, drawings, silhouettes and sculptures of Schnitzler that exist despite the author's reluctance to see himself depicted in non-photographic media. Urbach's essay is complemented beautifully by Julia Ilgner's detailed discussion of how Schnitzler used professional photography to stage his public persona as a writer. In particular, Ilgner examines how photographic portraits of Schnitzler function as tokens of commitment, commodities and fetishized items of celebrity worship.

The second group of essays focuses broadly on Schnitzler's collection of and encounters with art. Julia Ilgner and Martin Anton Müller introduce an inventory of the works of art Schnitzler owned and reconstruct in rich detail the shifting art decorations in the interiors of Schnitzler's different residences. Achim Aurnhammer and Ralf von den Hoff present research that is in equal measure pioneering and fascinating when they venture into the topic of Schnitzler's engagement with antiquity. Eva Höfflin-Grether examines Schnitzler's diary responses to works of art he encountered during his trips to the Netherlands and Scandinavia in 1896 and to Italy in 1901. Höfflin-Grether reminds us that, since Schnitzler's affinity to music was greater than his inclination to engage with painting and sculpture, it should not surprise us that Schnitzler brought with him to Italy first and foremost his *Baedecker*, Goethe's *Italienische Reise* [*Italian Journey*], and Heine's *Reisebilder* [*Travel Pictures*], rather than art-historical treatises. The section is rounded out by Nikolas Immer's analysis of Schnitzler's reception of Jacob Burckhardt, whose *Cicerone* was another volume that Schnitzler brought along to Italy. Via a discussion of his 1901 Renaissance drama, *Der Schleier der Beatrice* [*Beatrice's Veil*], Immer positions Schnitzler in the context of the *fin-de-siècle* Renaissance revival.

The third group of essays examines references to specific art objects in Schnitzler's literary works. Barbara Beßlich and Judith Becker focus their attention on his prose fiction, and in particular on *Die griechische Tänzerin* [*The Greek Dancing Girl*], *Die Fremde* [*The Stranger*], and *Frau Bertha Garlan* [*Bertha Garlan*]. All these narratives feature encounters of various characters with statues, and as Beßlich and Becher show, readers experience these encounters through the figural perspectives of the characters, for whom the statues function as projection screens of half-conscious desires. Günter Schnitzler, in his detailed analysis of the function of works of art in Schnitzler's 1903 *Der einsame Weg* [*The Lonely Way*], captures the complex ways in which images simultaneously arrest and animate the temporal structures of the play's sparse plot, thus playing off against each other the semiotics of language and image to generate a tense temporality on stage that ultimately collapses past, present and future into each other.

The rich concluding section focuses on book design and illustrations. Susanne Neubrand provides a comprehensive inventory of illustrated editions of Schnitzler's works in the context of media history, in particular the re-emergence of artisanal printing and book design in the late nineteenth century. Roland Stark picks up where Neubrand leaves off and chronicles the design developments of numerous editions of Schnitzler's texts from the late nineteenth century into the 1920s. Dieter Martin sheds light on Schnitzler's relationship to the painter and illustrator Moritz Coschell. Martin provides a fascinating account of the often tense interactions between Coschell, Schnitzler and Schnitzler's publisher Samuel Fischer around Coschell's illustrations of *Anatol* and *Lieutenant Gustl*. Susanne Neubrand's essay analyses the relationship between Schnitzler and Ferdinand Schmutzer who, in contrast to Coschell, was already well known and established as the director of the Wiener Akademie der bildenden Künste [Vienna Academy of Fine Arts] when he became friends with Schnitzler. Neubrand focuses on the intermediality between Schnitzler's text and illustrations by Schmutzer for a 1912 luxury edition of *Die Hirtenflöte* [*The Shepherd's Pipe*] and a 1915 charity edition of *Der blinde Geronimo und sein Bruder* [*Blind Geronimo and his Brother*]. Likewise, Judith Beniston approaches several illustrated editions of *Reigen* [*La Ronde*] that appeared between 1920 and 1970 as intermedial translations in which gender politics become legible in the forcefield between Schnitzler, his text, the illustrations and the male and female artists who provided them. The volume concludes with Evi Zemanek's analysis of graphic novel adaptations of *Fräulein Else* and *Traumnovelle* [*Dream Story*] by Manuele Fior and Jakob Hinrichs, works that, as Zemanek shows, are intermedial in more ways than one, referencing as they do not only Schnitzler's texts, but also various film adaptations of them, contemporary and non-contemporary paintings and architecture, and pop culture.

With *Arthur Schnitzler und die bildende Kunst*, Aurnhammer, Martin and their contributors have provided us with an invaluable resource on Schnitzler's multifaceted engagement with art. The volume breaks significant new scholarly ground at the intersection of literary studies, art history and media history, and provides us with nuanced insights into the place of art in Schnitzler's life and oeuvre. The collection is certain to become a seminal reference point in future scholarly discussions of Schnitzler and the visual arts.

IMKE MEYER   UNIVERSITY OF ILLINOIS CHICAGO
doi:10.1353/aus.00019

Die Macht der Kunstkritik: Ludwig Hevesi und der Wiener Moderne. By ILONA SÁRMÁNY-PARSONS. Vienna and Cologne: Böhlau. 2022. 485 pp. 313 illustrations. €65. ISBN 978–3-205–21614–8.

Ilona Sármány-Parsons has produced a noteworthy and important study on the prolific Hungarian-Viennese author and art critic Ludwig Hevesi (1843–1910), whose career spanned half a century. Hevesi started his journalistic career in Budapest in the 1860s and moved to Vienna in 1875, where he advanced to become the grey eminence of the Viennese art scene. Hevesi was a keen observer and empathetic viewer, who had a refined and discriminating aesthetic sensibility; he was widely recognized by his contemporaries as a critic, art educator, taste maker, opinion leader and advocate. He saw everything worth seeing, knew everybody worth knowing and wrote about everything that merited his attention. His oeuvre includes several thousand newspaper articles and reviews on the visual arts, theatre and literature, in addition to over forty books, including biographies, travelogues, novels, and — later in his career — monographs on Austrian artists and surveys of Austrian art history.

Hevesi is perhaps best known for his advocacy of Gustav Klimt and the Viennese Secessionists, relatively late in his career. He was responsible for penning the motto of the Secession — 'Der Zeit ihre Kunst, der Kunst ihre Freiheit' [To every age its art, to art its freedom] — in 1897, and he wrote the first seminal retrospective on the movement in 1906: *Acht Jahre Secession: Kritik — Polemik — Chronik* [Eight Years of the Secession: Critique — Polemic — Chronicle]. However, the life, career and enormous influence of Hevesi have otherwise been curiously underexposed in the literature on Austro-Hungarian visual arts and culture in the Dual Monarchy in general and in the specialized literature on *fin-de-siècle* Vienna in particular.

Sármány-Parsons has authored a magisterial study that represents the culmination of forty years of teaching and research in Budapest and Vienna on the visual arts in the Dual Monarchy. It has the distinction of being the first full-length monograph on Hevesi as an art critic, and it fills a substantial gap in the voluminous literature on *fin-de-siècle* Vienna. One of its great additional strengths is that it goes far beyond the temporal and geographical limitations of turn-of-the-century Vienna by placing Hevesi in the broader context of the evolution of institutional practices in the visual arts in Austria-Hungary from 1848 until 1910.

Hevesi's output as an art critic included over 600 *feuilletons*, essays, articles and reviews of artists and exhibitions, and commentary on architecture and the applied arts. Sármány-Parsons organizes her analysis of Hevesi's voluminous writings year by year in detailed, source-based vignettes, starting with his arrival in Vienna in 1875 and ending with his death in 1910. Hevesi was a fine prose stylist, and Sármány-Parsons's account — accompanied by over 300 high-quality illustrations — brings critical episodes in the development of the visual arts in Vienna to life, such as the sensational career of Hans Makart, the stations of the construction of the Ringstraße, the infighting that preceded and followed the establishment of the Secession, or the founding of the Wiener Werkstätte. Sármány-Parsons uses Hevesi's oeuvre and his worldview as a point of departure to reconstruct the history of the manifold forces at work in the visual arts in Vienna from the mid-nineteenth to the early twentieth century.

Hevesi, a journalist and art critic, also became a first-rate art historian and the foundational historiographer in Austrian art history. His decades of running commentary on the visual arts provided the groundwork for his pioneering two-volume history *Österreichische Kunst im neuzenten Jahrhundert* [Austrian Art in the Nineteenth Century; Vol. 1, 1800–1848, Vol. 2, 1848–1900, Leipzig, 1903]: a synthetic work which effectively established the modern stylistic canon and periodization for Austrian visual arts in the nineteenth century. Hevesi's arguments for the autochthonous development of an Austrian *Kulturnation* in the visual arts also incidentally made him one of the forerunners of the construction of a distinct Austrian national identity in the twentieth century.

One of the great strengths of Sármány-Parsons's book is the extent to which she regularly places 'Austrian art' in broader contexts. Her study begins with a comparative analysis of the French, English and German schools of nineteenth-century art criticism upon which Hevesi relied, and she subsequently contextualizes Hevesi's work as part of an ongoing conversation he cultivated with his contemporaries in the field. She also maps out the interplay of stylistic influences and trends originating in Paris and London — starting with the World Exhibition in Paris in 1855 — and their impact on Vienna, often mediated by Munich or Berlin, and she keeps an eye on the discrete national developments of the arts in other parts of the Dual Monarchy too.

Finally, Sármány-Parsons regularly includes the institutional and sociological conditions of the 'art business' in her analysis. Her concerns range from the evolution of the sponsorship, organization and format of exhibitions and the development of the art market to the critical roles that public (imperial and municipal) and private (aristocratic, then increasingly *haute bourgeoisie*) patronage played in the production and consumption of art. Her multifaceted study of Hevesi will be of interest to many different audiences.

LONNIE R. JOHNSON

FULBRIGHT AUSTRIA, VIENNA
doi:10.1353/aus.00020

Erasures and Eradications in Modern Viennese Art, Architecture and Design. Edited by MEGAN BRANDOW-FALLER AND LAURA MOROWITZ. New York and London: Routledge. 2022. 262 pp. £135. ISBN 978-1-032-01052-6. Paperback 2024; £39.99. ISBN 978–1-032010-53-3.

Megan Brandow-Faller and Laura Morowitz have published a remarkable anthology, which is dedicated to marginalized protagonists of Viennese Modernism and examines the roles of historiography and traditional art-historical methodology. The editors are continuing a line of research that, from the 1990s onwards, focused on personalities from the so-called second row which enriches previous knowledge with hitherto unknown or little-noticed facts. However, this publication also explicitly endeavours to explore the multi-layered contexts within which the art of Viennese Modernism was able to develop. Thus, it takes greater account of approaches such as postcolonial and gender theory, as well as methodological criticism, which allow us to better understand historical processes while sharpening our awareness of our own blind spots.

The editors' introduction deals with the historiography of Viennese modernist art and provides various interpretations of why and under what conditions and influences Viennese modernist protagonists were taken into account or were sidelined by art-historical research or political actors. Following this, the anthology is divided into three sections. The first is dedicated to Jewish protagonists, the second to people who were marginalized due to their gender, and the third to people who were pushed into the shadows by other contexts or historiographical approaches. An interview with representatives of the Vereinigung bildender Künstler*innen Österreichs (VBKÖ; Austrian Association of Women Artists) concludes the book.

By juxtaposing Klimt's Elisabeth Lederer portrait with Moll's genre-like depiction of an interior, Laura Morowitz argues for analysis, not only of an object as depicted, but of its history as a whole. Using the example of Max Oppenheimer, Nathan J. Timpano shows that artists are not only defamed and removed from memory for reasons of their religious affiliation or sexual orientation, but that competition among artists, as mediated by art critics, also contributes to the forgetting of a person. With a similar focus, Elana Shapira analyses Josef Hoffmann's biography as that of an opportunist caught up in selfish career aspirations — especially against those contemporaries who contributed significantly to his media presence. Frances Tanzer uses the activities of the exiled art dealer Otto Kallir to show that remembering and forgetting are actively shaped by exhibition policy and by the ambiguity of constructed narratives (for example, the victim myth of modernism defamed by the National Socialists). Steven Beller demonstrates how ambivalently memory and forgetting manifest themselves in Vienna's urban space using the categories of demolished buildings, contested restitution of Jewish property, and newly erected monuments.

Andrea Winklbauer lists unnoticed female artists from Schiele's *Neukunst-gruppe* [New Art Group] and shows that the inclusion of applied arts in exhibitions could determine the participation of female artists. In Rae Di Cicco's contribution on Erika Giovanna Klien's kinetic works, the central role Franz Čižek played as a teacher at the Kunstgewerbeschule [School of Arts and Crafts] becomes clear, as does his importance as an art theorist for later interpretations of his students' works. Julia Secklehner uses the example of Anna Lesznai to present the significance of folk art for the artist's own identity, in terms of the ambivalent contrast between (modern-innovative) centre and (traditional) province. Michelle Jackson-Beckett addresses the party-political context in her article on the Beratungsstelle für Inneneinrichtung und Wohnungshygiene [Advice Bureau for Interior Design and Housing Hygiene] of Vienna's social democratic city government. Megan Brandow-Faller characterizes Emmy Zweybrück-Prochaska as an economically and pedagogically successful mediator between Viennese Modernism and the postwar USA.

By scrutinizing the colonial origins of the furnishing materials and collections in the Palais Stoclet in Brussels and the financial foundations of the client, Debora Silverman exposes the moral ambivalence of our continuing prosperity in the Western world. James Shedel describes the cultural struggle between supporters of tradition and modernity, exemplified in the founding of the Secession in 1897, as a basis for the conflicts of the interwar period, which split into left- and right-wing party-political camps and became increasingly radicalized. In Robert Örley, Christopher Long deals with an architect who was already brought out of the 'forgotten second row' in the 1990s, presenting him all the more clearly as a particularly innovative representative of Viennese Modernism's diversity. In his contribution on Josephine Baker, Roman Horak addresses the polemics across the political spectrum surrounding topics such as sexuality, skin colour and the 'primitive', as well as the contrast between popular mass culture and elitist high culture. In his contribution on church building in the interwar period, Matthew Rampley addresses the fact that this building type is given remarkably little space in the architectural history of modernism. He analyses the arguably one-sided attitude of contemporary critics who, depending on their political position, instrumentalize new building materials, innovative construction technologies and functional design differently for or against modernism. The interview epilogue with the VBKÖ links the book to the present by posing questions about current marginalization and the challenges of archival collecting.

Brandow-Faller and Morowitz's anthology offers a variety of different examples not only of Viennese, but of Central European Modernism, which show similar contexts and comparable processes. It offers many points of reference for a constructive critique of art-historical methods, focusing not only on innovation, but also on synthesis. In the historiographical analyses, however, more attention could have been paid to the historical circumstances that led to the neglect of individual personalities. It is undeniably true that the first comprehensive and major presentation of Viennese Modernism, which was organized in 1964 by the Kulturamt [cultural office] of the City of Vienna, dealt first and foremost with the big names that are still known today. But we should not forget that this exhibition first had to do some convincing in order to give the art of Viennese Modernism a value that the general public could appreciate — at a time when a lack of understanding resulted in a significant loss of monuments. One need only recall the all too frequent demolitions of Viennese Modernist buildings at the time, which were sacrificed to the contemporary fetishes of the 1960s and 1970s, above all to motorized private transport and a relentlessly technology-orientated modernization and profit-maximizing economization of society.

RICHARD KURDIOVSKY

AUSTRIAN ACADEMY OF SCIENCES
doi:10.1353/aus.00021

The Memoirs of Ceija Stojka: Child Survivor of the Romani Holocaust. By LORELEY FRENCH. New York: Camden House. 2022. 300 pp. £95. ISBN 978-1-64014-121-6.

In *The Memoirs of Ceija Stojka: Child Survivor of the Romani Holocaust*, Loreley French provides the first English-language translation of three memoirs as well as two poems by Austrian Romani writer, artist and Holocaust survivor Ceija Stojka. Stojka was born in 1933 and died in 2013. She became the first Romani from Austria, and one of the first in the German-speaking countries, to publish her memories of her experiences in the concentration camps of the Third Reich with *Wir leben im Verborgenen: Erinnerungen einer Rom-Zigeunerin* [*We Live in Secrecy: Memories of a Romni-Gypsy*, 1988]. She later published two more narratives: one about her life after the Second World War, *Reisende auf dieser Welt: Aus dem Leben einer Rom-Zigeunerin* [*Travelers in this World: From the Life of a Romni-Gypsy*, 1992], and one that further details her experiences in Bergen-Belsen, *Träume ich, dass ich lebe?* [*Am I Dreaming I'm Alive?*, 2003]. All of these were ground-breaking works, not only in that they illuminated the experiences of Roma in the Third Reich and represented a transition from a largely oral tradition of storytelling and record-keeping, but also for the first time gave readers insights into Romani cultural and social practices, norms and traditions. Thus, the translation of these three memoirs into English is in its turn an important and overdue contribution to the study of Holocaust memory and writing. French's book, with its inclusion of Stojka's family photographs and selected colour reproductions of her paintings, offers a rich compilation of Stojka's key texts for English-language readers.

French has previously written about Stojka's work (e.g. *Roma Voices in the German-Speaking World*, 2015) and regularly spent time with Stojka and her family over many years. She is therefore able to include extensive supplementary materials in *Memoirs* and provide a thorough overview of the historical and cultural contexts of Stojka's oeuvre, while also painting an intimate portrait of her life and family. Alongside the translations of the original texts, *Memoirs* comprises a preface, a thirty-six-page introduction, footnotes and annotations, a glossary on select places, people and events mentioned by Stojka, and an appendix with notes on names and family members. Throughout her translations of Stojka's works, French acknowledges the need, given the lack of widespread knowledge of Romani culture, 'to parse out some of the customs and beliefs that are important for understanding her values' (p. 6), hence the footnotes, glossary and appendix. Further, she emphasizes the necessity of writing a lengthy introduction to 'provide[] context for Stojka's memoirs within the history of Roma in Austria before 1933' (p. 6).

This thoroughly researched volume does indeed provide useful context for Stojka's writing for an English-speaking audience, and it does so in a way that dispels existing stereotypes and misinformation about Romani cultural and social practices, and is sensitive to the dearth of common knowledge about Romani history. Stojka's works offer an avenue for learning about Romani experiences of the Holocaust, the longer history of Roma in Austria, and about aspects of Romani daily life and cultural norms. The couching of her narratives within the introduction, footnotes and additional resources makes this volume ideal for academic and classroom settings. It offers valuable contributions to the fields of literary studies, German studies, Holocaust studies, Romani studies, women's studies, memory studies and life writing. Indeed, the bibliography from the introduction alone, though not comprehensive, already provides a useful starting point for discovering the burgeoning scholarship on Romani history and literature. Readers, in this sense, are in safe hands with French's long engagement with literary, Romani and women's studies. However, the insertion of French's voice, particularly through the frequent use of footnotes, does at times detract from Stojka's own distinct and strong voice, whose narratives have much to offer on their own. French acknowledges the difficulty of rendering Stojka's particular style of writing by noting that her 'clear, direct, unfiltered stream-of-consciousness' (p. 7), her colloquial Viennese dialect, and the Romani phrases she used with her family 'cannot be translated adequately' (p. 7). These limitations result in language that does not quite capture the warm tone of Stojka's original text. While French encourages readers to discover Stojka's original texts as their language skills allow, this also demonstrates the need for a literary translation of Stojka in addition to French's compilation geared towards scholarly interests.

Overall, while an English translation of Ceija Stojka that focuses on capturing her style and content is still wanting, French's book remains a welcome and needed addition to the existing scholarly work on Romani Holocaust writing. French states that 'inspired by Stojka's unending, prolific artistic and activist drive, I hope my translation will make her message urging us not to forget accessible to an ever-widening audience' (p. 7). This is a goal largely realized by French's volume.

MARIANNE C. ZWICKER

PHILLIPS EXETER ACADEMY

doi:10.1353/aus.00022

Konstellationen österreichischer Literatur: Ilse Aichinger. Edited by CHRISTINE
FRANK AND SUGI SHINDO. Vienna: Böhlau. 2023. 552 pp. €75. ISBN 978–3–
205–21668–1 (Print). ISBN 978–3–205–21669–8 (Open Access).

The title of this volume makes one wonder if it is part of an existing series,
which it is not. It is, so far, Ilse Aichinger alone whom the editors have chosen
as their fixed star from which to undertake a variety of explorations of other
points on the Austrian literary firmament. Aichinger was a precise and
unexpansive writer who more than once talked of her desire to disappear, often
into the darkness of a cinema auditorium. Precisely this quality makes her a
brilliant choice for such an expansive project. The constellations suggested
regarding her comprise 200 years of Austrian literature, subsumed in five
subsections. The first four of these, containing thirty contributions, proceed
roughly chronologically, from Adalbert Stifter to Peter Handke, and relate
entirely to male authors. The fifth section features twelve essays on Aichinger
and other female writers, ranging from Veza Canetti to Eva Menasse.

In the opening essay, Deborah Holmes explores Aichinger's links to
Grillparzer by way of the short prose text 'Mit Franz Grillparzer in die
Brigittenau' ['To Brigittenau with Franz Grillparzer'], collected in her
Unglaubwürdige Reisen [*Improbable Journeys*]. A trip to a hospital appointment
in Brigittenau recalls the first-person narrator's same route in the Grillparzer
novella *Der arme Spielmann* [*The Poor Fiddler*]. Jakob, the fiddler, is dedicated
to his art without being able to play well. Holmes deftly teases out the parallels
between Grillparzer's poor fiddler and a woman dressed in violet whom
Aichinger observes in the hospital waiting room and who seems to her, in her
apparent insignificance, an even more improbable traveller than herself. The
art of being attuned to the seemingly inconspicuous connects the two authors
and provides a fitting way into the heart of Aichinger's poetics.

It is most interesting to see how the contributors approach the exploration of
such constellations, especially where there are no obvious links, or the authors
referenced were never mentioned by Aichinger. Thomas Pekar meditates
on the parallels between Aichinger and Robert Musil, whom she held in
especially high esteem and mentions frequently in her work. The copy of
Der Mann ohne Eigenschaften [*The Man Without Qualities*] she was given
by Ingeborg Bachmann even had the status of a codeword between the two
authors. Conversely, in her essay, Vivian Liska deals with the fact that although
Aichinger's writing is frequently compared to Franz Kafka's, or even seen in
direct succession to it, she herself claimed to have been unable to read more
than a single short passage from one of his letters, precisely because she felt too
overwhelming a shadow. Aichinger uttered this claim in her acceptance speech
for the Kafka prize in 1983, and it is impossible to tell from her wording whether
that looming shadow she wants to avoid is meant as an anxiety of influence or
actual fear.

Christine Frank explores the axis Aichinger–Sigmund Freud, and Sugi

Shindo the connections between Aichinger and the triple constellation Freud–
Alfred Adler–Viktor Frankl. Frankl's characteristic optimism, as shown in
his maxim and book title *...trotzdem Ja zum Leben sagen* [*Yes to Life: In Spite
of Everything*], was just as characteristically countered by Aichinger in her
newspaper column 'Trotzdem Nein zum Leben sagen' [No to Life, in Spite
of Everything]. Thomas Wild reads Aichinger and Jean Améry together in
terms of a shared poetics of irreconciliation, and thereby brings into focus a
correspondence which is not immediately obvious, but which illuminates both
Aichinger's and Améry's work incisively.

Elfriede Gerstl, ten years Aichinger's junior, arguably has most in common
with her, and is underappreciated, as she has never conquered the German (as
opposed to Austrian) market. There are not only striking biographical parallels,
but also a shared preponderance for the laconic, for sparsity and reduction;
both programmatically give short prose pieces names such as 'Blitzlichter'
[Flashlights] or 'Denkkrümel' [Thought Crumbs]. In both cases, this is not to
be read as a traditional patriarchally ingrained female modesty, but as a form of
anarchic resistance against the literary establishment, the master thinkers, and
against an often all-too-easy coming to terms with the past. Christa Gürtler's
contribution sets out this remarkable connection brilliantly.

Irene Fußl, who co-edited the correspondence between Aichinger and
Ingeborg Bachmann, provides a concise account of their close friendship. This
did not last the course, but was vital for their position as young female writers
in the Viennese literary circles dominated by Hans Weigel and Hermann Hakel,
and subsequently as the only two female members of Gruppe 47 in its initial
stages.

The volume is available as a free download in Böhlau's expanding open access
format. It is a fantastic source of information on Austrian authors from the
so-called Biedermeier era to the present, as well as an opportunity for in-depth
engagement with the writers in question, and, perhaps most interestingly, a
source of information and inspiration on how to frame literary history and
cross-pollination in constellations emerging from a single author.

ANDREA CAPOVILLA   INGEBORG BACHMANN CENTRE, ILCS, LONDON
doi:10.1353/aus.00023

Oskar Kokoschka und Österreich: Facetten einer politischen Biografie. By
    BERNADETTE REINHOLD. Vienna: Böhlau. 2023. 338 pp. €35. ISBN 978–3–
    205–21588–2.

The 1985 exhibition *Traum und Wirklichkeit: Wien 1870–1930* was the catalyst for
a repositioning of present-day Vienna as a global cultural metropolis and heir
to the *fin de siècle*. Oskar Kokoschka is now established as an integral part of
the kaleidoscope of Viennese Modernism, and marketed as part of the triad of
painters Klimt, Schiele and Kokoschka. He lived through both world wars and
the best part of the twentieth century. Kokoschka died in 1986, the same year

as the Waldheim affair marked the start of Austria's official reckoning with the Nazi period and of acts of restitution. His turbulent political trajectory can be read almost as a foil to Austrian cultural politics and identity constructions, as Reinhold impressively shows. She is familiar with published and unpublished sources, and proceeds in her intellectual biography perhaps following Ilse Aichinger's axiom of 'Aufruf zum Mißtrauen' [appeal to mistrust]. Kokoschka exerted extensive influence over his biographers right from the start and topped his autobiographical narrative with *Mein Leben* [*My Life*] in 1971. As evident from her other publications and talks on Kokoschka's art, Reinhold's expertise as an art historian is formidable. Here, her focus is on Kokoschka's extensive corpus of writings, in the form of autobiographical texts and correspondence, and on socio-political history. This interdisciplinary enterprise has led to fascinating and convincing results.

Kokoschka's submission to the 'Kunstschau' [art exhibition] of 1908 and his departure from Art Nouveau aesthetics towards something harder and edgier caused a scandal with conservatives, but integrated him in the avant-garde and brought him especially close to Adolf Loos, who used his influence to secure commissions. Kokoschka produced some of his most exciting and influential work in this period. Undoubtedly, he cultivated an early image of the anarchic victim of bourgeois narrow-mindedness, and at the same time, as Reinhold shows, cast himself as a victim of the official cultural powers in Vienna for several decades to come, whereas the reality was at times rather more complex. Reinhold is the director of the Oskar Kokoschka Zentrum at the University of Applied Arts Vienna, the 'Angewandte', as it is commonly known, and she charts his relationship with this university, which was his alma mater, in its earlier incarnation as the Kunstgewerbeschule [School of Arts and Crafts]. When he studied there, it was a hothouse of progressive art and intermediality. A decisive and lasting influence on Kokoschka's pedagogical theory and practice was Franz Cižek, the pioneer of children's art education, whose teachings Kokoschka later combined with an adaptation of the writings of John Amos Comenius, a Moravian-born Renaissance philosopher and educator who also revolutionized early years education. His ideas, and, more abstractly, his authority, form a lasting part of Kokoschka's extensive self-fashioning as an educator and as an autobiographical persona characterized by original talent and a special innate gift of perception.

The early Kokoschka was a successful and much-admired artist in liberal circles. Conversely, the persistent right-wing condemnation of his earlier work in Austria was soon echoed in similar terms by the Nazis, who excised his paintings from public display under their rubric of degenerate art. Kokoschka was close to socialist Red Vienna, but did also try, albeit unsuccessfully, to gain official positions at the beginning of the Austro-fascist regime. This failure precipitated his move to Prague in 1934. Here he became an active part of left-wing antifascism. With the support of President Masaryk, whom he painted, he gained Czechoslovak citizenship. To avoid political persecution in 1938 he had to emigrate and settled in the UK, where he remained until 1953, taking British citizenship in 1947. Here he actively and ardently supported antifascist activities.

The *pièce de resistance* of Reinhold's account of Kokoschka's political trajectory concerns post-1945 Austria. Never settling in his homeland again, in 1953 Kokoschka moved permanently with his wife Olda to Villeneuve in Switzerland. He did, however, subscribe to a nostalgic conception of the *Donauraum* [Danube region] as Central European heritage, and defined himself in this period as quintessentially European in a much less concrete political manner. He also subscribed to the then dominant, but not unchallenged, view of Austria as Nazi Germany's first victim. At the same time, he harboured resentment towards Vienna and his perceived, and also partly real, lack of official recognition. Reinhold shows how some functionaries pulled strings in his favour, while others initially deliberately refused him state honours. Kokoschka did not shy away from forming a close allegiance with Friedrich Wels, who was a leading art dealer throughout the Nazi period and advanced with an unbroken career, as did so many, to become director of the Salzburg Residenzgalerie after the war. Wels championed Kokoschka's work and was instrumental in establishing the 'Schule des Sehens' [School of Seeing], which Kokoschka taught as a summer academy in Salzburg for a decade. Reinhold's study shows in great detail the tug of war between progressive and conservative forces playing out around the question of how to present and honour this distinguished artist. This tension does not always make for a smooth read, but the book is thoroughly researched and very rewarding for anyone interested in Austria's identity construction and cultural politics in the 1950s and 1960s, as well as in the political biography and self-fashioning of a fascinating artist.

ANDREA CAPOVILLA   INGEBORG BACHMANN CENTRE, ILCS, LONDON
doi:10.1353/aus.00024

Thomas Bernhard: Language, History, Subjectivity. Edited by KATYA KRYLOVA
   AND ERNEST SCHONFIELD. Leiden: Brill 2023 (Amsterdamer Beiträge zur
   neueren Germanistik 95). 382 pp. €125. ISBN 978–90–04–54579–3.

Based on an online conference held in 2020 at the Universities of Glasgow and Aberdeen, this volume comprises an impressive twenty contributions, all of which seek to engage with Bernhard's work in such a way as to counteract the author's 'Mozartisierung' (Alexander Schimmelbusch), his (mis)appropriation as a picturesque Austrian commodity. The editors Katya Krylova and Ernest Schonfield summarize his main themes in their introduction: 'Bernhard's writings invite unconventional responses on at least three levels, characterized as they are by: an innovative and inimitable (although much imitated) use of *language*, an unrelenting attention to Austrian *history* and contemporary politics, and an intensely psychological depiction of human *subjectivity*' (p.

1). In the analyses of individual texts and Bernhardian motifs that follow, these three related aspects are investigated in depth. The scholars and experts who make up the volume hail from Europe, the USA and Australia and their contributions are published in the original German and English, reflecting the international cosmos of Bernhard research.

Manfred Mittermayer's opening piece gives an overview of possible approaches to Bernhard, after which come three contributions dealing with the author's poetics and language. Rüdiger Görner focuses on the phenomenon of the 'Kunst des Künstlichen' [art of the artificial] and 'des Künstlichen in der Kunst' [the artificial in art], Susanne Lorenz considers the rhetorical 'Sprachfluchten' [linguistic flights] of Bernhard's figures in the context of the language critique that is evident in his writing, and Daniel Steuer gives an original interpretation of *Gehen* as a 'redemptive text'. The concept of pessimistic philosophy provides Ritchie Robertson with a foil against which to read Bernhard's debut novel *Frost*. The story *Ungenach* and 'prekäre Erbschaften' [precarious inheritances] are the focus of Simon Schoch's contribution. Juliane Werner compares 'Dreiecksdramen' [triangle dramas] by Bernhard and Jean-Paul Sartre, exploring the inescapable entanglements that are relationships in their work. The socio-political relevance and range of Bernhard's plays is investigated by Nikolaos-Ioannis Koskinas (on identity and memory in *Vor dem Ruhestand*), Adrien Bessire ('Österreichbeschimpfung, Publikumsbeschimpfung und Selbstbeschimpfung') and Patrick Siegmann (on the motif of hate in *Der Theatermacher* and *Heldenplatz*). Elizabeth Boa and Beate Sommerfeld contribute critical, deconstructivist readings of *Alte Meister*. Boa explores Reger's relationship to his late wife and his totalitarian elitism as patriarchal behaviour, whereas Sommerfeld interprets the force of his rhetorical brilliance and all-encompassing aesthetic philosophizing as an ambivalent practice somewhere between subversion and conformism. Stefan Hajduk and Jack Davis give two different readings of *Auslöschung*, in particular as regards its linguistic and poetic form and narrative perspective. Victoria Boldina looks at Bernhard's references to the Russian writer Nicolai Gogol. The investigation of intertextuality is continued by Hans-Walter Schmidt-Hannisa with an analysis of the satirical text *Goethe schtirbt* written on the occasion of the 150th anniversary of Goethe's death.

The closing section of the volume examines the author-persona projected by Bernhard and biographical aspects of Bernhard research. Byron Spring explores the author's self-staging in various texts with an autobiographical dimension (*Meine Preise, Ein Kind, Wittgensteins Neffe*) and Sheila Dickson takes as her topic self-disgust in works by Thomas Bernhard and Elfriede Jelinek. Anita Tuta analyses the two interviews *Drei Tage* [Three Days] and *Monologe auf Mallorca* [Mallorca Monologues]. The grand finale is Martin Huber's detailed investigation of Bernhard's reputation as a scandalous author and 'Nestbeschmutzer' [someone who dirties their own nest]. Huber shows how

Bernhard himself contributed to this strand of reception, strategically causing public offence and instrumentalizing scandal.

Thomas Bernhard: Language, History, Subjectivity is, as this brief summary already indicates, a substantial volume that effortlessly demonstrates Bernhard's continuing relevance as an author while underscoring the impossibility of reducing him to any one line or school of interpretation. The formal and aesthetic complexity of his works (linguistic critique, repetition, performative contradictions) is also indicative of the clear challenges posed to the subject position by historical experience after 1945. Bernhard can and must be understood as a political author, whose critique of Austria is part of a longer tradition of critical modernism, but is also intimately connected to his individual biographical experience, as well as the collective catastrophe of National Socialism.

The structure of the volume as a whole and the sequence of chapters has been carefully planned to good effect. From foundational reflections on Bernhard's poetics, its focus moves to the early fictional prose and plays to the later prose, before concluding with the person of the author himself, which cannot of course be separated from either his works or his authorial self-fashioning and identity claims. As the editors assert: 'The thematic strands — language, history, and subjectivity — run concurrently through many of the chapters, allowing for contributions to be productively brought into dialogue with each other' (p. 11). In over 350 pages, the volume amply fulfils these aims. It gives us a differentiated and multifaceted view of Thomas Bernhard, characterized by careful analysis of individual works, motifs and themes. Those familiar with the author will also find much here that is new and insightful. The volume is available as an e-book, meaning that individual contributions are easily accessible, but its paper version should nevertheless be considered an indispensable addition to any German Studies library.

BERNHARD JUDEX   UNIVERSITY OF SALZBURG/
                                        SALZBURG LITERATURE ARCHIVE
doi:10.1353/aus.00025

German-Jewish Life Writing in the Aftermath of the Holocaust: Beyond Testimony. By HELEN FINCH. Rochester, NY: Camden House. 2023. 218 pp. £80. ISBN 978-1-64014-145-2.

The subtitle of Finch's book points to its purpose: by directing us 'beyond testimony', she wishes to shed light on how her chosen authors, H. G. Adler, Fred Wander, Edgar Hilsenrath and Ruth Klüger, participate in 'Holocaust metatestimony', that is, '[bear] witness to the process of bearing witness' (p. 7). Simply put, these authors write about what it is like to have survived unimaginable trauma and then return to a society that has no interest in hearing what they have to say. Whether one should attribute such indifference to antisemitism, or to a more general metaphysical fear of the person, is not a question that Finch answers definitively, though the former receives more attention. A recognized scholar, Finch has already published on several of these authors. My preference would have been for a close reading of the prose in its historical context as in her previous published work, but her attempt to create a solid theoretical foundation often seems at odds with this more literary goal. While she succeeds in uniting the works as metatestimony, Finch is not concerned with what makes them worth reading in terms of aesthetics or human value. The authors are 'taboo-breakers' (p. 21) to be sure, but that is not in and of itself valuable. The question they ask is not new: can one find the human good in a fallen world? If the answer to this question is not to be found in a 'sentimental humanism' (p. 64) or a utopian 'faith in humanity' (p. 91) where can it be found, if at all? Finch clearly wants to anchor these authors in something (humanly) valuable, but she is not fully forthcoming about what that is.

The premise of this book is compelling, and its structure straightforward. In her introductory chapter, Finch employs a broad set of theorists to support reading the diverse spectrum of texts written by these authors as one body of work, as metatestimony. In contradistinction to testimonial literature, metatestimonial writing extends into the aftermath of survival post-Holocaust. These texts are disrupted by 'traumatic temporality' (p. 8), thus narrators are frequently revisited by their trauma in texts that are often non-linear, fragmented and incoherent. Finch enlists Michael Rothberg's concept of 'multidirectional memory', which links Nazi terror with the legacies of colonialism and slavery (p. 20), to analyse the ways three of her authors use this as a political practice. Finally, all four attempt to rejuvenate narrative traditions that were disrupted by the Holocaust: modernist narrative (Adler), oral forms of Jewish ghetto narrative (Wander, Hilsenrath), and a lost tradition of Jewish and women's writing (Klüger).

Adler's 'modernist marginalization in exile' (p. 26) is the subject of Chapter 1. As Finch notes, Adler's works, famously neglected in his lifetime, have recently experienced a surge of interest. After sketching the historical and aesthetic reasons for his neglect, she integrates multiple points of view in a discussion of *ressentiment* and forgiveness, contrasting these with Adler's theological response. Finch then reads *Die unsichtbare Wand* [The Invisible Wall, 1989] as 'fiction of *ressentiment*' (p. 56), while also noting that Adler's fiction allows for authentic reconciliation in the acknowledgement of humans as 'being[s] with a soul, personality, and dignity' (p. 49).

In Chapter 2, Finch discusses three of Wander's works to lay bare a 'particular tension in the temporality and historicity of Holocaust testimony, exemplified in bearing witness in the GDR' (p. 71), that is, the tension between personal trauma and the search for a communal narrative. Additionally, she notes his transgressive 'poetics of connection between colonialism and Holocaust memory' (p. 79) but cautions the reader that Wander's 'multidirectional memory' also displays 'the racialized limits of solidarity' (p. 84), as he does not allow space for Algerian voices in his 1966 Paris travelogue. Finch does not dwell on this failing, however, and ends the chapter on Wander's desire to recuperate a, potentially imaginary, lost Jewish idiom.

In Chapter 3, Finch turns to the more controversial Hilsenrath, who indulges in 'transnational transgression' (p. 108) and 'multidirectional memory' with his 'uncomfortable links' between Nazi genocide and other instances of nationalized, racialized violence (p. 110). At the same time, Hilsenrath's literary transgressions frequently culminate in 'dark celebrations of rape and sexual violence' (p. 108). Thus, Finch links, as other scholars have, his 'poetics of misogynist violence' and use of racialized Others to a 'poetics of revenge' against a perceived hypocritical and antisemitic German literary canon that sought to exclude the authentic voices of the victims (p. 112), including his own. One would have expected a stronger evaluative stance here: Finch cites conflicting scholarly opinions without coming to a definitive conclusion, aesthetic or moral, about whether these 'poetics of revenge' are generative of any value.

In Chapter 4's focus on Klüger's 'feminist rage', Finch analyses a variety of texts by Klüger in terms of their propensity to 'interrogat[e] the taboo' from the point of view of an 'uncomfortable Germanist' (p. 155). A large chunk of the chapter is dedicated to 'multidirectional witnessing and the temporality of trauma' (p. 178) in Klüger's final memoir, *unterwegs verloren* [Lost Along the Way, 2010], and how it complicates the feminist life writing project Klüger had begun with *weiter leben* [*Still Alive*, 1992]. The limits that personal trauma places on multidirectional witnessing are exposed when Klüger's attempt to connect two injustices (her memory of Nazi persecution and the history of transatlantic slavery) reanimates 'competitive memory' instead of creating solidarity (p. 187). Although Finch chides Klüger for this, she in large part avoids an evaluation of Klüger's writing or of the theories underpinning this section. Instead, the chapter tends to collapse the (im)possibility of a solidarity grounded in 'humanism' into one survivor's 'irreparably damaged' connection to her own humanity (p. 153).

Finch's stated wish is to advance scholarship on these prolific writers who have received less attention than more celebrated Gentile German authors who wrote about the Holocaust. But for this reader, Finch has not adequately explained why her chosen authors deserve particular attention beyond her abstract use of spatial metaphors (they are 'transnational' and 'transgressive' and inhabit 'double' spaces) or the circular claim that the marginalized are worthy of inclusion because they are marginalized. Finch begins with a compelling question: how do survivor-authors write about writing in a post-Holocaust world? However, her analysis is not sufficiently balanced with attention to the authors' use of language, in all its facets, in their *literary* life writing. Especially in the chapters on Adler and Wander, Finch uses select quotations from the texts as documentary-style evidence to support her claims. There would have been more scope for comparative analysis. In both Klüger and Adler, the use of the word 'Fall' is striking: For Klüger, it is the fall into trauma and for Adler, it is a fall from grace. Further, how would Wander's communal ethic have communicated with Hilsenrath's degradation of Others? And do Wander and Adler suggest a place where humanism can rest and restore itself while Klüger und Hilsenrath reject this possibility? An emotionally and philosophically persistent question in any study of trauma is: can an ideal survive in a broken world? A need to repress this direct question as antiquated could explain Finch's generally pejorative use of the term 'humanist', as if it had become forever stained by the atrocities of the Holocaust. But are her authors, in their appeal to traditions of poetic, aesthetic and cultural value, not asserting the need for a guiding humanist ideal?

TRACI S. O'BRIEN   AUBURN UNIVERSITY
doi:10.1353/aus.00026

The Middle Kingdoms: A New History of Central Europe. By MARTIN RADY.
    London: Allen Lane. 2023. 617 pp. £35. ISBN 978-0-241-50615-8.

The term 'Central Europe' has always lacked a precise definition. It was first used in 1805 by the German geographer Georg Hassel to denote the lands that were neither French (or occupied by France) nor Russian. Later, *Mitteleuropa* was sometimes used to denote the lands ruled by the Habsburgs or a planned German colonization of eastern and south-eastern Europe. After 1945, the Cold War divided Europe into East and West. After 1989–90, historians and political scientists adopted the term East Central Europe for the former Eastern Europe.

For Martin Rady, Central Europe begins at the Rhine and extends eastwards to Russia, and his book traces its history from Roman times to the present. Precise boundaries were never fixed and, initially, ruling dynasties in the region were often short-lived. The Carolingian empire and its successor kingdoms were replaced by the Holy Roman Empire, perhaps the most durable of all Central European entities. In time, the Hungarian kingdom and Polish-Lithuanian Commonwealth became established.

Broadly speaking, these lands on the fringes of the Roman Empire shared a common experience of repeated invasion from the East countered by state building and Christianization over a period of a thousand years. Huns, Avars, Goths, Slavs and Tartars were among the early invaders. In the seventeenth century, Swedish (and French) expansionism posed a threat. In the south-east, the Ottoman Turks maintained constant pressure from the fifteenth until the eighteenth century. In the north-east, Russia began to emerge as an aggressor as the Ottomans declined.

The centuries from the late Roman Empire to the end of the eighteenth century occupy some two-thirds of Rady's narrative. He illuminates the fluctuating fortunes of territorial entities and their rulers, and also the developments that were common to the whole of Central Europe. The establishment of Christianity was key to the reinforcement of political power, but it also generated religious movements that shaped both society and government. The Bohemian reformers of the fifteenth century and the Lutheran and other reformers who emerged in the following century are perhaps the best examples. The Central European reception of the Italian Renaissance was both prompt and every bit as creative and transformational as its Italian predecessor, and unique in its fusion of new Renaissance styles with older gothic traditions. Later, both the Enlightenment and nationalism developed distinctive forms in Central Europe.

The challenges faced by this vast frontier zone also generated distinctive ideas of government and law that emphasized the power of the state. That was always counterbalanced by the emergence of diets, assemblies, city councils and the like, which defended the rights of the people. Yet, on the whole, Central European tradition attached less significance to the liberty of the individual than came to be common in the Western European tradition. The Central European Enlightenment was shaped by the environment in which it developed as a doctrine of better government, and better behaviour of subjects or citizens, rather than as a manifesto for emancipation or unfettered liberty.

The period 1789–1815 was a decisive watershed. The Polish-Lithuanian Commonwealth had disappeared by 1795, its remnants distributed in the Third Partition between Austria, Prussia and Russia. It was not restored in 1815, and Central Europe as a whole was now dominated by the three partitioning powers. Rady suggests that modern nationalism originated in Central Europe at this time. Yet it proved no match for the dominant powers, especially as they too discovered nationhood and nationality, competing for power and, in the German case, ambitious for space both in Europe and in the wider world.

Rady moves at pace through the long aftermath of the 1848 Revolution, the First World War and its repercussions, the Nazi occupations, and the Soviet domination of Eastern Central Europe during the Cold War. In a concluding chapter entitled 'Post-Communism and the Lesson of Laibach', he argues that the legacy of communism lives on in unexpected ways. The music and culture that was repressed in the 1980s, for example, has become the mainstream. In Serbia and Croatia, it was Turbofolk; in Slovenia it was Laibach ('Freddie Mercury meets the Nazi cinema of Leni Riefenstahl', p. 499), a band championed by Slavoj Žižek. Both the band and the philosopher, Rady writes, are imbued with a 'potpourri of psychoanalysis, classical German metaphysics, and soft Marxism' (ibid.) and rail against the new market system of the 1990s and the tyranny of global capitalism. Yet, whatever they and their contemporaries might think about the current economic system, Rady hopes that the threat currently posed by Russia will reinforce their loyalty to the West.

Life on the eastern edge of Europe is as precarious today as it has been for nearly two millennia. Rady's marvellous book really is a new and original history of Central Europe. It deserves a very wide readership.

JOACHIM WHALEY   GONVILLE AND CAIUS COLLEGE, CAMBRIDGE

doi:10.1353/aus.00027

Interwar Salzburg: Austrian Culture beyond Vienna. Edited by ROBERT DASSANOWSKY AND KATHERINE ARENS. New York: Bloomsbury Academic. 2024. viii + 344 pp. £95. ISBN 979-8-7651-1258-8.

As this volume was going to press, the sudden, untimely death of Robert Dassanowsky was announced. In 'A final note from Katie Arens', his fellow editor pays tribute to Dassanowsky as a

> transformative visionary in Austrian studies and film studies [...] *Interwar Salzburg* will be his legacy, opening eyes and minds to new optics on how Austria and Central Europe continue to resonate on a scholarly landscape still overly dominated by the World Wars of the twentieth century. (p. 344)

As its subtitle indicates, *Interwar Salzburg* 'points the way to new considerations of how "Austria" needs to be rethought' (p. 13), challenging the Viennese bias of so much work in Austrian Studies by concentrating on a city/state which has 'retained an identity that has long been determined by its own geographic particularities that have defied the abilities of empires and nation-states to subsume it' (p. 16).

The first section, entitled 'Dreaming Salzburg: Hoping for hope, grasping at what it was and might have been ...', opens appropriately with Vincent Kling's translation of, and engaging commentary upon, Hermann Bahr's 'Die Hauptstadt von Europa: Eine Phantasie in Salzburg' [The Capital of Europe: A Fantasy in Salzburg, 1900], a speculative Viennese *feuilleton* underlining Bahr's often unsung role in the development of a festival in Salzburg. According to Michael Haas, Bahr envisioned a 'Mozartian Bayreuth', and to this day Salzburg retains 'its international profile as the city of Mozart and music' (p. 224). It is refreshing, then, that Arens's extended essay 'Salzburg's Age of Aquarius: Der Wassermann as an Austrian *Sonderweg* in the European Arts', focuses on Salzburg's locally inspired, bourgeois art community, which acted 'as a counterpoint to the elite art scene and its patronage in Vienna' (p. 45). The section concludes with further material relating primarily to visual culture: Dassanowsky's far from cursory 'Notes on Salzburg and Cinema 1911–1938' explores attempts to develop Salzburg as 'Austria's second film capital, grown out of the interdisciplinary artistic base of the city' (p. 100). By the 1930s, Max Reinhardt was at the heart of these plans, which finally evaporated when he fled Austria in 1938.

The second section, 'Choosing Salzburg: Cosmopolitan Refuge and the Search for a Third Way', consists of a single, lengthy essay by Christoph Dietz, 'The "World of Doomed Enchantment": Carl Zuckmayer and the "Henndorf Circle"' — Henndorf being the village on whose edge Zuckmayer settled in 1926. His country estate soon became a magnet for such disparate figures as Stefan Zweig, Max Reinhardt, Alexander Lernet-Holenia, Werner Krauß, Franz Theodor Csokor and Ödön von Horváth. Some even spoke of it as a 'branch office of the Salzburg Festival' (p. 288).

Whereas musical life is represented by a single contribution, Julia Hinterberger's examination of the conflicted role of the Mozarteum(s) between the wars, the volume's emphasis on visual culture is maintained in Julia Secklehner's essay 'Shadow Sides of Modernism: Poldi Wojtek's Designs for the Salzburg Festival and Austria's Conservative Modernity'. The famous logo by Wojtek, originally a poster for the 1928 Festival, was created under the influence of Vienna's progressive School of Applied Arts (Kunstgewerbeschule). However, she later became a Nazi, her rejection of modernism being 'symptomatic of much wider entanglements between conservatism and reactionary politics in the environment of the Salzburg Festival and interwar Austria more generally' (p. 262). These contributions by Hinterberger and Sacklehner appear in the third section, 'Being Salzburg: Cultures Found and Lost', which also contains 'Sport Cultures in Salzburg between State and Dictatorship' by Andreas Praher and 'Everyman and the New Man: Festival Culture in Interwar Austria' by Alys X. George, a contribution that was first published as an article in this journal. George contrasts the 'elitist' festival in Salzburg with more proletarian events in Vienna, while Praher deftly reveals how sport too, especially football and skiing, was 'deeply influenced by the main political forces in the First Republic' (p. 177).

The last section, 'Eyes on Salzburg: Salzburg as Other', juxtaposes two essays. In 'Jewish Identities and Antisemitism in Salzburg after 1918', Helga Embacher admits that with Salzburg's Jews comprising just 0.1 per cent of its population compared with Vienna's 9 per cent Jewish population, the numerical imbalance with the capital could scarcely be greater, yet the fate of Jewish citizens in both cities remained the same. Finally, exploring the history of cultural transfers between West and East, Alexander Vari's 'Hungarian Salzburgs: Salzburg and the Salzburg Idea as Inspiration for Mozart Concerts, Urban Tourism Development and Festivals in Interwar Hungary' brings this original, multifaceted volume to its close.

Overall, this challenging collection fulfils admirably the editors' ambition to show how, via the example of Salzburg, 'Austria' needs to be rethought, 'moving it away from too-simple historiographic models that juxtapose "the provinces" with "the capital"' (p. 13). As they rightly claim, 'Salzburg's stories tell much about an Austria that was moving far beyond Vienna 1900 to seek a future that it never found' (p. 13). It is the story of a resilient culture that needs to be heard with its own voice, and seen in its own right.

ANDREW BARKER

UNIVERSITY OF EDINBURGH
doi:10.1353/aus.00028

Oswald Menghin: Science and Politics in the Age of Extremes. By ROBERT OBERMAIR. Berlin: De Gruyter. 2024. viii + 675 pp. £91. ISBN 978-3-11-105320-2.

The title of this study echoes Eric Hobsbawm's *The Age of Extremes: A History of the World, 1914–1991* (1994). There, a radical historian with Austrian roots charted an era marked by the failure of nationalism, communism and capitalism alike. Here, on a far narrower scale but at even greater length, Robert Obermair tells an unsavoury tale of unbridled academic ambition and its political ramifications. Just thirty when appointed to the Chair of Prehistory at Vienna University, Oswald Menghin (1888–1973) became Rector in 1935; three years later, he was appointed Minister of Education in Arthur Seyss-Inquart's brief post-Anschluss cabinet. During this short period in high office, when he was instrumental in the ethnic cleansing of Austria's schools and universities, Menghin finally joined the Nazi party. In equal measure a fervent German nationalist, pious Roman Catholic, and ingrained antisemite, the South Tirolean author of *Weltgeschichte der Steinzeit* [World History of the Stone Age, 1931] and *Geist und Blut* [Spirit and Blood, 1934] was charged with war crimes in 1945. Now on the run, and facing a potential death sentence, he resurfaced in Buenos Aires in 1948. Having seamlessly reactivated his academic career in Argentina, he died there in 1973. Coloured by personal conviction and political bias, Menghin's prolific output was acclaimed throughout Europe — he remained a Fellow of the Royal Anthropological Institute of Great Britain and Ireland (p. 559) — but is now generally discredited.

This resumé contains most that we need to know about 'probably one of the best-known Austrian academics of his time' (p. 2), memorialized as the scheming Professor Schummerer in Franz Werfel's *Eine blassblaue Frauenschrift* [*Pale Blue Ink in a Lady's Hand*, 1941], a story set in 1930s Vienna. Via the life-story of this 'opportunist par excellence' (p. 589), Obermair explores in often stultifying detail the interface of Austrian scholarship and extreme right-wing politics, a milieu in which unhinged academics tried to murder their rivals (p. 179). Menghin's progress on two fronts — academically in both pre-war Austria and postwar Argentina, politically in both the Austrian corporate state and after the Anschluss — is noteworthy, rendering him at the very least an intriguing example of academic careerism. Crucially, this biography confirms that apparent caesuras in Austrian history, culture and politics, as in 1933, 1938 and 1945, can be moments that signify the opposite, and that ostensible change merely masks the persistence of pre-existing networks, modes of thought and behaviour. Thus in 1959, the rehabilitated fugitive was welcomed back to the Austrian Academy of Sciences; upon his death, Vienna University's Dean of Arts, the Germanist Werner Welzig, 'expressed his condolences [...] stating that Oswald Menghin was highly esteemed by the faculty' (p. 577).

It is often assumed that democrats on the left (often Jewish) in interwar Austria were not patriots — for example, Otto Bauer and Friedrich Adler

— whereas patriots on the right (often Catholic) were not democrats — for example Engelbert Dollfuss and Kurt von Schuschnigg. The reality was more complex, as Obermair repeatedly reveals when examining the responses of pan-German Catholics to the lure of anticlerical National Socialism (p. 446). Menghin, a God-fearing Catholic on the anti-democratic right, was hardly a patriotic Austrian: 'Immediately after WW1, I had made my position regarding the annexation and the Jewish question clear, and could therefore only view the efforts of the Dollfuss government as a sad confusion' (p. 181).

Already abridged from Obermair's doctoral dissertation, the book is still bottom-heavy with footnotes, and further pruning would not have gone amiss. The author justifies writing in English because of its status as the 'global language' and his wish to avoid a 'national' (by which is meant *großdeutsch*) perspective on historical developments (p. 45). Nevertheless, constant references to 12 March 1938 as an 'annexation' (with scare quotes) go unexplained. Inconveniently oblivious to Austrian sensibilities, 'global' English generally refers to the event as the Anschluss, in German, and unadorned. Obermair's style, suffused with Germanicisms and lexical missteps, can be distracting and even an obstacle to understanding. Paradoxically, in order to decipher this study, extensive prior knowledge of Austro-German usage and its contexts is key.

Particularly jarring is the persistent misapplication of the terms 'science'/ 'scientific' in the obsolete sense of pertaining to knowledge of any kind. This may be how *Wissenschaft/wissenschaftlich* are commonly used, but 'science'/'scientific' refer to the systematic study of the structure and behaviour of the physical and natural world, underpinned by mathematics. 'Wissenschaft' and 'science' (and their derivatives) are not coterminous; Menghin *et al* were scholars, not scientists. Hence *Science and Politics in the Age of Extremes* is a misleading title for this unforgiving dissection of a man who exemplified what Julien Benda condemned as *La Trahison des clercs* (1927).

Nevertheless, there is much of value in this exhaustive study: Obermair is an ingenious, tenacious and original researcher. Relentlessly, he reveals how a complicit leader of the conservative intellectual elite, propelled by antisemitism, Roman Catholicism and German nationalism, helped yoke Austria's name in perpetuity to some of the worst excesses committed in the Age of Extremes. Sadly, it may come as little surprise that in September 2022 a portrait of Oswald Menghin was still on display in Vienna University's Institut für Urgeschichte und Historische Archäologie [Department of Prehistoric and Historical Archaeology] (p. 588).

ANDREW BARKER

UNIVERSITY OF EDINBURGH

doi:10.1353/aus.00029

Kafka: Making of an Icon. Edited by RITCHIE ROBERTSON. Oxford: Bodleian
   Library Publishing. 2024. 192 pp. £35. ISBN 978-1-85124-622-9.

Metamorphoses: In Search of Franz Kafka. By KAROLINA WATROBA. London:
   Profile Books. 2024. 256 pp. £18.99. ISBN 978-1-80081-274-1.

The centenary of Kafka's death in 2024 brought with it a new surge of activities,
events and works celebrating Kafka's work and legacy. In Oxford, home to
the largest archive on Kafka, there seems to have been an unending stream of
conversation, campaigns, critical and creative engagements with Kafka, and
not least the exhibition *Kafka: Making of an Icon*, accompanied by a book of
the same name. Kafka as icon — it is a bold claim for an author who famously
asked for his unpublished writings to be burnt, yet the title promises to explain
Kafka's now iconic status, as well as itself contributing to his iconization. The
bright pop colours of the cover image, depicting Kafka's face, pixellated, speaks
loudly to his assimilation into popular culture, but also invites us to look
beyond the surface image. The heavy hardback volume has a lot to live up to if
it is to offer accessible but also deep insight into Kafka's life, work and profound
impact.

The essays in the book, by six Oxford Kafka scholars, manage to strike the
right tone of informative, up-to-date scholarship, beginning with editor Ritchie
Robertson's introduction to Kafka's life and environment, in which he reflects
on Kafka's nationality and the Prague that shaped Kafka's world. All the
essays are accompanied by extensive colour illustrations, which in themselves
are fascinating to browse through — these include archival materials such as
photographs, postcards, writings and drawings by Kafka, as well as images
of creative works inspired by him. Approaching Kafka visually is of course
a core concept of the exhibition, but it also ties in with the claim that Kafka
was a highly visual writer, as Carolin Duttlinger expands upon in Chapter 2.
Duttlinger argues that Kafka's early drawings served as an outlet for a creative
impulse that he later channelled into writing; she also discusses Kafka's
encounters with film and photography.

The creation of the 'Kafkaesque' aesthetic through the representation of
space and place is addressed in an essay by Barry Murnane. Through his
reading of Kafka's three novels, Murnane highlights the disorientating effects
of mixing realistic spaces with abstract fantastic spaces, and juxtaposes detailed
description with a lack of overall perspective. Spatial movement is the subject
of another essay by Carolin Duttlinger. Through discussion of postcards, travel
diaries and literary writing, Duttlinger explores how Kafka's work was inspired
by his travels in Central Europe, France and Italy, as well as by imaginative
travel through reading. Attention is also drawn to Kafka's awareness of
European colonialism.

Kafka's 'animal stories' have place in this volume as well. Barry Murnane
explores the deep identification with non-human animals in Kafka's work, and

argues that Kafka's later stories, in particular, move away from anthropomorphic allegory and towards representations of non-human sentience and ontologies. Ritchie Robertson adds further to the volume through his perspectives on Kafka's Jewish identity, highlighting the author's interest in Jewish culture and Yiddish language, as well as exploring his sense of religious feeling more generally.

The fact that we can gain such insight into Kafka's world is of course thanks to the preservation of his manuscripts, a substantial portion of which ended up in the Bodleian Library. Katrin Kohl and Meindert Peters explain how this came about, and discuss the challenges involved in editing the unfinished manuscripts. They also reflect on the many translations and adaptations of Kafka's work into media, including film, radio, plays, comic books and art installations. The diverse legacy of his work is explored further in the final chapter on Kafka's global afterlives, by Katrin Kohl and Karolina Watroba. A year after being published, *The Metamorphosis* had already inspired a sequel by a little-known Prague author, and over a century later, sequels and adaptations are still being produced, helping people grapple with the coronavirus pandemic, Brexit or other unsettling experiences in a wide range of contexts. Kohl and Watroba highlight the enduring popularity of Kafka's work in Asia, and particularly Korea. They argue that the 'Kafkaesque' as a 'brand' has become infinitely transferable or adaptable and has inspired an evolving legacy of readings and creative transformations. The final chapter rounds off a well-balanced set of essays, suitable both for a general reader wishing to gain insight into the writer and his work, and as a touchpoint of contemporary scholarship, offering informative perspectives on key facets of Kafka's life and legacy. The extensive colour images add to the book's appeal, making it an impactful means of exploring Kafka today.

In the context of such extensive attention to Kafka, it might seem that there is little scope for new and original thinking about an author whose work has been so exhaustively analysed. And yet Karolina Watroba manages to offer just that in her book *Metamorphoses: In Search of Franz Kafka*. Unlike the more formal, scholarly perspective of *Kafka: Making of an Icon*, Watroba offers a wonderfully readable, personal exploration of Kafka's impact and legacy, seeking to understand not just what makes Kafka Kafka, but why his work has resonated with so many readers. While the book is richly informed, it is Watroba's voice and presence that make it shine. She sets out to discover what we might learn about literature and about ourselves 'by telling Kafka's story [...] through the story of his readers around the world, over the past century' (p. 3). The chapters take us to readers in Oxford, Berlin, Prague, Jerusalem and Seoul, beginning with Watroba's own encounters with Kafka as an Oxford scholar, and moving to wider settings — via travel or through reading — as the book progresses.

Metamorphoses opens with a dinner at an Oxford college, where Watroba met a visiting scholar who turned out to be distantly related to Kafka, and who recognized the author's satirical, self-deprecating humour as part of her own cultural heritage. The encounter prompts reflection on the relationships between books and their readers, with Watroba arguing that understanding 'where readers are coming from — both literally and figuratively — can help us see with much more clarity why and how books matter' (p. 11). Reading Kafka through this lens leads to discussion of ways in which *The Metamorphosis* resonated with recent experiences of the coronavirus pandemic and Brexit.

The second chapter takes us to readers who don't 'get it' — to one of Kafka's first readers, who was unable to make sense of *The Metamorphosis*, and to Richard Dawkins, who tweeted that he didn't 'get' the story either. Through such readers, Watroba reflects on the expectations that readers bring to literary texts, such as wanting the meaning to be clear. At a broader level, Watroba argues against the expectation that literature is tied to a homogeneous cultural formation, which Kafka's work clearly resists. Indeed, his evasion of simple labels — German, Czech, Jewish — Watroba claims, was central to his literary imagination (p. 52). Making a persuasive case for embracing Kafka's complexity, her explorations take in facets of Kafka's texts and identity, such as his social relationships, that have often been edited out.

Watroba is surprisingly sympathetic to the commodification of Kafka, making the case that Kafka's revival in Prague, via tourist souvenirs and monuments, attests to a form of peaceful political transformation in a country which has seen violent ruptures in cultural continuity (p. 98). Watroba's study of Kafka reception, both in Prague and elsewhere, is interwoven with analysis of major Kafka texts as well as discussion of archival material, such as the author's unpublished Hebrew vocabulary notebooks. This approach leads to explorations that are fluid and open to unexpected connections — the discovery, say, of a Hebrew play inspired by Kafka's notebooks — and which diversify the perspectives through which Kafka's work might be seen.

The global reach of the 'search for Kafka' becomes most apparent in the final chapter — Seoul — which investigates Kafka's presence in East Asia. Reading through writers influenced by Kafka, across Japan, China and Korea, Watroba also reaches back into Kafka's work to reflect on relationships between books and readers. She makes a persuasive case for attending to wider readerships rather than thinking along narrowly national or linguistic lines. For example, Kafka's literary imagination appears to adapt surprisingly well to expressing feminist concerns about women's social roles in South Korea. The discussion of work by authors such as Bae Suah also becomes a way of attending to other voices connected to Kafka, such as that of Milena Jesenská, thereby constantly reading Kafka as embedded within ever expanding contexts.

While Watroba's 'search' for Kafka may be too circuitous for those who want to pin the author down or go deep into textual exposition, Watroba makes an excellent case for her refreshingly varied exploration of why Kafka matters to so many readers. The bright, chatty tone feels like listening to a friend discussing a topic they know and care about a great deal. For those relatively new to Kafka, this is an enjoyable way in, and even more seasoned Kafka scholars will find much that is original, inspiring and thought-provoking.

TARA BEANEY UNIVERSITY OF ABERDEEN
doi:10.1353/aus.00030

Streetscapes of War and Revolution: Prague, 1914–1920. By CLAIRE MORELON. Cambridge: Cambridge University Press. 2024. xi + 327 pp. £85. ISBN 978-1-009-33530-0.

In June 1923 *Sozialdemokrat*, the chief organ of the German Social Democratic Workers' Party in the Czechoslovak Republic, carried an article titled 'Was the communist leader Beuer an abuser of soldiers [*ein Soldatenschinder*]?' The piece went on to explain that Gustav Beuer, a former lieutenant in the Austro-Hungarian army and now district Communist party (KSČ) secretary in the north Bohemian textile town of Reichenberg (Liberec), had been accused, at a recent Social Democrat rally, of having acted with undue brutality towards the reserve troops under his command during the war. Beuer denied this and was suing his alleged detractors. Yet, the paper continued, there were several more witnesses ready to confirm that he had indeed been a *Soldatenschinder*. For instance, it quoted Johann Kubatsch, a waiter from Reichenberg, who testified:

> I had a sick stomach and Beuer ordered me to the firing range in temperatures below 30 degrees [Fahrenheit], so that I also got chilblains... He made us soldiers sleep in a stable and in rows one on top of the other, and because I shook out my shirt full of fleas, he sentenced me to eight days barrack arrest. (*Sozialdemokrat*, 143, 22 June 1923)

This little episode, although taking place in another Czech town and in a predominantly German-speaking region, is relevant to Claire Morelon's brilliant new study of Prague in the years 1914–20 for several reasons. First, it confirms her view that the wartime shift from empire to republic was far from smooth, with political fault lines running not only between, but within nationality groups and social classes. Second, though, it suggests that calls among both nationalists and democrats for 'revolutionary purity [and] purges of Austrianity' (p. 291) in the early 1920s were not just rooted in broader fears of a return to autocratic government after the popular upheavals of 1917–20 in Russia and across much of Eastern, Central and Western Europe. In fact, feelings of uncertainty also emerged from something more immediate and tangible, namely the 'everyday sensorial experiences' of war and revolution on the home front (p. 2). While the guns fell silent on the battlefields in October–November 1918, early postwar urban life was characterized by ongoing food and coal shortages, large-scale industrial unrest and, on top of this, the 'more ephemeral' manifestations of unsolved conflict between citizens and the state over basic issues of social justice and human dignity (p. 3).

To put it another way, for Morelon 'Austria-Hungary did not lose the war primarily on the battlefields, but rather in the streets' of its major cities and lesser garrison towns, ensuring that the empire's collapse was a process lasting many years — indeed from 1914 to 1920 — rather than resulting from one single event (p. 5). Moreover, in the Bohemian lands and Moravia, it was a process that drew on and recast a whole variety of social relations, whether between soldiers and civilians, self-styled patriots and would-be liberators, men and women, producers and consumers, urban dwellers and their rural co-citizens and — albeit without blocking these other categories — between Czechs and Germans and between ideologically committed Leninists and their more nationally minded or grass-roots oriented critics in the socialist camp.

What makes Morelon's study unique and yet, at the same time, illuminating of the broader Central European experience of war and the passage to postwar is her decision to make urban space itself the chief 'object of enquiry' (p. 297) rather than particular national or social groups, political movements or economic interests. This allows her to explain why Prague — although situated far from the major battlefields and avoiding the worst violence and harshest forms of wartime Habsburg military-bureaucratic rule — nonetheless underwent a gradual but catastrophic loss of belief in state authority on its streets and squares. There are echoes here of the earlier work of Belinda Davis on Berlin and Maureen Healy on Vienna, especially when Morelon highlights the darker emotions brought forth by the chaos in food supply, namely the antisemitism, animosity towards refugees and alleged 'profiteers', and an all-round nervous disorderliness seen and heard in markets, municipal offices and even on the city's trams.

Overall, Morelon makes a strong case for (re)spatializing the Austro-Hungarian war experience by bringing it 'home' to Prague and delving into the unfamiliar and alarming sensations encountered in its many streetscapes. Her book is a significant addition to the growing body of literature on cities at war. However, I am not entirely convinced by her argument that the unresolved political tensions of the years 1914–20 reflected a discordance between a 'reduced experience of modernity' and popular 'aspirations to shape the future' (p. 17). I would rather frame this differently, as an ongoing clash between rival visions of (accelerated) modernity — despite the continued darkness and cold in the streets and other sensorial markers of wartime and postwar austerity. The insistence of the Czechoslovak Republic's first president, Tomáš Masaryk, on riding from the railway station to Prague Castle in a car, rather than the horse-drawn imperial carriage made ready for him by well-wishers, smacks to my mind of something new; after describing this scene, it seems odd to speak of an 'impregnation of the old imperial framework' (p. 268). Counting against this, too, was the ubiquity of American flags and visual references to Woodrow Wilson in Prague's streets in December 1918. Meanwhile, and despite attempts by Social Democrats to cast their Communist Party rivals as the reincarnation of wartime 'Austrian' mindsets, the decision of the KSČ to organize itself along supra-national lines from 1921 also offered something different: the invocation of proletarian internationalism and class solidarity over ethnic or imperial allegiance. In short, the 1920s in Prague, as much as in Vienna and Berlin, were an interim period, a time of breakneck social change, oscillating hopes and premonitions of disaster. And this applied at all spatial levels, whether the local-urban, the national or the regional.

MATTHEW STIBBE   SHEFFIELD HALLAM UNIVERSITY
doi:10.1353/aus.00031

Abstracts

Unterwegs zu Bachmann (via Melville): Re-reading 'Unter Mördern und Irren'
By CAITRÍONA LEAHY

This article re-reads Bachmann's 1961 short story 'Unter Mördern und Irren' in tandem with Herman Melville's 1853 short story 'Bartleby, the Scrivener'. Bachmann's murderer who will not murder, it is argued, emulates Melville's scrivener who will not scriven, and in the texts' shared exposition of the act of not doing, Bachmann's concern with the terms and conditions of agency across her literary and essayistic work comes to light. This plays out in dialectical relationships between the individual and the collective, between reading and reasoning, and between copying and murdering. It binds the contemporary reader, reading Bachmann now, into a literary and philosophical lineage that radically questions the possibility of its own agency.

Dieser Artikel unternimmt eine Neulektüre von Ingeborg Bachmanns Kurzgeschichte 'Unter Mördern und Irren' (1961), indem diese zu Herman Melvilles Kurzgeschichte 'Bartleby, the Scrivener' (1853) in Beziehung gesetzt wird. Bachmanns Mörder, der nicht mordet — so die im Artikel vertretene These — tritt in die Fußstapfen von Melvilles Schreiber, der nicht schreibt. Die von beiden Texten geteilte Herausstellung des Aktes der Verweigerung wirft ein neues Licht auf Bachmanns Beschäftigung mit den Begrifflichkeiten und den Bedingungen von Handlungsfähigkeit, die ihr gesamtes literarisches und essayistisches Werk durchzieht. Entwickelt wird dieses Anliegen über dialektische Beziehungen zwischen Individuum und Kollektiv, zwischen Lesen und Begründen und zwischen Nachahmen und Auslöschen. Auf diese Weise werden heutige Leser:innen in eine literarische und philosophische Erbfolge eingebunden, die die Möglichkeit der eigenen Handlungsfähigkeit radikal in Frage stellt.

From *Todesarten* to Artensterben: Re-reading Bachmann through an Ecocritical Lens
By CONOR BRENNAN

This article attempts to read Bachmann ecocritically by analysing the role of suffering animals and the symbolism of butchery and meat in the *Todesarten* cycle. The article suggests two different ways of understanding Bachmann's associative prose: as 'multidirectional' narration on the one hand, and as an aesthetic of 'archetypes' on the other. While Bachmann herself attended to the plight of animals only as cipher or site of identification for the suffering

Austrian Studies 32 (2024), doi:10.1353/aus.00032, pp. 287–96
© Modern Humanities Research Association 2024

of her female protagonists, I argue that her conception of the novel cycle as 'a single great study of all possible ways of dying' invites us to think beyond this comparison and to reverse the direction of identification, counting animals among the real victims of *Todesarten*.

Der Beitrag versucht eine ökokritische Lektüre, indem er die Rolle der leidenden Tiere und die Symbolik des Schlachtens und des Fleisches im *Todesarten*-Zyklus analysiert. Er schlägt zwei mögliche Herangehensweisen an Bachmanns assoziative Prosa vor: als 'multidirektionale' Erzählung einerseits und als eine Ästhetik der 'Archetypen' andererseits. Bachmann selbst betrachtete das Leid der Tiere nur als Chiffre oder Identifikationsbild für das Leiden ihrer Protagonistinnen. Angesichts ihrer Konzeption des Romanzyklus als 'eine einzige große Studie aller möglichen Todesarten' liegt es jedoch nahe, über diesen Vergleich hinauszudenken und die Richtung der Identifikation umzukehren. Dadurch werden Tiere zu den wirklichen Opfern der *Todesarten*-Texte gezählt.

Scientific Coloniality, Nubia and the Dynamics of Dispossession in *Das Buch Franza*
By TERESA LUDDEN

The web of associations in *Das Buch Franza* can be read as allusions to colonial logics of dispossession that generate property and knowledge. The key phrase 'the private thirst for knowledge of a scientist' alludes to Western epistemological enclosure and the production of race. I read scientific praxis as a material economy that emerges through the libidinal economy of White Archaeology and as a reference to colonial extraction. I foreground the importance of Wadi Halfa in relation to the UNESCO campaign to salvage the ancient monuments from the floodwaters of the Aswan High Dam. I re-read the Nubian desert as a symbol of material heterogeneity linked to the alluvial resistance of the Halfawis.

Das Assoziationsgeflecht im *Buch Franza* kann als Anspielung auf koloniale Enteignungslogiken gelesen werden, die Eigentum und Wissen generieren. Der Schlüsselbegriff 'private Wissensdurst eines Wissenschaftlers' spielt auf die westliche erkenntnistheoretische Abschottung und Rassenproduktion an. Ich verstehe wissenschaftliche Praxis als eine materielle Ökonomie, die durch die libidinöse Ökonomie der Weißen Archäologie entsteht, und als Verweis auf die koloniale Extraktion. Ich stelle die Bedeutung von Wadi Halfa im Zusammenhang mit der UNESCO-Kampagne zur Rettung der antiken Denkmäler aus den Überschwemmungen des Assuan-Staudamms in den Vordergrund. Ich lese die nubische Wüste als Symbol der materiellen Heterogenität, die mit dem alluvialen Widerstand der Halfawis verbunden ist.

Sexual-Political Positioning in Ingeborg Bachmann's Poem 'Liebe: Dunkler Erdteil' [Love: The Dark Continent]
By THOMAS PEKAR

The article analyses Bachmann's poem 'Liebe: Dunkler Erdteil' (1957) from two perspectives. First, it is contextualized within the political climate of the late 1950s, focusing on its exoticized Egyptian setting, particularly in light of the 1956 Suez Crisis and the decolonization process. Second, it explores the poem's depiction of masochistically oriented sexuality from a psychoanalytical perspective. Ultimately, these two aspects are combined to offer a sexual-political interpretation of the poem.

In dem Artikel wird Bachmanns Gedicht 'Liebe: Dunkler Erdteil' unter zwei Aspekten analysiert: Zunächst wird es im politischen Zeitkontext der späten 1950er Jahre in Hinsicht auf den Handlungsort des Gedichtes kontextualisiert, der in einem exotisierten Ägypten gesehen wird. Insbesondere die Suezkrise von 1956 im Zusammenhang mit dem Prozess der Dekolonialisierung wird für relevant gehalten. Zum anderen wird vor allem aus psychoanalytischer Perspektive ein Zugang zu der sich im Gedicht artikulierenden masochistisch orientierten Sexualität gesucht, um am Ende diese beiden Aspekte zu einem sexual-politischen Verständnis des Gedichtes zusammenzufügen.

Ingeborg Bachmann *In Egypt* with Robert Musil, Paul Celan, and Anselm Kiefer: An Exercise in Speculative Philaelogy (or *Art Will Survive its Ruins*, Artists Will Not)
By ARTUR R. BOELDERL

The article seeks to establish an underlying philological, if speculative, condition of the possibility for 'Egypt' to function as the 'common ground' between Musil, Celan, Bachmann and Kiefer, which has been merely touched upon hitherto rather than taken into account as seriously as it deserves to be. In the common words of the former two: 'Everything is more than it is' (Musil) — 'everything is less than it is, everything is more' (Celan), and the way in which everything is simultaneously less and more than it is, is Egyptian — as both Bachmann and Kiefer help us to realize respectively.

Der Aufsatz ist darum bemüht, eine zwar spekulative, aber dennoch philologisch belegbare unterschwellige Bedingung der Möglichkeit zu etablieren, wie 'Ägypten' als 'gemeinsamer Boden' zwischen Musil, Celan, Bachmann und Kiefer fungieren kann, was bisher nur angedeutet, jedoch nicht mit gebührendem Ernst in Betracht gezogen worden ist. In den gemeinsamen Worten der beiden Erstgenannten: 'Alles ist mehr, als es ist' (Musil) — 'alles ist weniger, als es ist, alles ist mehr' (Celan), und die Art und Weise, wie alles zugleich weniger und mehr ist, als es ist, ist ägyptisch — was Bachmann und Kiefer uns auf je eigene Weise zu erkennen helfen.

Intermedial Relations and Plant Poetics in Ingeborg Bachmann, Cy Twombly and Anselm Kiefer
By LINA UŽUKAUSKAITĖ

The article analyses selected paintings by Cy Twombly and Anselm Kiefer which feature quotations from Ingeborg Bachmann's poetry. The various modes of referentiality between text and image are examined, which unfold in intermedial actions as dynamic processes of combination and rivalry between media. The analysis makes visible the boundary crossing between media as well as the intermedial expansion of language and the mutual fertilization of the disciplines. The intermedial analysis is deepened by taking into account the works' transmedial dimensions in dialogue with plant poetics — including Jacques Derrida's term 'grafting' — as well as the findings of interdisciplinary and cultural plant studies.

Der Artikel analysiert ausgewählte Gemälde von Cy Twombly und Anselm Kiefer sowie die darin enthaltenen literarischen Zitate von Ingeborg Bachmann. Untersucht werden die verschiedenen Modi der Referenzialität zwischen Text und Bild, die sich in intermedialen Aktionen als dynamischen Prozessen der Kombination und Rivalität zwischen den Medien entfalten. Die Kunstwerkanalyse macht die Überschreitung medialer Grenzen sowie die intermediale Spracherweiterung und die gegenseitige Befruchtung der Disziplinen sichtbar. Die intermediale Analyse wird vertieft, indem transmediale Dimensionen der Werke samt ihren Verfahren im Dialog mit der Pflanzenpoetik — einschließlich von Jacques Derridas Begriff 'Aufpropfung' — und die Erkenntnisse der interdisziplinären und kulturellen Plant Studies berücksichtigt werden.

Inhabiting the Mind of a Multilingual Interpreter: Translation, Displacement and Revelation in Bachmann's 'Simultan'
By CLAUDIA J. FISCHER and VERA SAN PAYO DE LEMOS

The concept of translation as movement, change and displacement finds in Ingeborg Bachmann's short story 'Simultan' a remarkably vivid literary expression. Various discourse patterns intermingle, mirroring the main character's quest to communicate with the outer world, as well as with her inner self. In this multi-layered narrative, where signs elude certainty, revelation emerges as a recurrent theme, ultimately leading towards an ending that hints at a realm beyond knowledge. Analysable within the theoretical framework of Transfiction Studies, this story highlights characters confronting the limits of language. Its multilingualism and persistent oscillation between the narrator's points of view create an instability that reflects the translating process, always implied in human communication, or, as Ingeborg Bachmann puts it when referring to 'Simultan': '[J]eder muss den anderen ein wenig übersetzen.'

Der Prozess des Übersetzens als Bewegung, Veränderung und Entwurzelung findet in Ingeborg Bachmanns Kurzgeschichte 'Simultan' einen besonders lebendigen literarischen Ausdruck. Verschiedene Diskursmuster greifen ineinander und spiegeln die Bemühungen der Hauptfigur wider, sich sowohl mit der Außenwelt als auch mit sich selbst auseinanderzusetzen. In dieser vielschichtigen Erzählung, in der menschliche Kommunikation oft unzulänglich erscheint, spielt Erleuchtung eine immer bedeutendere Rolle und führt letztlich zu einem über das reine Wissen hinausgehenden Verständnis. Die hier im Rahmen der *Transfiction Studies* analysierte Geschichte handelt von Figuren, die mit den Grenzen der Sprache konfrontiert sind. Die Mehrsprachigkeit und der ständige Wechsel zwischen Erzählperspektiven erzeugen eine Instabilität, die der menschlichen Kommunikation inhärent ist; oder, wie Ingeborg Bachmann es in Bezug auf 'Simultan' ausdrückt: '[J]eder muss den anderen ein wenig übersetzen.'

Philip Boehm Revisits *Malina*
By EWA SIWAK

This article adopts Antoine Berman's concepts of the translator's 'position', 'project' and 'horizon' to compare two translations of Ingeborg Bachmann's *Malina* by Philip Boehm. My analysis shows that the first translation, published in 1990, highlights the novel's roots in the Austrian intellectual and literary tradition but overlooks Bachmann's protofeminist voice. Boehm's 2019 retranslation attends to *Malina's* politics and stylistics; his strategies complement Bachmann's aesthetics and accentuate the novel's work of mourning. Both target texts reflect collective and individual factors: they react to contemporaneous ideologies, align with their decades' approaches to Bachmann, as well as illustrating how Boehm's position and practice evolved.

In dem Aufsatz werden Antoine Bermans Konzepte der 'Position', des 'Projekts' und des 'Horizonts' des Übersetzers herangezogen, um Philip Boehms zwei Übersetzungen von Ingeborg Bachmanns *Malina* zu vergleichen. Meine Analyse zeigt, dass die erste Übersetzung (1990) die Wurzeln des Romans in der intellektuellen und literarischen Tradition Österreichs hervorhebt, doch Bachmanns protofeministische Stimme übersieht. Boehms Neuübersetzung (2019) wendet sich *Malinas* Politik und Stilistik zu; seine Strategien ergänzen Bachmanns Ästhetik und heben die Trauerarbeit des Romans hervor. Beide Zieltexte spiegeln kollektive und individuelle Faktoren wider: Sie reagieren auf zeitgenössische Ideologien, orientieren sich an der Sichtweise ihres jeweiligen Jahrzehnts in Bezug auf Bachmann und veranschaulichen, wie sich Boehms Position und Praxis entwickelt haben.

Care (Work) and Female Authorship in Ingeborg Bachmann's *Malina*
By ANNA SEETHALER

The article explores the interplay of the staging of care work and authorship in Bachmann's novel *Malina*. Within the novel care work is practised by the first-person narrator in the form of self-care, thus creating an artistic figure. The article argues that care and authorship are staged as opposites that cannot coexist in a manner that echoes the killing of the 'Angel in the House' by Virginia Woolf. Against the backdrop of female writing in the twentieth century, Bachmann's novel demonstrates the processed tension between care work and authorship as literarily productive.

Der Aufsatz untersucht das Zusammenspiel der Inszenierung von Care-Arbeit und Autorschaft in Bachmanns Roman *Malina*. Es wird deutlich, dass die Ich-Erzählerin im Roman Care-Arbeit in Form von Self-Care ausübt und damit eine Kunst-Figur schafft. Der Artikel argumentiert, dass Care-Work und Autorschaft als Gegensätze inszeniert werden, die nicht koexistieren können, in einer Weise, die an die Tötung des 'Angel in the House' von Virginia Woolf erinnert. Vor dem Hintergrund weiblichen Schreibens im 20. Jahrhundert präsentiert Bachmanns Roman die prozessierte Spannung von Sorgearbeit und Autorschaft als literarisch produktiv.

The School of Depth: Ingeborg Bachmann Meets Clarice Lispector
By MERCER GREENWALD

This article compares Ingeborg Bachmann's 'Undine geht' and Clarice Lispector's *Água Viva*. I posit that the primary site of the writers' mutual attunement in these texts is what I term the 'poetics of depth'. Centrally operating within this poetics of depth are figures of the mirror, the echo and the fragmentation of the apostrophic subject. In this essay, I aim to examine the correspondences between these two writers and demonstrate the critical distance that these texts demand from their readers.

Der Beitrag vergleicht Ingeborg Bachmanns 'Undine geht' und Clarice Lispector's *Água Viva*. Die verbindende Gestimmtheit der Schriftstellerinnen ist, so meine These, in einer 'Poetik der Tiefe' zu finden. Von zentraler Bedeutung in dieser Poetik der Tiefe sind die Figurationen des Spiegels, des Echos und der Fragmentarisierung des apostrophierten Subjekts. Ich untersuche die Korrespondenzen zwischen diesen Autorinnen und zeige die kritische Distanz, die diese Texte von ihren Leser:innen verlangen.

Anna Maria Ortese and Ingeborg Bachmann: Visual Anxiety between Naples and Vienna
By ROBERTO INTERDONATO

This article explores the profound affinity between Ingeborg Bachmann and Italian writer Anna Maria Ortese (1914–98). After an initial reflection on Ortese's esteem especially for Bachmann's Neapolitan elegy 'Lieder auf der Flucht', the article compares the collections *Il mare non bagna Napoli* by Ortese and *Simultan* by Bachmann, and more specifically their short stories 'Un paio di occhiali' and 'Ihr glücklichen Augen', to identify the blindness thematized by the two short stories as an ophthalmological metaphor of affect. The article argues that this metaphor is a rhetorical device to illuminate the mental, emotional and bodily pain of marginalized individuals and to diagnose alienation in 'anaesthetized' Italian and Austrian postwar societies.

Dieser Artikel untersucht die tiefe Affinität zwischen Ingeborg Bachmann und der italienischen Schriftstellerin Anna Maria Ortese (1914–98). Nach einer anfänglichen Reflexion über Orteses Wertschätzung für Bachmanns 'Lieder auf der Flucht', werden die Sammlungen *Il mare non bagna Napoli* von Ortese und *Simultan* von Bachmann und insbesondere deren Erzählungen 'Un paio di occhiali' und 'Ihr glücklichen Augen' in Beziehung gesetzt, um die in den beiden Erzählungen thematisierte Blindheit als eine ophthalmologische Metapher des Affekts zu identifizieren. Der Artikel argumentiert, dass diese Metapher ein rhetorisches Mittel ist, das den mentalen, emotionalen und körperlichen Schmerz marginalisierter Individuen beleuchtet und Entfremdung in 'betäubten' italienischen und österreichischen Nachkriegsgesellschaften diagnostiziert.

'I have to like a person's voice, otherwise it won't come to anything': Embodiment and Neurodiversity in *Malina*, 'Alles' and 'Ihr glücklichen Augen'
By LISELOTTE VAN DER GUCHT and GUNTHER MARTENS

This article explores the relevance of the neurodiversity paradigm for the interpretation of Ingeborg Bachmann's work, specifically focusing on her short stories 'Alles' and 'Ihr glücklichen Augen', and a passage from *Malina*. Drawing on concepts from neurodiversity studies like hypersensitivity, synaesthesia and proprioception, we demonstrate how Bachmann's writings offer a nuanced and empathetic portrayal of cognitive differences and challenge conventional understandings of disability and neuronormativity. In this way, our analysis allows for a deeper understanding of the characters and their complex relationships with language, the body, and the world around them. Given Bachmann's interest in medical and psychiatric reports, her use of medical terms and the role of sensory processing in her work, the article makes a case for including Bachmann in recent debates in critical disability studies and Medical Humanities.

Der Beitrag untersucht die Relevanz des Paradigmas der Neurodiversität für die Interpretation von Ingeborg Bachmanns Oeuvre und konzentriert sich dabei auf ihre Kurzgeschichten 'Alles' und 'Ihr glücklichen Augen', sowie auf eine zentrale Szene in *Malina*. Anhand von Begriffen wie Hypersensibilität, Synästhesie und Propriozeption zeigen wir, wie Bachmanns Texte eine nuancierte und einfühlsame Darstellung kognitiver Unterschiede bieten und geläufige Auffassungen von Behinderung und Neuronormativität in Frage stellen. Auf diese Weise ermöglicht unsere Analyse ein tieferes Verständnis der Figuren und ihrer komplexen Beziehungen zur Sprache, zu Körper und zur Umwelt. In Anbetracht von Bachmanns Interesse an medizinischen und psychiatrischen Berichten, ihrer Verwendung medizinischer Begriffe und der Rolle der sensorischen Verarbeitung in ihrem Werk plädiert der Artikel dafür, Bachmanns Texte im Rahmen der Methodologie der Disability Studies und der Medical Humanities zu untersuchen.

A Place of Disturbance: Ingeborg Bachmann and Witold Gombrowicz in Postwar Berlin
By TILL GREITE

The article deals with one of the most memorable constellations in literary postwar Berlin: the encounter between Ingeborg Bachmann and the Polish émigré Witold Gombrowicz in 1963. This unlikely pairing is illuminated against the backdrop of an institutional project in the dubious atmosphere of Cold War Berlin: the founding of the first Artist-in-Residence programme. The project was initiated by Walter Höllerer and his partners from the American Ford Foundation in response to the construction of the Berlin Wall. But instead of engaging themselves in the showcase politics of West Berlin, the two writers explored a deeply disturbing place: a city that was haunted at every turn by the 'uncanny' of recent history.

Der Beitrag beschäftigt sich mit einer der denkwürdigsten Konstellationen im literarischen Nachkriegsberlin: der Begegnung Ingeborg Bachmanns mit dem polnischen Exilanten Witold Gombrowicz im Jahr 1963. Diese unwahrscheinliche Paarung in der zweifelhaften Atmosphäre Berlins im Kalten Krieg wird vor dem institutionengeschichtlichen Hintergrund des ersten Artist-in-Residence-Programms beleuchtet, das durch Walter Höllerer und seine Partner der amerikanischen Ford Foundaton initiiert wurde, um der nach dem Mauerbau kulturell darbenden Weststadt neue Impulse zu verleihen. Doch anstatt sich in den Dienst der offiziellen Schaufensterpolitik zu stellen, erkundeten beide in ihren parallel entstehenden Werken einen tief verstörenden Ort: einer, der auf Schritt und Tritt vom 'Unheimlichen' der jüngsten Geschichte heimgesucht wurde.

'Ich kann nur gut allein sein': Love and Friendship in the Correspondence of Ingeborg Bachmann and Hans Werner Henze
By TOBIAS HEINRICH

The article investigates the correspondence between Ingeborg Bachmann and the composer Hans Werner Henze. The letters explore the tension between friendship and love by simultaneously developing but also rejecting the project of an artistic-romantic partnership between Bachmann and Henze. In Bachmann's case, these plans put into question the core of her own identity as a writer and as a woman. In this confrontation with the foundation of her own self, the letters and their language become key documents for our understanding of the relationship between life and literature.

Der Beitrag widmet sich der Korrespondenz zwischen Ingeborg Bachmann und dem Komponisten Hans Werner Henze. Die Briefe loten das Spannungsfeld zwischen Freundschaft und Liebe aus, indem sie das Projekt einer künstlerisch-romantischen Lebensgemeinschaft zwischen Bachmann und Henze zugleich entwickeln und auch wieder verwerfen. Für Bachmann geht es in diesen Entwürfen um das Fundament der eigenen Identität als Schriftstellerin und als Frau. In dieser Auseinandersetzung mit dem Kern des eigenen Selbst werden die Briefe und ihre Sprache zu Schlüsseldokumenten, um das Verhältnis zwischen Leben und Literatur nachzuvollziehen.

'Aber inwendig werde ich eines Tages das Du vollenden': The Use of Personal Pronouns in Ingeborg Bachmann's *Malina*
By SEBASTIAN SCHÖNBECK

At one point in Ingeborg Bachmann's novel *Malina* (1971), the narrator dreams of finding a specific second-person singular, a unique 'you', for Ivan and Malina. This passage refers to the provisional character of every pronoun, to its seemingly arbitrary quid pro quo. Based on this passage, the essay analyses and contextualizes Bachmann's use of personal pronouns in the Frankfurt lectures and in the novel. I show how the uncertainty of pronominal references in *Malina* leads to a complex and ambiguous constellation of characters. Furthermore, the article places Bachmann's writing in relation to other discursive fields such as linguistics and sociology, in which Émile Benveniste and Norbert Elias explored personal pronouns from their disciplinary perspectives in the 1950s and 1960s.

An einer Stelle in Ingeborg Bachmanns Roman *Malina* (1971) träumt die Erzählerin davon, für Ivan und Malina eine bestimmte zweite Person Singular, ein eindeutiges 'Du', zu finden. Diese Stelle verweist auf den provisorischen Charakter eines jeden Pronomens, auf sein scheinbar willkürliches quid pro quo. Ausgehend von dieser Stelle analysiert und kontextualisiert der Aufsatz Bachmanns Gebrauch von Personalpronomen in den Frankfurter Vorlesungen und im Roman. Er zeigt, wie die Unsicherheit der pronominalen Bezüge in *Malina* zu einer komplexen und mehrdeutigen Figurenkonstellation führt. Darüber hinaus setzt der Aufsatz Bachmanns Schreiben in Beziehung zu anderen diskursiven Feldern wie der Linguistik und der Soziologie, in denen in den 1950er und 1960er Jahren etwa Émile Benveniste und Norbert Elias die Personalpronomen aus ihren disziplinären Blickwinkeln erforschten.

High Noon: How to Tear Open a Vertical
By SABINE I. GÖLZ

Bachmann's work calls for a fundamental reorientation in our theories and interactions with texts. This is necessary to overcome the deeply ingrained misogyny to which the literary and critical canon has apprenticed us, and which we unwittingly perpetuate. This article shows that key poems — 'Die Gestundete Zeit', 'Anrufung des großen Bären', 'Tage in Weiß', 'An die Sonne' — work towards a radical break with an interpretative horizon governed by gendered signifying procedures. The Frankfurt Lectures continue this effort. In a coda, I show how we can deconstruct the conventional theorization of writing as coding (exemplified by an essay by Friedrich Kittler) in the spirit of Bachmann's poetics.

Die Lektüre von Bachmanns Werk erfordert eine grundsätzliche Neuorientierung in unserem theoretischen und praktischen Umgang mit Texten. Dies ist notwendig, um der Misogynie des literarischen und theoretischen Kanons entgegenzuwirken, die sich unterschwellig in unserer gesamten 'normalen' Interpretationspraxis fortschreibt. Anhand von vier Gedichten und der zentralen Frankfurter Vorlesung zeigt dieser Artikel, dass alle diese Texte auf einen radikalen, befreienden Bruch mit jenem destruktiven Interpretationshorizont hinarbeiten. Eine Coda demonstriert exemplarisch an einem Essay von Friedrich Kittler, wie das traditionelle Modell, das Schreiben als Codieren versteht, mit Bachmanns Hilfe dekonstruiert werden kann.

www.ingramcontent.com/pod-product-compliance
Ingram Content Group UK Ltd.
Pitfield, Milton Keynes, MK11 3LW, UK
UKHW031025120325
456161UK00005B/404